New Testament Philology

New Testament Philology

Essays in Honor of David Alan Black

Edited by MELTON BENNETT WINSTEAD

PICKWICK *Publications* · Eugene, Oregon

NEW TESTAMENT PHILOLOGY
Essays in Honor of David Alan Black

Copyright © 2018 Wipf and Stock Publishers. All rights reserved. Except for brief quotations in critical publications or reviews, no part of this book may be reproduced in any manner without prior written permission from the publisher. Write: Permissions, Wipf and Stock Publishers, 199 W. 8th Ave., Suite 3, Eugene, OR 97401.

Pickwick Publications
An Imprint of Wipf and Stock Publishers
199 W. 8th Ave., Suite 3
Eugene, OR 97401

www.wipfandstock.com

PAPERBACK ISBN: 978-1-5326-1894-9
HARDCOVER ISBN: 978-1-4982-4487-9
EBOOK ISBN: 978-1-4982-4486-2

Cataloging-in-Publication data:

Names: Winstead, Melton Bennett, editor.

Title: New Testament philology : essays in honor of David Alan Black / edited by Melton Bennett Winstead.

Description: Eugene, OR : Pickwick Publications, 2018 | Includes bibliographical references.

Identifiers: ISBN 978-1-5326-1894-9 (paperback) | ISBN 978-1-4982-4487-9 (hardcover) | ISBN 978-1-4982-4486-2 (ebook)

Subjects: LCSH: Bible. New Testament—Criticism, interpretation, etc. | Greek philology. | Bible. New Testament—Language, style.

Classification: LCC BS2395 N33 2018 (print) | LCC BS2395 (electronic)

Manufactured in the U.S.A.   06/06/18

To David Alan Black in honor of your groundbreaking
and inspiring work in New Testament studies, and for your diligence
and excellence as a professor, Christian brother, and missionary.

Contents

Permissions | ix
List of Contributors | xi
Introduction | xiii

Chapter 1
Who is Resisting—the Righteous One or Someone Else?:
   James 4:6 and 5:6 | 1
      —William Varner

Chapter 2
"Give Me This Water(!)": A Samaritan Woman, Jesus, and an Imperative
   Walk Into a Pub. . . . Communicative Intentions in John 4:15 | 14
      —Joseph D. Fantin

Chapter 3
Verbal Aspect and Imperatives: Ephesians as a Test Case | 34
      —Benjamin L. Merkle

Chapter 4
Semitic Wordplay Behind the Greek of the New Testament | 52
      —Michael B. Shepherd

Chapter 5
An Overview of the Gnomic or Logical Future Tense
   in the Pauline Corpus | 69
      —Philip La G. Du Toit

Chapter 6
The Role of Chiasm for Understanding Christology
   in Hebrews 1:1–14 | 84
      —Victor (Sung Yul) Rhee

Chapter 7
The Virginal Conception: An Exegesis of Luke 1:35 | 109
      —Stephen Stout

Chapter 8
Is Relevance Theory Relevant for Biblical Studies? | 125
—Margaret Sim

Chapter 9
Disarming Significant Textual Issues in Jude: A Text Critical Study and Interpretation of Jude 5 and 12 | 143
—Herbert W. Bateman IV

Chapter 10
The Linguistic Features of Second Timothy and Its Purpose | 159
—David R. Beck

Chapter 11
Scripture Memorization and Theological Education: καθ' ὑπερβολὴν ὁδός ("A Most Excellent Way") | 176
—Radu Gheorghita

Chapter 12
Defining Discourse Analysis as an Important New Testament Interpretive Framework | 194
—Stanley E. Porter

Chapter 13
Legal Metaphors in 2 Thessalonians 1 and 2: God's Just Judgment on the Day of the Lord | 212
—Terry Wilder

Chapter 14
"Participatory" Language in Ephesians Mediated through Σύν Compounds | 228
—Mel Winstead

Permissions

Scripture quotations taken from the New American Standard Bible® (NASB), Copyright © 1960, 1962, 1963, 1968, 1971, 1972, 1973, 1975, 1977, 1995 by The Lockman Foundation. Used by permission. www.Lockman.org

The Holy Bible, English Standard Version® (ESV®) Copyright © 2001 by Crossway, a publishing ministry of Good News Publishers. All rights reserved.

Scriptures taken from the Holy Bible, New International Version ®, NIV®. Copyright © 1973, 1978, 1984, 2011 by Biblica, Inc. Used by permission of Zondervan. All rights reserved worldwide. www.zondervan.com. The "NIV" and "New International Version" are trademarks registered in the United States Patent and Trademark Office by Biblica, Inc.

Scripture quotations marked (NLT) are taken from the Holy Bible, New Living Translation, copyright © 1996, 2004, 2007, 2013, 2015 by Tyndale House Foundation. Used by permission of Tyndale House Publishers, Inc., Carol Stream, Illinois 60188. All rights reserved.

Select Scripture quotations are from the New Revised Standard Version Bible, copyright © 1989 National Council of the Churches of Christ in the United States of America. Used by permission. All rights reserved worldwide.

Biblia Hebraica Stuttgartensia, edited by Karl Elliger and Wilhelm Rudolph, Fifth Revised Edition, edited by Adrian Schenker, © 1977 and 1997 Deutsche Bibelgesellschaft, Stuttgart. Used by permission.

Greek Bible text from: Novum Testamentum Graece, 28th revised edition, Edited by Barbara Aland and others, © 2012 Deutsche Bibelgesellschaft, Stuttgart.

Permission is granted for reprinting: Rhee, Victor (Sung Yul). "The Role of Chiasm for Understanding Christology in Hebrews 1:1–14." *JBL* 131 (2012): 341–62. The reprint is for inclusion in *New Testament Philology: Essays in Honor of David Alan Black*. Edited by Melton B. Winstead. Published by Pickwick, 2018.

List of Contributors

Herbert W. Bateman, IV is Professor of New Testament, President of Cyber-Center for Biblical Studies, and Kregel Publications Acquisitions Editor.

David R. Beck is Associate Dean of Biblical Studies and Professor of New Testament and Greek, Southeastern Baptist Theological Seminary.

Philip La G. Du Toit, Senior Lecturer, New Testament, North-West University, South Africa.

Joseph D. Fantin is Associate Professor of New Testament, Dallas Theological Seminary.

Radu Gheorghita is Associate Professor of Biblical Studies and Director of the Romanian D. Min. Program, Midwestern Baptist Theological Seminary.

Benjamin L. Merkle, Professor of New Testament and Greek, Southeastern Baptist Theological Seminary.

Stanley E. Porter is President and Dean, Professor of New Testament, and Roy A. Hope Chair in Christian Worldview at McMaster Divinity College, Hamilton, Ontario, Canada.

Victor (Sung Yul) Rhee is Professor of New Testament Languages and Literature, Talbot School of Theology/Biola University.

Michael B. Shepherd, Associate Professor of Biblical Studies, Cedarville University.

Margaret Sim is a former Senior Lecturer in Biblical Studies at Africa International University and a current translation consultant for SIL.

Stephen O. Stout is Adjunct Professor, Charlotte Christian College and Theological Seminary; Pastor, Shearer Presbyterian Church (PCA), Mooresville, NC.

William Varner, Professor of Biblical Studies, The Master's University.

Terry L. Wilder is Wesley Harrison Chair and Professor of New Testament and Associate Dean, PhD Program at Southwestern Baptist Theological Seminary.

Melton B. Winstead, Assistant Professor of New Testament and Dean of Students, Southern Evangelical Seminary.

Introduction

PHILOLOGY[1] IS THE COMPREHENSIVE study of a written text including structure, etymology, word history, grammar, morphology, and more.[2] Further, as Söderblom stated, "Philology is the eye of the needle through which every theological camel must enter the heaven of theology."[3] The discipline is not a lost art, is necessary for a comprehensive understanding of a Scripture passage, and holds a treasury of knowledge for understanding a text. The essays collected here perform the same kinds of research as scholars who have gone before, and all demonstrate a passion and love for the word of God.

Perhaps more than any New Testament scholar in the last few decades, my mentor, David Alan Black has contributed to the love of the Koine Greek language as it pertains to New Testament studies. A glance at his list of publications proves this.[4] But only reading and learning his written texts will offer the student a partial glimpse of Dr. Black's love for God's Word. It is imperative to meet Dr. Black and listen to his lectures (and, if possible, to sit

---

1. A dictionary definition of philology is "the study of literature and of disciplines relevant to literature or to language as used in literature" (http://www.merriam-webster.com/dictionary/philology).

2. Douglas Estes, *Questions and Rhetoric*, alerts us to the complexities involved in grammar and linguistics (30–31); and see Black's discussion in *Linguistics for Students*, 4–5. Some scholars probably rightly compartmentalized "philology" to the analysis of a written text, and "linguistics" to analysis of the spoken word. But since Adolph Deissmann, in his 1908 book *Philology and the Greek Bible: Its Present and Future*, seemed to equate or at a minimum, strongly tether Greek grammar to philology, and since the topics researched by older philologists and modern New Testament Greek linguists overlap, this collection of essays will use "philology" and "linguistics" interchangeably and as umbrella terms to cover topics that include grammar, verbal aspect, textual criticism, structural analyses, etc.

3 Quoted in D. A. Carson, *Exegetical Fallacies* (Grand Rapids, MI: Baker Academic. Kindle Edition, 2013) 27.

4. Dr. Black's C.V. can be accessed at http://apps.sebts.edu/FacultyUploads/David%20Alan%20Black%20CV.pdf, and can also be found in *Getting into the Text*, edited by Daniel Akin and Thomas Hudgins (published by Pickwick).

in one of his semester-long classes) to get a full appreciation for his passion, compassion, and desire to inspire.

The goal of this book is to demonstrate for students the value of continued research in the Greek New Testament. The essays demonstrate how research is currently being done, utilizing such tools as grammatical studies, discourse analysis, textual criticism, verbal aspect, and other linguistic analyses.

Chapter 1 is titled "Who is Resisting—the Righteous One or Someone Else: James 4:6 and 5:6?," by William Varner. In it Varner takes a comprehensive approach and offers a non-traditional interpretation of James 5:6 for who it is that is resisting you if and when you put to death the righteous man (is it the righteous man or someone else?). This chapter is an exercise in discourse analysis and textual criticism.

In Chapter 2, Joseph Fantin offers a study of the imperative mood in general and of the imperative used by the woman at the well in John 4, specifically. Fantin discusses the possible categories of the imperative mood, considers the social mores of first-century Israel, concludes with how he thinks the Samaritan responded to Jesus, and offers quite an invitation himself at the end of the essay.

In Chapter 3, Merkle offers what I think is one of the clearest explanations available concerning the relationship between word choice and verbal aspect. Merkle's thesis is solidly convincing when he explains that verbal aspect should be tweaked to understand that in many cases, a Koine writer had little or no choice in choosing for one tense-form over another.

Michael Shepherd's Chapter 4 will be a favorite for biblical theology students. Shepherd offers a masterful piece analyzing many Greek words in the New Testament that have a Hebraic background. It is in knowing these backgrounds that the key to many clearer interpretations of biblical passages can be found.

Chapter 5, by the South African scholar Philip Du Toit, is an analysis of a particular category of the future tense. He delineates between a gnomic future and the pragmatics of a logical future which result from certain conditions in a context. Du Toit's research will help with interpretation and will probably need to be considered in future grammars when discussing the future tense.

Chapter 6, by Victor Rhee, is a reprint from the *Journal of Biblical Literature*. In this chapter, Rhee offers a literary analysis of the rhetorical features in the opening chapter of the letter to the Hebrews (this is a fitting essay to include since Black wrote so much on Hebrews).

Chapter 7, by Stephen Stout, is exegesis of Luke 1:35. In this essay, Stout deals with the early creedal understanding of the virgin birth. Stout demonstrates the unparalleled importance of the virgin birth for New Testament Christianity because in it is found the reason why Jesus could be sinless.

Chapter 8 is a discussion of Relevance Theory, by European scholar Margaret Sim. In this chapter, Sim demonstrates how literary tools like allusion and metaphor are used in communication. Sim uses categories from the research into modern communication such as "representation," "naïve optimism," "cautious optimism," and "sophisticated understanding" as tools for understanding certain phrases in scripture.

Chapter 9 is a comprehensive application of textual criticism to certain verses in Jude. Herb Bateman takes an eclectic approach to TC in order to choose for a certain reading in several problem sections in Jude. If a student wants to see how TC actually works, Bateman's essay is a great place to start.

In Chapter 10, David R. Beck analyzes the purpose and character of 2 Timothy. He accomplishes this by discussing the linguistic features of the epistle and interacting with modern commentators as they have portrayed the theology of 2 Timothy. Through accepting the authenticity of 2 Timothy as a real letter from the historic apostle under particular historic circumstances, Beck views the letter as a viable tool for training in modern ministry.

Chapter 11 on scripture memorization by Radu Gheorghita is a most refreshing and challenging essay. Gheorghita challenges the evangelical theological academy to re-visit a long-standing, but fallen by the wayside, tradition of memorizing vast portions of the Bible. Gheorghita not only advocates memorizing sections of the Bible in the original languages, but offers a simple and organized method for doing so.

Chapter 12 on "Defining Discourse Analysis as an Important New Testament Interpretive Framework," was written by Stanley Porter (no stranger to New Testament studies). Porter offers a brief history of DA, discusses models of the discipline, and informs the reader of the various critical elements of DA such as context, co-text, and the difference between the top-down, bottom-up approaches. Porters ends with explaining the value of DA for interpretation.

Terry Wilder wrote Chapter 13 on the Legal Metaphors in 2 Thessalonians. His is a very tightly argued and convincing piece. In it Wilder analyzes the various Greek terms in the passage that are used in the legal field and finishes with an exposition of the passage. He is able thus to point out the judicial setting of the eschatological teaching in 2 Thessalonians and to offer practical advice based on the interpretation.

In the last essay, "'Participatory' Language," I attempt to offer a defense of why utilizing linguistics is imperative in studying the New Testament. I do this by means of an example—that of noting the prepositional compounds used by the apostle Paul. He clustered several of the compound words in Ephesians 2 and 3 with each section contributing to the doctrines of salvation and ecclesiology, respectively. More specifically, these prepositions were utilized with verbs and nouns, respectively. This study demonstrates the explanatory power of an in-depth usage of New Testament Greek.

In this *Festschrift* honoring Dave Black, my desire is that students be inspired to passion about knowing and loving the Word of God. I think that has been Dr. Black's life-long goal. Prayerfully, it will be yours.

Chapter 1

Who is Resisting—the Righteous One or Someone Else?

James 4:6 and 5:6

—WILLIAM VARNER
 The Master's University

PERSONAL INTRODUCTION

When I began to teach Intermediate Greek at the university level, I utilized a couple of grammars and found them adequate but not that helpful pedagogically. Then I discovered *It's Still Greek to Me* by David Black and I have used it with my students ever since. When I decided to adopt a more linguistic approach to teaching advanced Greek and discourse analysis, I discovered *Linguistics for Students of New Testament Greek* by David Black, and I have used it with my students ever since. When I was looking for a simple introduction to NT textual criticism for beginning students, I discovered *New Testament Textual Criticism: A Concise Guide* by David Black, and I have used it ever since. Finally, when I desired to teach my students a basic exegetical approach to the New Testament for the purpose of exposition, I discovered *Using New Testament Greek in Ministry* by David Black, and I have used it ever since. Therefore, the following proposal which utilizes a discourse approach to the Greek text of James is offered to David in appreciation for his influence on my teaching the Greek New Testament. He not only helped to form my thinking on the value of a linguistic approach to Greek but he also has helped me to communicate these insights to my students.

ABSTRACT

The two passages—Jas 4:6 and 5:6—at first do not appear to be directly related because of the distance between them. A theological tendency by many evangelicals is to identify quickly τὸν δίκαιον in 5:6 as the Messiah. We should not allow that assumption to trump the context and the use of the term in non-canonical texts. A literary assumption held by many is that the subject of the verb in 5:6 is τὸν δίκαιον as well. By relating 5:6 to 4:6, my suggestion is that the subject of the verb ἀντιτάσσεται in 5:6 is the expressed subject of the same verb earlier in 4:6—God. The sentence should also be read as a question expecting a positive answer. Therefore, the Prov 3:34 quotation in 4:6 functions as a statement not only at the paragraph level of 4:1–10 but also as a question at the wider discourse level of 4:1—5:6.

INTRODUCTION

An overly simple but not inaccurate definition of discourse analysis is that the method emphasizes that we ought to be "looking at grammar above the level of the sentence." Reed affirms what many other writers have also recognized — that the first and most often mentioned tenet of discourse analysis is *to examine language at a level beyond the sentence*.[1] Dave Black also observed: "The study of larger units of language (larger than just words and clauses) is normally called *discourse analysis*, or *text-linguistics*."[2] Biber, Conrad, and Reppen are more specific. "Discourse analyses focus on language characteristics that extend across clause boundaries."[3] This is perhaps the most distinguishing tenet of discourse analysis. Wallace declares "that one does not truly understand the meaning of a linguistic category until one comprehends its function in a text." He adds that much of modern linguistics has all but ignored such a critical affirmation.[4] Sadly, much traditional biblical exegesis, while always nodding its approval on the importance of *context*, has oftentimes ignored this principle in practice. The analysis of

---

1. Reed, "Discourse Analysis," 189–94. The reader is referred to the rest of this chapter for more detailed discussion of these four tenets and for further guidance on "doing discourse analysis" ("Discourse Analysis," 194–213).

2. Black, *Linguistics*, 170.

3. Biber, Conrad, and Reppen, *Corpus Linguistics*, 106.

4. Wallace, "Figure and Ground," 201.

words and clauses is vastly important, but their importance is constrained by the perspective of the larger discourse in which they are found. It is probably helpful to view all the linguistic elements of a text as comprising different "levels of discourse," with individual words on the bottom level and then clauses, clause complexes, sentences, paragraphs, and the entire discourse on the ascending levels, similar to a pyramid.[5]

One of the many benefits of utilizing discourse analysis in the interpretation of the New Testament is its reminder to focus on the discourse as a whole (holistic analysis) while not neglecting the "minutiae" of the specific text. Interpreters have often focused on a "bottom up" analysis while neglecting a "top down" analysis. A full discourse analysis of a text does not neglect one at the expense of the other. This chapter focuses on two apparently disparate texts that at first may appear to be unrelated to each other, but when viewed in light of the discourse as a whole yield an insight on the proper interpretation of both.

How then can this approach to a "whole text" help us discern a pattern that impacts interpretation? Two passages in James, 4:6 and 5:6, at first do not appear to be directly related because of the distance between them. For one of the texts (5:6) I resist a traditional translation and interpretation and propose altering it from an indicative declaration to an interrogative condemnation. While my main purpose is to propose this different approach to Jas 5:6c, I will attempt first to situate both of these texts within their overall context in James. I will then propose that Prov 3:34 serves to link together these passages and that reading 5:6c as a question is consistent both with its immediate context and also at the wider discourse level of 4:1—5:6.

JAMES 4:6

μείζονα δὲ δίδωσιν χάριν; διὸ λέγει ὁ θεὸς ὑπερηφάνοις ἀντιτάσσεται, ταπεινοῖς δὲ δίδωσιν χάριν, "But He gives more grace. Therefore, it says, 'God opposes proud people, but gives grace to humble ones.'"

The interpretation of the previous verse, Jas 4:5 (ἢ δοκεῖτε ὅτι κενῶς ἡ γραφὴ λέγει, Πρὸς φθόνον ἐπιποθεῖ τὸ πνεῦμα ὃ κατῴκισεν ἐν ἡμῖν), is a *crux interpretum* in James but will not concern us in this paper. I will, however, affirm that the difference between what James denies in 4:5 and what he affirms in 4:6 is strengthened by the δὲ following μείζονα in 4:6a

---

5. Porter conveys this analogy by the figure of a pyramid, with "word" as the base and successive levels as "phrase," "sentence," "pericope," and finally "discourse" as the cap of the pyramid (*Idioms*, 298). Longacre describes the levels from the top-down as "discourse, paragraph, sentence, clause, phrase, word and stem" (*Grammar*, 291–94).

and contrasts the promise of God with what he has just denied, i.e., that "the Spirit does not speak in this way." The sense of the verse, therefore, would be as follows: "Rather than desiring envy, He gives all the more grace" (μείζονα δὲ δίδωσιν χάριν). James already had in view the passage of the OT which he now quotes. The subject is the same as in the former sentence. The adjective μείζονα (comparative of μέγας) again contrasts the divine grace that follows with the worldly human attitude of the previous verse. Blomberg and Kamell suggest that this may be a case of the Koine comparative form being used for the positive ("great"), but they do not provide any other examples of this usage.[6] It is better, therefore, to suggest that this is an example of the comparative adjective being used for the Greek *elative* ("very great").[7]

The quotation from the LXX of Prov 3:34 in 4:6b ("He resists proud ones, but gives grace to humble ones") expands on what he has affirmed about God's grace and prepares the reader for what follows in 4:7-10. The word describing the first group, ὑπερηφάνοις ("proud ones"), is in the dative case and functions as the direct object of the verb "opposes" (ἀντιτάσσεται).[8] The second group, ταπεινοῖς ("humble ones"), is the more common dative of indirect object. The lack of articles before each of the substantives (like the LXX but different from the MT) denotes not "*the* proud" and "*the* humble" as social classes of people, but "proud" and "humble" as traits that are characteristic of anyone who can be one but become the other, which the following call to humility in 4:7-10 makes clear. The same ideas are found in Job 22:29, which utilizes the corresponding cognate verbs: "Because He has humbled (ἐταπείνωσεν) him, you will say, 'He has behaved proudly (ὑπερηφανεύσατο), but He will save the lowly.'"

In my commentary, I have argued that this quotation from Prov 3:34 functions as a "structural lynchpin" for the entire paragraph of 4:1–10.[9] Edgar explains both the anaphoric and cataphoric functions of the quotation:

> The first line of the quotation 'God opposes the arrogant' looks back to the enemies of God, who stand over against God at the climax of vv. 1–4, while the second line of the quotation 'but

---

6. Blomberg and Kamell, *Zondervan Exegetical Commentary*, 193. See 1 Cor 13:13 for an example of the comparative functioning as a superlative (Wallace, *Greek Grammar*, 299–300).

7. Wallace lists examples of comparative adjectives used this way in Acts 13:31 (πλείους), in Acts 17:22 (δεισιδαιμονεστέρους), and in Matt 13:32 (μικρότερον— "debatable"). Wallace, *Greek Grammar*, 300–301.

8. Ibid., 142–44. The special anaphoric role of this same construction of verb plus dative of direct object in 5:6 (οὐκ ἀντιτάσσεται ὑμῖν) will be explained in the comments on that verse.

9. Varner, *James*, 143–55.

to the lowly (ταπεινοῖς) he gives grace' anticipates the following verses, which culminate in the command: 'Humble yourselves (ταπεινώθητε) before the Lord and he will exalt you.'[10]

The message conveyed by the intertexture of 4:4–6 has been plainly conveyed. That message is that arrogant and proud people do not acknowledge their dependence on God but choose to live according to the order of the world and as enemies of God. By contrast, God gives grace to lowly people (ταπεινοὶ) who are acknowledging their dependence on God.[11]

Because James desires not only to be a negative condemner of arrogance but also a positive encourager of humility, he thus desires to assure his readers of divine grace and forgiveness. Therefore, he turns from the subject of God's opposition to the idea of God's approval in the second line of this quotation (ταπεινοῖς δὲ δίδωσιν χάριν). This is a general statement and we should not automatically connect it to the poor who are often included among the "humble" elsewhere in the book (1:9). Those people, whatever their socio-economic status, who align themselves with the poor in spirit are the ones who receive this grace. We all have known many poor people who walk humbly before God in trust and faith, but there are also many poor people who curse God whom they blame for their own poverty.

Richard Bauckham has noted that in his only actual citations of OT Scripture, James clearly employs the word γραφή (2:8 and 4:5). In each of these two passages James also reveals his own hermeneutical "keys" to the two main sections of OT literature. "Thus Lev 19:18b (in 2:8) serves as James's hermeneutical key to the Torah and Prov 3:34 (in 4:6) serves as James's hermeneutical key to the wisdom literature."[12] In the case of the Leviticus reference in 2:8, James also follows Jesus in recognizing this verse as the summary of the entire Torah. His utilization of the Proverbs reference here in 4:6 also expresses quite neatly the theme of "reversal in status" which is also quite prominent in Jesus' teaching (e.g., Matt 5:3–6; 10:23, 25, 31, 33–34).[13]

---

10. Edgar, *Has God Not Chosen the Poor?*, 187.

11. For the idea that Jas 4:4–6 is a midrashic commentary on the account of Noah in Gen 6–8, see Prockter, "James 4:4–6," 625–27. Prockter utilizes the rabbinic notion of the יֵצֶר הָרַע (*evil inclination*), which Noah resisted and thus experienced grace from above. The linguistic parallels, however, between James and the LXX of Gen 6 are simply not as clear as Prockter desires them to be.

12. Bauckham, *James*, 155.

13. Further reflection on James's intertextual skill is offered by Carson: "The same OT passage is quoted in 1 Pet. 5:5, one of the many close connections between James and 1 Peter. The grace that we require (4:6a) to face God's jealous longing for us (4:5b) is given to the humble. God sets himself against the proud (a common theme in the

THE CONTEXT OF JAMES 5:6

Before linking Jas 5:6 to 4:6, we must situate the statement within in its previous context. The linguistic and semantic characteristics of Jas 5:1–3 apply also to 5:4–6, but even more intensely. The "meta-comment," Ἄγε νῦν, opened 5:1, while 5:4 opens with a similar "orienter" (ἰδού) that directs the reader to the words that follow. The singular form of the verbs Ἄγε and ἰδού when addressing plural groups illustrates their roles as "frozen imperatives." The strong accusatory tone directed toward the rich in 5:1–3 is actually heightened in 5:4–6 with some greater specifics of the accusations being described. The personification of their corroded riches by their "testifying" and "eating" flesh in 5:3 is developed further by the day laborers' defrauded wages described as crying out against their heartless employers (5:4). Eschatological themes were earlier expressed by future tenses (5:3), allusions to Isaiah (5:1, 3), and reference to the "last days" in 5:3b. These themes are again stressed in the same ways in 5:4–6 by references to a future judgment and a clear allusion to the "day of slaughter" by Jeremiah. Below is a clausal display of Jas 5:4–6:

5:4

ἰδοὺ	ORIENTER
ὁ μισθὸς τῶν ἐργατῶν τῶν ἀμησάντων τὰς χώρας ὑμῶν ὁ ἀπεστερημένος ἀφ' ὑμῶν κράζει,	AFFIRMATION PRESENT
καὶ αἱ βοαὶ τῶν θερισάντων εἰς τὰ ὦτα κυρίου σαβαὼθ εἰσεληλύθασιν.	AFFIRMATION PERFECT

5:5

ἐτρυφήσατε ἐπὶ τῆς γῆς, καὶ ἐσπαταλήσατε	ACCUSATION AORIST
ἐθρέψατε τὰς καρδίας ὑμῶν ἐν ἡμέρᾳ σφαγῆς,	ACCUSATION AORIST

5:6

κατεδικάσατε,	ACCUSATION AORIST

OT—e.g., Ps. 18:27; 34:18; Isa. 61:1; Zeph. 3:11–12). James applies a common wisdom contrast to the particular situation that he is addressing, but this particular situation is embedded in the fundamental problematic of how sinful human beings are established in relationship with their Creator—a challenge that runs throughout the Bible, finding ready exposition in the Wisdom literature and in this embodiment of it" ("James," 1008).

ἐφονεύσατε τὸν δίκαιον,	ACCUSATION AORIST
οὐκ ἀντιτάσσεται ὑμῖν;	QUESTION PRESENT

As can be seen in this sentence flow analysis, after the initial orienter ἰδοὺ, 5:4–6 conveys its message through eight primary clauses characterized by the use of asyndeton (lack of conjunctions, except in 5:4, 5). Two of those clauses contain secondary participial clauses (5:4). In both of these, the subject of the clause is fronted (ὁ μισθὸς, αἱ βοαὶ) and calls our attention to the cries of the defrauded laborers (present κράζει) and how these cries have entered (perfect εἰσεληλύθασιν) God's ears. This threefold combining of (1) an imperative orienter; (2) the initial placement of the subjects; and (3) the aspectually prominent present/perfect tenses combine to convey a greater degree of prominence both for these cries expressed to God and also for His willingness to hear those cries.

We now turn our attention to the specific issues raised in Jas 5:6. The verse initially states simply: κατεδικάσατε, ἐφονεύσατε τὸν δίκαιον, "You condemned; you murdered the righteous person." The actions of the rich and greedy landowners also included judicial acts of condemnation (κατεδικάσατε) and even murder (ἐφονεύσατε). The verb καταδικάζω is constantly found in a forensic context, as a sentence of condemnation given against someone for committing a crime (Herodotus, 1.45; Job 34:29; Josephus, *Ant.* 7.271; Matt 12:37; Acts 25:15). This judicial thrust of Jas 5:6 recalls for the reader the earlier, vividly described court scene in 2:1–4. In that passage, it was said that the rich often drag poor believers into court and deal with them unjustly (2:6–7). It is a description of the abuse of power by the powerful against the powerless. The only other appearance of this verb form in the NT offers an interesting parallel: "And if you had known what this means, 'I desire mercy, and not sacrifice,' you would not have condemned (κατεδικάσατε) the guiltless" (Matt 12:7 ESV). Psalm 10 describes such a scene that was all too familiar in ancient Israel. "He sits in ambush in the villages; in hiding places he murders the innocent. His eyes stealthily watch for the helpless; he lurks in ambush like a lion in his thicket; he lurks that he may seize the poor; he seizes the poor when he draws him into his net" (Ps 10:8–9 ESV).

The murder accusation (ἐφονεύσατε τὸν δίκαιον) may be hyperbolic in its rhetoric or possibly juridical in its language.[14] Interesting linguistic and semantic parallels are found in Sirach 34:25–27: "The bread of the needy is the life of the poor (πτωχῶν); whoever deprives them (ὁ ἀποστερῶν) of it is a murderer. To take away a neighbor's living is to commit murder (φονεύων);

---

14. Huther, *Critical and Exegetical Handbook*, 207; Martin, *James*, 181.

to deprive an employee of wages (ὁ ἀποστερῶν μισθόν [cf. Jam 5:4]) is to shed blood." We cannot, therefore, reject outright the idea that this should be taken in a very literal sense, and that the Sirach passage should also be taken literally. If laborers who depend on receiving their pay at the end of the day (Matt 20:1–16) are thus defrauded, the loss of their promised daily bread may actually lead to the deaths of family members. These heartless employers, therefore, are directly to blame for their laborers' suffering and even for their families' deaths.[15]

Now we consider the traditional interpretation of this verse. An impressive amount of scriptural evidence can actually be assembled for the idea that the substantive τὸν δίκαιον, which serves as the direct object of the predicate ἐφονεύσατε, refers to *the* Righteous One—namely, the Messiah. "The righteous one" was a title applied to Jesus by early Messianic sermonizers. See its use by Peter in Acts 3:14 (τὸν ἅγιον καὶ δίκαιον); Stephen in Acts 7:52 (τοῦ δικαίου); and Paul in Acts 22:14 (τὸν δίκαιον).[16] Linguistic roots for this title can also be found in OT texts such as its possible Messianic use in Isaiah 3:10 (τὸν δίκαιον) and its more likely use as a Messianic title in Isaiah 53:11 (LXX δίκαιον; MT צַדִּיק עַבְדִּי).[17]

A number of commentators have suggested that *Wisdom of Solomon* 2:10–20 may also be influencing the language here.[18] The passage does share many unique verbal connections with James. The substantive δίκαιος appears three times in that passage as the object of attacks by wicked people (2:10, 12, 18) and it is clearly identified there as referring to a righteous (δίκαιον) poor man (2:10). Two verbs in the passage also appear in James and describe mistreatment of the poor (καταδυναστεύσωμεν in 2:10/Jas 2:6; κατεδικάσωμεν in 2:20/Jas 5:6). The righteous person, however, is not a Messianic term in *Wisdom of Solomon*, since the substantive is paired with a "widow" (χήρας) in *Wisdom* 2:10, which is of course another collective victim mentioned by James (1:27). Therefore, if this passage influenced James, it is probably best to view the substantive adjective τὸν δίκαιον in 5:6 as a collective term for the righteous poor, who are the subjects of the oppression described in the context.

---

15. Moo, *Letter of James*, 219.

16. Note also that each of these uses includes the article before δίκαιος, thus substantivizing the adjective.

17. I worked in an evangelistic outreach to Jewish people for seventeen years and I have authored a book on the Messianic idea (*The Messiah: Revealed, Rejected, Received*). I acknowledge, therefore, that I have a strong inclination to find references to the Messiah at every possible place that I can find. It is this theological inclination to find Jesus in this expression, however, that I have attempted to resist in this paper!

18. See, e.g., Dibelius and Greeven, *James*, 239–40.

We now turn our attention to Jas 5:6c: οὐκ ἀντιτάσσεται ὑμῖν, "Does He [God] not oppose you?" What has been written thus far has echoed other more traditional approaches to the meaning of this text. In this final clause, I will offer a non-traditional interpretation. This concluding clause suddenly switches from two plural aorist tense forms (κατεδικάσατε, ἐφονεύσατε) to a present tense form (ἀντιτάσσεται). This last clause refers to someone (singular) who, if it is a statement, *does not* resist these oppressors, or, if it is a question, *does* resist them. Identifying the subject of the verb ἀντιτάσσεται has been another of those important grammatical and hermeneutical issues in James. Is the subject the "righteous one" just mentioned, whoever that might be?[19] Furthermore, is the clause a negated indicative statement or is it a question, expressed with the negative particle οὐ/οὐκ/οὐχ that anticipates a positive response?[20] There are four basic answers to this issue that have been suggested and they are listed below. Afterward is my proposal of a possible additional solution to these conundrums.

(1) The sentence is indicative and the subject is the Righteous Messiah (a few commentators, who identify "the righteous one" as Messianic). The reference is to the submissive nonresistance of Jesus to His rich, Sadducean interrogators (patristic commentators such as Bede, Oecumenius, and Theophylact).[21]

(2) The sentence is indicative and the subject is the collective righteous sufferer (the majority of commentators).[22]

(3) The sentence is interrogative and the subject is the Messiah. This would imply a future sense given to the present verb. "He will resist you" in the eschatological judgment already mentioned.[23]

---

19. The presence of καί before the clause in some manuscripts (most importantly the tenth century 307) and the presence of *et* in the Clementine Vulgate are apparently efforts to read τὸν δίκαιον as the subject of the following verb (*Editio Critica Maior*, 87; see also NA28).

20. For the grammatical usage of asking questions in Greek with οὐ/οὐκ/οὐχ, see Blass and Debrunner, *Greek Grammar*, §427, 2; Robertson, *Grammar*, 917; Bauer, Danker, Arndt, and W. Gingrich, *Greek-English Lexicon*, 734. Surprisingly, Wallace does not clearly describe this usage (cf. 450).

21. Cited by Johnson, *Letter of James*, 304.

22. See Mussner, *Der Jakobusbrief*, 193; and Adamson, *Epistle of James*, 188, among several others.

23. Ropes, *Critical and Exegetical Commentary*, 292.

(4) The sentence is interrogative but has a rhetorical twist that implies that the poor *are* resisting their treatment with protests before God's throne.[24]

In agreement with views (3) and (4), it is best to view the final sentence as a question. Westcott/Hort and the SBL Greek NT also punctuate their texts in this way.[25] Taking the clause as a question instead of a declaration has not been a rare solution to the issue and finds a number of advocates, some of whom were previously cited. But who exactly is the subject of the verb ἀντιτάσσεται? With the help of a discourse perspective, I will argue that God should be considered as the subject of this rhetorical question: "Does He [God] not oppose you?" One of the keys to this approach is the sudden switch in tense from the series of five consecutive aorist verbs to this single present verb, ἀντιτάσσεται, and the earlier appearance of that very same present tense-form of the verb in 4:6: ὁ θεὸς ὑπερηφάνοις ἀντιτάσσεται.

Luis Alonso Schökel first suggested this interpretation of Jas 5:6c in 1973, and he listed no less than fifty previous authors on James who had *not* recognized this important connection between Jas 5:6 and Jas 4:6. A vital implication of recognizing this connection is that 5:6c then becomes a question, with God as the one who is doing the opposing.[26] Schökel's simple argument is that ἀντιτάσσεται has appeared earlier in this exact tense-form in 4:6, where it is part of a quotation from the LXX of Prov 3:34: "God opposes [ἀντιτάσσεται] the proud, but gives grace to the humble." Jas 5:6c, therefore, concludes the subsequent commentary by James on 4:6 and refers anaphorically to that quotation in 4:6. "This explains the surprising present ἀντιτάσσεται and the lack of a specific subject."[27] This proposal also helps to explain the lack of a conjunction that would connect the clause to what precedes. For example, some have suggested that the sense of the verse is: "You murdered the righteous one, *but* he does not oppose you." The asyndeton, however, supports the idea that someone other than "the righteous one" who was just mentioned is the actual subject of ἀντιτάσσεται.[28]

---

24. Davids, *Epistle of James*, 180.

25. Westcott and Hort, *Greek New Testament*, 609; SBL Greek New Testament *in loco*.

26. Schökel, "James 5, 2 [sic] and 4, 6," 73–76. His list of authors is on page 75. Additional post-1973 authors could now be added to his list. Luke Johnson was the first major commentator who espoused the view that God is the subject of the verb (Johnson, *Letter of James*, 305). Some recent monographs have followed Schökel's suggestion. Penner, *Epistle of James*, 155–58; Edgar, *Has God Not Chosen the Poor?*, 203; Taylor, *Text-Linguistic Investigation*, 67–68.

27. Schökel, "James 5, 2 [sic] and 4, 6," 74.

28. If we again assume the possibility that Wis 2:6–20 could be a source for Jas

This approach appears to me to be satisfactory because of the following additional reasons. 1) The passage (5:1–6) has moved alternatively between a discussion of the behavior of the rich to their promised judgment, and the reading given here forms the logical response to their final murderous act. 2) The use of a rhetorical question here certainly fits James's diatribal style elsewhere in his book. If 5:6c is also counted as a question, there is a total of 24 questions asked in only 108 verses.[29] 3) If we resist the influence of Dibelius, who interpreted James's various sayings as largely unrelated *paranesis*, and we rather acknowledge the discourse unity of James, then the use of ἀντιτάσσεται in proximity to 4:6 is not accidental. In 4:6 God is said to *oppose* (ἀντιτάσσεται) *the arrogant*. James has now given two such examples of arrogance: the presumptuous businessmen in 4:13–17; and the arrogant landowners in 5:4–6 which climaxes with the just-mentioned accusation of judicial murder. That God *opposes* them makes a fitting conclusion. 4) The objection that the nearest antecedent to the subject of ἀντιτάσσεται is the previous substantive δίκαιον is countered when we recognize that God has been the most dominant "actor" in the larger preceding context (4:4, 5, 6, 7, 8, 10, 12, 15; 5:4), as He will continue to be in the subsequent context (5:7, 8, 9, 10, 11). With such numerous references, "God" does not need to be specifically mentioned by name again for readers who are aware of His participant role in the larger discourse. 5) Thus this neglected approach to the discourse unity of the book then continues with the following verse. If 5:6 concludes not with a statement about the righteous person's lack of opposition, but with an assurance of God's opposition to the arrogant, then the οὖν ("therefore") that follows in 5:7 makes even better sense (Μακροθυμήσατε οὖν, ἀδελφοί, ἕως τῆς παρουσίας τοῦ κυρίου).[30] Because God opposes their oppressors, the believers can patiently endure and await expectantly His coming.

Earlier we suggested that the call to repentance in 4:7–10 expounds the latter part of Prov 3:34 ("He gives grace to the humble"). The role of God as judge, beginning in 4:11 and continuing through the harsh words of 4:13–17 and 5:1–6, further develops the first half of the quotation ("He

---

5:6, it is interesting to note that when "the righteous person" in that passage, which is clearly a term for the collective righteous poor, is said to "oppose" those oppressing and condemning him, the verb in Wis 2:12 is ἐνανιοῦται—not a NT word and definitely not the verb ἀντιτάσσεται of 4:6 and 5:6.

29. See, for example, 2:5 (with οὐκ); 2:6 (οὐχ); 2:7 (οὐχ); 2:14; 2:16; 2:20; 2:21(οὐκ); 2:25 (οὐκ); 3:11–12 (4 t.); 3:13; 4:1 (οὐκ); 4:4 (οὐκ); 4:5; 4:12; 4:14; 5:13 (2 t.); 5:14.

30. In chapters four and five, James utilizes the conjunction οὖν four other times. It is important to note that in each of these examples, the conjunction follows a significant statement about God's attitude or actions (4:4; 4:7; 4:17; 5:16). If we assume that God is the subject of ἀντιτάσσεται, the same pattern is followed in Jas 5:7.

opposes the proud"). The powerful conclusion to James's prophetic attack, therefore, comes in the final clause of 5:6: "God opposes the arrogant. You rich oppressors have behaved arrogantly. *Should He not oppose you?*"

BIBLIOGRAPHY

Adamson, James B. *The Epistle of James*. The New International Commentary on the New Testament. Grand Rapids, MI: Eerdmans, 1976.

Bauckham, Richard. *James: Wisdom of James, Disciple of Jesus the Sage*. London: Routledge, 1999.

Bauer, W., F. W. Danker, W. F. Arndt, and F. W. Gingrich. *Greek-English Lexicon of the New Testament and Other Early Christian Literature*. 2nd ed. Chicago: University of Chicago Press, 1999.

Biber, D., S. Conrad, and R. Reppen. *Corpus Linguistics: Investigating Language Structure and Use*. Cambridge: Cambridge University Press, 1998.

Black, David Alan. *Linguistics for Students of New Testament Greek: A Survey of Basic Concepts and Applications*. Grand Rapids, MI: Baker, 1988.

Blass, Friedrich, and Albert Debrunner. *A Greek Grammar of the New Testament and Other Early Christian Literature*. Translated by Robert W. Funk. Chicago: University of Chicago Press, 1961.

Blomberg, Craig L., and Mariam J. Kamell. *Zondervan Exegetical Commentary on the New Testament*. Vol. 16, *James*. Grand Rapids, MI: Zondervan, 2008.

Carson, D. A. "James." In *Commentary on the New Testament Use of the Old Testament*, edited by G. K. Beale and D. A. Carson, 997–1014. Grand Rapids, MI: Baker Academic, 2007.

Davids, Peter H. *The Epistle of James: A Commentary on the Greek Text*. New International Greek Testament Commentary. Grand Rapids, MI: Eerdmans, 1982.

Dibelius, Martin, and Heinrich Greeven. *James: A Commentary on the Epistle of James*. Hermeneia—a Critical and Historical Commentary on the Bible. Philadelphia: Fortress, 1976.

Edgar, David H. *Has God Not Chosen the Poor?: The Social Setting of the Epistle of James*. Journal for the Study of the New Testament, Supplement Series 206. Sheffield: Sheffield Academic, 2001.

Huther, John. *Critical and Exegetical Handbook to the General Epistles of James and John*. Translated by Paton Gloag and Clarke Irwin. Critical and Exegetical Commentary on the New Testament. Edinburgh: T&T Clark, 1882.

Johnson, Luke Timothy. *The Letter of James: A New Translation with Introduction and Commentary*. Anchor Yale Bible 37A. New Haven: Yale University Press, 2008.

Longacre, Robert E. *The Grammar of Discourse*. New York: Plenum, 1983.

Martin, Ralph P. *James*. Word Biblical Commentary 48. Dallas: Word, 1998.

Mayor, Joseph B. *The Epistle of St. James: Greek Text with Introduction, Notes and Comments, and Further Studies*. London: Macmillan, 1913.

McKnight, Scot. *The Letter of James*. New International Commentary on the Old and New Testament. Grand Rapids, MI: Eerdmans, 2011.

Moo, Douglas J. *The Letter of James*. Pillar New Testament Commentary. Grand Rapids, MI: Eerdmans, 2000.

Mussner, Franz. *Der Jakobusbrief: Auslegung von Franz Mussner.* Freiburg: Basel, Wien, 1964.
Penner, Todd C. *The Epistle of James and Eschatology: Re-Reading an Ancient Christian Letter.* Journal for the Study of the New Testament, Supplement Series 121. Sheffield: Sheffield Academic, 1996.
Porter, Stanley E. *Idioms of the Greek New Testament.* 2nd ed. Sheffield: Sheffield Academic, 1994.
Prockter, L. J. "James 4:4–6: Midrash on Noah." *New Testament Studies* 35 (1989) 625–27.
Reed, Jeffrey T. "Discourse Analysis." In *Handbook to the Exegesis of the New Testament*, edited by Stanley E. Porter, 189–217. Leiden: Brill, 1997.
Ropes, James Hardy. *A Critical and Exegetical Commentary on James.* International Critical Commentary. New York: Scribner, 1916.
Schökel, Luis A. "James 5, 2 and 4, 6." *Biblica* 54 (1973) 73–76.
Taylor, Mark E. *A Text-Linguistic Investigation into the Discourse Structure of James.* Library of New Testament Studies 311. London: T&T Clark, 2006.
Varner, William. *The Book of James: A New Perspective.* Woodlands, TX: Kress Biblical Resources, 2010.
———. *James: A Commentary on the Greek Text.* Rev. ed. Joplin, MO: Fontes, 2017.
Wallace, Daniel B. *Greek Grammar Beyond the Basics: An Exegetical Syntax of the New Testament.* Grand Rapids, MI: Zondervan, 1996.
Wallace, Stephen. "Figure and Ground: The Interrelationships of Linguistic Categories." In *Tense-Aspect: Between Semantics and Pragmatics*, edited by Paul J. Hopper, 201–25. Amsterdam: Benjamins, 1982.
Westcott, B. F., and F. J. A. Hort, eds. *The Greek New Testament.* Peabody, MA: Hendrickson, 2007.

Chapter 2

"Give Me This Water(!)"

A Samaritan Woman, Jesus, and an Imperative Walk Into a Pub. . . . Communicative Intentions in John 4:15

—JOSEPH D. FANTIN
Dallas Theological Seminary

IT IS AN HONOR to contribute to a *Festschrift* for David Alan Black. Although Dr. Black is familiar to me only through his work, I have the utmost respect for him and I see him as a kindred spirit. Dr. Black has contributed widely to New Testament studies but there are two areas in which he has influenced academia and the church that have impacted me most. First, Dr. Black was one of the first New Testament scholars to explicitly use linguistic theory in his work. The first edition of his book, *Linguistics for Students of the New Testament* was published the year that I completed my formal linguistic training.[1] Second, Dr. Black desires to make Greek widely accessible. His little book, *It's Still Greek to Me*, is an excellent example of this.[2] This book came out of a series of Greek courses in which Black's objective was "to teach people how to use Greek effectively in their personal lives and ministries."[3] *It's Still Greek to Me* can be used by those who in the past finished intermediate Greek and are in need of a refresher or by students who never really grasped Greek while in school and still feel lost. In class, I

---

1. Black, *Linguistics*. See also Black, Barnwell, and Levinsohn, *Linguistics and New Testament Interpretation*.

2. Black, *It's Still Greek to Me*. See also *Using New Testament Greek*, and his introductory Greek text, *Learn to Read New Testament Greek*.

3. Black, *It's Still Greek to Me*, 11.

continually use Dr. Black's preposition illustration, "A Tale of Twelve Mice" to show the relationships between prepositions with the enthusiastic approval of the students.[4] At a time where trends seem to be going in the other direction, Dr. Black recognizes the importance of Greek for understanding and communicating God's word. Greek is not an academic discipline to further knowledge (although it contributes to knowledge). Rather, Greek is an essential tool for Christians to know God better and to impact the world for Christ. I would also like to add that I appreciate his student-friendly approach. Dr. Black suggests that a prerequisite to using *It's Still Greek to Me* is a "healthy sense of humor."[5]

INTRODUCTION

This brief article focuses on a small but potentially important aspect of Jesus' encounter with the Samaritan woman in John chapter 4. It contributes to the study of Greek but also should impact us personally as we consider this woman's approach to Jesus and Jesus' response.

In the middle of the story of the encounter between Jesus and the Samaritan woman, after Jesus offers her living water, the Samaritan woman responds with an imperative clause:

κύριε, δός μοι τοῦτο τὸ ὕδωρ, ἵνα μὴ διψῶ μηδὲ διέρχωμαι ἐνθάδε ἀντλεῖν (John 4:15), "sir, give to me this water that I may not thirst nor come here to draw."[6]

Generally, this verse garners little discussion. The woman simply asks for the water that Jesus is offering. Most scholars and exegetes focus on the fact that the woman misunderstands Jesus and a few even see sarcasm or a negative response from the woman. However, few, if any, consider implications if this imperative is treated as a normal imperative. The purpose of this article is to reevaluate the classification of the imperative in John 4:15 in light of a reconsideration of the usage called "request" or "entreaty."

---

4. Ibid., 85.

5. Ibid., 11. Part and chapter titles include: "Up the Greek Without a Paddle: This Thing Called Grammar," "Rho, Rho, Rho Your Boat: The Greek Verb System," "Tense Times with Verbs (2): Interpreting the Greek Tenses," and "It's a Small Word After All: Adverbs, Conjunctions, and Particles."

6. All Greek scripture passages are from NA28; translations are my own.

1. THE CONTEXT OF JOHN 4:15

John chapter 3 records an encounter between Jesus and Nicodemus. Nicodemus is a religious leader and comes to Jesus after dark, presumably because he wished to do so secretly.[7] As a religious leader, Nicodemus should have understood Jesus' words in response to his questions (although I confess, I am not sure how I would have responded in his place). He did not. In contrast, in chapter 4, Jesus breaks ancient custom and initiates a conversation with a Samaritan woman (4:7)[8] who was on the margins of society.[9] Ancient readers unaware of this story may have worried: if the religious leader failed to understand Jesus, what was going to happen to this poor woman? However, as we all know, that in contrast to Nicodemus, Jesus pursues this woman until she is open to his message (4:28-29). The woman does not initially understand the significance of this water and thinks that it is actual and/or magical which follows given the *misunderstanding* theme in John.[10] Jesus appears sensitive but does not shy away from exposing what was keeping her from full acceptance in her community (4:17-18). This could not have been easy for her. Nevertheless, Jesus has offered her something better than her community — living water — and she wants it and will accept it (4:15, 28). One remarkable aspect of this story, is that among the rare occasions where Jesus reveals his messianic identity in the Gospels, his exchange with this woman includes the clearest and most direct identification (4:26).

This exchange in which Jesus breaks social convention and draws this woman (and later her community) to himself includes much personal drama.[11] A righteous man pursues a marginalized woman without sexual intent

---

7. "Nicodemus came at night so he wouldn't be seen by men" (Dylan, "In the Garden.") See also Lincoln, *Gospel According to Saint John*, 149; Michaels, *Gospel of John*, 178.

8. Carson, *Gospel According to John*, 217-18.

9. There is no need to rehash in any detail the negative standing of this woman. She was a woman, a Samaritan, unmarried, alone at the well, and likely in a sinful relationship. With the possible exception of the sinful relationship (and I suspect this was a circumstance forced on her for survival), she had no control over any of these. What is important is that she was not an acceptable person from the perspective of society, especially Jewish society of which Jesus is a part. For detail on barriers faced by this woman, see Keener, *Gospel of John*, 591-601. For a challenging and insightful treatment of this passage, see Neyrey, "What's Wrong?," 143-71.

10. Barrett, *Gospel According to St. John*, 235; Beasley-Murray, *John*, 61; Bruce, *Gospel of John*, 106; Carson, *Gospel According to John*, 220; Haenchen, *John 1*, 221; Köstenberger, *John*, 151 (includes "irony"); Lincoln, *Gospel According to Saint John*, 174; Michaels, *Gospel of John*, 243; Schnackenburg, *Gospel According to St. John*, 432.

11. See the helpful discussion of this exchange in Brant, *John*, 83-85. Bruce Malina and Richard Rohrbaugh are much stronger and suggest that "from the view of Judean

(which may have initially been in the woman's mind when approached).[12] Jesus uses the metaphor of water to explain who he is and what he can do for her. The woman, wisely suspicious, questions Jesus until it is clear he is more than a normal man. She wants what he has to offer and he obliges. In the midst of this great story, I wish to concentrate on a single issue and see what it can add to the color of this story and in turn what we can learn about approaching God.

2. THE ISSUE (4:15)

In the middle of the story of the encounter between Jesus and the Samaritan woman, after Jesus offers her living water, the Samaritan woman responds with an imperative clause:

κύριε, δός μοι τοῦτο τὸ ὕδωρ, ἵνα μὴ διψῶ μηδὲ διέρχωμαι ἐνθάδε ἀντλεῖν (John 4:15)

"sir, give to me this water that I may not thirst nor come here to draw"

It is common for grammars to see certain imperatives as weaker, labeling them "request" or something similar[13] instead of the more common "command." Due to the wide gap in the social status between Jesus and the woman, it seems logical that the lower-status woman would not wish to "command" Jesus. This seems like an ideal example of a "request" usage.[14] Many commentaries either say nothing at all about this imperative[15] or simply suggest that the woman is asking or making a request of Jesus.[16] She may

---

values, then, this whole scene seems socially deviant" (*Social-Science Commentary*, 99).

12. It is possible that given Jesus' break in social convention, she initially believed he had some sort of sexual intention. Her response to Jesus' instruction to "go, call your husband" (4:16) is, "I do not have a husband" (4:17). This statement can contribute to this assumption. However, as her response to Jesus' follow-up suggests, her elusive response is most likely to hide her shameful situation and history (Keener, *Gospel of John*, 605–6). Further, if one initially thinks that Jesus had sexual intentions, the developing exchange dispels this notion.

13. Brooks and Winbery, *Syntax*, 116; Dana and Mantey, *Manual Grammar*, 176; Young, *Intermediate New Testament Greek*, 144.

14. Mathewson and Emig classify this as an "entreaty (request)" (*Intermediate Greek Grammar*, 187). By consulting scripture indexes or electronically searching documents, I was unable to find any other grammar that classified the imperative in John 4:15.

15. See for example, Barrett, *Gospel According to St. John*, 235; Bruce, *Gospel of John*, 106; Bultmann, *Gospel of John*, 187; Carson, *Gospel According to John*, 220; Haenchen, *John 1*, 221; Lincoln, *Gospel According to Saint John*, 174; Michaels, *Gospel of John*, 245; Thompson, *John*, 99–101; Weinrich, *John 1:1—7:1*, 471–78.

16. Beasley-Murray, *John*, 61; Brown, *Gospel According to John 1–12*, 177; Keener, *Gospel of John*, 605; Köstenberger, *John*, 152; Malina and Rohrbaugh, *Social-Science*

be echoing Jesus' use of the imperative in 4:7, δός μοι πεῖν ("give me something to drink.")[17] Some even suggest that the woman is being combative.[18] There can be significant differences of opinion in the manner in which the exchange between Jesus and the woman is understood. Many seem to see the woman as submissive while others see her challenging or engaging in more of a playful exchange.[19] Nevertheless, as is seen above, most seem to assume the woman is in some way "requesting" living water from Jesus. This seems fairly obvious. In fact, few question the validity of this approach. Interpreters quickly consider the imperative in John 4:15 a request and move on to other exegetical details that demand their attention. However, I would like slow down to revisit this conclusion and the underlying assumptions which lead to it. Why do we simply assume this is a weakened form of a command, namely, a request? I plan to proceed by first looking at the meaning and nature of the imperative, considering the validity of the weakened command classification "request" (entreaty),[20] reconsider the imperative in John 4:15, and briefly consider implications for Christian living.

3. THE MEANING OF THE IMPERATIVE MOOD

The choice of an imperative must bring something to the communication situation. There is little debate concerning the main meaning of this mood so I will be brief here.[21] In relation to other moods, Wallace describes the imperative as the "mood of *intention*, . . . the mood furthest removed from certainty, . . . [the mood which] moves in the realm of *volition* . . . and *possibility*."[22] A number of observations can be made here. The mood involves communicative intention and it is the furthest mood from reality in

---

Commentary, 98; Schnackenburg, *Gospel According to St. John*, 432. Although John McHugh uses "request" and "ask" to characterize this statement, his words are a little stronger than most; "it serves to underline the seriousness and the sincerity of the woman's request." *Critical and Exegetical Commentary*, 272.

17. Neyrey, *Gospel of John*, 90; Thompson, *John*, 99. This observation may be accurate no matter how one interprets the imperative verb. It does not necessarily have any significance on the usage of the woman's imperative.

18. See Brant, *John*, 84.

19. Compare Bruner's more meek description with Brant's more confrontive understanding: Bruner, *Gospel of John*, 252; and Brant, *John*, 84–85. Edward Klink states the woman's response is "likely a bit playful and probably also includes a chiding, 'Hey dreamer, this water sounds good to me!'" *John*, 240–41.

20. Only the label "request" will be used from here.

21. For a more thorough discussion, see Fantin, *Greek Imperative*, 121–98.

22. Wallace, *Greek Grammar*, 485 (italics original).

the sense that actuality is "to be realized by another."[23] Thus, fulfillment of the expressed intention is dependent upon the actions of the one to whom the imperative is aimed. This is why it is the mood furthest from certainty. Wallace's "volition" can be more formally labeled, volitional directive.[24] Thus, a communicator uses the imperative to express his desire (volition) to direct the actions of another:

ἀγαπᾶτε τοὺς ἐχθροὺς ὑμῶν καὶ προσεύχεσθε ὑπὲρ τῶν διωκόντων ὑμᾶς (Matt 5:44), "*love* your enemies and *pray* for those who persecute you."

Here Matthew records Jesus instructing (commanding) others to "love" and "pray for" their persecutors. By using the imperative, Matthew presents this as Jesus' desire to direct certain behaviors (in this case, attitudes).[25] In addition to this example, other passages could be discussed.[26] Imperatives reveal a willful, directive presentation of purpose, thus, the imperative mood brings volition and direction to the communication situation.

4. THE VALIDITY OF THE IMPERATIVE OF REQUEST

The imperative is a mood that expresses volitional-direction. It is chosen by the communicator to present a desire to direct another individual or party to do something. It is a volitional directive.[27] It only "presents" a volitional intention because it is not possible to know with entire certainty what another's true intention through language is. This is especially relevant for ancient literature in which we do not have access to the authors.

4.1. The Category Request

As is to be expected, "commands" (including negative commands, "prohibitions"[28]) are the most common function of the imperative mood.

---

23. Zerwick, *Biblical Greek*, 100.

24. Fantin, *Greek Imperative Mood*, 196–97.

25. This does not guarantee that the communicator using the imperative is sincere. It only presents the desire as coming from the communicator. Context is necessary to determine sincerity. In this case, there is nothing that would challenge Jesus' sincerity.

26. For other examples, see Fantin, *Greek Imperative Mood*, 136–53. Imperatives are found to be volitional directive no matter how one classifies them in traditional grammars.

27. For more developed definitions of the imperative mood, see Wallace, *Greek Grammar*, 485; and Fantin, *Greek Imperative Mood*, 196–97.

28. For a thorough study and description of prohibitions in the New Testament, see Huffman, *Verbal Aspect Theory*.

Boyer classifies 83% (1357 occurrences) of imperatives this way.[29] The second most common category is "request." Boyer's analysis concludes that 11% (188) fall within this category.[30]

The overwhelming percentage of "command" usages makes one wonder whether other classifications are necessary. Especially since one of those classifications is "greeting" which is clearly a fixed idiomatic expression (e.g., χαίρε) and no longer maintains its volitional force.[31] What is driving the decision to make these exceptions?

I need to clarify exactly what I object to regarding the label "request." I am not arguing against an imperative verb being used to "ask for" something. Because the imperative does not carry the ability to assure fulfillment, in a sense all non-idiomatic imperatives are asking for something. Indeed, a person can request something with a strong command. No, I am only challenging the "request" label when it is intended to express something weaker than command. In other words, I am arguing against the label "request" when its choice replaces the category "command."

4.2. The Classification Request Challenged

The following description of the "request" category is representative and will serve as a starting point for my critique: "When the strength of command would be improper because of the social positions of the parties involved, the imperative is reduced to the force of a request."[32] Some develop "social position" by suggesting the request imperative is primarily used by inferiors towards superiors but can occur with superiors addressing inferiors.[33] The latter is qualified, "since we are dealing with written documents, we cannot determine by tone of voice, gesture, or tacit 'please' when this general rule is broken."[34] Given that these politeness elements are not explicit (or even

---

29. Boyer, "Classification of Imperatives," 36. In addition, there are an additional twenty-eight occurrences he has classified differently but suggests "command" is an alternative classification ("Classification of Imperatives," 36n2).

30. Ibid., 36. In addition, there are seven other occurrences he has classified differently but suggests "request" is an alternative classification (ibid., 36n3). Boyer's category is labeled "requests and prayers" (ibid., 36); however, when one removes prayers, the percentage is likely much less.

31. Fantin, *Greek Imperative Mood*, 131–33.

32. Young, *Intermediate New Testament Greek*, 144.

33. Wallace, *Greek Grammar*, 488; Mathewson and Emig, *Intermediate Greek Grammar*, 185–86.

34. Mathewson and Emig, *Intermediate Greek Grammar*, 185–86. They are following Wallace, *Greek Grammar*, 488. Young mentions that there is no exact correlation

implicit) in the text, I think the notion of the "request" usage for superiors to inferiors can be dismissed. Authors understand that written language demands different means of expression than speech in certain instances. If an author wishes to weaken the force of an imperative in writing, he has the linguistic tools at his disposal to do so (as we will see below).

Basically then, the "request" classification is reserved for use by inferiors when addressing superiors (including prayers). When an imperative usage is found in only one context and that specific context can only have one imperative usage, there is a problem. What determines the usage is then more than our usual syntactical context which has a measure of subjectivity built in. Here the roles played by those of higher and lower social status in a communication situation determine the usage. In other words, when an inferior addresses a superior, the imperative must be a request. We must then ask, is it really a different usage of the imperative or is it simply the imperative in a specific environment?[35] Further, on what basis do we consider an imperative weakened? Can it involve something other than the social rank of the participants?

---

between social class and force and acknowledges the possibility of inferiors commanding superiors and superiors requesting something from inferiors (Young, *Intermediate New Testament Greek*, 144). However, no examples are given.

35. Although not a perfect analogy, this situation reminds me of an aspect of linguistics. Basic to various levels of linguistic analysis (phonology, morphology, etc.) are the notions of complementary and contrastive distribution. Consider phonology. It is important to determine whether two phonetic sounds (phones) represent two distinct phonemes or both represent a single phoneme that is expressed differently in distinct contexts. To provide a common, yet simple example, consider two English phones: [p] and [ph] ([p with aspiration]). Place these in a minimal pair (words that differ in only a single aspect). The former [p] is found after [s] in words such as "spot" [spot] and the latter, [ph] occurs elsewhere in words such as "pot" [phot]. Thus, these are not separate phonemes but coallophones of a single phoneme /p/. This is complementary distribution. Contrastive distribution happens when two sounds in a minimal pair contrast and result in different meanings. Thus, consider the minimal pair: [dot] "dot" and [phot] "pot." The single consonantal difference between the [d] and the [ph] results in different meanings. These represent different phonemes. This example is only intended for the purpose of illustration. Phonological analysis of the English phoneme /p/ is more complex than is presented here. For an introduction to phonological analysis and the notion of complementary distribution and minimal pairs, see Gleason, *Introduction to Descriptive Linguistics*, 14–26, 80 (for further information and limitations of complementary distribution, see Lockwood, *Introduction to Stratificational Linguistics*, 190–92). The usages "command" and "request" are in complementary distribution. The "request" usage only occurs in a single environment. The point is that "requests" are only found when inferiors address superiors but "commands" are not found in this environment. Thus, they are complementary and should not be considered separate usages.

Languages have many ways of communicating commands and similar directives. Consider the following English sentences:

1) Open the window; 2) Can you open the window?; 3) I'm hot.

Example 1 is an imperative command. The other two are not imperatives but given certain contextual features, both can serve as directives with the equivalent goal of the first example. Assuming the hearer's ability to open a window is not in doubt, example 2 is a directive using a question. In a warm context and assuming an open window can cool the room in which number three is spoken, this can be a subtle directive to open the window. In each of these examples, the speaker wants the window opened. He or she is not restricted to the imperative. In fact, the choice of examples 2 and 3 may be ways of avoiding the strong nature of the imperative. These can be seen as "requests" or "weakened commands." These may be ways socially inferior persons may express their desire to a superior. Thus, in English, one is not restricted to the imperative to express volitional-direction.

In addition to the imperative, Greek has several ways of expressing commands as well. These include the future indicative (Matt 4:10 [2x]), negative aorist subjunctives (2 Thess 3:13), aorist infinitive (Luke 5:12), and possibly even the present indicative (1 Tim 2:12). Thus, in Greek, like English, there are a number of available means to express direction that can avoid the strong force of the imperative mood.[36]

Considering the strict contextual features demanded for the "request" usage to be present and the availability of other means to express politeness, why do Greek grammars insist on keeping the usage?

It seems that the main reason for maintaining the "request" usage for the imperative is our own lack of comfort with commands being used in certain situations. Few of us feel comfortable with this woman "commanding" Jesus. Concerning the usage of request more generally, Mathewson and Emig, state this well, "we can state with confidence, based on his character, that Jesus *asked* the woman at the well for water rather than *ordering* her. We can also assume that Jesus taught his disciples to make humble requests of God rather than to place arrogant demands on him. It should go without saying that ontological inferiors ought not command God."[37] To be fair to Mathewson and Emig, this makes perfect sense. However, there are three issues that need to be addressed. First, it makes perfect sense in our context today. I do not think we can assume that the ancient world shared our

---

36. It is possible for some of these to be strong commands given the right participants and context.

37. Mathewson and Emig, *Intermediate Greek Grammar*, 185–86 (emphasis original). It is only a coincidence that in this description, John 4 (although not our verse) is being referred to.

sensitivities. Second, if these were so offensive, why use the imperative at all? There were other means of expressing volitional-direction. Third, it places too much of a burden on the grammar itself. It seems such statements demand of the imperative mood meaning that it may not be able to sustain. There is nothing explicit to indicate weakening. Would it not be preferable to take these examples and reevaluate our understanding of the imperative mood? The meaning of the mood must account for inferiors' use and prayers. We cannot assume the imperative mood in Greek is the same as it is in English or other languages. Maybe we need to broaden our understanding of the Greek imperative rather than narrow it by assuming a major usage and then another usage that is based on the roles performed by the participants involved in the communication situation.

There is no textual evidence to lead us to conclude that this was an uncomfortable situation. In English, if I were to use an imperative to a superior or inferior, the force would be the same. However, it may affect the hearers differently based on their rank. But again, the imperative is the same. I can choose to use another verbal mood if I wish to spare my superior the somewhat improper confronting nature of the imperative. However, I chose to use the imperative for a reason. Given Greek has similar mechanisms, we should at least consider that there may be a reason to use the imperative. After all, the fact that inferiors rarely use the imperative should give us pause to consider why one is being used when it is encountered.

The imperative is used and not another form for a reason. However, this does not mean that there are not strategies in languages in place to help "soften the blow" or "weaken the force" of the imperative. Consider again English:

1) Open the window; 2) Please, open the window; 3) Sir, open the window.

The verbs here are all volitional-directive imperatives but the force of the imperative sentences is different. The first, is a raw command. The second and third use politeness strategies in the form of external features to prepare the hearer. Interestingly, in traditional Greek grammars, some suggest that example two which explicitly uses "please" is the implied intention of the imperative when an inferior addresses a superior.[38]

If the identical sentences are used by different socially ranked people, I do not think that one would imply that the example stated by the inferior was a weakened request:

1) From a boss to his or her employee, "open the window," or, 2) From an employee to his or her boss, "open the window."

---

38. This seems to be implied by ibid., 185; quoted above.

Based on Greek usage criteria, the second example would be classified as a request. However, would anyone actually interpret it this way? Probably not. Instead, it comes across as rather offensive. However, consider the following options for example 2: 2b) From an employee to his or her boss, "please, open the window"; 2c) From an employee to his or her boss, "sir, open the window"; 2d) From an employee to his or her boss, "please sir, open the window."

These still are rather bold but at least there is an acknowledgement of the superiority of the boss. The imperative is still strong but the sentence is weakened. Consider the difference when the imperative is not used at all: 2e) From an employee to his or her boss, "could you open the window?"[39]

Most would agree that this is a request.

Greek also has several weakening features. These can be employed in both social rank directions; however, my examples here are all from lower-to-higher social rank. First, the speaker or the narrator may introduce the imperative with a word of "asking":[40]

δέομαι δέ σου, ἐπίτρεψόν μοι λαλῆσαι πρὸς τὸν λαόν. (Acts 21:39), "And I ask you, *permit* me to speak to the crowd." Second, the third person imperative can be used. This removes the direct focus away from the recipient of the imperative and provides distance or remoteness:

Πάτερ ἡμῶν ὁ ἐν τοῖς οὐρανοῖς·ἁγιασθήτω τὸ ὄνομά σου·(Matt 6:9), "Our Father, who is in heaven, *let* your name *be kept holy* (or your name *must be kept holy*)." Finally, for lower ranked individuals, terms of honor can be used to acknowledge the higher social rank of the addressee: κύριε, κατάβηθι πρὶν ἀποθανεῖν τὸ παιδίον μου (John 4:49), "Sir, *come down* before my son dies."

In each of these examples, an element is introduced that prepares the addressee and/or weakens the force of the entire imperative clause.[41] Whatever means of weakening is employed, an imperative is still being used. The imperative (commanding) force should not be ignored. To be clear, this does not weaken the imperative mood of the verb but rather the imperative clause itself. The reason these weakening devices are necessary is because

---

39. If the social distance is very large, one might need to even go further: 2f. From an employee to his or her boss, "sir, could you please open the window?"

40. For further discussion see, Fantin, *Greek Imperative Mood*, 224–26 (higher-to-lower rank), 223–36 (lower-to-higher rank).

41. It is possible that lexical word choice may also soften an imperative when such an option exists. However, there is not enough data in the New Testament to determine if this is the case. For a discussion of this phenomenon in classical Greek, see Miller, "Limitation of the Imperative," 399–436. See also Fantin, *Greek Imperative Mood*, 221–23.

the imperative mood itself is strong. Further, the act of addressing a superior in any manner was probably an act of boldness in some measure.

Given the negative social implications and risk of imperative used by lower ranked individuals, why would one choose to use it? The imperative may be used to express urgency, gain immediate attention, or express excitement.

Before moving onto our passage, one more issue must be briefly addressed. This is a major contribution and thus can only be mentioned here. I am convinced that there is much more to this issue than grammar. There is a lot about the interaction between peoples in the ancient world that we do not know; however, our knowledge in this area has significantly increased in recent decades. To further our understanding, we must incorporate this knowledge more critically into our discussion of the imperative mood. One fruitful avenue will be to consider implications of social interaction among levels of Roman and Jewish society, including but not limited to the patronage system.[42]

I have challenged the validity of the imperative mood category, "request." This category has a unique distribution. The full imperative clause is weakened by other features, not by the imperative mood itself. The vast majority of imperatives are commands in the traditional paradigm. There is no internal reason to assume imperatives be considered otherwise. The "result" category in the traditional paradigm is likely a creation due to our modern sensitivities. These are among the reasons that it is unnecessary to consider this a special category. Imperatives are commands. Nevertheless, there are means by which the larger imperative clause may be weakened.

5. JOHN 4:15

If the category of "result" is invalid, how do we treat the Samaritan woman's imperative directed towards Jesus in John 4:15? Is she rude? Again, the verse reads as follows:

κύριε, δός μοι τοῦτο τὸ ὕδωρ, ἵνα μὴ διψῶ μηδὲ διέρχωμαι ἐνθάδε ἀντλεῖν (John 4:15), "sir, *give* to me this water that I may not thirst nor come here to draw."

I will now proceed to defend the command usage in John 4:15 and then suggest implications of this identification.

---

42. A helpful introduction to the patronage system in New Testament times can be found in deSilva, *Honor, Patronage, Kinship, and Purity*, 95–156 and the literature cited there. For general discussion of Jewish patronage from the second century BC through the sixth century AD, see Sorek, *Remembered for Good*.

5.1. Commanding Jesus

In addition to our conclusion that "request" is not a valid category, there are several contextual reasons that a command is present here.

First, as already noted above, the use of an imperative is rarely used by lower ranked individuals addressing those of a higher rank. This itself should cause us to pause concerning the legitimacy of the category. This is the case here. In this conversation, Jesus uses the imperative six times (4:7, 10, 16 [3x], 21). The woman only uses it once. This indicates that an imperative can be intrusive and thus should not be used without good reason. Again, lower ranked people rarely use imperatives towards superiors. This is the norm. One way to emphasize or highlight something is to break the norm.

Second, the woman demonstrates sensitivity to Jesus elsewhere. There are two statements made by the woman that help illustrate this: Λέγει αὐτῷ [ἡ γυνή]· κύριε, οὔτε ἄντλημα ἔχεις καὶ τὸ φρέαρ ἐστὶν βαθύ· πόθεν οὖν ἔχεις τὸ ὕδωρ τὸ ζῶν; μὴ σὺ μείζων εἶ τοῦ πατρὸς ἡμῶν Ἰακώβ, ὃς ἔδωκεν ἡμῖν τὸ φρέαρ . . .; (John 4:11–12), "[The woman] said to him, 'sir, you do not have anything to draw with and the well is deep; where then do you get living water? You are not greater than our father Jacob who gave us this well. . .?'"

The woman does not believe Jesus.[43] The question introduced by the negative particle μή in verse 12 expects a negative answer.[44] but nevertheless she probes deeper. She may be simply playing with him but how realistic would such interaction be with a [more powerful] stranger? In light of her quick follow up to Jesus' response with her imperative, it may be that despite some objections noted above, John is presenting the woman's interest in Jesus as growing. Our next example is a subtle question: Λέγει αὐτῷ ἡ γυνή· οἶδα ὅτι Μεσσίας ἔρχεται ὁ λεγόμενος χριστός· ὅταν ἔλθῃ ἐκεῖνος, ἀναγγελεῖ ἡμῖν ἅπαντα, "The woman said to him, 'I know that Messiah is coming (the one who is called Christ), when that one comes he will tell us all things'" (John 4:25). Perhaps, the woman is simply making a statement; however, this is unlikely because her focus is on Jesus after what he has just revealed. The statement must be relevant and further the progress of the communication situation. Why introduce the "Messiah" now unless she wanted to know if she happened to be in his presence? The woman seems to want to ask Jesus if he is the Messiah[45] but is reluctant to do so for any number of reasons. She

---

43. Carson, *Gospel According to John*, 219.

44. Porter, *Idioms*, 277–78; McHugh, *Critical and Exegetical Commentary*, 270.

45. The Samaritans did not use the title "Messiah." The figure for whom they awaited was the "Taheb." This was not a Davidic figure but more of a Mosaic redeemer (Keener, *Gospel of John*, 619–20). There may be many reasons the term "Messiah" is used here.

may not have wanted to offend Jesus or put him in a position to have to deny the identification. Jesus' response suggests that he understands this intent and answers it straight away.

One may argue that I am assuming a lot here. It is impossible to know the woman's attitude during this conversation. This is true but one must acknowledge that this is what all interpreters of this passage do. We all consider the contextual clues and are undoubtedly influenced by our own experiences, then we try to make sense of the passage. We conclude what we are persuaded is most probable.

Third, whether one understands it literally or spiritually, "living water" is cool stuff. Who would not want it? The Samaritan woman needed to humiliatingly draw water daily. The opportunity to avoid this was appealing. If even a remote possibility, she could not let such an opportunity pass. Jesus' description makes it so appealing. Just prior to the woman's response expressing her desire for the living water, Jesus states: ... πᾶς ὁ πίνων ἐκ τοῦ ὕδατος τούτου διψήσει πάλιν· ὃς δ' ἂν πίῃ ἐκ τοῦ ὕδατος οὗ ἐγὼ δώσω αὐτῷ, οὐ μὴ διψήσει εἰς τὸν αἰῶνα, "all those who drink from this water will thirst again; but whoever drinks from the water which I will give to him [or her], will certainly not thirst forever." The use of emphatic negation (οὐ μὴ)[46] and the phrase indicating "eternity" or "forever" (εἰς τὸν αἰῶνα)[47] dramatically emphasize the "permanent satisfaction" regarding the need for water.[48]

Fourth, the objection that it is too offensive to be a "command" is not valid. As noted before, the Greek verb shows no linguistic difference between what traditional grammarians label a "command" and a "request." Other mood options existed but they were not used. This is probably the product of our own lack of comfort with this passage. Further, the woman uses a politeness strategy before her imperative clause. She calls Jesus "sir" (κύριε[49]) acknowledging his superiority. The result is that the imperative clause is not a demand.

---

46. "The negative is strengthened, not destroyed, by the two negatives." Robertson, *Grammar*, 1174.

47. This is the first of many uses of this phrase by John (6:51, 58; 8:35, 51, 52; 10:28; 11:26; 12:34; 13:8; 14:16). It is often translated with the previous negation as "never" (NASB, NIV, NRSV) or as "again" (ESV, NLT; in these cases, "never" translates the emphatic negation).

48. Klink, *John*, 240.

49. The vocative κύριε from κύριος is a term of respect. It has a range of meaning from "sir" to "Lord." Context determines the term's strength. In this case, there is no reason to assume the woman sees Jesus as a type of Lord figure or some sort of master. There are no Christological implications intended here (see options in BDAG, section 2; Köstenberger, *John*, 150).

Fifth, by labeling this a "command," we are not denying that there is an implied request for something. As noted above, commands are by their very nature volitional directive which express a desire for someone to do something. We must separate the nature of the imperative verb as command from the purpose of the clause which in this case is an expressed desire for Jesus to give the woman "living water."

5.2. Implications

As noted, the Samaritan woman uses the imperative only once in this conversation with Jesus. She is not being rude. Her general sensitivity and caution is evidenced by her round-about means of questioning Jesus (4:11, 25). Further, she qualifies her imperative clause with an honorific term, κύριε, indicating respect for Jesus. Nevertheless, she still uses the imperative. Why?

It seems probable that her use of this potentially offensive mood demonstrates her desperation and/or excitement about the potential of acquiring living water. McHugh suggests that the use of vocative κύριε demonstrates here "seriousness and sincerity."[50] As noted in the last section, even if the possibility was remote, it was worth the risk to possibly acquire living water. However, I think the imperative offers insight into her expectations. The use of this mood suggests she probably believed he could fulfill her request. Why potentially offend with an imperative unless her desire could be fulfilled? As seen above, some see the woman's imperative clause as a combative or mocking response. This would fit the data. The woman uses the command as a challenge, a means by which to call Jesus' bluff. However, Jesus' response demonstrates that he is willing to consider the woman's statement. If she was being combative, she may have taken offense at Jesus' venture into her private life and ended the conversation. Nevertheless, this perspective cannot be ruled out and such a position still fits well with the command usage of the imperative here.

It seems best to see this imperative as a command usage within a clause forcefully asking for living water. A potential for offense exists but this is minimized because the imperative is preceded by a term of honor acknowledging Jesus' superiority. It is a risk and it works. Ultimately, although she wanted physical water, she received true spiritual living water which was beyond anything she could have hoped for when she arrived and met the stranger at the well.

---

50. McHugh, *Critical and Exegetical Commentary*, 272.

6. IMPLICATIONS FOR CHRISTIAN LIVING

Much can be gleaned from this passage about how the believer can relate to God. Most of the so-called "request" imperatives occur in prayer.[51] The largest possible gap in social rank is between people and God. Yet, imperatives are used. Imperatives are also used consistently (842x) in the Greek translation of the Psalms (LXX).[52]

Jesus sets the example in his prayer in the upper room (John 17). Here Jesus uses the imperative four times (17:1, 5, 11, 17). In the first three examples, Jesus also uses honor terms (πάτερ [17:1, 5], πάτερ ἅγιε [17:11]). Jesus' instructions on prayer to his disciples in the form of a sample prayer (Matt 6:9–13) begin with an honorific term (πάτερ) and the first three imperatives are weaker third person imperatives (6:9–10). This is then followed by two second person imperatives, a negative aorist subjunctive,[53] and a final second person imperative: . . . Πάτερ ἡμῶν ὁ ἐν τοῖς οὐρανοῖς·; ἁγιασθήτω τὸ ὄνομά σου; ἐλθέτω ἡ βασιλεία σου; γενηθήτω τὸ θέλημά σου; ὡς ἐν οὐρανῷ καὶ ἐπὶ γῆς; τὸν ἄρτον ἡμῶν τὸν ἐπιούσιον δὸς ἡμῖν σήμερον; καὶ ἄφες ἡμῖν τὰ ὀφειλήματα ἡμῶν; ὡς καὶ ἡμεῖς ἀφήκαμεν τοῖς ὀφειλέταις ἡμῶν; καὶ μὴ εἰσενέγκῃς ἡμᾶς εἰς πειρασμόν; ἀλλὰ ῥῦσαι ἡμᾶς ἀπὸ τοῦ πονηροῦ (Matt 6:9–13); "Our *Father*, who is in heaven; *let* your name *be kept holy*; *let* your kingdom *come*; *let* your will *be done*; even on earth as in heaven; *give* to us today our daily bread; and *forgive* us our debts; as we forgave our debtors; and do not lead us into temptation; but *rescue* us from evil."

There is a further observation about John 4 worth noting. The woman did not really understand what Jesus was offering. He knew what she really needed and met this need. We do not need to know everything. We do not need to understand everything. We simply need to trust God that he will do what is best for us. We can even pray ignorantly in good faith and if what we ask for is not what is best for us, God will know what to do. He even protects us from ourselves.

I have attempted to take a contextual approach to John 4:15. This included both removing inaccurate information and adding insights from grammar and culture. In applying what we have learned, we must avoid extremes. We should boldly approach God. However, everything indicates

---

51. Mathewson and Emig, *Intermediate Greek Grammar*, 186.

52. See Fantin, *Greek Imperative Mood*, 246.

53. The negative aorist imperative is extremely rare. It occurs only eight times in the New Testament and always in the third person: Matt 6:3; 24:17, 18; Mark 13:15 (2x), 16; Luke 17:31 (2x). Eight occurrences is deceptively high. All but Matt 6:3 occur in parallel passages in Jesus' speech in the synoptic apocalypses. See Fantin, *Greek Imperative Mood*, 284–85. The negative aorist subjunctive is used in its place.

that the Samaritan woman and the examples of prayer here demonstrate respect. My proposal is that the "command" nuance present is not the same as a modern form of demanding. God deserves respect. Meditation on who God is and what he has done both in creation and in redemption should force us to our knees and to humbly acknowledge who he is and thank him for what he has done. In the past, some have gone to the extreme and have made God unapproachable. It is likely that our "request" category has some root in this belief. We must move beyond this. God wants a relationship with us. However, it is equally wrong to treat God like some buddy or cosmic Santa Claus to meet our physical and emotional needs. A true understanding of God will cause us to respond like the Samaritan woman. She left what she had (her water pot) and went to the city to tell others about Jesus (John 4:28).

I have emphasized prayer in this section. This is because the woman's approach to Jesus was a divine meeting. The closest we can come to this today, is prayer. However, an understanding of and appreciation for our access to God can apply to our entire life. We see a little more clearly how we are related to God. We can conclude that we can have a measure of boldness when we approach God. We can have confidence in our standing before him. We can be certain of God's love for us. As Jesus pursued the Samaritan woman, he has pursued us. As he initiated a relationship with her, he initiated his relationship to us. He made access to God possible (Heb 10:19–22). He has provided us with "living water." Let us confidently embrace this and drink.

BIBLIOGRAPHY

Barrett, C. K. *The Gospel According to St. John: An Introduction with Commentary and Notes*. 2nd ed. Philadelphia: Westminster, 1978.

Beasley-Murray, George R. *John*. 2nd ed. Word Biblical Commentary. Nashville: Nelson, 1999.

Black, David Alan. *It's Still Greek to Me: An Easy-to-Understand Guide to Intermediate Greek*. Grand Rapids, MI: Baker, 1998.

———. *Learn to Read New Testament Greek*. 3rd ed. Nashville: B&H, 2009.

———. *Linguistics for Students of New Testament Greek: A Survey of Basic Concepts and Applications*, 2nd ed. Grand Rapids, MI: Baker, 2000.

———. *Using New Testament Greek in Ministry: A Practical Guide for Students and Pastors*. Grand Rapids, MI: Baker, 1993.

Black, David Alan, Katharine Barnwell, and Stephen Levinsohn, eds. *Linguistics and New Testament Interpretation: Essays on Discourse Analysis*. Nashville: Broadman, 1992.

Blass, Friedrich, and Albert Debrunner. *A Greek Grammar of the New Testament and Other Early Christian Literature*. Translated and revised by Robert W. Funk. Chicago: University of Chicago Press, 1961.

———. *Grammatik des neutestamentlichen Griechisch*. 18th ed. Edited by Friedrich Rehkopf. Göttingen: Vandenhoeck & Ruprecht, 2001.
Boyer, James L. "A Classification of Imperatives: A Statistical Study." *Grace Theological Journal* 8 (1987) 35–54.
Brant, JoAnn A. *John*. Paideia. Grand Rapids, MI: Baker, 2011.
Brooks, James A., and Carlton L. Winbery. *Syntax of New Testament Greek*. Lanham, MD: University Press of America, 1979.
Brown, Raymond E. *The Gospel According to John 1–12: A New Translation with Introduction and Commentary*. Anchor Bible 29. New York: Doubleday, 1970.
Bruce, F. F. *The Gospel of John: Introduction, Exposition and Notes*. Grand Rapids, MI: Eerdmans, 1983.
Bruner, Frederick Dale. *The Gospel of John: A Commentary*. Grand Rapids, MI: Eerdmans, 2012.
Bultmann, Rudolf. *The Gospel of John: A Commentary*. Translated by G. R. Beasley-Murray et al. Philadelphia: Westminster, 1971.
Burton, Ernest deWitt. *Syntax of the Moods and Tenses in New Testament Greek*. 3rd ed. Edinburgh: T&T Clark, 1898.
Carmichael, Calum M. "Marriage and the Samaritan Woman." *New Testament Studies* 26 (1980) 332–46.
Carson, D. A. *The Gospel According to John*. Pillar New Testament Commentary. Grand Rapids, MI: Eerdmans, 1991.
Dana H. E., and Julius R. Mantey. *A Manual Grammar of the New Testament*. New York: Macmillan, 1927; reprint, 1957.
deSilva, David A. *Honor, Patronage, Kinship, and Purity: Unlocking New Testament Culture*. Downers Grove, IL: InterVarsity, 2000.
Dylan, Bob. "In the Garden." *Saved* [album]. N.p.: Columbia, 1980.
Eslinger, Lyle. "The Wooing of the Woman at the Well: Jesus, the Reader and Reader-Response Criticism." *Journal of Literature & Theology* 1 (1987) 167–83.
Fantin, Joseph D. *The Greek Imperative Mood in the New Testament: A Cognitive and Communicative Approach*. Studies in Biblical Greek 12. New York: Peter Lang, 2010.
Gleason, H. A., Jr. *An Introduction to Descriptive Linguistics*. Rev. ed. New York: Holt, Rinehart and Winston, 1961.
Haenchen, Ernst. *John 1: A Commentary on the Gospel of John 1–6*. Hermeneia. Translated by Robert W. Funk. Philadelphia: Fortress, 1984.
Huffman, Douglas S. *Verbal Aspect Theory and the Prohibitions in the Greek New Testament*. Studies in Biblical Greek 16. New York: Peter Lang, 2014.
Keener, Craig S. *The Gospel of John: A Commentary*. Vol. 1. Peabody, MA: Hendrickson, 2003.
Klink, Edward W., III. *John*. Zondervan Exegetical Commentary on the New Testament. Grand Rapids, MI: Zondervan, 2016.
Köstenberger, Andreas J. *John*. Baker Exegetical Commentary on the New Testament. Grand Rapids, MI: Baker, 2004.
Köstenberger, Andreas J., Benjamin L. Merkle, and Robert L. Plummer. *Going Deeper with New Testament Greek: An Intermediate Study of the Grammar and Syntax of the New Testament*. Nashville: B&H Academic, 2016.

Lincoln, Andrew T. *The Gospel According to Saint John*. Black's New Testament Commentary. London: Continuum, 2005; reprint, Peabody, MA: Hendrickson, 2005.

Lockwood, David G. *Introduction to Stratificational Linguistics*. New York: Harcourt, Brace, Jovanovich, 1972.

Malina, Bruce, and Richard Rohrbaugh. *Social-Science Commentary on the Gospel of John*. Minneapolis, MN: Fortress, 1998.

Mathewson, David L., and Elodie Ballantine Emig. *Intermediate Greek Grammar: Syntax for Students of the New Testament*. Grand Rapids, MI: Baker, 2016.

McHugh, John F. *A Critical and Exegetical Commentary on John 1–4*. International Critical Commentary. London: T&T Clark, 2009.

Michaels, J. Ramsey. *The Gospel of John*. New International Commentary on the New Testament. Grand Rapids, MI: Eerdmans, 2010.

Miller, C. W. E. "The Limitation of the Imperative in the Attic Orators." *American Journal of Philology* 13 (1892) 399–436.

Moule, C. F. D. *An Idiom Book of New Testament Greek*. 2nd ed. Cambridge: Cambridge University Press, 1959.

Moulton, James Hope, et al. *A Grammar of New Testament Greek*. 4 vols. Edinburgh: T&T Clark, 1908–76.

Neyrey, Jerome H. *The Gospel of John*. New Cambridge Bible Commentary. Cambridge: Cambridge University Press, 2007.

———. "What's Wrong with This Picture?: John 4, Cultural Stereotypes of Women, and Public and Private Space." In *The Gospel of John in Cultural and Rhetorical Perspective*, 143–71. Grand Rapids, MI: Eerdmans, 2009.

Porter, Stanley E. *Idioms of the Greek New Testament*. 2nd ed. Sheffield: Sheffield Academic, 1994.

Robertson, A. T. *A Grammar of the Greek New Testament in Light of Historical Research*. 4th ed. Nashville: Broadman, 1934.

Schnackenburg, Rudolf. *The Gospel According to St. John*. Vol. 1, *Introduction and Commentary on Chapters 1–4*. Herder's Theological Commentary on the New Testament. Translated by Kevin Smith. New York: Herder and Herder, 1968.

Sorek, Susan. *Remembered for Good: A Jewish Benefaction System in Ancient Palestine*. The Social World of Biblical Antiquity, Second Series 5. Sheffield: Sheffield Phoenix, 2010.

Thompson, Marianne Meye. *John: A Commentary*. New Testament Library. Louisville: Westminster John Knox, 2015.

Wallace, Daniel B. *Greek Grammar Beyond the Basics: An Exegetical Syntax of the New Testament*. Grand Rapids, MI: Zondervan, 1996.

Weinrich, William C. *John 1:1—7:1*. Concordia Commentary. St. Louis, MO: Concordia, 2015.

Winer G. B., and F. W. Moulton. *A Treatise on the Grammar of New Testament Greek, Regarded as a Sure Basis for New Testament Exegesis*. 3rd ed. Translated by F. W. Moulton. Edinburgh: T&T Clark, 1882; reprint, Eugene, OR: Wipf and Stock, 1997.

Young, Richard A. *Intermediate New Testament Greek: A Linguistic and Exegetical Approach*. Nashville: Broadman & Holman, 1994.

Zerwick, Maximilian. *Biblical Greek Illustrated by Examples*. Scripta Pontificii Instituti Biblici 114. Translated by Joseph Smith. Rome: Editrice Pontificio Instituto Biblico, 1963.

Chapter 3

Verbal Aspect and Imperatives
Ephesians as a Test Case

—BENJAMIN L. MERKLE
Southeastern Baptist Theological Seminary

THERE IS NO DOUBT that David Alan Black is a master teacher. His knowledge combined with his passion leave an inevitable mark on his students. It is no wonder that his classes are always full. But perhaps more than all of this is his love for the Lord Jesus Christ and his unwavering commitment to bring the gospel to all the nations. As his colleague for almost a decade now I can truly say that he is a role model for me and I am thankful to have the joy and privilege of working alongside of him for all these years.

INTRODUCTION

In a previous essay, I argued that modern interpreters who embrace verbal aspect theory are often guilty of placing too much interpretive weight on the tense-form (aspect) of verbs.[1] Whereas earlier interpreters often wrongly placed emphasis on the type of action conveyed by the tense-form, modern interpreters often place too much emphasis on the subjective choice of the tense-form used and are thus also guilty of over-interpreting verbs as being "marked" or receiving "prominence." In reality, usage of certain aspectual forms is simply the normal, expected form of that verb. In other words, sometimes an author does not make a subjective choice to portray an action

---
1. Merkle, "Abused Aspect," 57–74. This volume of the journal also includes a response from Stan Porter and a follow-up response from me (83).

in a certain way, but submits to convention and uses the normal or expected form which is often influenced by a particular verb's lexical meaning.[2]

The purpose of this essay is to further test the theory that the lexical meaning of a verb (i.e., whether it is telic or atelic) affects which tense-form is to be expected. That is, telic verbs tend to prefer the aorist whereas atelic verbs prefer the present (or imperfect) tense-form. Specifically, this thesis is tested on the forty imperatives found in the book of Ephesians. In this essay I will demonstrate that most of the imperatives in Ephesians are simply the expected form and therefore should not be over-interpreted. Those verbs that do not follow the expected pattern are given special attention as I offer a careful analysis of why the particular form is used as it relates to (1) verbal aspect, (2) the general distinction that aorist imperatives give a specific command and present imperatives give a general precept, or (3) some other contextual reason.

VERBAL ASPECT AND IMPERATIVES

There is a general consensus among modern scholars that NT Greek is aspect-prominent. In other words, in the Greek verbal system, the subjective portrayal of the action is prominent and not the time of the action. Of course, this emphasis is especially true with non-indicative verbs since time is not communicated by the verb's tense-form. In fact, based on their hortatory function, all imperatives relate to an action (or prohibition) that is to take place in the future.

So then, when it comes to imperatives, what is the meaning of a verb's aspect? Generally speaking, the aorist imperative (perfective aspect) portrays the action from an external perspective viewing the action as a whole without focusing on the unfolding internal details. In contrast, the present imperative (imperfective aspect) portrays the action from an internal perspective viewing the action as a process without focusing on the end of the action.[3] Verbal aspect theory relates to the semantic or unaffected meaning of the verb. That is, verbal aspect only gives us the basic perspective of how the author views the action of the verb but it is also necessary to take into consideration contextual features (the pragmatic or affected meaning) since a particular tense-form does not occur in isolation.

2. Even when the author does make a subjective choice, that choice may communicate the semantical portrayal of the aspect or prominence, but not both.

3. Fanning, *Verbal Aspect*, 326; McKay, "Aspect in Imperatival Constructions," 203–4.

It is far too simplistic, therefore, to think that whenever we come to an imperative (or any verb) we can simply identify the tense-form and conclude that the author subjectively chose to portray an action from a particular perspective. Such an explanation fails to take into consideration other important factors that contribute to the tense-form choice of an author.

VERBAL ASPECT AND CONTRIBUTING FACTORS

Because this basic aspectual distinction does not exist in isolation, it is necessary to consider other factors that might have influenced an author to choose a particular tense-form. Perhaps the two most influential factors that affect the author's tense-form choice are lexical and contextual factors.

Lexical Factors

A verb's semantic meaning often has a significant influence upon the tense-form that is selected by the author. This influence is due to the overlap in function of the verb's aspect and the inherent meaning of the verb. In other words, because the perfective aspect (aorist tense-form) is used by the author to portray the action as a whole, it is more natural to use the perfective aspect with verbs whose actions are normally completed in a relatively short period of time. For example, in the NT the imperative of βάλλω occurs fourteen times as an aorist but never as a present.[4] This usage is expected when one considers that the action to "throw" or "put" takes place almost instantaneously. Indeed, it is difficult to conceive of the imperfective aspect being used when there would be virtually no time to portray the action as in progress or incomplete.[5]

Conversely, because the imperfective aspect (present tense-form) is used by the author to portray the action as in progress, it is more natural to use the imperfective aspect with verbs whose actions normally are viewed as having no natural endpoint or are stative verbs. For example, in the NT the imperative of γρηγορέω occurs eleven times as a present but only once as an aorist.[6] Again, this usage is expected when one considers that the action

---

4. These stats, as well as others in this essay, include both commands and prohibitions (i.e., negated commands). For how negation can limit semantic potential, see Aubrey, "Greek Prohibitions," 486–538.

5. When an author uses a verb outside of its normal usage, a special nuance might be intended (e.g., inceptive/ingressive).

6. The only aorist imperative of γρηγορέω is found in 1 Pet 5:8 (γρηγορήσατε). We should be aware, however, that the author of 1 Peter has a propensity to use the aorist

of "keeping watch" is not normally completed in a short period of time but is an action that has no natural terminus. Indeed, it is difficult to conceive of the perfective aspect being used when the action is not easily portrayed as a whole.

Verbs of Motion

Verbs of motions are a class of verbs that tend to fall into a predictable usage. That is, based on the lexical meaning (at least originally), as imperatives, verbs of motion are almost always found in the present tense-form.[7] Thus, such verbs are idiomatically found in the imperfective aspect and so the form is not usually dependent on the author's subjective choice.[8] In fact, the present tense is used whether or not the imperative is intended as a specific command (where the aorist is overwhelmingly preferred).

Telic and Atelic Verbs

In addition to verbs of motion preferring the present tense-form, other verbs, based on their inherent lexical meaning, often prefer one tense-form over another.[9] Generally speaking, most verbs can be categorized as being either telic or atelic. A telic verb "refers to an action which does have an understood terminus, whether it takes some discernible amount of time ['performance'] or not ['punctual'] to perform this act."[10] In contrast, an atelic verb refers to a "state of being, a condition, a relationship, or even a certain kind of action that has no natural terminus implied in its being or accomplishment."[11]

These two categories can be further delineated. For instance, some telic verbs refer to actions that are limited in that they convey a climax,

---

form, even when the present is expected.

7. Verbs of motion that heavily favor the present tense-form include ἀκολουθέω, ἔρχομαι, περιπατέω, πορεύομαι, ὑπάγω, φεύγω, and φέρω. See Campbell, *Verbal Aspect*, 94–95; Fanning, *Verbal Aspect*, 341; McKay, "Aspect in Imperatival Constructions," 213; Bakker, *Greek Imperative*," 82.

8. Fanning rightly states that "the subsequent force of the idiom seems to overshadow any conscious choice on the part of the speaker" (*Verbal Aspect*, 341). He later adds that the tense-forms for certain verbs seem to be "a virtually fixed idiom rather than a free choice by the speaker" (*Verbal Aspect*, 348).

9. See Baugh, *Introduction to Greek Tense*.

10. Ibid., 10.

11. Ibid. See also Fanning who follows the Vendler-Kenney taxonomy to categorize kinds of verbs (*Verbal Aspect*, 127–63).

conclusion, or termination and yet still convey some perceived duration (performance).[12] Other telic verbs refer to an action that is done in a moment without taking any perceived or significant time duration for the action (punctual).[13] In contrast, atelic verbs convey a state (condition) or relationship (personal, temporal, or local), referring not to what someone *does* but what he or she *is* (or a relationship they have).[14] Activities are also viewed as having no set limit for their completion ("unbounded").[15]

Telic	Performance	Bounded actions with perceived duration	*Prefers:* Aorist
	Punctual	Bounded actions with little perceived duration	
Atelic	Stative	States and relationships	*Prefers* Present/ Imperfect
	Activity	Actions with no inherent termination	

The point to be gained from these distinctions is that the inherent semantic meaning of the verb (i.e., whether it is telic or atelic) limits the choice of the tense-form (aspect) used. That is, telic verbs are most semantically compatible with the aorist whereas atelic verbs are most semantically compatible with the present (or imperfect) tense-form. Thus, a verb's tense-form is not simply based on the subjective viewpoint that the author wishes to portray but is sometimes influenced by the verb's semantic meaning. In other words, a verb's lexical meaning often influences the tense-form more than the perspective the author consciously wills to communicate.

Contextual Factors

There are several contextual factors that contribute to the aspectual form that is used, including (1) literary genre, (2) idiolect, and (3) the specific command/general precept distinction. First, a text's literary genre can influence what tense-form is chosen since certain literary styles are prone to favor certain tense-forms. For example, historical narratives heavily favor the aorist tense-form whereas epistles favor the present tense-form. Thus, in

---

12. Examples include ἀνοίγω, δίδωμι, ἐνδύω, ἑτοιμάζω, and καλέω.

13. Examples include ἀγοράζω, βάλλω, εὑρίσκω, and πίπτω.

14. Examples include ἀγαπάω, ἀσθενέω, εἰμί, ἔχω, ζάω, μισέω, οἰκέω, πιστεύω, πλουτέω, and φοβέομαι.

15. Examples include ἀναγινώσκω, ἐσθίω, κηρύσσω, (possibly) λέγω/λαλέω, and ποιέω.

Paul's epistles, he uses the present imperative three times more frequently than the aorist imperative. When considering all epistles and Revelation, the present tense-form is used about twice as often as the aorist.[16] Additionally, in prayers where imperatives are used to make requests to God, the aorist is the predominant tense-form regardless of the lexical meaning of the verb. In this case, the literary genre (prayer) virtually determines the use of the tense-form.[17]

A second contextual factor relates to idiolect, or a particular author's individual propensity to favor a certain tense-form. As mentioned above, epistles heavily favor the present tense-form. Paul uses present imperatives about three times more than he uses aorist imperatives (330 present; 118 aorist). In contrast, 1 Peter contains twenty-five aorist imperatives but only ten present imperatives (a 2.5 to 1 ratio).[18]

The third, and most significant, contextual factor is the specific command versus general precept rule. This well-known, yet debated, "rule" states that when an author wants to communicate a command that is to be done on a specific occasion (single occurrence),[19] the aorist tense-form is used.[20] Conversely, when an author wants to communicate a command that is to be done as a general precept (multiple occurrence),[21] the present tense-form is used. Because of the significant number of exceptions, some authors doubt this particular "rule." A couple of comments are in order here. First, it is misleading to call this a "rule" since that communicates the idea that such a grammatical guideline was known and followed. But this is saying too much. Instead, scholars are merely identifying a certain noticeable trend.

---

16. All epistles and Revelation contain 451 presents and 259 aorists. The Gospels and Acts contain 456 presents and 651 aorists.

17. See, e.g., Bakker, *Greek Imperative*, 12; Fanning, *Verbal Aspect*, 380.

18. See Robertson, *Grammar*, 856; Campbell, *Verbal Aspect*, 87; and Forbes, *1 Peter*, 4–7. Fanning offers four reasons for the use of the aorist when a present is expected: (1) ingressive; (2) urgency; (3) consummative; and (4) use of traditional material (*Verbal Aspect*, 370–79).

19. A specific command, as defined by Fanning, is "an order or request for action to be done in a particular instance. The speaker commands or prohibits some attitude or action, but does so only in reference to the immediate circumstances and hearers involved: he does not intend to regulate conduct in broader terms" (*Verbal Aspect*, 328).

20. See, e.g., Blass, Debrunner, and Funk. *Greek Grammar of the New Testament*, 172 (§335); Fanning, *Verbal Aspect*, 325–88; Fanning, "Approaches to Verbal Aspect," 55; Zerwick, *Biblical Greek*, 79 (§243).

21. A general precept, as defined by Fanning, is "a moral regulation which is broadly applicable; a rule for conduct to be applied in multiple situations; a command or prohibition to be followed by an individual or a group not only in the immediate situation in which it is given, but also in subsequent (repeated or continuing) circumstances in which the precept is appropriate" (*Verbal Aspect*, 327–28).

Second, although there are exceptions, it is a helpful guideline. To ignore such a pattern of usage due to the presence of exceptions is to ignore important information at hand.[22] In other words, there is a reasonable explanation as to why there is a somewhat consistent pattern.

Indeed, the specific command (with aorist imperatives) versus general precept (with present imperatives) is affirmed by most grammarians.[23] This guideline helps explain why aorist imperatives are more frequent in narratives whereas present imperatives are more frequent in epistles.[24] Because narratives typically report the events that took place between particular individuals or groups, a specific command is expected. For example, Pilate stated before his Jewish audience, "judge (κρίνατε) him by your own law" (John 18:31).[25] Here, the aorist imperative is expected because Pilate is giving a specific command that is not intended to be repeated. Thus, this type of perceived action fits with the perfective aspect that views that action as a whole. Somewhat predictably, all five uses of the aorist imperative of κρίνω involve a specific command (see Acts 4:19; Rom 14:13; 1 Cor 10:15; 11:13). In contrast, as part of Jesus' teaching on the Sermon on the Mount, he declared, "Judge (κρίνετε) not, that you be not judged" (Matt 7:1). Here, the present imperative is used because Jesus is giving a general precept that is to be repeated whenever the situation might call for such a response. Thus, this type of perceived action fits with the imperfective aspect that views the action as in process or on-going. Unsurprisingly, the seven uses of the present imperative of κρίνω involve a general command (see Luke 6:37; John 7:24 [x2]; Rom 14:3; 1 Cor 4:5; Col 2:16).

Thus, there is a natural relationship between a verb's aspect and the specific command/general precept distinction. Because the perfective aspect communicates an author's portrayal of an action in its entirety or as a whole, it is natural for this aspect to be used when communicating a specific command since such an action is to be done in its entirety on that particular occasion.[26] Conversely, because the imperfective aspect communicates an author's portrayal of an action in progress or on-going, it is natural for

---

22. For a more nuanced explanation of this pattern, see Aubrey, "Greek Prohibitions," 486–538.

23. See, e.g., Fanning, *Verbal Aspect*, 327–40, Wallace, *Greek Grammar*, 719, 721; Blass, Debrunner, and Funk, *Greek Grammar*, 172 (§335).

24. See Fanning, *Verbal Aspect*, 329, 331.

25. Unless otherwise indicated, all Scripture quotations are from English Standard Version.

26. See Fanning, *Verbal Aspect*, 329; Wallace, *Greek Grammar*, 485; Blass, Debrunner, and Funk, *Greek Grammar*, 172 (§335); Young, *Intermediate New Testament Greek*, 142; Dana and Mantey, *Manual Grammar*, 300.

this aspect to be used when communicating a general precept since such an action is to be repeated on appropriate occasions (customary).[27] Thus, as Fanning notes, there is a "natural and plausible connection between the aspectual values of present and aorist and the normal difference which a speaker would envisage between a general precept and a specific command."[28]

We can summarize our discussion by noting that both the lexical meaning and context influence the aspect used. The lexical meaning directly influences the aspect because the way an action is *performed* affects the way it can be *portrayed*. The context also affects the aspectual choice because if an author envisions the readers only responding once to the command, then it is more natural to use the aorist form whereas the present form is naturally favored for commands that are to be repeatedly obeyed or carried out as the appropriate situation arises. Thus, the aspect (tense-form) used with imperatives is often not the result of a pure, subjective choice of the author.

OVERVIEW OF IMPERATIVES IN EPHESIANS

We will now turn our attention to the imperatives used in the epistle to the Ephesians. We will proceed by first looking at the present imperatives followed by the aorist imperatives. There are forty imperatives in Ephesians: thirty-four present tense-forms, with twenty-eight non-repeated forms, and six aorist tense-forms. Of the forty imperatives, thirty-eight are used for general precepts (thirty-three presents and five aorists) and only two for specific commands (1 present [ἔγειρε, 5:14] and 1 aorist [ἀνάστα, 5:14]). Because of the number of imperatives, I will group them into categories when appropriate. For example, the twenty-eight non-repeated present tense-forms will be grouped according to (1) expected and (2) unexpected forms.

---

27. See Fanning, *Verbal Aspect*, 329; Wallace, *Greek Grammar*, 485; Zerwick, *Biblical Greek*, 79 (§243); Robertson, *Greek Grammar*, 172 (§335).

28. Fanning, *Verbal Aspect*, 329. The statistical count of the uses of imperatives confirms this general principle. Fanning notes that for specific commands the aorist is used 280 times whereas the present is used only 86 times (a 3.3 to 1 ratio, or 70 percent). For general precepts, the present is used 449 times whereas the aorist is used only 145 times (a 3 to 1 ratio, or 68 percent) (see ibid., 332).

Present Imperatives in Ephesians

Expected Present Imperatives

By "expected" and "unexpected" we are specifically referring to the relation of the verb's tense-form to its lexical meaning. That is, because of a verb's inherent lexical meaning, it will often favor one tense-form over another. For instance, verbs that have no natural terminus favor the present tense-form. Of the twenty-eight non-repeated present imperatives, twenty-three of them are the expected form and only five are unexpected. We must remember, however, that not only is the lexical meaning influencing the tense-form, but the intended application of the imperative (the specific command/general precept distinction) is also influencing the verb's tense-form.

Verbs of Motion

There are three different verbs of motion used as imperatives in Ephesians and all of them are in the present tense-form. The first is ἐκπορευέσθω ("*Let no corrupting talk come out of your mouths,*" 4:29), which occurs only once as an imperative in the NT but four times in the LXX—all in the present tense-form.[29] The second imperative in this category is περιπατεῖτε ("*walk in love,*" 5:2; "*Walk as children of light,*" 5:8). In the NT, the present tense-form is used fourteen times but the aorist form is never used. The use of the present imperatival form of περιπατέω in parallel construction with aorist imperatives also confirms its idiomatic usage.[30] Again, one wonders how much choice an author has when using περιπατέω as an imperative. The imperatival form is used in nine different books (all four Gospels, Acts, and four different Pauline epistles) with five different authors (Matthew, Mark, Luke, John, and Paul) and every occurrence is in the present tense-form. The last verb of motion is ἔγειρε ("*Awake,* O sleeper," 5:14) which occurs eighteen times in the present tense-form and only twice in the aorist. In the eighteen present forms, all but one of them (Matt 10:8) is used as a command for a specific occasion. Thus, the idiomatic usage of this verb which favors the present form is not usually affected by the specific command/general precept distinction. Like περιπατέω, ἐγείρω is often found in parallel constructions with aorist imperatives.[31]

---

29. The imperative form of πορεύομαι occurs twenty-three times in the present tense-form and five times in the aorist.

30. See Matt 2:20; 25:9; Mark 2:9; John 20:17; Acts 8:26; 20:10; see also Luke 5:24; John 5:8, 11, 12.

31. See Mark 2:9; Luke 6:8; Rev 11:1; see also Mark 2:11; Luke 5:24; John 5:8.

Here is a summary of the verbs of motion:

Eph	Verbs of Motion	Present Impv	Aorist Impv
4:29	ἐκπορευέσθω	1	0
5:2	περιπατεῖτε	14	0
5:14	ἔγειρε	18	2
Total		33	2

States

In Ephesians there are ten stative imperatives and all are found in the present tense-form. We will focus our attention on the six verbs that occur more than one time in the NT as imperatives.[32] In chapters 1–3, μνημονεύετε ("*remember* that at one time you Gentiles in the flesh," 2:11) is the only imperative. The present tense-form is expected because μνημονεύω is an atelic stative verb that does not have a perceived terminus. Consequently, in the NT the present tense-form occurs nine times whereas the aorist form never occurs.[33]

The imperative γίνεσθε ("*Be* kind to one another," 4:32; "*be* imitators of God," 5:1; "do not *become* partners with them," 5:7; "do not *be* foolish," 5:17) is also undoubtedly a stative verb. As such, it naturally favors the present tense-form with thirty-six presents and nine aorists. But why the nine uses in the aorist tense-form? To answer this question, each use must be examined independently. The aorist form in Matt 6:10 is found in the Lord's Prayer, and in prayers to deity the aorist form is consistently used. The other four uses in Matthew (8:13; 9:29; 15:28; 26:42) all include a similar phrase coming from the lips of Jesus ("let be done . . ."), referring to something being done on a specific occasion. Furthermore, both Acts 1:20 and Rom 11:9 quote Psalm 69 (vv. 25 and 22, respectively). Not only are these verbs found in the LXX, but they point to a specific situation and do not indicate a general practice. In 1 Cor 3:18 Paul states, "Let no one deceive himself. If anyone among you thinks that he is wise in this age, let him become a fool that he may become (γενέσθω) wise." Here, the imperative occurs in the apodosis of a conditional statement. As such, it is not something that is conceived as a general precept but only when a certain condition is met. Finally, 1 Pet 1:15 has the aorist imperatival form, but we must remember

---

32. The other four verbs are ὀργίζεσθε (4:26 [LXX: 5 present; 1 aorist]); λυπεῖτε (4:30 [LXX: 5 present; 1 aorist]); ἀπατάτω (5:6); and μεθύσκεσθε (5:18). Each one of these imperatives occurs just one time in the NT (present tense-form) and all are used to convey general precepts.

33. LXX: 7 present; 1 aorist (2 Sam 14:11).

that the author of 1 Peter has a propensity to use the aorist form, even when a present form is expected.

The imperative βλέπετε ("*Look* carefully then how you walk," 5:15) is also a stative verb because watching or looking is not so much what you do but involves who you are. The present tense occurs twenty-eight times (in the imperative mood) whereas the aorist form only occurs once.[34] In addition, the uses are general precepts and not specific commands. The one use of the aorist, however, clearly involves a specific command. In Acts 3:4, Peter said to the crippled beggar, "Look (βλέψον) at us." This occurrence is the only time the verb is used to indicate a physical sight (look) as opposed to a figurative sense (watch out).

The imperative συνίετε ("*understand* what the will of the Lord is," 5:17) occurs twice in the present tense-form and once in the aorist. The other present form is found in Matt 15:10 where Jesus tells the crowd, "Hear (ἀκούετε) and understand (συνίετε)." Both of these uses refer to general precepts. Interestingly, the aorist form occurs in the parallel passage in Mark 7:14. But Mark's version is slightly different: "Hear (ἀκούσατε) me, all of you, and understand (σύνετε)." Why does Mark's version employ an aorist form? First, both imperatives are aorist forms (whereas in Matthew's version both are present). Second, instead of the general command to "hear" and "understand," the direct object "me" is added along with the emphatic use of πάντες. These additions may have caused the author to shift perspectives or to view the imperatives as specific commands.

The imperative ἀγαπᾶτε ("*love* your wives," 5:25; "*let* each one of you *love* his wife as himself"; 5:33) also represents a stative verb that has no natural terminus. As an imperative it occurs nineteen times in the present tense-form and only once in the aorist. The only aorist form is found in 1 Pet 1:21 ("love [ἀγαπήσατε] one another earnestly from a pure heart") which is not surprising since the author of 1 Peter favors the aorist even when the command involves a general precept.

The imperative ἐνδυναμοῦσθε ("*be strong* in the Lord," 6:10) is the final stative verb. As an imperative, this verb occurs twice in the present tense-form and never in the aorist. The command also represents a general precept and so the present form is expected.

---

34. LXX: 5 present; 1 aorist (Jdt 9:9).

Here is a summary of the atelic stative verbs:

Eph	Atelic Stative Verbs	Present Impv	Aorist Impv
2:11	μνημονεύετε	9	0
4:26	ὀργίζεσθε	1	0
4:30	λυπεῖτε	1	0
4:32	γίνεσθε	36	9
5:6	ἀπατάτω	1	0
5:15	βλέπετε	28	1
5:17	συνίετε	2	1
5:18	μεθύσκεσθε	1	0
5:25	ἀγαπᾶτε	19	1
6:10	ἐνδυναμοῦσθε	2	0
Total		100	12

Activities

There are ten imperatives in Ephesians that can be categorized as activities. Again, we will focus our attention on the four verbs that occur more than one time in the NT as imperatives.[35] The imperative λαλεῖτε ("let each one of you *speak* the truth with his neighbor," 4:25) is difficult to categorize because it is not obvious as to whether "speaking" is an atelic or telic action. Based on the NT usage, however, it appears to be conceived of as an atelic action. It occurs nine times in the present form and never in the aorist.[36] Another possibility is that this verb more closely follows the specific command versus general percept rule. Fanning notes that verbs of speaking, including λαλέω, "offer the speaker a more open choice than do other verbs between viewing the utterance as a whole (aorist) or seeing it in its progress or repetition (present)."[37]

The imperative ἁμαρτάνετε ("Be angry and *do* not *sin*," 4:26) occurs four times in the present tense-form and never in the aorist. Interestingly, it does occur once in the aorist tense-form in the LXX (and twice in the present tense-form). In 1 Sam 19:4 we read, "And Jonathan spoke well of

35. The other six verbs are ἐπιδυέτω (4:26); κοπιάτω (4:28); ὀνομαζέσθω (5:3); συγκοινωνεῖτε (5:11); παροργίζετε (6:4); and ἐκτρέφετε (6:4). Each one of these imperatives occurs just one time in the NT (present tense-form) and all are used to convey general precepts.

36. It must be admitted, however, that in the LXX the usage of λαλέω is markedly different (15 presents; 95 aorist).

37. Fanning, *Verbal Aspect*, 351–52.

David to Saul his father and said to him, 'Let not the king sin (ἁμαρτησάτω) against his servant David, because he has not sinned against you, and because his deeds have brought good to you.'" In all the present tense-form uses (in the NT and LXX), the imperative represents a general precept. In 1 Sam 19:4, however, the command relates to a specific occasion. Perhaps the author uses the aorist tense-form to present the action from a holistic viewpoint and a command that is intended for a specific occasion fits with that presentation.

The imperative ὑπακούετε ("*obey* your parents in the Lord," 6:1; "*obey* your earthly masters with fear and trembling," 6:5) occurs four times in the present tense-form and never in the aorist. All the commands are intended as general precepts.

Finally, the imperative τίμα ("*Honor* your father and mother," 6:2) occurs eight times in the present tense-form and only once in the aorist.[38] The only aorist form is found in 1 Pet 2:17, which is common for Peter to use the aorist form even when the command is a general precept.

Here is a summary of atelic activity verbs:

Eph	Atelic Activity Verbs	Present Impv	Aorist Impv
4:25	λαλεῖτε	9	0
4:26	ἁμαρτάνετε	4	0
4:26	ἐπιδυέτω	1	0
4:28	κοπιάτω	1	0
5:3	ὀνομαζέσθω	1	0
5:11	συγκοινωνεῖτε	1	0
6:1	ὑπακούετε	4	0
6:2	τίμα	8	1
6:4	παροργίζετε	1	0
6:4	ἐκτρέφετε	1	0
Total		31	1

Unexpected Present Imperatives

There are five present forms that do not seem to fit the expected usage. In other words, based on their lexical meaning, we would expect these verbs to occur in the aorist tense-form but they occur in the present tense-form.[39]

---

38. LXX: 10 presents; 2 aorists.

39. This number does not include verbs that occur only once as an imperative in the NT.

The first is the imperative δίδοτε ("*give* no opportunity to the devil," 4:27). There is no doubt that δίδωμι is a telic verb. It occurs only four times in the present tense-form but thirty-two times in the aorist. This usage is confirmed by the LXX which has only five present tense-forms but 148 aorist forms. The question then is why does Paul use the present form here in Ephesians and why does Luke use it in three other places (Luke 6:30, 38; 11:3)? First, the present forms occur in the teachings of Jesus and Paul that are intended as a general practice. Second, when comparing Luke's use of the present with Matthew's use of the aorist in parallel passages, we see an interesting distinction.

In Matt 5:42 we read, "*Give* to the one who begs from you" (τῷ αἰτοῦντί σε δός). Notice, however, that Luke adds the word πᾶς, "*Give* to everyone who begs from you" (παντὶ αἰτοῦντί σε δίδου, 6:30). Consequently, it is possible, if not likely, that the addition of παντί turns the phrase from a specific command ("give to *the one who begs* from you") to a general precept ("give to *everyone who begs* from you"), at least conceptually. Furthermore, in the Lord's Prayer, Matthew's version states, "Give us *this day* our daily bread" (τὸν ἄρτον ἡμῶν τὸν ἐπιούσιον δὸς ἡμῖν σήμερον, 6:11). But Luke's version is slightly different: "Give us *each day* our daily bread" (τὸν ἄρτον ἡμῶν τὸν ἐπιούσιον δίδου ἡμῖν τὸ καθ᾽ ἡμέραν, Luke 11:3). Again, notice that Luke adds the adverbial phrase καθ᾽ ἡμέραν ("each day" or "day by day") instead of "today" (σήμερον). This is one of the rare exceptions where an aorist form is not used in a prayer. Perhaps this is an example of an adverbial phrase clarifying an imperfective idea. Thus, in Eph 4:27 Paul most likely uses the present tense-form because he is offering a general command that he envisioned as being obeyed daily.[40]

Next is the imperative κλεπτέτω ("*Let* the thief no longer *steal*," 4:28). As an imperative, the verb κλέπτω occurs only here in the present tense-form but two times in the aorist. Thus, it is likely that this verb is viewed as a telic action and that Paul went against the expected form because it is a general precept.

The imperative ἐλέγχετε ("instead *expose* them," 5:11) also conveys a telic action. Interestingly, the present form occurs four times and the aorist form occurs only twice.[41] The other three uses of the present (1 Tim 5:20; Titus 1:13; 2:15) all are in the context of a general precept. In contrast, the aorist form in Matt 18:15 occurs in the context of a specific command:

---

40. Furthermore, the previous verse mentions not letting the sun go down on your anger, so the idea of doing something daily is in the immediate context.

41. LXX: 2 present; 5 aorist.

"If your brother sins against you, go and rebuke (ἔλεγξον) him in private" [CSB]).[42]

The imperative πληροῦσθε ("*be filled* with the Spirit," 5:18) occurs only here in the present tense-form but twice as an aorist. The telic nature of this verb is clarified by the LXX which includes only one present form and six aorist forms. In Eph 5:18, the present form is used because the command is a general precept.

Finally, the imperative ποιεῖτε ("Masters, *do* the same to them," 6:9) does not seem to fit into the typical telic/atelic distinction. The imperative occurs twenty-two times in the present tense-form and twenty-three times in the aorist form.[43] Nearly all of the twenty-three aorist forms, however, are found in contexts where a specific command is given[44] whereas the present forms are often found when the command is intended as a general practice. Another distinction is that in the Gospels the aorist is typically found when Jesus is speaking or responding to a specific group or an individual whereas the present is used when Jesus is teaching the crowds.

Expected Aorist Imperatives in Ephesians

Because Ephesians does not contain any unexpected uses of the aorist imperative, all six verbs will be discussed in this category. These verbs are expected because they are all telic verbs that occur in the aorist tense-form. Of the six verbs (αἴρω, ἀνίστημι, ἐνδύω, ἀναλαμβάνω, ἵστημι, and δέχομαι), only the first verb αἴρω (ἀρθήτω, "*Let* all bitterness and wrath and anger and clamor and slander *be put away* from you," 4:31) occurs in the present tense-form in the NT (Luke 9:3; 23:18; Acts 21:36; 22:22). As an imperative, it occurs four times in the present tense-form and twenty-two times in the aorist tense-form. A few observations can be made. First, we should note that only Luke employs the present tense-form. Thus, it may be a distinction of idiolect. Second, the last three uses are very similar and might be idiomatic ("Away with this man," Αἶρε τοῦτον [Luke 23:18]; "Away with him!" Αἶρε αὐτόν [Acts 21:36]; and "Away with such a fellow from the earth!" Αἶρε ἀπὸ τῆς γῆς τὸν τοιοῦτον [Acts 22:22]).

Besides αἴρω, none of the other aorist verbs occur in the present tense-form as imperatives in the NT. Although one could argue that this is a mere coincidence or that the sample size is too small, the larger corpus of the LXX

---

42. The other use of the aorist form is in 2 Tim 4:2.

43. The LXX presents a greater distinction with forty-one present tense-forms and 115 aorist tense-forms.

44. One clear exception is 1 Pet 3:11.

confirms this trend. For these six verbs, the usage in the LXX is even more dramatic with only two present tense-forms but 184 aorist tense-forms. Such disparity suggests that with certain imperatives, the author often does not have much of a choice but conforms to the normal or expected use of the verb.

The next aorist imperative ἀνάσται ("*arise* from the dead," 5:14) is a good example of the lack of choice in tense-form selection. In the Bible the imperative of ἀνίστημι occurs 101 times (91 [LXX]; 10 [NT]), all in the aorist tense-form. Although this example is somewhat of an exception, it is instructive because it reminds us that sometimes an author is not making a subjective choice but is "forced" to use a particular form based on convention.

The third aorist imperative ἐνδύσασθε ("*Put on* the whole armor of God," 6:11) occurs five times in the aorist tense-form but never in the present form. This usage is expected because this verb conveys an action that can be completed in a relatively short period of time (at least conceptually, i.e., according to the metaphor).[45] In other words, it normally does not take long for someone to "put on" an article of clothing. So, although in Eph 6:11 a believer needs to continually (or daily) put on the full armor of God, Paul expresses this idea using the aorist because the verb typically "requires" the aorist form. In other words, although this verb (as well as the following verbs) is found in the aorist tense-form, it certainly provides a command that needs to be repeated.

The fourth aorist imperative ἀναλάβετε ("*take up* the whole armor of God," 6:13) only occurs once as an imperative. The telic nature of this verb, however, is confirmed by the LXX which has six aorist imperatives but no present imperatives. In addition, if the verb is analyzed without the prepositional prefix (ἀνα-), the imperatival form of λαμβάνω occurs once in the present tense-form but eleven times in the aorist. This pattern continues in the LXX where the imperatival form of λαμβάνω occurs only once in the present tense-form but 169 times in the aorist.

The fifth aorist imperative στῆτε ("*stand*," 6:14) also conforms to the expected usage since standing is a telic verb that has a natural terminus taking very little time to accomplish. This tendency is confirmed by actual usage in the NT (0 presents and 6 aorists) and the LXX (1 present and 41 aorists). In addition, when considering parallel constructions of ἵστημι with another verb, we see further evidence that ἵστημι strongly favors the aorist. For example, in Luke 6:8 Jesus says to the man with the withered hand,

---

45. See Caird, *Language*, 152–55. Fanning states, "The use of the aspects here seem to be influenced more by the *vehicle* of the metaphor than by the *tenor* of it" (*Verbal Aspect*, 363, n. 40).

"Come and stand here" (Ἔγειρε καὶ στῆθι εἰς τὸ μέσον). Whereas ἔγειρε is a present tense-form imperative, στῆθι is an aorist. Another example is found in Jas 2:3 which states, "you say to the poor man, 'You stand (στῆθι) over there,' or, 'Sit down (κάθου) at my feet.'" Although the first verb is aorist and the second is present, it seems unlikely that the author is purposefully trying to portray the verbs differently. This analysis is confirmed by the usage of κάθημαι which never occurs as an aorist imperative but occurs nineteen times as a present imperative in the Bible (13 [LXX]; 6 [NT]).

Finally, the aorist imperative δέξασθε ("*take* the helmet of salvation," 6:17) also conveys a telic action that usually requires little time to complete. As an imperative, it never occurs in the present tense-form but is found sixteen times in the aorist form in the Bible (9 [LXX]; 7 [NT]).

Here is a summary of the aorist imperatives found in Ephesians.

Eph	Telic Verbs	Present Impv	Aorist Impv
4:31	ἀρθήτω	4	22
5:14	ἀνάστα	0	10
6:11	ἐνδύσασθε	0	5
6:13	ἀναλάβετε	0	1
6:14	στῆτε	0	6
6:17	δέξασθε	0	7
Total		4	51

CONCLUSION

I will offer four thoughts as I conclude this essay. (1) Verbal aspect studies still has a long way to go and needs correcting. The idea that we can simply identify the aspect (tense-form) of a verb and then comment about the author's subjective choice is too simplistic. (2) To maintain that the aorist is the "default" tense-form in the NT (or even in historical narratives) is vacuous. Not only do we need to consider the literary genre, but, especially with imperatives, we need to consider the lexical meaning and the context of the verb. (3) The general distinction that aorist imperatives refer to specific commands and that present imperatives refer to general precepts is helpful. The reason that this guideline is usually accurate is because it is natural for an author to use the aorist form (perfective aspect) when communicating a specific command since the action is to be completed in its entirety on that particular occasion. Conversely, it is natural for an author to use the present form (imperfective aspect) when giving a general precept since the action is to be repeated as necessary. (4) With imperatives, the author is often not making a subjective choice but is merely conforming to the normal or expected use of a term. Thus, we should be careful not to over-interpret imperatives based on the tense-form used.

BIBLIOGRAPHY

Aubrey, Michael. "Greek Prohibitions." In *The Greek Verb Revisited: A Fresh Approach for Biblical Exegesis*, edited by Steven E. Runge and Christopher J. Fresch, 486–538. Bellingham, WA: Lexham, 2016.

Bakker, Willem Frederik. *The Greek Imperative: An Investigation into the Aspectual Differences Between the Present and Aorist Imperatives in Greek Prayer from Homer Up to the Present Day*. Amsterdam: Adolf M. Hakkert, 1966.

Baugh, S. M. *Introduction to Greek Tense Form Choice in the Non-Indicative Moods*. Pdf edition, 2009. http://dailydoseofgreek.com/wp-content/uploads/sites/2/2015/09/GreekTenseFormChoice-Baugh.pdf.

Blass, F., A. Debrunner, and Robert W. Funk. *A Greek Grammar of the New Testament and Other Early Christian Literature*. Chicago: University of Chicago Press, 1961.

Caird, G. B. *The Language and Imagery of the Bible*. London: Duckworth, 1980.

Campbell, Constantine R. *Verbal Aspect and Non-Indicative Verbs: Further Soundings in the Greek of the New Testament*. Studies in Biblical Greek 15. New York: Peter Lang, 2008.

Dana, H. E., and Julius R. Mantey. *A Manual Grammar of the Greek New Testament*. Toronto: Macmillan, 1927.

Fanning, Buist M. "Approaches to Verbal Aspect in New Testament Greek: Issues in Definition and Method." In *Biblical Greek Language and Linguistics: Open Questions in Current Research*, edited by Stanley E. Porter and D. A. Carson, 46–62. Sheffield: Sheffield Academic, 1993.

———. *Verbal Aspect in New Testament Greek*. Oxford: Clarendon, 1990.

Forbes, Greg W. *1 Peter*. Exegetical Guide to the Greek New Testament. Nashville: B&H Academic, 2014.

McKay, K. L. "Aspect in Imperative Constructions in New Testament Greek." *Novum Testamentum* 27 (1985) 201–26.

Merkle, Benjamin L. "The Abused Aspect: Neglecting the Influence of a Verb's Lexical Meaning on Tense-Form Choice." *Bulletin for Biblical Research* 26 (2016) 57–74.

Robertson, A. T. *A Grammar of the Greek New Testament in the Light of Historical Research*. 4th ed. Nashville: Broadman, 1934.

Wallace, Daniel B. *Greek Grammar Beyond the Basics: An Exegetical Syntax of the New Testament*. Grand Rapids, MI: Zondervan, 1996.

Young, Richard A. *Intermediate New Testament Greek: A Linguistic and Exegetical Approach*. Nashville: B&H, 1994.

Zerwick, Maximilian. *Biblical Greek: Illustrated by Examples*. Rome: Scripta Pontificii Instituti Biblici, 1963.

Chapter 4

Semitic Wordplay Behind the Greek of the New Testament

—MICHAEL B. SHEPHERD
Cedarville University

INTRODUCTION

SEMITIC (BOTH HEBREW AND Aramaic) influence throughout the Greek of the New Testament is well-known and well-documented.[1] This influence is primarily due to two main factors among others. First, the spoken language of first-century Jews living in Israel was Aramaic. This includes Jesus and the NT authors with the exception of Luke (see, e.g., Matt 5:22; 27:33, 46; Mark 5:41; 10:51; 14:36; 15:22, 34; John 1:42; 19:17; 20:16; Rom 8:15; Gal 4:6; 1 Cor 16:22; 2 Cor 1:22; 5:5; Eph 1:14; Rev 22:20).[2] Thus, not only would writing in Greek (or dictating to an amanuensis [e.g., Rom 16:22]) require translation, but also any oral and written sources behind

---

1. E.g., Ernesti, *Institutio interpretis*, 41–57; Moulton, *Grammar*; Robertson, *Grammar*, 88–107; Hill, *Greek Words*; Black, "New Testament Semitisms," 215–23; Voelz, "Semitic Influence," 115–29; and Black, *Aramaic Approach*.

2. References to "the Hebrew dialect" (e.g., Acts 21:40; 22:2; 26:14) are thus references to the language in which the Hebrews spoke, namely, Aramaic. See Beattie and Davies, "What Does Hebrew Mean?," 71–83. This is not to deny evidence for widespread use of Greek (or Latin) in first-century Israel (see John 19:20), especially among non-Jews. See Gleaves, *Did Jesus Speak Greek?* But the mere presence of such evidence should not be used simply to infer what is contrary to the evidence of the NT documents themselves.

the Greek NT, as well as any initial drafts of NT compositions, would have more than likely been in Aramaic in most cases.³ The second factor is the Septuagint. Translations of the Hebrew Scriptures for Greek-speaking Jews (e.g., those living in Alexandria, Egypt) were for the most part designed to bring the target audience to the source language (Hebrew) rather than to bring the source language to the target audience.⁴ This means that the translation technique is largely "literal" or formally equivalent (as opposed to dynamically equivalent), resulting in translation Greek (which is un-Greek-like and Hebraic) rather than freely-composed Greek.⁵ When the NT authors wanted to explain Jesus and the gospel from the Hebrew Bible to the Greek-speaking Roman Empire, they turned to the Greek Bible and found a storehouse of Hebrew-Greek words, grammatical forms, and syntactical constructions they incorporated into the very language of their work.⁶ The Septuagint essentially became the grammar, lexicon, and conduit for the communication of the theology of the Hebrew Bible in the NT.

The present essay is devoted to the lesser-known (and in some cases unrecognized) phenomenon of Semitic wordplay behind the Greek of the NT. There are, of course, several fairly well-known examples such as Matt 1:21 and Matt 2:23. The Greek text of Matt 1:21 presupposes a typical Hebrew wordplay (cf., Gen 29:31—30:23) involving the root ישע in the angel's explanation of the name of Jesus to Joseph: "She will bear a son, and you will call his name Jesus (ישוע), for he will save (יושיע) his people from their sins."⁷

---

3. "Matthew had first preached to Hebrews, and when he was on the point of going to others he transmitted in writing in his native language [i.e., Aramaic] the Gospel according to himself" (Eusebius, *Ecclesiastical History*, 250–51).

4. See Kraus, "Comtemporary Translations," 69.

5. "A Hebraism may be defined as a Greek word, phrase, or syntagma which expresses certain characteristic Hebrew elements in Greek in a non-Greek fashion. Sometimes an isolated parallel to the Hebraism may be spotted in a secular Greek source, but the word or element should nevertheless be considered a Hebraism if the great frequency of its occurrences shows that its appearance its conditioned by Hebrew rather than Greek usage." Tov, *Greek and Hebrew Bible*, 88.

6. This is not unlike what happens today when a pastor who knows biblical Hebrew nevertheless has to communicate with his congregation by means of some sort of English translation. Many of the most commonly used formally equivalent English translations (e.g., KJV) preserve Hebrew idioms that are not native to English, but because of the influence of the Bible those idioms have now found their way into the usage of the English language.

7. Explanation of names in Hebrew narrative are rarely intended to be strict etymologies (see Barr, *Semantics of Biblical Language*, 109). Often, such explanation simply involves wordplay that associates a name with a word highlighting something about the character in the story. For example, see the sustained sound play on Noah's name involving multiple words in Gen 5:29; 6:6, 8 (Sailhamer, *Pentateuch as Narrative*, 124).

This play does not translate into Greek (or English). Likewise, according to Matt 2:23, the settling of Joseph and his family in the city of Nazareth was to fulfill something spoken by the prophets—namely, that the Messiah would be called a Nazarene. This is rather dumbfounding in translation, but it involves a wordplay between נצרי ("Nazarene") and the Hebrew word נצר ("sprout, shoot") in the messianic prophecy found in Isa 11:1.[8] The following discussion seeks not only to survey and to bring to light the widespread occurrence of Semitic wordplay but also to propose new examples and to reflect on the purpose of wordplay. In some cases, wordplay seems to have exegetical or theological purpose. In others, it is possible that wordplay has more of an aesthetic value that contributes to the reader's enjoyment of the text.[9] Of course, these are not mutually exclusive reasons for the use of wordplay.

MATTHEW AND MARK

The Sermon on the Mount

One of the oft-noted differences between Matthew's account of the Sermon on the Mount (Matt 5–7) and Luke's (Luke 6:17–49) is the fact that Matthew says Jesus "went up into the mountain" (Matt 5:1), while Luke indicates that Jesus descended the mountain with his disciples and "stood on a level place" (Luke 6:17; cf., Luke 6:12). Apart from the fact that Matthew's expression—"went up into the mountain"—is a Hebrew idiom (see Exod 19:3; 24:18; 34:4),[10] his decision to highlight Jesus' ascent into the mountain is perhaps

---

8. It is worth noting in this mention of examples from Matthew that his book begins with a well-recognized instance of Hebrew *gematria*. Matthew designates Jesus "the son of David, the son of Abraham" (Matt 1:1). The numerical value of David's name in Hebrew is fourteen. Thus, in the genealogy of Jesus there are fourteen generations from Abraham to David, fourteen from David to the Babylonian exile, and fourteen from the Babylonian exile to the Christ (Matt 1:17).

9. Benjamin Sommer mentions this as a reason for allusion in the prophetic literature: "While many literary critics focus on more hermeneutically oriented aspects of allusion, this element of play, of sensual enjoyment, in allusion should not be overlooked. I think it often is one of the most important reasons for allusion; at times, it may be the only one. We ought not forget that luxuriating in 'the pleasure of the text' is perhaps the most crucial aspect of reading literature, and the element of play in allusions encourages just this. The element of play helps explain why allusion usually is covert: it is more challenging, and more fun, for the reader to have to produce the identification" (*Prophet Reads Scripture*, 19).

10. Matthew also uses a Hebrew idiom in Matt 5:1: "he opened his mouth and taught them" (see Ps 78:2; Job 3:1; 33:2; Dan 10:16). Luke uses a different idiom: "he lifted up his eyes to his disciples and said" (Luke 6:20; see Brown, Driver, and Briggs,

based in part on a Semitic soundplay between the Hebrew word תורה ("Torah") and the Aramaic word טורא ("the mountain"). After all, Jesus states that he has not come to abolish the Torah (νόμος = "Torah" in the LXX) or the Prophets but to fulfill them (see Matt 1:22–23; 2:5–6, 15, 17–18; 3:3; 4:14–16). Moreover, the six antitheses in Matt 5:21–48 are Jesus' exposition of the Torah. The Sermon on the Mount is thus the *torah* ("Torah") on *tura* ("the mount").

Matthew 7:6

The Greek text of Matt 7:6 translates: "Do not give what is holy (τὸ ἅγιον) to dogs or cast your pearls before pigs." Because of the seemingly unusual parallel between "what is holy" and "pearls," it has been suggested that "what is holy" is a mistranslation of the Aramaic word קִדְשָׁא ("ring").[11] In a purely consonantal Aramaic text, this word would be identical to קַדְשָׁא ("what is holy"). According to the supposedly original Aramaic, the parallel would be between "ring" and "pearls," perhaps alluding to Prov 11:22 ("A gold ring in a pig's snout is a woman beautiful and turning away from discretion"). But Charles Quarles has demonstrated that the Greek text ("what is holy") makes good sense in context.[12] He argues that "what is holy" is holy meat (Lev 8:31; 10:14). Dogs were to be kept from this kind of meat (4QMMT 51–54). Meat from an animal killed by predators was to be thrown to the dogs (Exod 22:30 [Eng., 22:31]). Thus, it is not necessary to characterize the Greek text as a mistranslation. But it is also not necessary to choose only one or the other option for translation of קדשא. Double entendre is a well-recognized literary technique both inside and outside biblical literature in both ancient and modern texts. It is entirely possible that the more unusual option for קדשא was chosen for the Greek text ("what is holy") in order to prompt the reader to think of the expected parallel ("ring") at the same time.[13]

Brown-Driver-Briggs Hebrew, 670). Furthermore, note the use of Hebrew parallelism in Matt 5:3–10; Luke 6:20–21.

11. See Black, *Aramaic Approach*, 200–203. See also Targum Job 42:11.

12. Quarles, *Sermon on the Mount*, 289–95.

13. Other examples of double entendre elsewhere in the Greek NT may include multiple plausible renderings of the Aramaic ד, which can be a relative, a sign of the "genitive," or a variously translated conjunction (Black, *Aramaic Approach*, 70–92). See, e.g., Mark 4:12; John 1:3 (note the parallelism).

Matthew 15:15; 16:23; 21:37, 42

Other potential Semitic wordplays in Matthew include but are not limited to Matt 15:15; 16:23; 21:37, 42. The unique (at least for the Greek NT) choice of the imperative φράσον ("explain") in Matt 15:15 (cf., Mark 7:17) may be an attempt to imitate the Hebrew/Aramaic root פרשׁ ("explain"). In Matt 16:23 (also Mark 8:33), Jesus addresses Peter as σατανᾶ (Aramaic: שָׂטָנָא). This is usually translated/transliterated "Satan," but it could just as easily be translated "adversary" (cf., 2 Sam 19:23).[14] Perhaps both the Aramaic and the Greek in this case are intentionally ambiguous. Finally, the parable of the vineyard and the tenants in Matt 21:33-46 (also Mark 12:1-12; Luke 20:9-19) climaxes with the sending of the "son" who is subsequently killed, resulting in the handing over of the vineyard to other tenants. Jesus concludes the parable by citing Ps 118:22-23, which speaks of the "stone" rejected by the builders. In this scenario, the "stone" (אבן) is the "son" (בן). The play on the two Hebrew words finds a parallel in the Targum of Ps 118:22, which interprets the "stone" to be the "son" (lit., "the boy" among the sons of Jesse).[15] This shared interpretation of Ps 118:22 is the basis for its citation with reference to the parable in Matthew (see also Mark and Luke).[16]

Mark 9:49

Both Matt 5:13 and Luke 14:34-35 contain Jesus' saying about salt losing its saltiness and thus becoming good for nothing except to be thrown out. Mark 9:50 has a shorter form of this, but prior to this verse, Mark 9:49 has something unique following the reference to the "fire" of Gehenna never being extinguished in Mark 9:48. This verse is represented differently in the textual witnesses: (1) Codex Vaticanus: "For every one will be salted with fire"; (2) Codex D: "For every sacrifice will be salted with salt"; and (3) Codex Alexandrinus: "For every one will be salted with fire, and every sacrifice will be salted with salt." According to Bruce Metzger, the first reading is

---

14. A similar issue occurs in 1 Chr 21:1 (cf., 2 Sam 24:1). Some contend for the translation "Satan" based on Zech 3:1; Job 2:3 (see Klein, *1 Chronicles*, 418-19). Others argue for "adversary" (as in "foreign adversary") based on the use of the term in the Chronicler's sources: 1 Sam 29:4; 1 Kgs 5:18; 11:14, 23, 25 (see Sailhamer, *Introduction to Old Testament Theology*, 302-8).

15. There may also be an implied play in the Hebrew text of Ps 118:22 on אבן (בן) and הבונים ("the builders"). See Gen 16:2; 30:1, 3; Isa 54:13 (MT and 1QIsaa). See also Matt 23:31; Luke 11:48.

16. See Shepherd, "Targums," 931-34. See also Evans, "Aramaic Psalter," 44-91.

to be preferred.[17] The reading in Codex D was originally a marginal gloss from Lev 2:13, and the reading in Codex Alexandrinus is thus considered a conflation of readings 1 and 2. Apart from the fact that there is no actual evidence of a marginal gloss from Lev 2:13, there is more than one way to reconstruct the history of the textual variation here. It is quite possible that the longer reading in Codex Alexandrinus is to be preferred. Readings 1 and 2 are the products of scribal oversight, created by homoioteleuton and homoioarchton, respectively. The reading in Codex Alexandrinus also preserves a wordplay between אֵשׁ ("fire") and אִשֶּׁה ("offering made by fire") when the Greek text is back-translated into Hebrew. The Greek word θυσία ("sacrifice") in Codex Alexandrinus is used several times by the LXX translator in the immediate context of Lev 2:13 to translate אִשֶּׁה (see Lev 1:9, 13, 17; 2:2, 3).

LUKE-ACTS[18]

Luke 1:13–14

It is well known that Luke-Acts is a two-volume work addressed to the Roman official Theophilus (Luke 1:3; Acts 1:1). Luke writes his prologue in good classical Greek style (Luke 1:1–4; cf., *Ant.* 1), but the remainder of his work is in Semitic Greek like Matthew, Mark, and John. This is due to the fact that the compilation and composition of the book consists of various Hebrew and Aramaic (and possibly Semitic Greek) eyewitness accounts, both oral and written. Already in Luke 1:13–14 there is a Greek wordplay that finds its basis in the Hebrew name יוֹחָנָן ("John," "The LORD is gracious"). The angel says to Zechariah that there will be "joy to you" (χαρά σοι)—which is the Hebrew idiom for possession ("you will have joy")—and many "will rejoice" (χαρήσονται) at John's birth. Both the Greek phrase and the Greek verb create a sound play on the Greek noun χάρις ("grace"), which, back-translated into Hebrew, is חֵן ("grace") from the verbal root in John's name.[19]

17. Metzger, *Textual Commentary*, 87.

18. Acts is included in the heading to this section not because of the presence of specific examples from Acts, but because Luke-Acts is a single work. It is to be noted, however, that Codex D may be the best place to look for Aramaisms in Acts given its proximity to Luke's Aramaic sources when compared to the Alexandrian or Byzantine text forms (see Black, *Aramaic Approach*, 28–34).

19. It is also possible for an author to play on the similarity between a Greek word and a Hebrew or Aramaic word. For example, in Luke 22:15 Jesus says to the disciples, "I have greatly desired to eat this Passover (πάσχα = Aramaic פִּסְחָא) with you before I

Luke 2:30; 19:9–10

Luke features at least a couple of plays on the meaning of Jesus' name ("salvation"). When Simeon praises God at the presentation of Jesus in the Temple, he says, "For my eyes have seen your salvation" (Luke 2:30). Simeon has seen ישוע ("Jesus," "salvation") who "will save" (יושיע) his people from their sins (Matt 1:21; Luke 1:31; 1 Tim 1:15). Also in the story of Zacchaeus, which is unique to Luke's Gospel, Zacchaeus pledges to give half of his possessions to the poor and to pay back fourfold to anyone he has cheated (Luke 19:8). Jesus ("salvation") then says to him, "Today salvation has come to this house, because he too is a son of Abraham. For the Son of Man came to seek and to save the lost" (Luke 19:9–10; cf., 1 Tim 1:15). On the surface this looks like salvation by works (cf., Luke 11:41; 12:33),[20] and the usual resolution of the problem is to say that Zacchaeus' pledge is a reflection of a genuine change of heart.[21] But there is no indication of such change. Rather, it seems that "salvation" in Luke 19:9 is a reference to self (see also John 4:22). Jesus is explaining why he has come to the house of a crooked tax collector. It is because he too is a son of Abraham, and it is precisely lost individuals like Zacchaeus that the Son of Man came to seek and to save.

Luke 11:41; 12:33; 14:5

In Matt 23:26, Jesus tells the scribes and the Pharisees, "Clean (καθάρισον = דכו) first the inside of the cup, so that also its outside may be clean." Luke 11:41 has instead, "But the things inside give alms (δότε ἐλεημοσύνην = זכו), and look, all things will be clean for you." The Aramaic behind Luke's text is neither a mistranslation nor a misinterpretation of the Aramaic behind Matthew's text as Julius Wellhausen, and later, Matthew Black, had it.[22] Rather, Luke's text represents deliberate exegesis of Matthew's text, which is based on the similarity of the Aramaic words. It is a translation of Jesus' metaphor.

Luke 12:33 also mentions giving alms. Black noted a soundplay at the end of this verse when back-translated into Aramaic: "where a thief does

---

suffer (παθεῖν from πάσχω)." Incidentally, the beginning of this quote features a common Hebraism/Septuagint-ism. The Greek of the Septuagint typically renders the Hebrew construction involving a finite verb and an infinitive absolute from the same root with a finite verb and either a cognate noun in the dative or a cognate participle (see Tov, *Greek and Hebrew Bible*, 247–56).

20. Zacchaeus' name is related to the same Aramaic root that is translated "give alms" in Luke 11:41.
21. E.g., Bock, *Luke*, 1522.
22. Black, *Aramaic Approach*, 2.

not approach (*qarebh*), and a moth (*ruqba*) does not corrupt (*marqebh*)."[23] Unlike the previously discussed examples, this one seems to have little exegetical significance. Nevertheless, it is memorable and pleasant to the eye and to the ear. Another similar example is Luke 14:5: "Which of you, if a son (*bᵉra*) or an ox (*bᵉʿira*) falls into a pit (*bēra*), will not immediately pull him up on the Sabbath day?" Black's suggestion that this should be "an ox (*bᵉʿira*) or an ass (*bar ḥamra*)" is not necessary.[24]

Luke 24:32

One of the reasons that appeal to Semitic sources behind the Greek of the NT has either failed to gain traction or is losing traction in some circles is the frequent claim that the Greek text mistranslates the Semitic source. This is unfortunate because the claim is entirely unnecessary. For instance, in Luke 24:32 the disciples who have been with Jesus on the road to Emmaus say to one another, "Was not our heart/mind burning within us as he spoke to us on the way, as he opened to us the Scriptures?" The suggestion is that the Greek καιομένη ("burning," i.e., "warmed and enlightened") translates the Aramaic word יקיד, which is a misreading of the graphically similar Aramaic word יקיר ("heavy," i.e., "slow to understand").[25] This latter Aramaic word is in the Old Syriac of Luke 24:32. It is perhaps also behind the reading κεκαλυμμένη ("veiled"; cf., 2 Cor 3:15) in Codex D. Furthermore, יקיר ("heavy") is likely behind Jesus' description of the disciples in Luke 24:25: "O foolish and slow (βραδεῖς = יקיר) in heart/mind to believe in all that the prophets spoke." But Luke 24:25 is a description of the disciples prior to Jesus' exposition of Moses and the Prophets (Luke 24:27). The text of Luke 24:32 is their self-description after his exposition. Thus, it appears more probable that the two verses play on two very similar Aramaic words. Prior to Jesus' exposition the disciples were יקיר ("heavy," "slow to understand"), but after his exposition they were יקיד ("burning," "warmed and enlightened").[26] According to this reading, the Old Syriac and Codex D of

---

23. Ibid., 178.
24. Ibid., 168.
25. Ibid., 254–55.
26. Cf., *Song of Songs Rabbah* 42: "Ben-Azzai was sitting and interpreting [making midrash], and fire was all around him. They went and told Rabbi Akiva, 'Rabbi, Ben-Azzai is sitting and interpreting, and fire is burning all around him.' He went to him and said to him, 'I heard that you were interpreting, and the fire burning all around you.' He said, 'Indeed.' He said, 'Perhaps you were engaged in the inner-rooms of the chariot [theosophical speculation].' He said, 'No. I was sitting and stringing the words of the Torah [to each other], and the Torah to the Prophets and the Prophets to the Writings,

Luke 24:32 represent a misreading of the originally intended יקִד ("burning") as יקִר ("heavy").

JOHN

John 4:10–14

John's presentation of the conversation between Jesus and Nicodemus in John 3 exploits the semantic range of the Greek word ἄνωθεν. When Jesus tells Nicodemus that a person must be born ἄνωθεν to see the kingdom of God (John 3:3), Nicodemus understands him to mean that someone must be born "again" literally and physically (John 3:4). But Jesus clarifies that he means a person must be born "from above" spiritually (John 3:5). A similar play on the potential referents of "living water" (ὕδωρ ζῶν) occurs in John 4, but this time it is that of the Hebrew phrase behind the Greek that the writer exploits (see the Greek phrase in the LXX). The Hebrew phrase מים חיים can refer to literal "fresh water," "running/flowing water," or "spring water" (Gen 26:19; Lev 14:5, 50; 15:13; Num 19:17; Zech 14:8; Song 4:15).[27] It can also refer to spiritual "life-giving water" (Jer 2:13; 17:13; cf., Ps 36:10 [Eng., 36:9]; Prov 13:14; 14:27; 16:22). Thus, when Jesus tells the woman at the well that if she knew who was speaking to her she would have asked, and he would have given to her "living water" (John 4:10), the woman understands him to mean that he somehow has "fresh water" (John 4:11–12). Jesus then clarifies that he means spiritual "life-giving water" (John 4:13–14).

---

and the words were as radiant/joyful as when they were given from Sinai, and they were as sweet as at their original giving. Were they not originally given in fire, as it is written, "And the mountain was burning with fire" [Deut. 4:11]?'" (quoted in Boyarin, *Intertextuality*, 109–10). "Ben Azzai does not speak of having achieved the original meaning or inner meaning or hidden meaning of the Torah, but only of having read in such a way that he reconstituted the original *experience* of revelation. He did what he did, not by linking texts with their meanings but by linking texts with texts, that is, by revealing the hermeneutic connection between the Prophets and Writings and the Torah." Boyarin, *Intertextuality*, 110. See also *Lev. Rab.* 16:4.

27. Compare the use of the language "bitter" and "sweet" in Exod 15:23, 25; Jas 3:11–12.

THE PAULINE EPISTLES

Romans 4:11

Given Paul's stated background and Hebrew learning (Acts 23:6; 26:5; 2 Cor 11:22; Gal 1:13-14; Phil 3:5-6),[28] it is to be expected that back-translation from the Greek of his letters to Hebrew might prove to be helpful in interpretation. Perhaps the most exegetically significant example of this occurs in Rom 4:11. At the outset of Paul's letter to the Romans, the programmatic passage in Rom 1:16-17 sets forth Paul's doctrine of justification by faith with a citation from Hab 2:4b, which is based on the reference to Abram's justification by faith in Gen 15:6 (cf., Gal 3:1-14). Thus, in Romans 4, Paul begins with Gen 15:6 (Rom 4:3, 9, 22) and calls Abraham the father of all who believe (Rom 4:11, 16). This designation is primarily based on Paul's exegesis of the change of the patriarch's name from "Abram" to "Abraham" (אברהם [*Avraham*]) in Gen 17:5 (Rom 4:17-18; see also Neh 9:7; 1 Chr 1:27). The explanation given for this change is that God has appointed him to be "father of a multitude of nations" (אב המון גוים [*av hamon goyim*]). This creates a soundplay between *Avraham* and *av hamon goyim*, using the sounds "av" and "ham." But what does it mean that Abraham will be the father of a multitude of nations (cf., Gen 28:3; 35:11; 48:4)? Rashi initially interpreted this to mean that Abraham would be the father of the whole world, but then he explained "nations" in Gen 17:6 to be Israel (from Jacob) and Edom (from Esau) (see Gen 25:23).[29] The problem is that the text says "a multitude of nations," not "two nations." Paul understands that Abraham is primarily the father of one nation in the biblical narrative. Therefore, he takes "father of a multitude of nations" to mean that because of Gen 15:6 he is the spiritual father of all who believe. Back-translated into Hebrew, it becomes apparent that the phrase "father of all who believe" (אב לכל המאמינים [*av lkhol hamaaminim*] in Rom 4:11 is Paul's own soundplay on *Avraham* and *av hamon goyim*.

Romans 5:12

The dependent clause at the end of Rom 5:12 (ἐφ' ᾧ πάντες ἥμαρτον) is another example from Paul's letter to the Romans that requires knowledge of Hebrew. This verse states that just as sin came into the world through

---

28. Note Paul's preference, which is almost unique to him in the NT except for John 1:42, for the Aramaic form of Peter's name, "Cephas" (1 Cor 1:12; 3:22; 9:5; 15:5; Gal 1:18; 2:9, 11, 14).

29. Scherman, *Chumash*, 73.

one "man" (Adam), and through sin death, so also death came to all "men/people" (*adam*). The Latin Vulgate then mistranslates the final clause as *in quo omnes peccaverunt* ("in whom all sinned"). The Greek phrase ἐφ' ᾧ does not mean "in whom" (*in quo*), that is, in Adam. It is a translation of the Hebrew phrase אשר על, which functions as a causal conjunction ("because") in biblical Hebrew (see BDB, 758): "because all sinned." Paul's reading of the narrative in Genesis 3 focuses not only on the entrance of death into the world (Gen 2:17; 3:3–4; 4:8, 14–15, 23–24) but also on exegesis of אדם, which can be "man," "mankind," or "Adam." Sin came into the world through one אדם ("man/Adam"), and through sin, death. So also, death came to all אדם ("mankind/humanity"), because all (i.e., אדם ["Adam/mankind"]) sinned (cf., Gen 6:5).

1 Corinthians 7:9

Paul mentions his training in the Torah at the feet of Gamaliel (Acts 22:3) who is depicted both in the NT (Acts 5:34–39) and in the later rabbinic literature as a well-respected teacher. It is no surprise then to find examples of the influence of this great teacher on Paul's instruction. There is a teaching attributed to Gamaliel that plays on the similarity of the three Hebrew words איש ("man"), אשה ("woman"), and אש ("fire"). The letters י and ה join the איש ("man") and the אשה ("woman"). These letters also spell יה ("Yah[weh]" or "the LORD"). Thus, the LORD joins the man and the woman in marriage (cf., Matt 19:6). But if the letters י and ה are removed from the איש ("man") and the אשה ("woman"), then all that is left is אש ("fire"). Therefore, Paul says that it is better to marry than to burn (1 Cor 7:9; cf., Prov 6:27; Matt 19:10; 1 Tim 5:14).

1 Corinthians 16:22

At the end of 1 Corinthians (1 Cor 16:22), Paul uses an Aramaic expression (in Greek letters, μαραναθα) whose interpretation depends upon how the letters are divided.[30] Early uncial manuscripts like Sinaiticus leave this expression undivided as part of their continual script. Some witnesses divide it as μαραν αθα (= מרן אתא), which could mean either "Our Lord has come" or "Our Lord is coming" (if אתא is re-vocalized as a participle). The verb could also be re-vocalized as an imperative (see Syriac). If the expression is divided μαρανα θα (= מרנא תא), then it would most certainly be an imperative:

---

30. See Fee, *First Epistle*, 838–39.

"Our Lord, come." This is apparently the way the same Aramaic expression is translated in Rev 22:20. It is generally agreed that μαραναθα is also used in this manner in *Didache* 10:6 where it is the conclusion to a prayer intended for use after communion. But there are other possibilities. The letters אתא could be reanalyzed as the noun את ("sign") plus the suffixed definite article א: "Our Lord is the sign" (see BDAG, 616). The sense of this would be that the Lord is the *Aleph* and the *Taw* or the *Alpha* and the *Omega* (the first and last letters of the alphabet), the beginning and the end (Isa 41:4; 44:6; 48:12; Rev 1:8, 17; 2:8; 21:6; 22:13).[31] Given the ambiguities of Paul's use of the expression in 1 Cor 16:22, it is possible that he intentionally leaves it open to multiple readings—a wordplay of sorts.

2 Corinthians 4:17

In 2 Cor 4:17, Paul says that our momentary lightness of affliction is working for us an eternal "weight of glory" (βάρος δόξης) beyond all measure. The Greek word βάρος ("weight") in the LXX translates כָּבֵד ("heaviness"). The word δόξα ("glory") is most commonly used in the LXX to translate כָּבוֹד or כָּבֵד ("heaviness"). Philip Hughes has suggested that Paul is not consciously combining two senses of the Hebrew word ("abundance" and "honor"):

> Attractive though the suggestion must be to those whose business is with words, we do not hesitate to answer in the negative, since an etymological refinement of this kind, being irrelevant to his main purpose, which is doctrinal and certainly not philological, would not consciously have been devised by the Apostle.[32]

In response to this assessment, it is important to note that a combination of two senses of the Hebrew word is not the only explanation of what is happening here between Paul's Greek text and the underlying Hebrew language. Secondly, words should be the business of every exegete, otherwise interpretation becomes a mere impression of themes ungrounded in the grammar and syntax of the text itself. And thirdly, Hughes concedes that the Hebrew word means "heaviness." He also concedes that the Greek words are both used to translate this Hebrew word. So, where is the etymological refinement? An etymological fallacy involves the resurrection of a supposed original meaning to explain a word that no longer bears that meaning

---

31. This is the way Codex Alexandrinus interprets the definite direct object marker את in Amos 9:12 when it translates it as "the Lord" (see Acts 15:17; see also Zech 12:10).

32. Hughes, *Paul's Second Epistle*, 158.

according to common usage. By Hughes's own admission, that is not the case here. Furthermore, it is beyond comprehension how Hughes can say that the meaning of the words is irrelevant to Paul's purpose, since it is precisely the point of the verse to contrast momentary lightness with eternal heaviness.

It is quite plausible that Paul's play on words in 2 Cor 4:17 is intended to be exegetical. If he had simply said that our momentary lightness of affliction is working an eternal "glory" (δόξα), then the contrast between "lightness" and "heaviness" would not be very clear (cf., Rom 8:17–18; 1 Pet 5:10). The Greek word δόξα ("glory") means "brightness" or "splendor" (cf., Hebrew הדר, הוד), so a reader not familiar with the way this word has absorbed the sense of כָּבוֹד ("heaviness") from its use in the LXX would not see the contrast with "lightness." Thus, he clarifies with βάρος that it is the Hebrew "weight" or "heaviness" of glory that he has in mind.

THE GENERAL EPISTLES AND REVELATION

1 Peter 1:15–16

In 1 Pet 1:15, the apostle calls on his readers to be holy or set apart in all their conduct "according to [or, like/as] the Holy One who called you." He then cites Lev 19:45b (see also Lev 20:7) in 1 Pet 1:16: "You will be holy [or, set apart], for I am holy [or, set apart]." Peter's exhortation in 1 Pet 1:15 appears to be based on an exegetical play on the clause כי קדוש אני ("for holy am I") as כקדוש ("like the Holy One"): "You will be holy like the Holy One." Just as God set himself apart from the other so-called gods in the original exodus (Exod 12:12; Num 33:4), so Israel was to be set apart from the other peoples by following the instruction in Leviticus 11. Likewise, Jesus has distinguished himself as the leader of a new exodus (Num 23:22; 24:8; Hos 2:16–17 [Eng., 14–15]; 8:13; 9:3; 11:1, 5, 11; Matt 2:15; Luke 9:31; Jude 5). Therefore, his people are to be set apart to him in all that they do.

2 Peter 3

In Peter's second letter (2 Pet 3:1), he urges his readers to remember the things spoken before by the prophets and the apostles (2 Pet 3:2, 16), specifically the things about the last days (2 Pet 3:3; see Gen 49:1; Num 24:14; Deut 4:30; 31:29; Isa 2:2; Jer 30:24; Ezek 38:16; Hos 3:5; Mic 4:1; Dan 2:28; 10:14; 1–2 Thess; 2 Tim 3), judgment in the Day of the Lord (2 Pet 3:10; see Joel 2:2; Amos 5:18; Obad 15; Zeph 1:7, 15; Mal 3:23 [Eng., 4:5]), and the new creation (2 Pet 3:13; see Isa 65:17). There are those who say, "Where is the promise of his coming? For since the fathers fell asleep, all things have thus remained from the beginning of creation" (2 Pet 3:4; cf., Ezek 12:21–28). Peter goes on to respond to this with a citation from Psalm 90 (2 Pet 3:8–9), but first the reference to creation prompts him to correlate the water of creation (Gen 1:2, 6–10; Ps 24:2), the water of the flood (Gen 7), and the fire of the final judgment (2 Pet 3:5–7). The accounts of creation, the flood, and the exodus all feature the dividing of the water and the appearance of dry ground (Gen 1:2, 9–10; 8:1–3, 13–14; Exod 14:21–22). The flood story is paradigmatic for depictions of future judgment, only the judgment cannot be by a flood of water (Gen 9:15). Thus, in the judgment of Sodom and Gomorrah God rains fire instead (Gen 19:24; cf., Gen 7:4; see also Ezek 38:22). The present creation is now reserved for judgment by fire to make way for the new creation (2 Pet 3:7, 12–13). But is there also a reference to fire in the creation account? Peter may be alluding to an ancient play on the word שמים ("heavens, sky") from Gen 1:1 referenced in the commentary of the great medieval commentator Rashi (see also *b. Hag.* 12a, where it is attributed to the Tannaim [first and second centuries A.D.]). According to this play, the word שמים ("heavens, sky") consists of the word אש ("fire") and מים ("water").

Revelation 1:8; 21:6

In Rev 1:8, the Lord God says that he is the *Alpha* and the *Omega*, the first and last letters of the Greek alphabet (see also Rev 21:6; 22:13). He is the beginning and the end, the first and the last (Rev 1:17; 21:6; 22:13). It is generally recognized that this language comes from Isa 41:4; 44:6; 48:12. But the use of the letters of the alphabet for this purpose has a precedent in Hebrew. There are at least two places in the Hebrew Bible where the untranslated definite direct object marker את (*Aleph* and *Taw*, the first and last letters of the Hebrew alphabet) has been or can be interpreted as a reference to the LORD. The first part of Amos 9:12 in the MT translates, "that they may possess (יירשו) the remnant of Edom (אדום)." In Codex Alexandrinus (LXX) the same part of Amos 9:12 translates, "that the remnant of mankind (= אדם) may seek (ידרשו) the Lord (את)." The other example comes from Zech 12:10 where the object marker appears at first glance to be an intrusion to the syntax. About a third of the way into the verse the LORD says, "And they will look at me את whom they pierced and mourn for him . . . ." Because of the difficulty of the idea of piercing the LORD, and because of the added difficulty of the following third person pronoun "him" (cf., John 19:37), the object marker is placed directly next to the pronoun "me" to clarify that the pronoun refers to the LORD, even though it should already be evident that the LORD is the speaker.

Revelation 10:10

When John says that the little scroll was in his mouth as sweet as honey, but also that when he ate it his stomach was made bitter (Rev 10:10), he depends upon two texts in particular: Jer 15:16 and Ezek 2:8–3:3.[33] Nevertheless, neither of these two texts contains the key word "bitter." The choice of this word is likely based on a play between the Hebrew word מר ("bitter") and the Hebrew word מרי ("rebellious") in Ezek 2:8. This is similar to the double entendre in Exod 15:23 where כי מרים הם can be read, "For they [i.e., the waters] were bitter [מָרִים]," or it can be read, "For they [i.e., the people] were rebellious [מֹרִים]."[34] In other words, while John himself found the message of the scroll to be acceptable, he also faced the bitterness of rejection by a rebellious people (Rev 1:9), not unlike the prophets before him (Jer 20:8–9; Ezek 2:5).

Revelation 13:18

Gematria, the practice of assigning numerical value to the letters of a word, is its own kind of wordplay. Perhaps no other passage in the Bible has drawn more attention to this practice than Rev 13:18 where the number of the antichrist is said to be 666. Because attempts to identify the antichrist on the basis of this number have ranged from the plausible to the ridiculous, many interpreters balk at any such attempt. Yet the text invites the reader who has understanding to calculate the number of the beast, for it is the number of a man (see Dan 7:8, 24–27). The most common interpretation says that the man is "Nero Caesar" (666 = קסר נרון), but this then requires the non-preterist to say that the historical Nero was merely a prefiguration of the antichrist.[35] It is odd that interpreters tend to look outside the book for a historical figure whom the number represents. Very little effort has been made to understand the gematria to be internal to the book itself. The final enemy to be defeated goes by a couple of different names in the chap-

---

33. See Shepherd, *Text in the Middle*, 145–46.

34. See the discussion of the Mekilta commentary on this passage in Boyarin, *Intertextuality*, 66.

35. See, e.g., Osborne, *Revelation*, 520–21.

ters that follow Rev 13:18. The first is Babylon (Rev 14:8; 16:19; 17:5; 18:2, 10, 21; cf., Isa 14:12; 21:9; Jer 51:8). The code name for Babylon in the book of Jeremiah is Sheshak (Jer 25:26; 51:41), which, according to *atbash* (the interchange of the first letter of the alphabet and the last, the second letter and the second to last, and so on), is Babylon (see *Tg. Jon.* Jer 25:26; 51:41). The second name for the enemy is Gog (Rev 20:8; see Num 24:7 [LXX]; Ezek 38–39). The numerical value of Babylon (34 = בבל), Sheshak (= ששך 620), and Gog (12 = גוג) is 666. Thus, the number does not point to someone in history but to a future and final enemy as depicted in the Hebrew Bible.

CONCLUSION

Not only is it imperative to know Hebrew, Aramaic, and translation-Greek in order to understand the grammar, syntax, and semantics of the Greek NT, but it is also important for the exegete to look for potential Semitic wordplay behind the Greek text. The above treatment has revisited some previous suggestions, some more well-known than others, and in most cases has offered new explanations of the examples. Several new proposals have also been made. It is evident from the discussion that the purposes for the wordplays range from the aesthetic to the exegetical and theological. Therefore, in future investigations of this phenomenon it is of utmost importance for the interpreter to recognize that wordplay is often more than a mere rhetorical flourish.

BIBLIOGRAPHY

Barr, James. *The Semantics of Biblical Language*. Oxford: Oxford University Press, 1961; Reprint, London: SCM, 1983.
Bauer, W., F. W. Danker, W. F. Arndt, and F. W. Gingrich. *Greek-English Lexicon of the New Testament and Other Early Christian Literature*. 2nd ed. Chicago: University of Chicago Press, 1999.
Beattie, D. R. G., and Philip R. Davies. "What Does Hebrew Mean?" *Journal of Semitic Studies* 56 (2011) 71–83.
Black, David Alan. "New Testament Semitisms." *The Bible Translator* 39 (1988) 215–23.
Black, Matthew. *An Aramaic Approach to the Gospels and Acts*. 3rd ed. Oxford: Oxford University Press, 1967; Reprint, Peabody, MA: Hendrickson, 1998.
Bock, Darrell L. *Luke*. Vol. 2, *9:51—24:53*. Baker Exegetical Commentary on the New Testament. Grand Rapids, MI: Baker Academic, 1994.
Boyarin, Daniel. *Intertextuality and the Reading of Midrash*. Bloomington: Indiana University Press, 1990.

Brown, F., S. R. Driver, and C. A. Briggs. *The Brown-Driver-Briggs Hebrew and English Lexicon: With an Appendix Containing the Biblical Aramaic.* Boston: Houghton, Mifflin, and Company, 1906; Reprint, Peabody, MA: Hendrickson, 2001.

Ernesti, J. A. *Institutio interpretis Novi Testamenti.* 3rd ed. Leipzig: Weidmann & Reich, 1774.

Eusebius of Caesarea. *The Ecclesiastical History.* Vol. 1, Books I–IV. Translated by Kirsopp Lake. Loeb Classical Library. Cambridge: Harvard University Press, 1926.

Evans, Craig A. "The Aramaic Psalter and the New Testament: Praising the Lord in History and Prophecy." In *From Prophecy to Testament: The Function of the Old Testament in the New*, edited by Craig A. Evans, 44–91. Peabody, MA: Hendrickson, 2004.

Fee, Gordon D. *The First Epistle to the Corinthians.* New International Commentary on the New Testament. Grand Rapids, MI: Eerdmans, 1987.

Gleaves, G. Scott. *Did Jesus Speak Greek? The Emerging Evidence of Greek Dominance in First-Century Palestine.* Eugene, OR: Pickwick, 2015.

Hill, David. *Greek Words and Hebrew Meanings.* Cambridge: Cambridge University Press, 1967.

Hughes, Philip Edgcumbe. *Paul's Second Epistle to the Corinthians: The English Text with Introduction, Exposition and Notes.* New International Commentary on the New Testament. Grand Rapids, MI: Eerdmans, 1962.

Klein, Ralph W. *1 Chronicles.* Hermeneia. Minneapolis, MN: Fortress, 2006.

Kraus, Wolfgang. "Contemporary Translations of the Septuagint: Problems and Perspectives." In *Septuagint Research: Issues and Challenges in the Study of the Greek Jewish Scriptures*, edited by Wolfgang Kraus and R. Glenn Wooden, 63–83. Atlanta: SBL, 2006.

Metzger, Bruce M. *A Textual Commentary on the Greek New Testament.* 2nd ed. Stuttgart: German Bible Society, 1994.

Moulton, J. H. *A Grammar of New Testament Greek.* Vol. 2. Edited by Wilber Francis Howard. Edinburgh: T&T Clark, 1919.

Osborne, Grant R. *Revelation.* Baker Exegetical Commentary on the New Testament. Grand Rapids, MI: Baker Academic, 2002.

Quarles, Charles. *Sermon on the Mount: Restoring Christ's Message to the Modern Church.* Nashville: B&H, 2011.

Robertson, A. T. *A Grammar of the Greek New Testament in the Light of Historical Research.* Nashville: Broadman, 1934.

Sailhamer, John H. *Introduction to Old Testament Theology.* Grand Rapids, MI: Zondervan, 1995.

———. *The Pentateuch as Narrative.* Grand Rapids, MI: Zondervan, 1992.

Scherman, Rabbi Nosson, ed. *The Chumash.* Brooklyn: Mesorah, 2006.

Shepherd, Michael B. "Targums." In *Dictionary of Jesus and the Gospels*, edited by Joel B. Green, 931–34. 2nd ed. Downers Grove, IL: InterVarsity, 2013.

———. *The Text in the Middle.* New York: Peter Lang, 2014.

Sommer, Benjamin. *A Prophet Reads Scripture: Allusion in Isaiah 40–66.* Stanford: Stanford University Press, 1998.

Tov, Emanuel. *The Greek and Hebrew Bible: Collected Essays on the Septuagint.* Atlanta: SBL, 2006.

Voelz, James W. "Semitic Influence on the Greek of the New Testament." *Concordia Journal* 20 (1994) 115–29.

Chapter 5

An Overview of the Gnomic or Logical Future Tense in the Pauline Corpus

—PHILIP LA G. DU TOIT
North-West University, South Africa

INTRODUCTION

As INDICATED IN MOST New Testament Greek grammars, in the New Testament the future tense is mainly used as a predictive future (e.g., τέξεται in Matt 1:21; δώσω and διψήσε in John 4:14), an imperatival future (e.g., φονεύσεις, μοιχεύσεις, κλέψεις and ψευδομαρτυρήσεις in Matt 19:18; ἔσεσθε in 6:5), and a deliberative future (e.g., δώσομεν in Mark 6:37; ζήσομεν in Rom 6:2). More rare uses are the so called gnomic future (e.g., ἀποθανεῖται in Rom 5:7; χρηματίσει in 7:3) and the future which is used as an equivalent to a subjunctive (e.g., with οὐ μή in John 4:14; with a ἵνα clause in Gal 2:4; in an indefinite relative clause in Mark 8:35).[1] The focus of this contribution is primarily to explore the gnomic future and the so-called logical future in the Pauline corpus, and secondarily to compare it with the subjunctive use of the future in the Pauline corpus. The eventual aim will be to describe the gnomic future or this kind of use of the future tense in more detail and to review the prevalence of such usage in Paul.

---

1. Wallace, *Greek Grammar*, 568–71. Rom 5:7 (ἀποθανεῖται) and 7:3 (χρηματίσει) are most often cited in Greek grammars as examples of the gnomic future (e.g., Blass, and Debrunner, *Greek Grammar*, §349; Robertson, *Grammar*, 876; Burton, *Moods and Tenses*, 36; Blass, *Grammar*, 201).

As Wallace points out, there is a tendency in Greek grammars to retreat from a multitude of grammatical categories, for specific categories are restricted to semantic situations.[2] In terms of the future tense, Porter for example challenges the traditional understanding of the future tense by pointing to its use in "distinctly non-future contexts,"[3] which includes its gnomic use, its use in conditional sentences, and its use as a parallel to the subjunctive. For Porter, the future tense originated "as a non-Indicative form, thus in some way related to or extending the Subjunctive meaning."[4] The approach to the gnomic future in Paul that will be pursued here, is thus not so much to determine such an inherent function of the future tense as it is to describe the way in which it is used in a specific *context*. As Black rightly pointed out in terms of ways in which the future tense is used, it "is the *context* and not the tense that determines these meanings."[5]

A PRELIMINARY DEFINITION OF THE GNOMIC AND LOGICAL FUTURE

Robertson describes the gnomic future as follows: "In the gnomic future the act is *true of any time* . . . In indirect discourse the time is relatively future to that of the principal verb, though it *may be absolutely past*."[6] In a similar way, Blass and Debrunner state that the "future indicative is used . . . occasionally as a gnomic future in order to express that which is to be expected under certain circumstances."[7] In terms of the gnomic future, Wallace states that the "idea is not that a particular event is in view, but that such events are true of life,"[8] and then quotes Robertson: "In the gnomic future the act is true of any time."[9] But Wallace omits the fact that Robertson leaves open the possibility that the gnomic future might denote something that is relatively future to that of the principal verb, but *may be absolutely past* (as quoted above). When the two examples that Robertson provides in illustrating this possibility are considered (Matt 20:10; John 21:19),[10] it shows

---

2. Wallace, *Greek Grammar*, xii–iii.
3. Porter, *Verbal Aspect*, 439.
4. Ibid., 412.
5. Black, *Learn to Read*, 21, emphasis added; cf. Wallace, *Greek Grammar*, xiv.
6. Robertson, *Grammar*, 876, emphasis added.
7. Blass and Debrunner, *Greek Grammar*, §349; cf. Burton, *Moods and Tenses*, 36; Blass, *Grammar*, 201.
8. Wallace, *Greek Grammar*, 571.
9. Robertson, *Grammar*, 876.
10. Ibid.

how the gnomic future can be used within a context where the future tense denotes something that ultimately (in terms of absolute time) lies in the past: (1) In Matt 20:10, in the parable of the workers in the vineyard, Jesus says: "But when the first came, they thought they will receive [λήμψονται, future] more, but each of them also received [ἔλαβον, aorist] a denarius." (2) In John 21:19, after Jesus' death and resurrection, the text reads: "He said this to show the kind of death by which he will glorify [δοξάσει, future] God. After this he said to him, 'Follow me.'" In both examples the future tense is not used in such a way that the actions lie in the speaker's absolute future, but such as that the actions lie in the speaker's *absolute past*.

A certain usage of the future that is often found in commentaries (see below) is the so-called *logical future*. In Roberts's Greek grammar, he refers to the "Future logical" by using the illustration, εἰ ποιήσει ταῦτα, σχήσει καλῶς, which he translates with "If he will do this, *it will be* well with him."[11] It therefore seems that the future indicative can be understood as a logical future where it stands in certain types of comparative or conditional sentences, a function that might be related to the future tense's probable descent from the aorist subjunctive.[12] In the sentence, "By believing in Christ we will be saved," the condition (to believe) could have been met, resulting in being saved already. The verb "will be saved" can thus be understood as a "logical future" in this sentence. In other words, if the condition has already been met, the salvation may be absolutely past. If the logical future is compared to the way in which grammarians define the gnomic future (see above), there seems to be a considerable amount of overlap, especially if Blass and Debrunner's definition that the gnomic future expresses something which is to be expected under certain circumstances (see above), is considered. This is in fact the exact tendency that can be identified in the interchangeable way in which commentators refer to the gnomic and the logical future.

THE GNOMIC AND THE LOGICAL FUTURE IN COMMENTARIES AND OTHER SECONDARY LITERATURE

Romans

In respect of the letter to the Romans, Jewett refers to λογισθήσεται in 2:26 as a "logical future," a future that is required by the "if" (ἐάν) clause. Jewett

11. Roberts, *Grammar*, 140, emphasis added.
12. Porter, *Verbal Aspect*, 412; Wallace, *Greek Grammar*, 571; Robertson, *Grammar*, 354.

argues that in context, the uncircumcision of the one keeping the righteous requirement of the Law that "shall be counted" as circumcision, should not be interpreted as a reference to eschatological judgement.[13] In other words, his argument implies that the future tense is not used to indicate an event that is necessarily future of the speaker, but constitutes a logical result following the condition. But this is where the terminology between the gnomic and logical future starts to overlap. Fung refers to δικαιωθήσεται in 3:20 as a "gnomic-logical future" that does not refer to the future judgment, but in quoting Murray, it rather refers to the "certainty and universality"[14] of what is said.[15] Similarly, Bultmann refers to δικαιωθήσονται in 2:13 as having no temporal meaning, but as a logical and/or gnomic formulation.[16] The idea would be that justification would be a general, logical consequence of being able to do the Law. Another example of mixed terminology in reference to the future tense, is where Moo refers to δικαιώσει in 3:30 as "simply a logical future, with gnomic significance."[17] Other writers that refer to δικαιώσει in 3:30 as a logical future include Bell, Fung, Käsemann, Cranfield, Schrenk, Bultmann, and Denney.[18] The notion would be that God's justification on the basis of faith is not something that is only effected in the distant future, but becomes a reality at the moment of faith.

Romans 5:17 and 19 provide interesting and significant examples of the logical or gnomic future. As Moo indicates, that those who receive grace and the gift of righteousness "will reign" (βασιλεύσουσιν) according to 5:17, is best understood as a logical future, for the future is "not so much in time as Paul writes but future from the standpoint of the reign of death in Adam."[19] Similarly, Paul states in 5:19 that "just as by the one man's disobedience the many were made [κατεστάθησαν, aor.] sinners, so by the one man's obedience the many *will be made* [κατασταθήσονται, fut.] righteous."[20] That Paul has a logical future in mind with κατασταθήσονται is

---

13. Jewett, *Romans*, 234.

14. Murray, *Epistle to the Romans*, 107.

15. Fung, *Epistle to the Galatians*, 233; cf. Bultmann, *Theology*, 274.

16. Bultmann ("Δικαιοσύνη Θεοῦ," 15) includes Rom 2:13 in list of future verbs in Romans and Galatians that have "keinen zeitlichen Sinn, sondern sind logische bzw. gnomische Formulierungen."

17. Moo, *Epistle to the Romans*, 252.

18. Bell, "Myth of Adam," 31; Fung, *Epistle to the Galatians*, 233; Käsemann, *Commentary*, 104; Cranfield, *Critical and Exegetical Commentary*, 222; Schrenk, "δίκη," 218; Bultmann, *Theology*, 274; Denney, "Paul's Epistle," 614.

19. Moo, *Epistle to the Romans*, 340; cf. Murray, *Epistle to the Romans*, 198; Denney, "Paul's Epistle," 630.

20. NRSV, emphasis added.

suggested by Bell, Moo, Fitzmyer, Fung, Bultmann, Schrenk, and Lagrange.[21] Jewett regards κατασταθήσονται either as an eschatological future or a logical future without pertinently choosing for one.[22] Although Dunn does not ultimately opt for a logical future here, he sees it as a possibility on the basis of its parallel relationship with the aorist verb κατεστάθησαν.[23] Although Cranfield does not specifically assign the designation "logical future" to κατασταθήσονται, he argues that this verb, "while it could refer to the final judgment . . . is probably better understood, in agreement with 5.1 and 9, as referring to the *present life* of believers."[24] Many other commentators interpret κατασταθήσονται as having a logical rather than an eschatological or absolute future or sense.[25] The interpretation of κατασταθήσονται in 5:19 as a future that denotes a present or realized reality, which can be interpreted as a logical future, thus finds wide support among commentators.

Romans 6:1–14 is another passage where commentators find logical futures, probably because of the realized significance of life that results from dying with Christ in baptism (cf. ζῶντας in vv. 11 and 13). Wilckens finds a logical future in the rhetorical question of verse 2, which asks: "we who died to sin, how shall we still live [ζήσομεν] in it?"[26] But it is especially the verbs ἐσόμεθα in verse 5 and συζήσομεν in verse 8 that are often interpreted as logical futures.[27] The logic behind this reasoning is that unification with Christ in his resurrection (καὶ τῆς ἀναστάσεως ἐσόμεθα, v. 5) is not something that is awaited eschatologically, but is already a reality in the life of the believer. Similarly, our life with Christ (συζήσομεν αὐτῷ, v. 8) is already a present reality. In the same vein, Fitzmyer understands the future κυριεύσει in verse 14 in a logical way and not as a mere "temporal future":[28] being under grace, sin *will have no dominion* over believers.

A pertinent example of a logical future within a conditional sentence (with ἐάν) is Rom 10:9, where Paul writes that those who believe "will be

---

21. Bell, "Myth of Adam," 31; Moo, *Epistle to the Romans*, 345, Fitzmyer, *Romans*, 421; Fung, *Epistle to the Galatians*, 233; Bultmann, *Theology*, 274; Schrenk, "δίκη," 218; Lagrange, *Saint Paul*, 112.

22. Jewett, *Romans*, 386.

23. Dunn, *Romans 1–8*, 258.

24. Cranfield, *Critical and Exegetical Commentary*, 291, emphasis added.

25. E.g., Wilckens, *Der Brief*, 328; Schlier, *Der Römerbrief Kommentar*, 175; Ridderbos, *Aan de Romeinen*, 178; Schrenk, "δίκη," 191; Murray, *Epistle to the Romans*, 206; and several others.

26. Wilckens, *Der Brief*, 11.

27. Kruse, *Paul's Letter*, 262; Jewett, *Romans*, 406; Wright, "Letter," 539–40; Mounce, *Romans*, 150, 152; Fitzmyer, *Romans*, 435; and several others.

28. Fitzmyer, *Romans*, 447.

saved" (σωθήσῃ). Jewett argues that this future is logical rather than temporal "showing the consequence of the mouth's confession and the heart's conviction."[29] Osborne and Moo argue in a similar manner.[30] According to this logic the saving (10:9) is thus not necessarily at the eschaton, but becomes a reality as soon as the condition of belief is met. A similar example presents itself in 11:24. Within the logical construction of verse 24 starting with εἰ, the verb ἐγκεντρισθήσονται can be understood as a logical future:[31] if it is true that Gentiles can be grafted onto the tree, it follows logically that the same can be true of those "according to nature." The same goes for σωρεύσεις in 12:20, which is another example of a logical result flowing forth from a certain condition (ἐάν). Yet Yarbrough reads σωρεύσεις as a non-eschatological future that constitutes a proverbial truth, and relates it to the gnomic future.[32] Finally, the judgment that those will receive (λήμψονται) who resist according to 13:2 can be read as a logical future.[33]

The Corinthian Correspondence

Instances of the gnomic or logical future can also be found in the Corinthian correspondence. The verb κληρονομήσουσιν in 1 Cor 6:10 can be understood as a logical future in that the non-inheritance of God's kingdom is the logical result of persisting in the sins that Paul mentions.[34] In 2 Cor 3:7–8, Paul draws a comparison between the "ministry of death" that came with glory (v. 7) and the ministry of the Spirit. He asks the rhetorical question if the ministry in the Spirit will not have more glory. The verb ἔσται (v. 8) is understood as a logical future by Harris, Matera, Thrall, and others.[35] This means that the ministry is future from the Sinai-event and subsequent to the glory of Moses,[36] but past from Paul's point of view (cf. v. 3). The general saying in 9:6 that those who sow sparingly "will reap" sparingly, and that those who sow bountifully "will reap" (θερίσει, X2) bountifully, reads like a

---

29. Jewett, *Romans*, 630.
30. Osborne, *Romans*, 207; Moo, *Epistle to the Romans*, 658.
31. Cottrell, *Romans*, 389; Denney, "Paul's Epistle," 682; Weiss, *Der Brief*, 492; cf. Kim, "Reading," 327.
32. Yarbrough, "Theology of Romans," 48, 58.
33. Käseman, *Commentary on Romans*, 357.
34. Lewis, *Looking for Life*, 86.
35. Harris, *Second Epistle to the Corinthians*, 286; Matera, *II Corinthians*, 83; Thrall, *Critical and Exegetical Commentary*, 245; and others.
36. Thrall, *Critical and Exegetical Commentary*, 245.

general truth. Harris thus understands the verb θερίσει as a gnomic future.[37] Similarly, he reads καυχήσομαι (X2) in 12:5 as a gnomic future.[38] Finally, in 13:11 Paul directs the congregation to perfect themselves, to encourage themselves, to mind the same thing, to be at peace, and then tells them that the God of love and peace "will be" (ἔσται) with them. Grammatically, God's love and peace can be understood as the logical result following their actions. The verb ἔσται can thus be read as a logical future.[39]

Galatians

In the letter to the Galatians, at least three logical or gnomic futures can be identified. In 2:16, Paul writes that a person is not justified (δικαιοῦται) by the works of the Law, but through faith in Christ. He follows up this statement by a parallel statement, indicating that on the basis of the works of the Law, no one "will be justified" (δικαιωθήσεται). In stating the converse of the present reality of justification (δικαιοῦται) through faith, Fung describes δικαιωθήσεται as "a gnomic-logical future."[40] Similarly, Bultmann explains the same verb as having no temporal meaning, but as a logical and/or gnomic formulation.[41] On the same theme, Paul quotes from Hab 2:4 in Gal 3:11: "the righteous shall live by faith" (cf. Rom 1:17). Lenski reads ζήσεται as a logical future.[42] Lastly, Paul's saying that each one will bear (βαστάσει) their own load in 6:5 can be understood as a general truth and thus as a gnomic future.[43]

PRELIMINARY CONCLUSIONS

From the above data, it should be clear that there exists a considerable amount of overlap between the designations gnomic and logical future. These designations seem to be applied similarly in terms of denoting *relative time*.[44] The designation *gnomic future* however seems to lean more toward

37. Harris, *Second Epistle*, 633.
38. Ibid., 847.
39. Furnish, *II Corinthians*, 586.
40. Fung, *Epistle to the Galatians*, 233.
41. Bultmann, "Δικαιοσύνη," 15 (see above for the German).
42. Lenski, *Interpretation of St. Paul's Epistles*, 145.
43. Kim, "Reading," 326; Martyn, *Galatians*, 543; Vaughan and Gideon, *Greek Grammar*, 143; Burton, *Critical and Exegetical Commentary*, 334.
44. Cf. Robertson, *Grammar*, 876; Blass, *Grammar*, 201.

denoting a *general truth* (esp. Rom 5:7; 7:3), whereas the *logical future* seems to lean more toward denoting a *logical result* (derived from the context), which does not necessarily lie in the actual future (esp. Rom 5:19, see above).[45] The frequency in which commentators interpret the future tense in Paul as a logical future or the future being logical, suggests that a future is used in a *relative* context more often than what otherwise might be expected. It is another question whether the logical future could be considered as a subset or a certain variant of the gnomic future. While Wallace's remark that the gnomic future is rare,[46] and seems to argue against such a possibility, Robertson's remark about the *relative* future just after mentioning the gnomic future (citing Matt 20:10; John 21:19)[47] does seem to leave such a possibility open, which in turn would imply that the gnomic future, if it includes a relative or logical future, is not necessarily that rare. The same possibility seems to be left open in Blass and Debrunner's more general definition for the gnomic future: that "which is expected under certain circumstances."[48]

THEOLOGICAL REASONS FOR PAUL'S USE OF A LOGICAL FUTURE

Apart from the logical flow of thought or the logical construction of sentences, one could ask if there are theological reasons for Paul to occasionally utilize a logical future. As indicated earlier, the realized significance of the new life that results from dying with Christ is evident in Rom 6:1–14. Earlier, in Rom 5, a close relationship between the concepts of salvation and righteousness/justification can be identified.[49] Righteousness, justification and salvation (as denoted by their cognate terms) all correspond to the same new reality in Christ for those who believe. While these concepts have future significance in terms of awaiting eschatological fulfilment, all of them additionally contain a realized or present aspect in the Pauline corpus. Apart from the realized significance of the new creation for those in Christ[50] and the present reality of the Spirit in believers' lives (Rom 8:10),

45. Cf. Roberts, *Grammar*, 140.

46. Wallace, *Greek Grammar*, 571.

47. Robertson, *Grammar*, 876.

48. Blass and Debrunner, *Greek Grammar*, §349; cf. Burton, *Moods and Tenses*, 36; Blass, *Grammar*, 201.

49. The close relationship between salvation and concepts revolving around righteousness and justification is evident in Rom 5:9–10, 18–19 (σῴζω, vv. 9, 10; δικαιόω, v. 9; καταλλάσσω, v. 10; δικαίωμα, v. 18; δικαίωσις, v. 18; δίκαιος, v. 19).

50. See παρῆλθεν (second aor. ind.) and γέγονεν (second perf. ind.) in 2 Cor 5:17;

the realized or present aspect can especially be derived from the occurrence of the verbs δικαιόω, καταλλάσσω, and σῴζω in their perfect/aorist indicative or -participle forms, and their present indicative or -participle forms.[51] In terms of Pauline eschatology, Hagner states:

> Contrary to popular misunderstanding, the Christian faith is far more a celebration of eschatological reality already accomplished than a celebration of future eschatology — "pie in the sky in the bye and bye." Eschatology is about the present as well as the future.[52]

It is especially significant that Rom 8:24 portrays salvation as being realized (σῴζω, aor. ind.) even though it carries a future component, a notion confirmed by Schreiner, Wright, Fee, Moo, Morris, Bruce, Cranfield, Foerster, and Ridderbos.[53] The modifying phrase τῇ ἐλπίδι is probably best understood in terms of an associative sense: "we were saved, *with hope* as the ever present companion of this salvation."[54] This present or realized aspect to salvation is arguably one of the most important reasons why scholars understand Paul to utilize a logical future more often than usually acknowledged. The effect of a logical future is that the reality denoted by the verb may already have come into effect even though it might await future completion.

συνεσταύρωμαι (perf. ind.), ζῶ and ζῇ (both pres. ind.) in Gal 2:19–20. See also 2 Cor 1:20 where Paul confirms the present significance of all of God's promises in Christ.

51. *Aorist indicative*: δικαιόω: Rom 4:2; 8:30; 1 Cor 6:11 (cf. 1 Tim 3:16); καταλλάσσω: Rom 5:10; σῴζω: Rom 8:24 (cf. Titus 3:5). *Aorist participle*: δικαιόω: Rom 5:1, 9 (cf. Titus 3:7); καταλλάσσω: 2 Cor 5:18 (cf. σῴζω: 2 Tim 1:9). *Perfect indicative*: δικαιόω: Rom 6:7 (cf. *perfect participle*: σῴζω: Eph 2:5, 8). *Present indicative*: δικαιόω: Gal 2:16; 3:8, 11; 5:4. *Present participle*: δικαιόω: Rom 3:24, 26; 4:5; 8:33; καταλλάσσω: 2 Cor 5:19; σῴζω: 1 Cor 1:18; 15:2; 2 Cor 2:15.

52. Hagner, *New Testament*, 403.

53. Schreiner, *Romans*, 439; Wright, "Letter to the Romans," 598; Fee, *Paul*, 61; Moo, *Epistle to the Romans*, 521; Morris, *Epistle to the Romans*, 325; Bruce, *Romans*, 174; Cranfield, *Critical and Exegetical Commentary*, 419; Foerster, "σῴζω, σωτηρία, σωτήρ, σωτήριος," 994; Ridderbos, *Aan de Romeinen*, 189.

54. Moo, *Epistle to the Romans*, 521–22, emphasis added; cf. Schreiner, *Romans*, 439; Mounce, *Romans*, 186; Dodd, *Epistle to the Romans*, 148. Even by understanding τῇ ἐλπίδι as a modal dative: "in hope" (e.g., Fee, *Paul*, 61; Fitzmyer, *Romans*, 515; Bruce, *Romans*, 174; Käsemann, *Commentary on Romans*, 439; Cranfield, *Critical and Exegetical Commentary*, 419), the realized significance of salvation is retained (e.g., Fee, *Paul*, 61; Bruce, *Romans*, 174; Cranfield, *Critical and Exegetical Commentary*, 419).

OTHER POSSIBLE LOGICAL FUTURES IN PAUL?

I have argued elsewhere that σωθήσεται in Rom 11:26 can also be understood as a logical future.[55] Some of the main grammatical and semantic reasons for this possibility are the following:

(1) Syntactically, Rom 11:26 is similar to 5:19, which can be understood as a logical future (see above). While the structure of 5:19 is ὥσπερ ... οὕτως + future indicative [κατασταθήσονται], the structure of 11:26 is οὕτως + future indicative [σωθήσεται] ... καθώς. In both 5:19 and 11:26 οὕτως can be translated as "in this manner." Both adverbial markers καθώς and ὥσπερ signify comparison.[56] In terms of the syntax, the difference between these two sentences is word order. Although the normal word order between the comparative adverbial marker and the future indicative is as within 5:19 (ὥσπερ/καθώς/ὡς, followed by οὕτως), there are exceptions in Paul. For example, Phil 3:17 has οὕτως first, followed by καθώς. 1 Cor 3:15; 4:1; 9:26; and 2 Cor 9:5 have οὕτως, followed by ὡς. 1 Thess 2:4 has καθώς, followed by οὕτως and ὡς. It is noteworthy that in these examples, οὕτως refers to that which stands after καθώς, and not to something preceding οὕτως. As a translated example, instead of writing "as (ὡς) not beating air, so (οὕτως) I fight," Paul writes "so (οὕτως) I fight, as (ὡς) not beating air" (1 Cor 9:26). In accordance with these examples, it is possible that οὕτως ... καθώς in Rom 11:26 could be read without a comma after σωθήσεται, implying that οὕτως might (additionally) refer to that which stands after καθώς (that which is written). Οὕτως in 11:26 might therefore pertain to both the preceding condition set forth by the subjunctive εἰσέλθῃ in verse 25 (the coming in of the Gentiles) and to καθὼς γέγραπται (that which is written), or a measure of ambiguity in terms of the referent of οὕτως might be implied. Οὕτως in 11:26 might therefore pertain to both the preceding condition set forth by the subjunctive εἰσέλθῃ in verse 25 (the coming in of the Gentiles) and to καθὼς γέγραπται (that which is written). In other words, the manner in which (οὕτως) Israel is saved pertains to both the condition of the Gentiles coming in (v. 25) and the way in which Israel's salvation is foretold in Scripture (vv. 26b–27). If οὕτως therefore also stands in a dependent relationship with καθὼς γέγραπται, it strengthens the notion that οὕτως in 11:26 denotes manner (see above). In addition, the syntactical similarity between 5:19 and 11:26 might argue for viewing the future tense in 11:26 also as a logical future (as in 5:19).

---

55. Du Toit, "Salvation," 432–40; cf. Kim, "Reading," 326.
56. BDAG, καθώς, §1; ibid., ὥσπερ, a.

(2) With respect to Paul's use of οὕτως and καθώς in Rom 11:26, it is likely that Paul applies Scripture here in 11:26–27 not merely to reinforce or confirm his teaching, contra Moo,[57] but to denote the *manner in which* Israel will be saved,[58] making the coming in of the fullness of the Gentiles (ἄχρις . . . εἰσέλθῃ) and that which is written (καθὼς γέγραπται . . .) to relate to the same event. In other words, it seems possible that the salvation of "all Israel" intricately stands in both (a) a *comparative* relationship with καθὼς γέγραπται . . . , which constitutes the *manner in which* salvation is effected, and (b) in a *conditional* relationship with ἄχρις οὗ τὸ πλήρωμα τῶν ἐθνῶν εἰσέλθῃ, which constitutes the *condition* for salvation.

(3) The future ἥξει in 11:26b can be understood as a *futurum propheticum*.[59] In other words, the prophecy is looking forward, but in Paul's quote, it could have been fulfilled already. In reference to Zion in 9:33 (cf. Zion in 11:26), Fitzmyer considers it possible that the words in 11:26b can be understood as "somehow having been fulfilled."[60] Byrne puts it even more clearly:

> It is much simpler to see Paul understanding the prophecy as speaking out of its proper time reference, pointing to a 'coming' (of a 'deliverer') which for Isaiah lies in the future but which for Paul has already been realized in the original appearance and saving work of Christ.[61]

The salvation of all Israel could thus be future (σωθήσεται) of the prophecy of 11:26a and being written in the future tense to correspond with the future ἥξει of the prophecy. In other words, if the Deliverer coming out of Zion in Christ's first advent describes the *manner in which* "all Israel" will be saved, then it could follow *logically* that the salvation of Israel has *already been effected in Christ's first advent*.

(4) If ἐγκεντρισθήσονται in 11:24 can be understood as a logical future (see above), it would be in the same line of thought to consider σωθήσεται in 11:26 as a logical future, too. However, a future element in the completion of salvation is not necessarily hereby denied (cf. Ezek 36–37). But the point is that historical Israel's salvation can be understood as effected through the same event as for any believer in Christ—that being Christ's death and resurrection.

---

57. Moo, *Epistle to the Romans*, 724, 727.
58. Wright, "Letter to the Romans," 693; cf. Longenecker, "Different Answers," 98.
59. Fitzmyer, *Romans*, 625.
60. Ibid.; cf. Holwerda, *Jesus and Israel*, 173.
61. Byrne, *Romans*, 355.

(5) The language around the Deliverer can be understood as pertaining to Christ's first advent. In 9:33 Paul refers to Zion within the context of the stumbling stone, which is Christ.[62] Zion therefore seems to refer to Jerusalem as the place of Christ's death and resurrection[63] rather than to the heavenly Jerusalem, contra Jewett or Moo.[64] If Christ is the Deliverer and comes out of the earthly Jerusalem, then Paul's entire claim on Scripture in 11:26b–27 pertains to Christ's first advent.[65]

In many of the above examples of (possible) logical futures in Paul, they seem to stand in certain types of comparative or conditional sentences. Such a use of the future might be related to the future tense's probable descent from the aorist subjunctive (see above). If a logical future could be associated with a kind of substitute for the aorist subjunctive, other possible contenders for being logical futures in Paul, could be the following:

Note the similarity between Rom 5:19 (ὥσπερ ... οὕτως ... + fut. ind.), which has been argued to be a logical future, and 5:21 (ὥσπερ ... οὕτως ... + aor. subj.). In these two verses, which stand in close proximity with each other, it seems as if Paul uses the aorist subjunctive and the future indicative in an interchangeable way. Other examples (apart from Rom 2:26; 10:9; and 12:20) of possible logical future indicatives in Paul that follow ἐάν, and thus function as a kind of substitute for the aorist subjunctive, include Rom 9:27; 11:23; 1 Cor 14:7, 9; 2 Cor 10:8; and Gal 5:2; 6:7. The latter text could in fact be both a logical and a gnomic future.

CONCLUSION

In conclusion, it could be argued that the logical future is a kind of subset to the gnomic future (esp. Robertson), and that there exists a considerable amount of overlap in the way that exegetes use these designations, especially in terms of denoting relative time. However, the gnomic future leans more toward denoting a general truth (e.g., Rom 5:7; 7:3), whereas the logical future leans more toward denoting a logical result following a certain condition. In Paul, the logical future closely corresponds to the future indicative's use as a kind of substitute for an aorist subjunctive, occurring in sentences

---

62. Even Moo (*Epistle to the Romans*, 728) admits that "[i]t would make sense to interpret 'out of Zion' in 11:26 in light of this earlier text" (cf. Longenecker, "Different Answers," 117).

63. Fitzmyer, *Romans*, 625.

64. Jewett, *Romans*, 704; Moo, *Epistle to the Romans*, 728.

65. So, e.g., Kim, "Reading," 465; Zoccali, "And So All Israel," 312; Wright, "Letter to the Romans," 692. See Du Toit ("Salvation") for the theological arguments for viewing the salvation of all Israel as being realized already.

with ὥσπερ (e.g., Rom 5:19) or ἐάν (e.g., Rom 2:26). In sum, the prevalence of the gnomic and/or logical future in the Pauline corpus is probably higher than is usually acknowledged. It has to be noted though that the designation "logical future" is strictly speaking not well accounted for in Greek grammars, and is therefore not so much a firm grammatical category inherent to the future tense itself as it is a category that is derived from the use of a future within a specific (conditional) context. It is thus more of a theological category than it is a firm grammatical category.[66]

BIBLIOGRAPHY

Bauer, Walter, Fredrick W. Danker, W. F. Arndt, and F. W. Gingrich. *Greek-English Lexicon of the New Testament and Other Early Christian Literature*. 3rd ed. Chicago: University of Chicago Press, 2000.

Beasley-Murray, G. R. *Baptism in the New Testament*. Exeter: Paternoster, 1972.

Bell, R. H. "The Myth of Adam and the Myth of Christ in Romans 5.12–21." In *Paul, Luke and the Graeco-Roman World: Essays in Honour of J. M. Wedderburn*, edited by C. Claussen, J. Frey, and B. Longenecker, 21–36. Sheffield: Sheffield Academic, 2002.

Black, David A. *Learn to Read New Testament Greek*. 3rd ed. Nashville: B&H, 2009.

Blass, F. *Grammar of New Testament Greek*. Translated by H. St. J. Thackeray. New York: Macmillan, 1905.

Blass, F., and A. Debrunner. *A Greek Grammar of the New Testament and Other Early Christian Literature*. Translated by R. W. Funk. Cambridge: Cambridge University Press, 1961.

Bruce, F. F. *Romans: An Introduction and Commentary*. Tyndale New Testament Commentaries. Downers Grove, IL: InterVarsity, 1985.

Bultmann, R. "Δικαιοσύνη Θεοῦ." *Journal of Biblical Literature* 83 (1964) 12–16.

———. *The Second Letter to the Corinthians*. Translated by R. A. Harrisville. Minneapolis, MN: Augsburg, 1985.

———. *Theology of the New Testament: With a New Introduction by Robert Morgan*. Vol. 1. Translated by K. Grobel. Waco: Baylor University Press, 2007.

Burton, Ernest DeWitt. *A Critical and Exegetical Commentary on the Epistle to the Galatians*. International Critical Commentary. New York: Scribner, 1920.

———. *Moods and Tenses in New Testament Greek*. Chicago: University of Chicago Press, 1906.

Byrne, B. *Romans*. Sacra Pagina 6. Collegeville, MN: Liturgical, 1996.

Cottrell, J. *Romans*. College Press NIV Commentary. Vol. 2. Joplin: College Press, 1998.

Cranfield, C. E. B. *A Critical and Exegetical Commentary on the Epistle to the Romans*. Vol. 1. International Critical Commentart. Edinburgh: T&T Clark, 1975.

Denney, J. St. "Paul's Epistle to the Romans." In *The Expositor's Greek Testament*, edited by W. R. Nicoll, 555–725. Vol. 2. Grand Rapids, MI: Eerdmans, 1902.

Dodd, C. H. *The Epistle to the Romans*. London: Collins Fontana, 1963.

Dunn, James D. G. *Romans 1–8*. Word Biblical Commentary 38a. Dallas: Word, 1988.

---

66. Cf. Jewett, *Romans*, 386.

Du Toit, Philip la G. "The Salvation of 'All Israel' in Romans 11:25–27 as the Salvation of Inner-Elect, Historical Israel in Christ." *Neotestamentica* 49 (2015) 417–52.

Fee, Gordon D. *Paul, the Spirit, and the People of God*. Grand Rapids, MI: Baker Academic, 1996.

Fitzmyer, J. A. *Romans*. Anchor Bible 33. New York: Doubleday, 1993.

Foerster, W. "σῴζω, σωτηρία, σωτήρ, σωτήριος." In *Theological Dictionary of the New Testament*, edited by G. Friedrich, 980–1012. Translated and edited by G. W. Bromiley. Vol. 6. Grand Rapids, MI: Eerdmans, 1971.

Fung, R. Y. K. *The Epistle to the Galatians*. New International Commentary on the New Testament. Grand Rapids, MI: Eerdmans, 1988.

Furnish, Victor P. *II Corinthians: Translated with Introduction, Notes, and Commentary*. Anchor Yale Bible 32. New York: Doubleday, 1984.

Godet, F. *Commentary on St. Paul's Epistle to the Romans*. Vol. 1. Edinburgh: T&T Clark, 1881.

Hagner, Donald A. *The New Testament: A Historical and Theological Introduction*. Grand Rapids, MI: Baker Academic, 2012.

Harris, Murray J. *The Second Epistle to the Corinthians*. New International Greek Testament Commentary. Grand Rapids, MI: Eerdmans, 2005.

Holwerda, D. E. *Jesus and Israel: One Covenant or Two?* Grand Rapids, MI: Eerdmans, 1995.

Jewett, Robert. *Romans: A Commentary*. Hermeneia. Minneapolis, MN: Fortress, 2006.

Käsemann, Ernst. *Commentary on Romans*. Translated by G. W. Bromiley. London: SCM, 1980.

Kim, D. "Reading Paul's καὶ οὕτως πᾶς Ἰσραὴλ σωθήσεται (Rom 11:26a) in the Context of Romans." *Calvin Theological Journal* 45 (2010) 317–34.

Kruse, C. G. *Paul's Letter to the Romans*. Pillar New Testament Commentary. Grand Rapids, MI: Eerdmans, 2012.

Kühl, E. *Der Brief des Paulus an die Römer*. Leipzig: Quell & Meyer, 1913.

Lagrange, M.-J. *Saint Paul: Epître aux Romains*. Paris: Gabalda, 1950.

Lange, J. P., and F. R. Fay. *The Epistle of Paul to the Romans*. Translated by J. F. Hurst. New York: Scribner, 1899.

Lenski, R. C. H. *The Interpretation of St. Paul's Epistles to the Galatians, to the Ephesians, and to the Philippians*. Minneapolis, MN: Augsburg, 1937.

Lewis, J. G. *Looking for Life: The Role of "Theo-Ethical Reasoning" in Paul's Religion*. New York: T&T Clark, 2005.

Longenecker, Richardn"Different Answers to Different Issues: Israel, the Gentiles and Salvation History in Romans 9–11." *Journal for the Study of the New Testament* 36 (1989) 95–123.

Martyn, J. L. *Galatians: A New Translation with Introduction and Commentary*. Anchor Yale Bible. New York: Doubleday, 1997.

Matera, F. J. *II Corinthians: A Commentary*. Louisville; London: Westminster John Knox, 2003.

Moo, Douglas J. *The Epistle to the Romans*. New International Commentary on the New Testament. Grand Rapids, MI: Cambridge: Eerdmans, 1996.

Morris, Leon. *The Epistle to the Romans*. Grand Rapids, MI: Eerdmans, 1988.

Mounce, R. H. *Romans*. New American Commentary. Nashville: B&H, 1995.

Murray, John. *The Epistle to the Romans: The English Text with Introduction, Exposition and Notes*. Vol. 1. New International Commentary on the New Testament. Grand Rapids, MI: Eerdmans, 1959.

Osborne, G. R. *Romans*. IVP New Testament Commentary 6. Downers Grove: IVP Academic, 2004.

Plummer, A. *A Critical and Exegetical Commentary on the Second Epistle of St. Paul to the Corinthians*. International Critical Commentary. New York: Scribner, 1915.

Porter, Stanley E. *Verbal Aspect in the Greek of the New Testament with Reference to Tense and Mood*. Studies in Biblical Greek 1. New York: Peter Lang, 1989.

Ridderbos, H. *Aan de Romeinen*. CNT. Kampen: Kok, 1959.

———. *Paulus: Ontwerp van zijn Theologie*. Kampen: Kok, 1966.

Roberts, J. W. *A Grammar of the Greek New Testament for Beginners*. Edited by D. L. Potter. Abilene, TX: Abilene Christian College, 2006.

Robertson, A. T. *A Grammar of the Greek New Testament in the Light of Historical Research*. 3rd ed. New York: Hodder & Stoughton, 1914.

Schlier, H. *Der Römerbrief Kommentar*. Herders. Freiburg: Herder, 1977.

Schreiner, Thomas R. *Romans*. Baker Exegetical Commentary on the New Testament. Grand Rapids, MI: Baker Academic, 2005.

Schrenk, G. "δίκη, δίκαιος, δικαιοσύνη, δικαιόω, δικαίωμα, δικαίωσις, δικαιοκρισία." In *Theological Dictionary of the New Testament*, edited by G. Kittel, 178–225. Translated and edited by G. W. Bromiley. Vol. 2 Grand Rapids, MI: Eerdmans, 1964.

Thrall, M. E. *A Critical and Exegetical Commentary on the Second Epistle to the Corinthians*. Vol. 1. International Critical Commentary. Edinburgh: T&T Clark, 1994.

Thyen, H. *Studien zur Südenvegebung im Neuen Testament und seinen alttestamentlichen und jüdischen Voraussetzungen*. Forshungen zur Religion und Literatur des Alten und Neuen Testaments 96. Göttingen: Vandenhoeck & Ruprecht, 1970.

Vaughan, C., and E. Gideon. *A Greek Grammar of the New Testament*. Nashville: Broadman, 1979.

Wallace, Daniel B. *Greek Grammar Beyond the Basics: An Exegetical Syntax of the New Testament*. Grand Rapids, MI: Zondervan, 2002.

Weiss, B. *Der Brief an die Römer*. 9th ed. Göttingen: Vandenhoeck & Ruprecht, 1899.

Wilckens, Ulrich. *Der Brief an die Römer*. Vol. 2. Evangelisch-katholischer Kommentar zum Neuen Testament. Zürich: Neukirchen-Vluyn, 1980.

WrightnT. "The Letter to the Romans: Introduction, Commentary, and Reflections." In *The New Interpreter's Bible*, edited by Leander E. Keck, 394–770. Vol. 10. Nashville: Abingdon, 2002.

Yarbrough, Robert W. "The Theology of Romans in Future Tense." *Southern Baptist Journal of Theology* 11 (2007) 46–57.

Zoccali, C. "'And So All Israel Will Be Saved': Competing Interpretations of Romans 11.26 in Pauline Scholarship." *Journal for the Study of the New Testament* 30 (2008) 289–318.

Chapter 6

The Role of Chiasm for Understanding Christology in Hebrews 1:1-14[*]

—VICTOR (SUNG YUL) RHEE
Talbot School of Theology/Biola University

ALBERT VANHOYE, IN HIS book entitled, *La structure littéraire de l'Épître aux Hébreux*, discusses different literary devices employed by the author of Hebrews.[1] Through a careful analysis of these devices in Hebrews, he proposes that the overall structure of the book is symmetrical (or chiastic).[2] In addition, he suggests that many passages of Hebrews are written in a chiastic manner.[3] However, he fails to identify the overall symmetrical patterns of 1:1-4 and 1:5-14. In recent years scholars have recognized the complexity of the literary design of Heb 1:1-14. Some share the opinion that the exordium (1:1-4) is so intricately organized in form and style that it is probably one of the finest literary works in the whole NT.[4] Others have even observed the presence of a chiastic structure in this passage.[5] Richard

---

[*] This essay was published originally in the *Journal of Biblical Literature*. See Rhee, "Role of Chiasm," 341–62. Permission for the reprint was given by the Society of Biblical Literature. The title and contents of this publication are basically the same as the original, but I have made slight modifications for corrections and clarity.

1. Vanhoye, *La Structure littéraire*, 37.

2. Ibid., 149. Vanhoye understands 9:11–12 to be the center of the book, and vv. 13–14, the counterpart of vv. 11–12.

3. See ibid., 70 (1:5), 75 (2:3), 76 (2:4), 80 (2:14–15), 88 (3:3), 110 (5:1–10), 152 (9:18–22), 167 (10:11–14), 199 (12:8).

4. See Black, "Hebrews," 175–76; Attridge, *Epistle to the Hebrews*, 36.

5. See Ebert, "Chiastic Structure," 167; Lane, *Hebrews 1–8*, 6–7.

Bauckham maintains that the catena of the OT quotations in 1:5–13 has a chiastic arrangement.[6] Moreover, others have come to realize that there are literary and conceptual correlations between 1:1–4 and 1:5–14. For instance, William L. Lane suggests that there exists a synthetic parallelism between the two passages.[7] Likewise, John P. Meier argues that there is a general agreement between 1:1–4 and 1:5–14, even though the symmetry lacks one-to-one correspondence.[8] These scholars have provided helpful insights for a better understanding of the structure and theology of Hebrews 1:1–14. However, they might have overlooked the possibility that the author of Hebrews may have intended vv. 1–4 and vv. 5–14 to be in a perfect symmetry with the idea of different stages of Christ's existence (i.e., exaltation, preexistence, and incarnation). I propose that Heb 1:1–14 was designed as a chiastic structure by the author, which may be illustrated as follows:

A The function of the Son: God's final spokesperson (vv. 1–2a).

  B The Son in his exaltation: heir of all things (v. 2b).

    C The Son in his preexistence: bearer of God's nature, creator, and sustainer of the world (vv. 2c–3b).

      D The Son in his incarnation: purifier of sins (v. 3c).

        E The Son in his exaltation: he sat down at the right hand of God, with the result that he became superior to the angels (vv. 3d–4).

        E' The Son in his exaltation: because of God's enthronement of the Son at the right hand, he is superior to the angels (v. 5).

      D' The Son in his incarnation: the Son who is brought into the world is superior to the angels because they worship him (v. 6).

    C' The Son in his preexistence: the Son is superior to the angels because he is God (vv. 7–12).

  B' The Son in his exaltation: the Son is superior to the angels because the Father has exalted him at his right hand (v. 13).

A' The function of the angels: the Son is superior to the angels because they are the ministering spirits for the sons who will inherit salvation (v. 14).

The analysis of 1:1–14 indicates that in 1:5–14 the author repeats and further elaborates the themes he introduced in the exordium (vv. 1–4) in an

---

6. Bauckham, "Monotheism and Christology," 175–76.
7. Lane, *Hebrews 1–8*, 22.
8. Meier, "Symmetry and Theology," 523.

inverted order. In this proposed chiastic structure one can see that sections from A to E show why the Son is qualified to be the authority for speaking the final revelation of God. Nils W. Lund asserts that in a chiastic structure the center is where the turning point takes place and that a shift of thought in the center is continued to the end of the system.[9] I detect this type of pattern from sections E' to A' (1:5-14). In section E' (v. 5) there is a shift of thought from "God's final revelation through the Son" to "the Son's superiority to the angels," which continues to end of the passage (A', v. 14). The author emphasizes why the Son is superior to the angels by employing the three stages of the Son's existence, as he did in vv. 1-4. This type of chiastic pattern in the NT has been observed by many scholars in recent years. A survey of the literature indicates that the definition of chiasm is not limited to the parallelism of words or phrases but includes an inversion of ideas or concepts in a broad sense. For example, Vanhoye asserts that conceptual ideas should be allowed in the discussion of the literary structure in Hebrews.[10] Based on this premise, he suggests that Hebrews has a chiastic arrangement at the conceptual level, which can be illustrated as follows:[11]

I Eschatology (1:5—2:18)
  II Ecclesiology (3:1—5:10)
    III Sacrifice (5:11—10:39)
  IV Ecclesiology (11:1—12:13)
V Eschatology (12:14—13:19)

Likewise, Craig Blomberg, in his discussion of criteria for identifying chiastic structures, suggests that conceptual parallelism, as well as verbal, should be used in identifying chiastic structures.[12] Using this as a guideline, he asserts that 2 Cor 1:12—7:16 is chiastically arranged at the conceptual level.[13] These examples suggest that the term is used to designate an inversion of concepts and ideas as well as words or phrases in a given passage. In this essay I will adopt the definition of chiasm in this sense for the purpose of examining the structure of Heb 1:1-14. More specifically, I intend to demonstrate the validity of the newly proposed chiastic structure in this passage by comparing each corresponding section at both the microscopic level (i.e.,

---

9. Lund, *Chiasmus in the New Testament*, 40-41.

10. Vanhoye, *La Structure Littéraire*, 237.

11. Ibid., 240. I have indicated the verse divisions for clarity based on Vanhoye's analysis of Hebrews. His division of "V. Eschatology" is 12:14—13:18. I have added 13:19 to his division (see pp. 205, 217).

12. Blomberg, "Structure," 7.

13. Ibid., 8-21.

words and phrases) and the macroscopic level (i.e., theological ideas and concepts).

I. SECTIONS A (1:1–2A) AND A' (1:14)

(The Function of the Son and the Angels)

According to the proposed chiastic structure of Heb 1:1–14, sections A (vv. 1–2a) and A' (v. 14) are arranged in an inverted manner. These outer sections of the chiasm describe the function of the Son and of the angels.

Section A (1:1–2a)

In this beginning section the author sets forth the function of the Son as the final spokesperson for God. A careful examination of this section shows that it comprises a single sentence, which may be illustrated as follows:

1:1 Πολυμερῶς καὶ πολυτρόπως πάλαι
in many portions and in many ways long ago

ὁ θεὸς
God

λαλήσας τοῖς πατράσιν ἐν τοῖς προφήταις
after having spoken to the fathers by the prophets,

1:2a ἐπ' ἐσχάτου τῶν ἡμερῶν τούτων
in these last days

ἐλάλησεν ἡμῖν ἐν υἱῷ
has spoken to us by (his) Son

This diagram enables one to see that the main clause is "God has spoken to us by (his) Son (v. 2a)."[14] This main clause is modified by two adverbs (πολυμερῶς, πολυτρόπως) and a participial phrase (λαλήσας τοῖς πατράσιν ἐν τοῖς προφήταις). What is the significance of the expressions "in many portions" (πολυμερῶς) and "in many ways" (πολυτρόπως)? These two terms are so closely related that they are considered by some to be synonyms.[15] However, there seems to be a slight difference between the two. The first adverb suggests that God's speaking in the OT was fragmented, coming in multiple segments or portions in different times. The second term implies the diverse

---

14. For the structural analysis of Heb 1:1–4, see Übelacker, *Der Hebräerbrief*, 78.
15. Black, "Literary Artistry," 45. See also Ellingworth, *Epistle to the Hebrews*, 91.

ways in which God spoke through the prophets.[16] Both words speak of the progressive nature of God's revelation, which is completed in the Son. The modifiers, along with the main clause, clearly describe the function of the Son; the Son is the final spokesperson of God's revelation. The idea of the function of the Son is further enforced by the qualitative use of the noun υἱός without the definite article. This anarthrous usage emphasizes the quality, nature, or essence of the noun[17] and draws attention to the essential character of the one who is the Son (i.e., by such a one who is the Son).[18] The point is that God has given the Son the authority to deliver the final revelation to us. The verses speak of the Son's role in bringing about God's full and complete revelation in these last days.

Section A' (1:14)

The function of the Son in section A (vv. 1–2a) is in contrast to that of the angels in the counterpart of the chiasm in section A' (v. 14). The thread that connects these two sections has to do with the functions. On the one hand, the Son is the one through whom God has spoken the final word (A); the Son has the function of being the spokesperson of the finality of God's revelation. On the other hand, the angels have the role of being merely the ministering spirits sent out on account of those who will inherit salvation (A').

These two sections also correspond to each other in the concept of eschatology. In section A (vv. 1–2a) the idea of eschatology is expressed with the phrase "in these last days" (ἐπ' ἐσχάτου τῶν ἡμερῶν τούτων [v. 2a]). The phrase ἐπ' ἐσχάτου τῶν ἡμερῶν is used four times in the LXX (Num 24:14; Jer 23:20; 25:19; Dan 10:14). An examination of the context of these passages indicates that the phrase is an expression for the future, which has an eschatological sense.[19] Interestingly, the author of Hebrews adds "these" (τούτων) to this LXX term, which connotes that the last days have already begun with the first advent of Christ.[20] In Heb 1:2 the phrase refers to the period between Christ's first advent and his second coming. The dawn of the new age has begun, while the final last day has not yet come.[21]

---

16. Attridge, *Epistle to the Hebrews*, 37. See also Koester, *Hebrews*, 176–77; Braun, *An Die Hebräer*, 20.

17. Wallace, *Greek Grammar*, 244.

18. Lane, *Hebrews 1–8*, 5.

19. Attridge, *Epistle to the Hebrews*, 39.

20. Ellingworth, *Epistle to the Hebrews*, 93.

21. Barrett, "Eschatology," 391.

In A' (v. 14) the concept of eschatology is described in terms of "those who will inherit salvation" (τοὺς μέλλοντας κληρονομεῖν σωτηρίαν). The idea of the end time is described in various ways in Hebrews. For example, it is expressed as "the world to come" (2:5), "Sabbath rest" (4:3, 5, 9, 11), "the age to come" (6:5), "the hope set before us" (6:18), "the day drawing near" (10:25), "he who is coming . . . will not delay" (10:37), "a kingdom that cannot be shaken (12:28), and "a city which is to come" (13:14). The time of those who will inherit salvation (1:14) is related to the second coming of Christ. The word σωτηρία, which is used in this verse, occurs also in 9:28. A careful examination of the context in 9:26–28 indicates that "salvation" in 9:28 has a clear reference to the parousia. In 9:26 the author states that Jesus has been manifested to put away sin by the sacrifice of himself. The phrase "once at the end of the ages" (ἅπαξ ἐπὶ συντελείᾳ τῶν αἰώνων) suggests that putting away sin took place during the time of Christ's incarnation, and more specifically, on the cross. Then in 9:28, the author goes on to indicate that Christ will appear a second time for the salvation of those who eagerly wait for him. In this verse the phrase "apart from sin" (χωρὶς ἁμαρτίας) suggests that Christ's second coming will have nothing to do with the removal of sin but will be for the salvation of believers in the eschatological sense.[22] It is evident from the investigation of σωτηρία in 1:14 and 9:28 that the time of those who will inherit salvation will be at the second coming of Christ. The work of salvation began with the first advent of Christ, but the consummation of it will be realized with his second advent.

In summary, an examination of section A (1:1–2a) and section A' (1:14) reveals that they complement each other with the idea of the function of the Son and that of the angels. They also show parallelism in the concept of eschatology: section A speaks of the present aspect of eschatology, while section A' describes the future aspect of eschatology. Therefore, it is reasonable to consider sections A and A' counterparts, as suggested in the proposed chiastic structure.

II. SECTIONS B (1:2B) AND B' (1:13)

(The Son in His Exaltation)

As illustrated in the proposed chiastic structure, beginning from section B (1:2b) to section B' (1:13) the counterparts of the chiasm are arranged according to various stages of the Son's existence (i.e., exaltation, preexistence,

---

22. Attridge, *Epistle to the Hebrews*, 266.

incarnation).[23] In sections B (v. 2b) and B' (v. 13) the author begins with the exaltation of the Son. The former section speaks of the Son's exalted status as the heir of all things, while the latter depicts the Son's superiority to the angels in his exaltation.

Section B (1:2b)

After having stated the main idea that God has spoken to us in his Son (1:1–2a), the author further develops it in 1:2b–4 by the use of the relative pronouns (ὅν, οὗ, ὅς in vv. 2–3) and the participles (ὤν, φέρων in v. 3; γενόμενος in v. 4) to elaborate on the nature, work, and the position of the Son. In section B (v. 2b) the author begins with the exaltation of the Son. The expression "whom he appointed heir (κληρονόμος) of all things" is probably an allusion to Ps 2:8. This is evidenced by the author's quotation of Ps 2:7 in 1:5. The idea of the heir, which is introduced here, is further developed in other parts of the book (κληρονομέω, 1:4, 14; 6:12; 12:17; κληρονόμος, 1:2; 6:17; 11:7; κληρονομία, 9:15; 11:8). These verses reveal explicitly and implicitly that the concept has something to do with the promises of God. Lane suggests that there is a literary connection between 1:2b and Gen 17:5 (i.e., "whom he appointed heir of all things" [Heb 1:2b]; "I have appointed you the father of many nations" [Gen 17:5]). From this he deduces that the appointing of Abraham as heir marks the beginning of redemptive history and the appointing of the Son is the accomplishment of the work of redemption.[24]

Then what is the inheritance that the Son has come to possess? The Greek word for "all things" (πάντων) can be either masculine or neuter. In the immediate context, the words such as "world" (τοὺς αἰῶνας) in v. 2c and "all things" (τὰ πάντα) in v. 3 suggest that it may be considered neuter, referring to the universe. However, the term could also refer to the human race. The word studies on κληρονομέω ("to inherit") and its cognates in Hebrews indicate that the inheritance involves people who were either revered ancestors in the OT (6:12; 11:7–8) or believers in the NT period (1:14; 9:15). In addition, the author uses the neuter form of πᾶς in other parts of Hebrews to indicate humanity. For example, the reference to "all things" (πάντα) in 2:10 and 3:4 involves the people of God (i.e., "in bringing many sons to glory" [2:10]; "whose people we are" [3:6]). For this reason, it may be concluded that the inheritance includes both the universe and humanity.

---

23. Section B (1:2b) reads, ὃν ἔθηκεν κληρονόμον πάντων ("whom he appointed heir of all things").

24. Lane, *Hebrews 1–8*, 12.

Philip Edgcumbe Hughes rightly states, "[H]is inheritance is the innumerable company of the redeemed and the universe renewed by virtue of his triumphant work of reconciliation."[25] As the finality of God's revelation, the Son accomplished the beginning of redemptive history and became the heir of all things. The inheritance was already inaugurated with the first advent and will have the final fulfillment at the second coming of Christ (1:13–14; 6:17; 9:15).

Section B' (1:13)

As seen in the proposed chiastic structure, the Son's exaltation is reiterated in section B' (1:13) with a slightly different emphasis. Verse 5 and v. 13 form an *inclusio* with a similar rhetorical formula of introducing the quotations. This literary device is employed to mark the beginning and the end of the unit vv. 5–14. This may be illustrated as follows:[26]

- v. 5 "To which of the angels did he ever say . . ." (Τίνι γὰρ εἶπέν ποτε τῶν ἀγγέλων), followed by the quotations of Ps 2:7 and 1 Sam 7:14.
- v. 13 "But to which of the angels has he ever said . . ." (πρὸς τίνα δὲ τῶν ἀγγέλων εἴρηκέν ποτε . . .), followed by the quotation of Ps 110:1 (109 LXX).

The major difference between the two verses is the use of different tenses (εἴρηκέν [perfect] in v. 13; εἶπέν [aorist] in v. 5). Whereas the latter describes the action of speaking in the past, the former expresses the action in the past with the abiding consequence of the speech. The author's use of the perfect tense in v. 13 implies that he is more interested in the period of inauguration as sitting at the right hand of God, rather than in the single event of Christ's exaltation.[27]

In this verse (v. 13) the author brings in Ps 110:1 (109:1 LXX) to conclude the argument for the supremacy of the Son to the angels. In this quotation, the author follows the LXX exactly. The context of Ps 110 is that of a king of Israel who reigned with the power and authority of the Lord himself.[28] In the early church, Ps 110:1 was frequently applied to Christ to express the notion that Christ was exalted in the right hand of God.[29] In

---

25. Hughes, *Commentary*, 39.
26. See Vanhoye, *La Structure Littéraire*, 74.
27. Ellingworth, *Epistle to the Hebrews*, 131.
28. Hay, *Glory at the Right Hand*, 20.
29. Ibid., 52–103; see 163–64 for direct quotations and allusions.

Hebrews also, this verse is quoted (1:13) and alluded to (1:3; 8:1; 10:12–13; 12:2) to indicate the enthronement of the Son. In the context of 1:5–14 the idea of Christ's exaltation is expressed in v. 5 with the quotation of Ps 2:7 and reinforced in v. 13 with Ps 110:1.

The thought of Christ's exaltation in v. 13 also goes back to v. 2b in the exordium. God's appointing of the Son as the heir of all things in v. 2b and God's command to sit at his right hand in v. 13 correspond to each other with the theme of the enthronement and exaltation of the Son. These findings support the suggestion in the proposed chiastic structure that v. 2b (B) is the counterpart of v. 13 (B') with the idea of Christ's exaltation.

III. SECTIONS C (1:2C-3B) AND C' (1:7-12)

(The Son in His Preexistence)

After having described the Son from the standpoint of his exaltation (B and B'), the author then proceeds to emphasize the Son's preexistent stage in sections C (1:2c–3b) and C' (1:7–12). These two sections are parallel with the idea of the Son's role as the creator and his attributes as God in his preexistent stage.

Section C (1:2c–3b)

What evidence is there to indicate that section C (1:2c–3b) refers to the preexistence of the Son? First, his preexistence may be demonstrated from the Son's role as the mediator of the creation. Hebrews 1:2c reads, "through whom also he made the world" (δι' οὗ καὶ ἐποίησεν τοὺς αἰῶνας). The word translated here as "world" is from αἰών, which has the following range of meaning: (1) eternity, (2) time of the world, and (3) world equivalent to κόσμος.[30] In Hebrews it primarily has a temporal sense of either "age" (6:5; 9:26), or "forever" (1:8; 5:6; 6:5; 6:20; 7:17, 21, 24, 28; 9:26; 11:3; 13:8). However, here and 11:3, it has a spatial idea of "the world." Moreover, the plural form αἰῶνας means "worlds" or "spheres" (i.e., the entire universe).[31] In this verse the author points out that the Son is the agent through whom the whole universe came into existence.

Next, the idea of the Son's preexistence can be shown from his nature. In 1:3a it is conveyed by the participial phrase ὢν ἀπαύγασμα τῆς δόξης καὶ

---

30. Sasse, "αἰών, αἰώνιος," 197–208.
31. Ibid., 204.

χαρακτὴρ τῆς ὑποστάσεως αὐτοῦ ("being the radiance of his glory and the imprint of his nature" [my translation]). The term χαρακτὴρ has the meaning of "a mark impressed on an object such as a coin."[32] The idea is that the Son of God bears the very mark of his nature, "just as the image and superscription on a coin exactly correspond to the device on the die."[33] It speaks of the essential nature of Christ in his preexistence stage, which is manifested in his incarnation and exaltation. The word ἀπαύγασμα can have either a passive meaning of "reflection" or an active meaning of "radiance."[34] If, on the one hand, the word is understood as having the meaning of "reflection," the interpretation of the phrase would be the glory of God manifested in the perfection of his manhood (i.e., in his incarnation).[35] If, on the other hand, the word has the sense of "radiance," then it would refer to the Son's glory in his preexistent stage. The active understanding is more likely to be what the author has in mind in this context because it is more consistent with the meaning of χαρακτὴρ. Ulrich Wilckens observes that these two statements are placed together intentionally to indicate that they are synonymous. His logic is that since God's glory is his nature, the function of the Son expressed by ἀπαύγασμα and χαρακτὴρ must be the same.[36] For this reason, it seems best to understand both terms as referring to the Son's glorious nature in his preexistent stage, rather than the glory of God revealed in his incarnation. The significance of these two phrases describing the nature of the Son is that Jesus has the full participation in the nature of the Father and a unique relationship with the Father.[37] The Son is qualified to be the final spokesperson for God because he himself bears God's glory and the impression of God's nature in his preexistent state.

Third, the Son's preexistent stage can be seen in the idea that he is the sustainer of the world (1:3b). The verse begins with another participle (φέρων): φέρων τε τὰ πάντα τῷ ῥήματι τῆς δυνάμεως αὐτοῦ ("and upholding all things by the word of his power"). In v. 3a the emphasis is on the Son's essential nature, but here attention is directed toward what the Son does; he upholds all things by the word of his power. In this verse the word "uphold" (φέρω) has the meaning of "carrying" or "bearing" in the sense of "sustaining."[38] The phrase "by the word of his power" should be under-

32. BDAG, 1077.
33. Bruce, *Epistle*, 48.
34. BDAG, 99.
35. Hughes, *Commentary*, 42.
36. Wilckens, "χαρακτὴρ," 421; see also Hughes, *Commentary*, 42, n. 13.
37. Fanning, "Theology of Hebrews," 373.
38. BDAG, 1052.

stood as "by his powerful word."³⁹ The Son is not only the direct agent of the creation, but also the one who is holding (φέρων) the world together. While the participle ὤν in v. 3a speaks of a timeless preexistence of the Son with God even prior to the creation of the world, φέρων in v. 3b indicates that the Son's function of sustaining the world had a beginning in the past.[40] This observation allows one to see that, as with ὤν, the participial phrase with φέρων implies the preexistence of the Son. The Son's being the radiance of God's glory and upholding all things by the word of his power refer to the preexistent state of Christ as the creator and sustainer of the world.[41]

Section C' (1:7-12)

It is clear from section C that the Son is described as being the creator and sustainer of the world. He is also portrayed as the one who possessed the attributes of God in his preexistent stage. In the counterpart of the chiasm (section C', 1:7-12) these thoughts are further developed by way of a comparison between the Son and the angels. The Son is superior to the angels because he has an abiding and eternal character: (1) his throne is eternal (vv. 7-9), and (2) he himself is eternal (vv. 10-12).

Eternality of his throne (1:7-9). In order to set forth the superiority of the Son to the angels in his attributes, the author introduces a quotation from Ps 45:6-7 (44:7-8 LXX). The context of the OT is that of the celebration of the royal wedding, in which a bride and groom are in the ceremony.[42] In the present context this quotation is applied to Christ.

To what stage of Christ's existence do these verses refer? Does the author have the preexistence or the exaltation in mind? Opinions are divided among scholars.[43] For example, Lane observes that the author's quotation of Ps 45:6-7 in vv. 8-9 is an implicit reminder of 2 Samuel 7, in which the establishment of an eternal throne is prophesied. He asserts that vv. 8-9 have the same idea of enthronement as in v. 3c in the exordium (i.e., "he sat down at the right hand of the Majesty on high").[44] Likewise, Kenneth

---

39. The genitive δυνάμεως is an attributive genitive.
40. Meier, "Structure and Theology," 182-83.
41. For exaltation, see Schenck, *Cosmology and Eschatology*, 87.
42. Craigie, *Psalm 1-50*, 337.
43. For preexistence, see Meier, "Symmetry and Theology," 515-16; Ellingworth, *Epistle to the Hebrews*, 122; Moffatt, *Critical and Exegetical Commentary*, 14. For exaltation, see Lane, *Hebrews 1-8*, 29; Hughes, *Commentary*, 64; Schenck, "Celebration," 474-75.
44. Lane, *Hebrews 1-8*, 29.

Schenck argues that the idea of "anointing" and "the exaltation of a king" in Ps 45:6–7 is the language of enthronement, which the author of Hebrews applies to Christ.[45]

However, the following evidence suggests that Christ's preexistence is in view. First, the preexistence is implied by the way God (the Father) addresses the Son. B. F. Westcott, taking ὁ θεὸς as either subject or predicate, translates ὁ θρόνος σου ὁ θεὸς in v. 8 as "God is Thy throne" or "Thy throne is God" (i.e., your kingdom is founded upon God).[46] But this rendering is difficult to reconcile with the context of vv. 7–9. In these verses the author makes a contrast between the angels and the Son by the use of the μέν . . . δὲ construction (v. 7 and v. 8). The angels, on the one hand, are mutable in nature, in that they can be made into winds and flame of fire (v. 7). The Son, on the other hand, has an eternal quality (vv. 8–9). Daniel B. Wallace rightly points out that the rendering of v. 8 as "your throne is God" (or God is your throne) loses the adversative force of δὲ, which may lead to the understanding that both the angels and the Son are under the reign of God.[47] For this reason it seems more natural to take ὁ θεὸς as the nominative for vocative, thus rendering v. 8 as, "your throne, O God, is forever and ever."[48] This rendering is more in line with the author's intent to draw a contrast between the angels and the Son. If God (the Father) addresses the Son as God, then it can be said that the preexistence of Christ is implied.

Second, the phrase "forever and ever" (εἰς τὸν αἰῶνα τοῦ αἰῶνος) in v. 8 denotes the eternity of Christ's throne, which includes the period of his preexistence. Although it does not exclude the exaltation of Christ, the emphasis certainly falls on the preexistent stage of Christ because in vv. 10–12, the author describes the Son as the creator of heaven and earth. This point will be elaborated further below in the discussion of the eternality of the Son in vv. 10–12.

Third, the description of the Son's attribute as "the one who loves righteousness and hates lawlessness" (v. 9) has to do with the eternal aspect of Christ. Hughes asserts that this expression does not refer simply to the eternal holiness of the Son but is applied specifically to the life and ministry of Christ in his incarnation.[49] However, if we consider that v. 9 is a continuation of the thought in v. 8, then it seems logical to see that the Son's character

---

45. Schenck, "Celebration," 474.

46. Westcott, *Epistle to the Hebrews*, 25; See also Moffatt, *Critical and Exegetical Commentarty*, 11.

47. Wallace, *Greek Grammar*, 59.

48. Ibid. See also Harris, "Translation and Significance," 129–62.

49. Hughes, *Commentary*, 65.

of "loving justice and hating lawlessness" is related to the idea of "forever and ever." Both ideas in vv. 8–9 imply the preexistence of Christ.

Fourth, the word χρίω ("anoint") in v. 9 is a symbol of joyfulness in timeless eternity rather than anointing at the exaltation.[50] Schenck argues that the word "anointing" in v. 9 echoes the royal title of "Christ" (i.e., the anointed one), and that it is the language of enthronement.[51] However, the expression "oil of gladness" (ἔλαιον ἀγαλλιάσεως) can be understood metaphorically as "oil, namely joy."[52] Meier offers further insight by pointing out that the author does not describe the exaltation and enthronement in terms of anointing elsewhere in Hebrews.[53] The implication of this observation is that "anointing" does not necessarily refer to the exaltation of Christ.

Careful scrutiny of the terms and ideas in vv. 7–9 indicates that these verses do not point to the exaltation of Christ. Rather, they refer to the preexistence of Christ. This idea is parallel to section C (vv. 2c–3b), which describes the Son as the bearer of God's nature, the creator and sustainer of the universe. This point will become more clear with the analysis of vv. 10–12.

Eternality of the Son himself (vv. 10–12). In order to elaborate on the eternal quality of the Son in his preexistent stage, the author introduces another quotation from the Psalter (102:25–27 [101:26–28 LXX]) in vv. 10–12. The Son is superior to the angels because he is the creator of the universe (v. 10) and the possessor of an eternal nature (vv. 10–12). This quotation is in the context of suffering and discipline due to sin (cf. Ps 102:10, 23–24). The psalm is the prayer of a man who pours out his lament before the Lord in his affliction.[54] In the present context the psalm is applied to Christ. The title "Lord" (κύριε) in the LXX refers to Yahweh, but here in Heb 1:10–12 it undoubtedly refers to Christ. In vv. 8–9 the author introduced the OT quotations with the expression πρὸς δὲ τὸν υἱόν. The conjunction καί at the beginning of v. 10 clearly indicates that the quotation that follows in vv. 10–12 is a continuation of the eternal aspect of the Son mentioned in vv. 8–9.

Again, one needs to ask whether vv. 10–12 speak of the preexistence or exaltation of Christ. Schenck argues that the main point of vv. 10–12 is Christ's lordship over the creation as the enthroned cosmic Lord

---

50. Meier, "Symmetry and Theology," 515.

51. Schenck, "Celebration," 474. See also Attridge, *Epistle to the Hebrews*, 60; Koester, *Hebrews*, 195.

52. The genitive ἀγαλλιάσεως ("of gladness") can be taken as the genitive of apposition.

53. Meier, "Symmetry and Theology," 515.

54. VanGemeren, "Psalms," 644–45.

in fulfillment of Psalm 8.⁵⁵ He maintains that Christ was the creator of the world not in a literal sense but in a figurative way; namely, he is the embodiment of God's creative wisdom.⁵⁶

Yet a careful examination of this passage makes clear that it has to do with the eternality of Christ in a literal sense, with an emphasis on the preexistent stage of Christ. The statement "You, Lord, laid the foundation of the earth in the beginning and the heavens are the works of your hands" (v. 10) is a reminiscence of God's act of creation in Genesis 1; Christ is the creator as the preexistent Son. Christ's eternality is further developed by comparing his permanent nature with the mutability of the creation (vv. 11–12). The expressions such as "they will perish," "they will become old," "you will roll them up like a mantle," "they will be changed like a garment" are contrasted with the descriptions "you remain," "you are the same," and "your years will not come to an end." Different tenses are used in describing the creation in vv. 10–12 (aorist, ἐθεμελίωσας [v. 10]; present, εἰσιν [v. 10]; future, ἀπολοῦνται [v. 11], παλαιωθήσονται [v. 11], ἑλ ξεις [v. 12], ἀλλαγήσονται [v. 12]). The implication is that the author has the entire history of the creation in mind.⁵⁷ However, the emphasis falls on the eternality and immutability of the Son in his preexistent stage.⁵⁸

The attribute of the eternality of Christ can be seen also from the comparison between v. 8 and v. 12 (v. 8: "you throne, O God, is forever and ever"; v. 12: "but you are the same and your years will not come to an end"). Lane observes that the author has purposely arranged the quotations so that they begin and end with the idea of the Son's eternal nature.⁵⁹ The conceptual link between these two quotations reinforces the durability and permanence of the Son.⁶⁰ Contrary to Schenck's assertion that the citations in vv. 8–12 refer to Christ's enthronement only, the entire passage speaks of the unchangeable nature of the Son, with the stress on the preexistence of Christ.

What is the point of the discussion in vv. 7–12 (C')? It is to demonstrate that this passage finds its counterpart in vv. 2c–3b (C). While section

---

55. Schenck, "Celebration," 475.

56. Ibid., 476.

57. Meier, "Symmetry and Theology," 518.

58. In contrast to this view, Schenck holds that in 1:10–12 it is not Christ's role as creator that is the main point but the eternity of his throne. Nevertheless, Schenck acknowledges that these verses express the idea of Christ's preexistence ("Keeping His Appointment," 113).

59. Lane, *Hebrews 1–8*, 30.

60. Bateman, *Early Jewish Hermeneutics*, 230–31.

C describes Christ's nature and activity as the preexistent Son, section C' speaks of the Son's superiority to the angels in his preexistent stage.

IV. SECTIONS D (1:3C) AND D' (1:6)

(The Son in His Incarnation)

In sections D (1:3c) and D' (1:6) the author shifts the focus from the preexistence of the Son to his incarnate stage. In section D (v. 3c), on the one hand, the aspect of incarnation was expressed with the Son's role as the purifier of sins.[61] In section D', on the other hand, it is described in terms of the Son's superiority to angels as the firstborn. Meier, illustrating the different stages of the Son's existence from the ring structure, asserts that the reference to the Son's purification of sins (1:3c) finds no correlation in the catena of the seven OT quotations.[62] However, I contend that its counterpart is in v. 6, as pointed out in the proposed chiastic structure.

Section D (1:3c)

After describing the Son's preexistent stage with two participial phrases in 1:2c–3b (section C), the author employs another participial phrase in v. 3c, "after making purification of sins" (καθαρισμὸν τῶν ἁμαρτιῶν ποιησάμενος), to express the idea of Christ's incarnation. This verse is the summary of the accomplishment of Jesus in his earthly life; he brought about the purification of sins through the sacrificial death on the cross. In the LXX the verb καθαρίζω and its cognates are related to the removal of the defilement of sin, either in connection with the altar or the people (see Exod 29:37; 30:10; Lev 16:19, 30). After introducing this concept here with "purification" (καθαρισμός), the author further develops it in other parts of the book (9:13, 14, 22, 23; 10:2, 22).[63] With this term the author also anticipates the theme of Christ's high priesthood, which he delineates throughout the epistle (2:17; 3:1; 4:14; 5:1; 7:26; 8:1; 9:11).

---

61. Verse 3c reads, καθαρισμὸν τῶν ἁμαρτιῶν ποιησάμενος ("after making purification of sins"). Note: Correction was made from my *JBL* article, 354n61.

62. Meier, "Symmetry and Theology," 523; for Meier's ring structure, see, "Structure and Theology," 189.

63. Lane, *Hebrews 1–8*, 15.

Section D' (1:6)

In v. 6 the author introduces another quotation, the source of which is unclear. It is possible that he has Ps 97:7 (96:7 LXX) in mind (MT: "worship him, all you gods"; LXX: "Let all his angels worship him," προσκυνήσατε αὐτῷ πάντες οἱ ἄγγελοι αὐτοῦ). But it is more likely that he is quoting from Deut 32:43 [LXX], replacing "sons of God" with "angels of God."[64] In order to determine whether D' (v. 6) can be considered the counterpart of D (v. 3c), one must consider the time reference to God's bringing the firstborn into the world (v. 6). Does it refer to the parousia (second advent),[65] the exaltation,[66] or the incarnation of Christ?[67] Answering this question requires the consideration of the following issues.

"*Again*" (πάλιν). Westcott, who takes this as a reference to the parousia, believes that it is more natural to connect the adverb "again" (πάλιν) with the verb "bring" (εἰσαγάγῃ). This allows him to understand v. 6 as "when he again brings the firstborn into the world." For this reason, he maintains that the introduction of the quotation refers to the second coming of Christ.[68] However, an examination of the term πάλιν goes against Westcott's assertion. This Greek term is used 10 times in Hebrews. When an OT quotation does not follow, it always has a temporal sense (5:12; 6:1, 6). But when it is accompanied by a quotation, it functions as a formula of introduction (1:5; 2:13 [twice]; 4:5, 7). If this observation is correct, then it is reasonable to consider the use of the adverb πάλιν in v. 6 as a connective introducing an additional quotation.[69] Taking the word as a formula of introduction allows one to relate it to the verb λέγει ("he says"). In this way one can see that v. 6 is the continuation of what God says in v. 5 (i.e., "again he says, when he brings the firstborn into the world"). The use of πάλιν militates against the parousia view.

"*Bring*" (εἰσαγάγῃ). Westcott asserts that the phrase "when he brings in" (ὅταν . . . εἰσαγάγῃ) looks forward to an event to be fulfilled in the future,

---

64. See Koester, *Hebrews*, 193; Ellingworth, *Epistle to the Hebrews*, 118–19; Bruce, *Epistle to the Hebrews*, 56–57.

65. Westcott, *Epistle to the Hebrews*, 21–23; Käsemann, *Wandering People*, 99–101; Braun, *An Die Hebräer*, 36.

66. Jewett, *Letter to Pilgrims*, 30; Bruce, *Epistle to the Hebrews*, 57–58; Lane, *Hebrews 1–8*, 26–28; Schenck, "Celebration of the Enthroned Son," 469–85; Koester, *Hebrews*, 192; Ellingworth, *Epistle to the Hebrews*, 118.

67. Hughes, *Commentary*, 58; Attridge, *Epistle to the Hebrews*, 56.

68. Westcott, *Epistle to the Hebrews*, 22.

69. See Lane, *Hebrews 1–8*, 26.

not an event already completed.⁷⁰ It is true that in many instances a clause with ὅταν and a temporal adverb may indicate an event that lies in the future from the perspective of the time of the main verb.⁷¹ However, this does not necessarily lead to the conclusion that the event of angels worshiping God will take place at the parousia. The future reference to the quotation is from God's point of view when the author of the passage wrote in the OT period.⁷² In this sense the phrase "bringing the firstborn into the world" is more likely to refer to the first advent of Christ. Moreover, Attridge notes that the phrase "introduction into the world" is a common expression (both Hebrew and Greek) for giving birth.⁷³ It appears that the author has the incarnation of Christ in mind in v. 6. This point will become more evident in the following discussion.

"*Firstborn*" (πρωτότοκος). In the LXX, the word "firstborn" refers to a family relationship, among many meanings. The firstborn in the family had distinct privileges and responsibilities (Gen 25:29–34 [cf. Heb 12:16]; 49:3–4; Deut 21:15ff; 2 Chr 21:3); he was the representative of his family who administered the property and interests of the father for the good of the family.⁷⁴ In Hebrews, the term also carries the idea of family relationship—between Christ (1:6) and believers (12:23). The immediate context of 1:6 indicates that Jesus, as the firstborn Son, is the heir of all things (1:2). He is the representative of the family who brings the believers to glory (2:10). In addition, the plural form of πρωτότοκος in 12:23 clearly denotes the family relationship between Jesus (i.e., "the Son") and the believers (i.e., "sons"). Believers are heirs of promise because Jesus was appointed heir of all things by the Father.

What is the time reference of God's bringing the firstborn in v. 6? Craig R. Koester asserts that in v. 6 the idea of "firstborn" is associated with Christ's exaltation because it further develops the idea of divine begetting in v. 5. He states that Jesus, as the firstborn from the dead, is uniquely the heir of all things.⁷⁵ Paul Ellingworth likewise argues that, just as Christ's supremacy was expressed by "firstborn from the dead" in Col 1:18 and Rev 1:5, the author of Hebrews also confirms his conviction about Christ's superiority in his exaltation with this term. Thus, the author's understanding

---

70. Westcott, *Epistle to the Hebrews*, 22–23.

71. Wallace, *Greek Grammar*, 479.

72. Hughes has a similar view (*Commentary*, 58).

73. Attridge, *Epistle to the Hebrews*, 56n67. See also Moffatt, *Critical and Exegetical Commentary*, 10.

74. Westcott, *Epistle to the Hebrews*, 23.

75. Koester, *Hebrews*, 192; See also Lane, *Hebrews 1–8*, 26–27.

of v. 6a is that God has brought Christ from the dead into the glory of the heavenly assembly.[76] Both Koester and Ellingworth see that the time reference of bringing the firstborn is clearly the exaltation.

In response to this view it may be noted that in v. 6 the author uses the term "firstborn" alone without a modifier (i.e., there is no additional expression such as "from the dead" as in Col 1:18 and Rev 1:5).[77] Since the word is used absolutely, it does not necessarily refer to either the resurrection or the exaltation of Christ. Rather, it appears that the term corresponds to the earlier use of the "Son," which occurs without a modifier (1:2).[78] If this observation is correct, then the author may have had in mind with this term the preexistent Son of God, who is the creator and sustainer of the universe, who disclosed God's revelation partially in the prophets and fully in his incarnation.[79] The designation of Christ as the "firstborn" may refer to the eternal divine sonship of Christ.[80] This leads to the inference that the time of God's bringing the Son is more likely to have been at the incarnation of Christ.

"*Into the world*" (εἰς τὴν οἰκουμένην). The proponents of the exaltation view interpret "the world" in v. 6 as the heavenly world.[81] For example, Schenck asserts that οἰκουμένη in v. 6 has to be the heavenly world because the referent of the "the world to come" in 2:5 is not the present earth but the coming habitable world. He supports his view by pointing out that the heavenly realm of the author of Hebrews is the homeland of God's people (11:13–16; 13:14) and the unshakable kingdom (12:28) that is to come. For Schenck, the term οἰκουμένη in both 1:6 and 2:5 has a metaphorical reference to the heaven as the truly civilized world (as opposed to the inhabited earth).[82] In other words, the place where God brings the first born into the world is the heavenly world, where the Son is *now* seated at the right hand of the Majesty on high, receiving worship from the angels.[83]

However, the enthronement view in 1:6 set forth by Schenck needs to be reconsidered. His understanding of οἰκουμένη as "the eschatological, heavenly world to come" raises the difficulty of relating the time reference

76. Ellingworth, *Epistle to the Hebrews*, 118.
77. Michaelis, "πρωτότοκος," 880.
78. Ibid.
79. Lindars, *Theology*, 4.
80. Attridge, *Epistle to the Hebrews*, 57. Hughes holds a similar view (*Commentary*, 60).
81. See Lane, *Hebrews 1–8*, 27; Koester, *Hebrews*, 192; Ellingworth, *Epistle to the Hebrews*, 118.
82. Schenck, "Celebration of the Enthroned Son," 478–79.
83. I have added the word "*now*" to reflect my understanding of Schenck's view.

of the entrance of the firstborn at the exaltation; the exaltation has already taken place at the ascension, whereas the world to come is still in the future. If the author of Hebrews has the eschatological world in mind in 1:6 as in 2:5, then it would be more natural to hold that the time of God's bringing the firstborn will be at the second coming of Christ, not at the enthronement.

Moreover, the use of οἰκουμένη in both the LXX and the NT goes against the understanding of the term in 1:6 as "the metaphorical heavenly world." In the LXX the word is used primarily in three senses: (1) the inhabited places on earth (e.g., Exod 16:35; Prov 8:31; Isa 10:14; 10:23; 13:5; 23:17), (2) the world God has created (e.g., 2 Sam 22:16; Pss 17:16; 18:5; 23:1; Prov 8:26; Isa 14:17; Jer 10:12; Dan 3:45), and (3) people in the world (Pss 9:9; 97:9). A word study reveals that the term is never used in the LXX to refer to the inhabited place in heaven in a metaphorical sense. In the NT οἰκουμένη occurs fifteen times (Matt 24:14; Luke 2:1; 4:5; 21:26; Acts 11:28; 17:6; 17:31; 19:27; 24:5; Rom 10:18; Rev 3:10; 12:9; 16:14). An examination of the use of the term in these passages indicates that it refers almost exclusively to the inhabited world on earth.[84] The way the author of Hebrews uses the term suggests that it probably does not have the same meaning in the two occurrences in the epistles (1:6; 2:5). In 1:6, οἰκουμένη is used without a modifier, while in 2:5 the participle μέλλουσαν is added as a modifier (i.e., the world to come). Since the term οἰκουμένη had a primary meaning of "the inhabited world on earth" in both the LXX and the NT periods, it is likely that in 1:6 the author of Hebrews had in mind "the inhabited world on earth." In the absence of a modifier, οἰκουμένη in v. 6 probably denotes not the heavenly world but the earthly one.[85] In 2:5, however, the author adds μέλλουσαν to let the readers know that he is speaking of a different οἰκουμένη (i.e., the world to come with the second coming of Christ on earth).

In summary, a close look at the author's expressions in section D' (1:6), "again" (πάλιν), "bring" (εἰσαγάγῃ), "firstborn" (πρωτότοκος), and "into the world" (εἰς τὴν οἰκουμένην), suggests that God's bringing the firstborn is more likely to have taken place at the incarnation of Christ. This section corresponds to D (1:3d-4), as illustrated in the proposed chiastic structure; as the firstborn Son in his preexistence, Christ came to the world for the purification of sins.

---

84. The only exception is Acts 17:31, which has a reference to the people in the world.

85. Michaelis, "πρωτότοκος," 880.

V. SECTIONS E (1:3D-4) AND E' (1:5)

(The Son in His Exaltation)

Finally, in sections E (1:3d-4) and E' (1:5), the author returns to the discussion of the exalted stage of the Son. According to the proposed structure, these sections are the center of the chiasm, in which the main point of the passage is highlighted. In both sections the exaltation is expressed with the Son's enthronement and his superiority to the angels. While section E describes the superiority of the Son to the angels in his exaltation, E' explains why he is superior by employing OT quotations.

Section E (1:3d-4)

The incarnation of the Son (i.e., after making purification of sins, 1:3c) naturally leads to the exaltation (i.e., he sat down at the right hand of the Majesty on high, 1:3d). Verse 3d is an allusion to Ps 110:1, which is specifically quoted in 1:13 and alluded to in other parts of the epistle (8:1; 10:12; 12:2). The phrase "sitting at the right hand" indicates power and honor. The author implies that, with the fulfillment of the psalm by Jesus, the messianic age has begun and the Son has a share in the glory and power of the Father.[86] The addition of the modifiers "of the majesty" (μεγαλωσύνης) and "on high" (ἐν ὑψηλοῖς) intensifies the Son's supreme exaltation without compromising the rank and rule of God the Father.[87]

The exaltation of the Son is further elucidated in v. 4 by another participle, γενόμενος ("having become"), an adverbial participle expressing the idea of result. The outcome of the Son's exaltation is the inheritance of a more excellent name than the angels. The comparison between the Son and the angels is emphasized with terms such as "so much ... than (or, as)" (τοσούτῳ ... ὅσῳ), "better" (κρείττων), and "more excellent" (διαφορώτερον). By employing these words, the author introduces the theme of superiority of the Son to the angels, which he further develops in 1:5-14 and in 2:5-18.

Section E' (1:5)

The idea of the Son's superiority to the angels continues in section E' (v. 5). The two parts of the center of the chiasm (E and E') are linked to each other by the hook word "angels" (ἀγγέλων) in verses 4-5, and by the conjunction

---

86. Grundmann, "δεξιός," 37-40.
87. Lane, *Hebrews 1-8*, 16.

γὰρ in v. 5. By these structural markers the author indicates that in section E' he intends to elaborate on the superiority of Christ to the angels in his exalted state.

In v. 5 the author quotes two passages from the OT. The first quotation is from Ps 2:7, in which the psalmist speaks of the rebellion of the nations against God and his anointed. The psalmist warns that if the kings of the nations do not pay homage to God's anointed, they will not escape the consequences of God's wrath. Christians in the first century applied this psalm to Christ in his baptism (Matt 3:16–17; Mark 1:10–11; Luke 3:21–22) and exaltation (Acts 13:33–34).[88] Hebrews 1:5 begins with a rhetorical question, "To which of the angels did he ever say, 'you are my Son, today I have begotten you'?" The question expects a negative answer; God did not make this statement to any angels.

There are some places in the OT where the phrase "the sons of God" (בני האלהים) refers to heavenly beings (Gen 6:2, 4; Job 1:6; 2:1; 38:7—in the three passages from Job the LXX translates the word "sons" as "angels" [ἄγγελοι]). Apparently, the LXX understood the phrase "the sons of God" as "the angels of God." If the interpretation of the Hebrew Bible by the LXX is correct, then it may be said that angels are sometimes referred to as the sons of God in the OT. But a survey of the singular form "angel" in the OT shows that there is no mention of an "angel" being the son of God. It appears that the author of Hebrews also reflects this understanding, which is evidenced by the singular form τίνι in v. 5.[89] The phrase τίνι . . . τῶν ἀγγέλων ("to which of the angels") implies that God never called any "angel" his son, unlike his anointed in Ps 2:7.

The second quotation is from 2 Sam 7:14 (cf. 1 Chr 17:14). In this passage Nathan, relating God's response to David's desire to build a house for the ark of God, prophesies that David's son will build a house for God, and that God will establish his kingdom forever. The prophecy was partially fulfilled in Solomon, but the context indicates that the fulfillment goes beyond Solomon's reign. The early church understood this prophecy to have been fulfilled in Christ (Luke 1:32–33; Acts 13:23). In this verse the author of Hebrews also follows this tradition of the messianic interpretation.[90]

An important issue pertaining to these two quotations is the question of when the Son was begotten.[91] Attridge argues that the quotation in Ps 2:7 speaks of the Son's eternal generation. He asserts that the word "today" is

---

88. Attridge, *Epistle to the Hebrews*, 53.

89. Note: Correction was made from my *JBL* article, 360 (changed from v. 6 to v. 5).

90. Koester, *Hebrews*, 192.

91. For different views see Ellingworth, *Epistle to the Hebrews*, 113.

used in a metaphorical or allegorical sense to denote the eternal generation of the Son.[92] According to Attridge, the author shows an obvious tension in dealing with the two traditions of Christ's preexistence and exaltation and has combined the two merely to set forth the superiority of the Son to any other agent of God's purposes. The author did not intend to provide a systematic Christology that would effect the reconciliation.[93]

The following evidence, however, suggests that the quotations in v. 5 are more likely to refer to the exaltation of Christ.[94] First, the conjunction "for" (γὰρ) in v. 5 is a further elaboration of the idea mentioned in vv. 3d–4, that the Son has obtained a higher position than the angels as a result of having sat down at the right hand of God. Therefore, it seems logical to conclude that the author uses the two quotations to confirm the exaltation of Christ. The proposed chiastic structure of 1:1–14 also shows that the quotations in v. 5 (E') need to be interpreted in light of vv. 3d–4 (E). Second, the author's use of Ps. 2:7 along with Ps 110:4 in 5:5–6 shows that "today" should be understood in terms of the exaltation. It is apparent that these two quotations are brought together to imply that the time when Christ was begotten as the Son was the same time that he was appointed high priest.[95] In other words, God's begetting of the Son has to do with the enthronement of the Son at the exaltation. This leads to the inference that the quotation of Ps. 2:7 in Heb 1:5 refers to Christ's exaltation. It may be said that the quotation of 2 Sam 7:14 speaks of this also; it is a repetition of the content of Ps 2:7 in a different manner.[96] This is supported by the use of the verb εἶπέν ("he said"), which is used only once in v. 5 in quoting the two OT passages. With the adverb "again" (πάλιν), the author indicates that the second quotation is closer to Ps 2:7 than the one that follows in v. 6.[97]

The above evidence demonstrates that the quotations of E' (1:5) speak of the exaltation of Christ. As I have pointed out in my proposed chiastic structure, E' (1:5) corresponds to E (1:3d–4). These two sections of the center of chiasm are parallel, with the theme of Christ's superiority to the angels as the exalted Son.

---

92. Attridge, *Epistle to the Hebrews*, 54.

93. Ibid., 55. See also Moffatt (*Critical and Exegetical Commentary*, 9–10), who tends to follow this view.

94. For exaltation view see Lane, *Hebrews 1–8*, 25–26; Ellingworth, *Epistle to the Hebrews*, 113–14; Bruce, *Epistle to the Hebrews*, 54.

95. Bruce, *Epistle to the Hebrews*, 54.

96. Meier, "Symmetry and Theology," 506.

97. Ellingworth, *Epistle to the Hebrews*, 114.

VI. CONCLUSION

The analysis of the structure and Christology of Heb 1:1–14 reveals that the author of Hebrews employed a very carefully designed chiasm to emphasize the three stages of Christ's existence. This study shows that the use of the chiasm is not limited to vv. 1–4 but extends to vv. 5–14. The investigation also demonstrates that the agreement between vv. 1–4 and vv. 5–14 is not just general, as some scholars assert, but much more specific. Both passages are designed in a perfect symmetry with each other with christological implications. As one can see from the proposed chiastic structure, the author describes the functions of the Son and the angels in A (vv. 1–2a) and A' (v. 14). Then, from sections B (v. 2b) to B' (v. 13), he goes on to explain the three aspects of Christ's existence (i.e., preexistence, incarnation, exaltation). In B and B' the emphasis is placed on the exaltation of the Son. The Son is the heir of all things in his exaltation (B), and he is superior to the angels (B'). The author then proceeds to emphasize the preexistent stage of Christ in C (vv. 2c–3b) and C' (vv. 7–12). These two sections correspond to each other with the idea of the Son's being the creator and his attributes as God in his preexistent stage. In D (v. 3c) and D' (v. 6) the focus is on the incarnation of Christ. The Son became a man to effect purification from sins (D, v. 3c); at the same time the Son is superior to the angels as the firstborn (D'). Finally, in the center of the chiasm (E, vv. 3d–4; E', v. 5), the author returns to the theme of the exaltation of the Son.

While E describes the Son's superiority to the angels in his exaltation, E' elucidates why the Son is superior by using the OT quotations. The author's purpose in placing exaltation at the center of the chiasm is to inform the readers that it is the main point of Heb 1:1–14. However, while emphasizing the Son's exaltation, the author does not minimize the importance of the other two aspects, because there can be no exaltation without preexistence and incarnation. Christ's exaltation necessitates the stages of preexistence and incarnation.

The three aspects of Christ's existence are crucial for the author because they are the basis for exhorting the readers to continue in faith in God. For this reason he introduces these concepts in 1:1–4, repeats them artistically in 1:5–14 in an inverted order, and further delineates them in other parts of the epistle (e.g., preexistence: 2:9; 10:5; 13:8; incarnation: 2:5–18; 5:7–8; 12:2–3; exaltation: 5:5–6, 9; 8:1; 12:2–3; 13:12) to encourage his audience not to forsake Christ, who is the author and perfecter of faith. For the author of Hebrews, the literary device of chiasm is a vehicle by which he conveys his teaching to his audience. Therefore, one must pay close attention to the various literary devices the author employs to have a better comprehension of the message of Hebrews.

BIBLIOGRAPHY

Attridge, Harold. W. *The Epistle to the Hebrews: A Commentary on the Epistle to the Hebrews*. Hermeneia. Philadelphia: Fortress, 1989.

Barrett, C. K. "The Eschatology of the Epistle to the Hebrews." *The Background of the New Testament and Its Eschatology: Essays in Honor of Charles Harold Dodd*, edited by William D. Davies and David Daube, 363-93. Cambridge: Cambridge University Press, 1954.

Bateman, Herbert W. *Early Jewish Hermeneutics and Hebrews 1:5-13: The Impact of Early Jewish Exegesis on the Interpretation of a Significant New Testament Passage*. American University Studies 7: Theology and Religion 193. New York: Peter Lang, 1997.

Bauckham, Richard. "Monotheism and Christology in Hebrews 1." In *Early Jewish and Christian Monotheism*, edited by Loren T. Stuckenbruck and Wendy Sproston North, 167-85. Journal for the Study of the New Testament, Supplement Series 263. London: T&T Clark, 2004.

Bauer, Walter, Frederick W. Danker, William F. Arndt, and F. Wilbur Gingrich. *A Greek-English Lexicon of the New Testament and Other Early Christian Literature*. 3rd ed. Chicago: University of Chicago Press, 2000.

Black, David Alan. "Hebrews 1:1-4: A Study in Discourse Analysis." *Westminster Theological Journal* 49 (1987) 175-94.

———. "Literary Artistry in the Epistle to the Hebrews." *Filologia Neotestamentaria* 7 (1994) 43-51.

Blomberg, Craig L. "The Structure of 2 Corinthians 1-7." *Criswell Theological Review* 4 (1989) 3-20.

Braun, Herbert. *An Die Hebräer*. Handbuch zum Neuen Testament 14. Tübingen: Mohr, 1984.

Bruce, F. F. *The Epistle to the Hebrews*. Rev. ed. New International Commentary on the New Testament. Grand Rapids, MI: Eerdmans, 1990.

Craigie, Peter C. *Psalm 1-50*. Word Biblical Commentary 19. Waco, TX: Word, 1983.

Ebert, Daniel J., IV. "The Chiastic Structure of the Prologue to Hebrews." *Trinity Journal* 13 (1992) 163-79.

Ellingworth, Paul. *The Epistle to the Hebrews: A Commentary on the Greek Text*. New International Greek Testament Commentary. Grand Rapids, MI: Eerdmans, 1993.

Fanning, Buist M. "A Theology of Hebrews." *A Biblical Theology of the New Testament*, edited by Roy B. Zuck and Darrell L. Bock, 369-416. Chicago: Moody, 1994.

Harris, Murray J. "The Translation and Significance of Ὁ Θεός in Hebrews 1:8-9." *Tyndale Bulletin* 36 (1985) 129-62.

Hay, David M. *Glory at the Right Hand: Psalm 110 in Early Christianity*. Society of Biblical Literature Monograph Series 18. Nashville: Abingdon, 1973.

Hughes, Philip Edgcumbe. *A Commentary on the Epistle to the Hebrews*. Grand Rapids, MI: Eerdmans, 1977.

Jewett, Robert. *Letter to Pilgrims: A Commentary on the Epistle to the Hebrews*. New York: Pilgrim, 1981.

Käsemann, Ernst. *The Wandering People of God: An Investigation of the Letter to the Hebrews*. Minneapolis, MN: Augsburg, 1984.

Kittel, G., and G. Friedrich, eds. *Theological Dictionary of the New Testament*. Translated by G. W. Bromiley. 10 vols. Grand Rapids, MI: Eerdmans, 1964.

Koester, Craig R. *Hebrews: A New Translation with Introduction and Commentary*. Anchor Bible 36. New York: Doubleday, 2001.

Lane, William. *Hebrews 1–8*. Word Biblical Commentary 47A. Dallas: Word, 1991.

Lindars, Barnabas. *The Theology of the Letter to the Hebrews*. New Testament Theology. Cambridge: Cambridge University Press, 1991.

Lund, Nils Wilhelm. *Chiasmus in the New Testament: A Study in Formgeschichte*. Chapel Hill: University of North Carolina Press, 1942. Reprint under the title *Chiasmus in the New Testament: A Study in the Form and Function of Chiastic Structures*. Peabody, MA: Hendrickson, 1992.

Meier, John P. "Structure and Theology in Heb 1:1–14." *Biblica* 66 (1985) 168–89.

———. "Symmetry and Theology in the Old Testament Citations of Heb 1:5–14." *Biblica* 66 (1985) 504–33.

Moffatt, James. *A Critical and Exegetical Commentary on the Epistle to the Hebrews*. International Critical Commentary. Edinburgh: T&T Clark, 1924.

Rhee, Victor (Sung Yul). "The Role of Chiasm for Understanding Christology in Hebrews 1:1–14." *Journal of Biblical Literature* 131 (2012) 341–62.

Sasse, Hermann. "αἰών, αἰώνιος." In vol. 1 of *Theological Dictionary of the New Testament*, edited by G. Kittel, 197–209. Translated and edited by G. W. Bromiley. Grand Rapids, MI: Eerdmans, 1964.

Schenck, Kenneth L. "A Celebration of the Enthroned Son: The Catena of Hebrews 1." *Journal of Biblical Literature* 120 (2001) 469–85.

———. *Cosmology and Eschatology in Hebrews: The Settings of the Sacrifice*. Society for New Testament Studies Monograph Series 143. Cambridge: Cambridge University Press, 2007.

———. "Keeping His Appointment: Creation and Enthronement in Hebrews." *Journal for the Study of the New Testament* (1997) 91–117.

Übelacker, Walter G. *Der Hebräerbrief Als Appell: Untersuchungen Zu Exordium, Narratio Und Postscriptum (Hebr 1–2 Und 13, 22–25)*. Vol. 1. Coniectanea Biblica: New Testament series 21. Stockholm: Almqvist & Wiksell International, 1989.

VanGemeren, Willem A. "Psalms." *The Expositor's Bible Commentary*. Edited by Frank E. Gaebelein. Vol. 5. Grand Rapids, MI: Zondervan, 1981.

Vanhoye, Albert. *La Structure Littéraire de l'Épître Aux Hébreux*. 2nd ed. Paris: Desclée De Brouwer, 1976.

Wallace, Daniel B. *Greek Grammar Beyond the Basics*. Grand Rapids, MI: Zondervan, 1996.

Westcott, B. F. *The Epistle to the Hebrews: The Greek Text with Notes and Essays*. London: Macmillan, 1889.

Chapter 7

The Virginal Conception

An Exegesis of Luke 1:35

—STEPHEN STOUT
Charlotte Christian College and Theological Seminary

PREFACE

THE MOST TERRIFYING MOMENT in my doctoral studies at Southeastern Seminary came in a one-on-one inquisition with Dr. David Black as the final exam for his seminar in Greek exegesis. Actually, he was most patient as I stumbled through my reading of a NT passage, and then he inquired most genuinely about my current pastorate. To this point, I had admired Dr. Black at a distance, but at that moment I came to view him as a concerned colleague in ministry, and I promised myself to be diligent to his urging of devoted studies of the Greek NT. This essay reflects the exegetical disciplines taught by Dr. Black, and I offer it to this *Festschrift* with gratitude for his love and commitment to the truths uncovered by careful study of the original language of the NT.

INTRODUCTION: IS THE VIRGIN BIRTH OUT-MODED?

There is general agreement that the Virgin Birth of Jesus has been considered an essential part of doctrinal orthodoxy from the beginning of Christian theology: the received form of the Apostle's Creed affirms of Jesus, "*qui conceptus est de Spiritu Sancto, natus ex Maria virgine.*"[1] Protestant catechetical instruction asked, "How did Christ, being the Son of God, become man?" and answered, "Christ the Son of God became man, by taking to himself a true body, and a reasonable soul, being conceived by the power of the Holy Ghost in the womb of the Virgin Mary, of her substance, and born of her, yet without sin."[2] Such a teaching may seem to be quite outmoded in the modern world, so this essay examines the birth announcement in Luke 1:35 to see what implications the virginal conception of Jesus might have toward twenty-first century Church life.

THE SOURCE OF LUKE 1:35, NATURAL OR SUPERNATURAL?

Where did the idea of a virgin conception originate? Luke's answer is simply stated in answer to Mary's question, "How can this be, since I am a virgin?" "And the angel answered and said to her . . ." (καὶ ἀποκριθεὶς ὁ ἄγγελος εἶπεν αὐτῇ, Luke 1:34).

Luke begins his narrative with a rather innocuous account of a childless Jewish couple, Zacharias and Elizabeth, when the story is interrupted by the appearance of an angel of the Lord while the old priest ministers in the Temple (Luke 1:11). This event is as troubling to Zacharias as it is to readers of any period, since angelic appearances are not the stuff of everyday experiences (Luke 1:12). Luke gives no apology for the existence of angels; he merely reports that the angel reveals a future prophecy concerning an unborn son in verbal, propositional form (Luke 1:13–16).

The angel Gabriel reappears to a young virgin named Mary, announcing, "Behold, you will conceive in your womb, and bear a son, and you shall name him Jesus" (Luke 1:31), a prediction that echoes Isa 7:14, "Behold, a virgin will be with child and bear a son, and she will call His name Immanuel," a prophecy that figures prominently in Matthew›s fulfillment motif (Matt 1:23). Upon later reflection, Mary may have observed that her experience was remarkably similar to an earlier event, when the angel of the Lord appeared to the mother of Samson and used comparable language, "Behold

---

1. Schaff, *History of Creed*, 21. The Apostle's Creed delineates two issues in this regard, that Jesus was "conceived of the Holy Spirit, born of the Virgin Mary." The latter statement confirms the historical event and maternity of the birth of Jesus, whereas the former describes that which is miraculous and unobservable.

2. *Westminster Larger Catechism*, Question 37, prooftexting John 1:14, Matt 26:38; Luke 1:27, 31, 35, and 42; Gal 4:4; Heb 4:15; and 7:26.

now, you are barren and have borne no *children*, but you shall conceive and give birth to a son" (Jdg 13:3).

Regardless, Luke concurs with the united testimony of Scripture, that angels not only exist but that God sends them to communicate with humans in propositional language, though the impression is that such angelic visitations are certainly not expected by those surprised and dismayed by their appearance, as is the case with Mary. Unlike so many critics who dismiss angelic revelation as ancient fables, the reader ought to be convinced that "the word spoken through angels proved unalterable" (Heb 2:2). It seems only natural that a supernatural conception of a supernatural person should be announced in a supernatural manner.

THE COMING OF THE HOLY SPIRIT UPON MARY

The first part of the answer of the angel to Mary is, "The Holy Spirit will come upon you," and while the meaning seems obvious, each word raises questions: does this refer to the Holy Spirit of God, or some other spirit? What does it mean that this Spirit comes upon Mary, and why in particular, is Mary the one upon whom the Spirit will come?

The Agent of this Coming: πνεῦμα ἅγιον

It may surprise some readers to discover that occasional scholars deny that the expression πνεῦμα ἅγιον refers to the Holy Spirit as the third person of the Triune God. Fitzmyer, for example, insists that a Trinitarian explanation imposes fourth century theology onto the text.[3] One reason for this view is that the expression πνεῦμα ἅγιον lacks the definite article, leading Plummer to insist, "It may be doubted whether the article is omitted because Holy Spirit is here a proper name; rather because it is regarded impersonally as the creative power of God (cf. Gen 1:2 and Luke 1:15)."[4] It should be noted, however, that when πνεῦμα ἅγιον appears in the NT, it refers to the Holy Spirit of God, not to some impersonal divine power.[5] Furthermore, the expression "son of God" (υἱὸς θεοῦ) at the end of this verse also lacks the

---

3. Fitzmyer, *Gospel According to Luke*, 351.
4. Plummer, *Critical and Exegetical Commentary*, 24.
5. The anarthrous expression, πνεῦμα ἅγιον, is found only twice in the LXX (Dan 5:12 and 6:4), but it is not a good translation of *ruah yatirah* (NAS, "extraordinary spirit"). The same expression is used eight times in the NT (Luke 1:35; 11:13; John 20:22; Acts 8:15, 17, 19; 19:2), and while the definite article is not used, the context clearly refers to the Holy Spirit.

definite article, yet it clearly refers to a proper title of Jesus, as Robertson points out that the article is often absent when used with proper and divine names.[6] Luke had his reasons for using or omitting the definite article, but the adjective "holy" clearly identifies this Spirit as divine, whether the designation is used with or without the article.[7]

The Means of this Coming: ἐπελεύσεται

But now, declares Gabriel, the Holy Spirit is about to do something new and unique with regard to Mary. Gabriel describes the action of the Holy Spirit as coming upon Mary,[8] language he perhaps borrowed from the LXX of Isa 32:15, "Until the Spirit is poured out (ἐπέλθῃ) upon us from on high." It is this divine coming which shall result in the conception, as the future tense indicates that Mary has not yet conceived–the passage gives no indication of that precise moment, although it may have happened when Mary consents, "Behold, the bondslave of the Lord; be it done to me according to your word" (Luke 1:38).

This coming-upon expresses a spiritual reality of the divine coming in visitation upon a human, in itself a profound experience. The most obvious parallel is found in the words of Jesus at His ascension, "[Y]ou shall receive power when the Holy Spirit has come upon you" (ἐπελθόντος τοῦ ἁγίου πνεύματος ἐφ᾽ ὑμᾶς, Acts 1:8); however, that prediction refers to a universal coming of the Spirit upon all the disciples, whereas this one refers to Mary alone. When it occurs, something that has never before happened shall take place: a holy child shall be conceived in the womb of a daughter of Eve.

The Recipient of this Coming: ἐπὶ σὲ.

This preposition phrase, "upon you" (ἐπὶ σὲ) applies only to Mary, who has been introduced already in 1:26–27 as "a virgin betrothed to a man whose

---

6. Robertson, *Grammar*, 795. The article does not appear with Holy Spirit until Luke 2:26, and then with a preposition (ὑπὸ τοῦ πνεύματος τοῦ ἁγίου).

7. Moule, *Idiom Book*, 112–13, states, "It seems to me rather forced to interpret the anarthrous use (e.g., in the Gospels) as uniformly meaning something less than God's Holy Spirit."

8. The verb ἐπελεύσεται is future middle indicative, third person singular from ἐπέρχομαι and means primarily to come upon someone or something (BDAG §2900.1.b). It is intensified not only by the prefix ἐπ- but also doubled by the preposition ἐπὶ following the verb. Of the nine times ἐπέρχομαι is used in the NT, seven are found in Luke-Acts (Luke 1:35; 11:22, 21:26; Acts 1:8; 8:24; 13:40, 14:19); the other two appearances are in Eph 2:7 and Jas 5:1.

name was Joseph, of the house of David. The virgin›s name was Mary."[9] She is, of course, the key figure in this entire narrative, one whom Elizabeth will later address as "the mother of my Lord" (Luke 1:43), a remarkable confession coming from the wife of a Jewish priest.[10] While Luke honors Mary's thoughtfulness (1:29, 35), obedience (1:38), blessedness (1:42, 48), and faith (1:45), her virginity makes this conception unique.[11] As already noted, Gabriel paraphrases Isa 7:14 in Luke 1:31, "Behold, you will conceive in your womb and bring forth a Son, and shall call His name Jesus." By this citation, Luke agrees with Matthew's fulfillment motif of the same passage, meaning that the virginal status of Mary qualifies her to fulfill this prophecy. While English versions still contest whether to translate the Hebrew *HaAlmah* as virgin or young woman,[12] it is clear that both Matthew and Luke explain παρθένος as meaning Mary had no sexual relations with any man: that is certainly how Mary understands her virginity when she states, "I know not a man."[13] By this admission, she echoes the description of Rebecca as "a virgin, neither had any man known her" (Gen 24:16); furthermore, Matthew insists that Mary was still a virgin when she gave birth to Jesus, but the miracle occurred not at birth but at conception. Perhaps the Church would be more biblically accurate in its doctrinal statements to use the term Virginal Conception, since that is precisely what the Evangelists teach.[14] The

9. The mother of Jesus is mentioned in the NT (1) as Μαρία, an indeclinable feminine proper noun (at Matt 1:16, 1:18, 2:11, 6:3, Luke 1:41), and (2) as Μαριάμ (Matt 13.55; Luke 1:27, 30, 34, 38, 39, 46, 56; 2:5, 16, 19, 34; Acts 1:14). There seems to be no difference between the two forms; however, it may be significant that Luke uses Μαριάμ every time in the Birth Narrative except for 1:41, since he may be linking the mother of Jesus to her namesake, Miriam the sister of Moses, the only woman in the OT (besides Rebecca in Gen 24:43) who is also called *HaAlmah* (maiden/virgin).

10. Perhaps if the Chalcedon Creed had described Mary as *kuriostokos* rather than *theotokos*, the history of Christology might have been less emotionally charged and Mary better served.

11. Luke's concern is not Mary's virginity after the birth of Jesus, a dogma of Roman Catholic tradition defended by Clark, "Virgin Birth," 576–93.

12. The ESV, NAS, and NIV read "virgin," whereas several others read "young woman" (*Bible Works 10*, Norfolk, VA: BibleWorks, LLC, 2014). It is difficult to see how a young maiden bearing a child would be a unique sign; however, a virgin giving birth would be a divine indicator.

13. Wilson, "Meaning of 'Alma,'" 315–16, notes, "The evidence that Mary was a virgin does not after all depend on the meaning of the word *'alma* and *parthenos* alone; for it is said, also, of Mary, that 'she had not known man.' This phrase is used in the OT of Rebecca 'a virgin that had not known man' (Gen. xxiv.16), of Jephthah's daughter (Jud. xi.39), and of the virgins of Jabesh Gilead (Jud. xxi.12)."

14. McCready makes this insightful observation, though he relegates it to a footnote: "I will use the term virgin birth throughout even though the correct term is *virginal conception*" (*He Came Down*, 107n6).

Apostle's Creed attempts to do justice to both events with the expressions, "conceived by the Holy Spirit, born of the Virgin Mary," assenting to both the divine origin of conception and the maternal process of birth with regard to Jesus. The language of Scripture and the Creed is unmistakable: the mother is Jesus is presented only in terms of virginity. The text assumes that the reader will accept this miraculous intervention of the Holy Spirit coming upon Mary.[15]

THE OVERSHADOWING OF THE POWER OF THE MOST HIGH UPON MARY: ΕΠΙΣΚΙΑΣΕΙ

Although "power of the Most High" (δύναμις ὑψίστου) suggests the sheer omnipotence of the Supreme God (as in Ps 47:2) in the gestation of Mary's baby, that power is displayed in a manner quite the opposite of a show of force, by an overshadowing (ἐπισκιάσει), which may be a figure of speech indicating nothing more than a description of God's care, as in Ps 91:4,[16] or perhaps an as allusion to the Spirit of the Lord hovering over creation in Gen 1:2.[17] Besides here in Luke 1:35, this verb ἐπισκιάζω is used only four more times in the NT, once of Peter›s shadow (Acts 5:15) and the other three times in conjunction with the cloud that overshadowed Jesus as His transfiguration (Matt 17:5; Mark 9:7; Luke 9:34). When Peter mentions the making of tabernacles at that event, he may be thinking of Exod 40:35, when Moses was unable to enter the tent of meeting because the cloud had settled (ἐπεσκίαζεν) on it, and the glory of the LORD filled the tabernacle. As God came to dwell visibly on the Mercy Seat, now He comes to dwell physically in the womb of Mary.[18] There is an obvious element of mystery involved

---

15. Wilson concludes, "The language itself is not the difficulty. The great and only difficulty lies in disbelief in predictive prophecy and in the almighty power of God; or in the desire to throw discredit upon the divine Sonship of Jesus" ("Meaning of 'Alma,'" 316).

16. The verb ἐπισκιάσει is the indicative future active third person singular of ἐπισκιάζω. It appears only nine times in the Bible (Exod 40:35; Ps 91:4; 140:7; Prov 18:11; Matt 17:5; Mark 9:7; Luke 9:34; 1:35; and Acts 5:15). Bock, *Luke*, 123, notes that Ps 91:4 ("He will cover you with His pinions, ἐν τοῖς μεταφρένοις αὐτοῦ ἐπισκιάσει σοι) gives a close OT parallel to Mary's experience.

17. Plummer, *Critical and Exegetical Commentary*, 24, suggests this allusion is to creation, but the imagery in Gen 1:2 is that of a mothering bird, not an overshadowing cloud. Witherington, "Birth of Jesus," 71, notes, "It may be that Luke intends for us to see here the beginning of the eschatological reversal of the curse on Eve (Gen 3:16)," an intriguing thought for which he gives no further support.

18. Plummer observes, "It is the idea of the Shekinah which is suggested here (Ex. 40:38). The cloud of glory signified the Divine Presence and power, and it is under such

here, as one contemplates how the overshadowing of God who is spirit can produce an offspring of Mary who is physical, although there is no sexual intercourse present here that is normally required to conceive a child.

THE IDENTITY OF MARY'S BABY

The final sentence of this verse ("and for that reason the holy offspring shall be called the Son of God.") directly identifies Mary's baby.[19] Chronologically, this confession is the first time Jesus is designated as the Son of God, making Luke 1:35 extremely significant in terms of Christology, as Bock notes.[20] Furthermore, the description of Jesus as "the Holy (One)" makes a profound statement about the nature of this child. This section will examine these concepts.

The Inference of the Identified One: διὸ καὶ

The conjunctions διὸ and καὶ indicate a grammatical continuity between the preceding statement ("the power of the Most High will overshadow you") and the following sentence. While most English versions translate διὸ by "therefore/wherefore," others render it "so that,"[21] leading one to inquire whether it expresses cause ("and so that, or, for that reason") or result ("therefore"). The matter may seem inconsequential until one reads Fitzmyer contending that διὸ "expresses a causal connection between the virginal conception and Jesus' divine sonship; it is another implication that Luke does not have a notion of Jesus' pre-existence."[22] However, it is tenuous to deny Jesus' pre-existence on the basis of a conjunction that is regularly used to express result.[23]

---

influence that Mary is to become a mother" (*Critical and Exegetical Commentary*, 24).

19. A minor textual variant exists in some Greek mss, with the addition of the prepositional phrase ἐκ σοῦ inserted after τὸ γεννώμενον. The reading lacks widespread support, leading Metzger to note, "The words ἐκ σοῦ/ are apparently an early addition prompted by a desire for greater symmetry after the two preceding instances of the second person pronoun" (*Textual Commentary*, 108).

20. Bock, *Luke*, 123.

21. The BBE and NJB translate διὸ. as "and so that," while the NAS and NAU render it "for that reason."

22. Fitzmyer, *Luke*, 351. He is apparently headed toward an adoptionist view of Jesus, that Jesus *became* the Son of God by the work of the Holy Spirit, as he adds, "Jesus is God's Son because of the Spirit's activity in causing the Virgin Birth."

23. LNLEX: *Louw-Nida Greek-English Lexicon*, §89.47 (*Bible Works 10*), defines διὸ as a "relatively emphatic marker of result."

The Gestation of the Identified One: τὸ γεννώμενον

Gabriel first emphasizes the gestation of Mary's child by describing her baby in terms of the normal processes of human development; however, as fitting for a unique birth, the verbal form τὸ γεννώμενον is unique to the Bible.[24] The question arises whether Gabriel refers to the act of birth,[25] to the moment of conception, or to the process of gestation. Because this verb appears in the present tense ("the one who is being") rather than the future tense ("the one who shall be"), it seems that Gabriel refers to Mary's present condition rather than her future delivery.[26] In this case, the preferred translation would be, "the one being gestated."[27]

Gabriel speaks as if the child has already been conceived in Mary, perhaps answering the question, when did the conception of Jesus actually occur. There is nothing else in the birth narrative to pinpoint a particular moment when Mary conceived her child, though some might argue that the conception would not (even could not) have occurred until Mary gave her assent in Luke 1:37. The important issue is that the Word has now become flesh (John 1:14): Mary's baby had true human gestation, taking upon himself a human body and presumably, a human soul as well, as Orthodox Theology maintains.[28]

---

24. Luke 1:35 contains the only biblical appearance of γεννάω as a present passive participle nominative neuter singular, and it is the only time the present passive is used as an appellative, as the subject of the sentence.

25. The closest appearance of γεννάω is in Luke 1:13, where Gabriel promised Zacharias, "Your wife Elizabeth will bear you a son" (ἡ γυνή σου Ἐλισάβετ γεννήσει υἱόν σοι); however, the verb appears there in the future tense and could refer either to conception or birth. Fitzmyer, *Luke*, 351, concedes, "It [γεννώμενον] could theoretically mean 'the one begotten,' but since the words are being addressed to the mother to be, it means rather 'the one being born.'"

26. One must wonder why Gabriel did not use the word συλλαμβάνω here, since it more specifically refers to conception rather than to birth. He does use συλλαμβάνω with reference to Elizabeth conceiving John (Luke 1:24; 1:36), as well as to Mary conceiving Jesus (Luke 1:31 and 2:21).

27. *Young's Literal Translation* comes the close to this preference, "Therefore also the holy-begotten thing shall be called Son of God." However, the word "begotten" is rather archaic and confused by the translation "only-Begotten" of μονογενής, which is related to γίνομαι rather than to γεννάω.

28. Bostock, "Divine Birth," 261, insists that the VB actually jeopardizes the humanity of Jesus, because it "implies that Jesus was somehow different from everyone else." The fact is, Jesus *is* different from everyone else in that He is sinless.

The Holiness of the Identified Baby: ἅγιον

It has been established that the noun ἅγιον serves as the subject of the participle τὸ γεννώμενον,[29] so that the word order used by Gabriel (τὸ γεννώμενον ἅγιον) emphasizes the holiness of the child even before His identity as the Son of God. This order is reasonable, because a child who is not holy cannot qualify as Son of God in any respect. Holiness is a key theme in this chapter: Luke has already mentioned the Holy Spirit in this verse (and in 1:15, 41, 67), and Mary confesses of the Mighty One, "Holy is His Name" (1:49; see also 1:70 and 1:72), so the idea of ethical purity permeates the entire section.[30]

The fact is, however, that Jesus is the only baby who can be described as holy, according to the verdict of Gen 8:21, that "the intent of man's heart is evil from his youth." Theology labels this malady original sin—that humans commit sin in practice because they are sinners by nature; as Eph 2:3 charges, "We were by nature children of wrath, even as the rest." This indictment of human nature does not and cannot apply to Jesus, because He is designated as the Holy One from His conception, and later His disciples confessed, "We have believed . . . that You are the Holy One of God" (John 6:69). Also, Jesus confirmed His own sinlessness with a rhetorical question, "Which one of you convicts Me of sin?" (John 8:46), a legal innocence Pontius Pilate repeatedly pronounced although he still delivered Jesus to be crucified in a shocking miscarriage of justice (Luke 23:4, 14, 15, 22; John 18:38; 19:4, 6; Acts 13:28).

2 Corinthains 5:21 also confirms the sinlessness of Jesus, "He made him who knew no sin *to be* sin on our behalf," as does 1 Pet 2:22, which asserts that Jesus "committed no sin." Likewise, Heb 4:15 observes that Jesus was "tempted in all things as *we are, yet* without sin," and Heb 7:26 affirms that Jesus is "holy, innocent, undefiled." Such descriptions of Jesus as "righteous" (1 John 2:29) and as "holy" (Rev 3:7) are unique among humanity.[31]

---

29. Although Moule, *Idiom Book*, 107, notes that "the Holy Child" is a "distinctly irregular usage," he cites Mark 11:10 as giving a parallel construction where the article is separated from the modified noun by a participle (ἡ ἐρχομένη βασιλεία).

30. One can make a good case that Scripture presents the holiness of God as His premier attribute. Holiness is so distinctive that God designates Himself (fifty-five times) as "the Holy One" (see Isa 40:25), and Rev 15:4 singles out this attribute, "Thou alone art holy." The holiness of God may come to the forefront in divine revelation in contrast to the unholiness of fallen sinners.

31. The only other human that Scripture describes as "a holy one" is Aaron in Ps 106:16, but it seems that Aaron's description as a holy one refers to his position as High Priest, not so much to his personal character.

It is reasonable to look to the conception of Jesus and ask if there is any relationship between the sinlessness of Jesus and his virginal conception as the Holy One. In his essay, "On the Virgin Conception and Original Sin," Anselm may have been the first to tackle this issue, insisting that "whatever the Son of God took to his person from the Virgin could contain no stain of sin,"[32] yet he attempts to absolve Jesus from original sin by seeming to deny that any infant possesses a sinful nature. If no baby has a sinful nature, then every baby would be as holy as the Son of God, voiding the uniqueness of the VB.

Godet also inquires of the connection between this miraculous birth of Jesus and his

perfect holiness and concludes, "The latter does not necessarily result from the former, for holiness is a fact of volition, not of nature. How could we assign any meaning to the moral struggles in the history of Jesus (the temptation, for example) if His perfect holiness was the necessary consequence of His miraculous birth?"[33] Godet, however, places the proverbial cart before the horse: he implies that humans are sinners because they sin, not that they sin because they are sinners. Following his view, any child could choose to become as holy as the Son of God, or conversely, that the Son of God could decide to become as unholy as any other child of Adam. Either way, Godet's view eliminates the need for a virginal conception.

Likewise, Raymond Brown insists that "while the virginal conception may enter into the mystery of Jesus' sinlessness, it is difficult to argue that in order to be free from original sin, Jesus had to be conceived of a virgin."[34] Following his view to its logical conclusion, there is no particular reason for the virginal conception at all. It would be nothing more than a theological oddity.

Thus, Gabriel indicates that the reason why Jesus was conceived virginally, apart from natural generation, is the identity of this baby as "Holy One." It is not that Jesus *becomes* holy, a divine work that is accomplished for redeemed sinners (1 Thess 3:13), but because he is the "Holy One" prior to

---

32. Anselm, *Major Works*, 367. He suggests that what infants receive from fallen parents is the *necessity* to sin, though he does not explain why this tendency would be a necessity.

33. Godet adds, "It [the VB] gave Him the liberty *not to sin*, but did not take away from Him the liberty of sinning." This assertion is a rather poor choice of words, especially when Jesus notes, "Truly, I say to you, everyone who commits sin is the slave of sin" (John 8:34). Jesus evidently did not think that committing sin was a liberty but an enslavement. Because Jesus had no inclination to sin (1 John 3:5), he never chose to sin but instead "always did the things pleasing to [the Father]" (John 8:29) (*Commentary on the Gospel*, 58).

34. Brown, *Virginal Conception*, 41.

and from the moment of His conception, the virginal conception apparently preserves His holiness of nature so that Jesus received none of the taint of sin that spoils every child of Adam.[35] Nor does the virginal conception make Jesus less human because he lacks two biological parents[36] or because he does not share a sinful nature with the rest of humanity;[37] rather, his human nature is similar to that of the First Man Adam, who was created as "very good" (Gen 2:4). Luke develops an fascinating anthropology of Jesus as the "son of Adam, Son of God" (Luke 3:38), who, as a child, "continued to grow and become strong, increasing in wisdom; and the grace of God was upon him" (Luke 2:40); as a twelve year-old adolescent who possessed awareness of his divine Sonship (Luke 2:49), yet who continued in subjection to his parents; and as a young adult who "kept increasing in wisdom and stature, and in favor with God and men" (Luke 2:52). In these processes of maturity, Jesus became the only normal human. In such case, the virgin conception makes Jesus the true human, the "Last Adam" (1 Cor 15:45). Furthermore, because Jesus committed no sin, he provides an example to follow in his steps (1 Pet 2:21–22).

Because the holiness of Jesus plays such a pivotal role in the scheme of salvation, it is

imperative to inquire, when, where, and how did Jesus acquire the ability never to sin and always to do what was pleasing to his Father, as he claimed (John 8:29)? Gabriel supplies the answer: the child being gestated in the womb of the Virgin Mary is the "Holy One," conceived without a sinful nature.

---

35. Lange, *Commentary on the Holy Scriptures*, 21, asks, "How could He be free from every taint of the power of sin, if He had been born by the fleshly intercourse of sinful parents?" He answers, "The strong and healthy graft which was to bring new life into the diseased stock, must not originate from this stock, but be grafted into it from without."

36. Brown, *Virginal Conception*, 143, raises this objection, that the virginal conception cannot be reconciled with the true humanity of Jesus, asking, how can he be human if he had only one parent? The obvious answer is that Adam and Eve were certainty human, although they had no parents at all!

37. Godet, *Commentary on the Gospel*, 58, argues that a sinless nature would have rendered the temptations of Jesus meaningless. To the contrary, the writer of Hebrews notes the reality of Jesus being "tempted in all things as we are, yet without sin" (χωρὶς ἁμαρτίας; Heb 4:15). It may be noteworthy that the object of the preposition χωρὶς is not a participle ("sinning") but a singular noun ἁμαρτίας, "a sin." The writer may be emphasizing that Jesus overcame without succumbing to a single sin, or that he overcame because he was "without a sin." Regardless, a sinless person feels the acuteness of sin far more than one desensitized to its power.

The Designation of the Identified One: κληθήσεται υἱὸς θεοῦ

Who then is this unique child? Gabriel declares, "He shall be called Son of God," making this the second time he has used a similar designation in this conversation, as he said to Mary in Luke 1:32 of her child, "He will be great, and will be called the Son of the Most High" (υἱὸς ὑψίστου κληθήσεται).[38] The angel repeats a common motif employed by God to designate the names and/or identities of significant individuals in patriarchal times,[39] so it is possible that Mary may have recognized this covenantal echo, given her extensive knowledge of Scripture exhibited in her *Magnificat*. This motif shows that to call someone a particular identity bestows special status upon that person, and in this case, even the grammar indicates that Gabriel designates Mary's child with a divine vocative: "The Holy One shall be called—Son of God!"[40]

That God has a Son, however, is not an entirely new thought, for the Psalmist calls on his readers to "Do homage to the Son, lest He become angry, and you perish *in* the way, for His wrath may soon be kindled" (Ps 2:12). This Son appears to stand with *YHWH* as His Anointed (2:2), "My King" (Ps 2:6), and the One of whom the Lord decrees, "'Thou art My Son, Today I have begotten Thee" (Ps 2:8, applied to Jesus in Acts 13:35, Heb 1:5 and 5:5). For this reason, some interpret the title, "Son of God" strictly as a Messianic type and not in ontological terms of divinity;[41] however, the closing benediction of Ps 2:12 ("How blessed are all who take refuge in Him") is also

---

38. Luke uses similar phrases with the same verb also at 1:60 and 2:23.

39. See Gen 17:5, 15; 21:12; and 35:10.

40. The entire sentence lacks a direct object: the noun υἱός appears in the nominative case along with τὸ γεννώμενον ἅγιον—these phrases are certainly set in apposition to each other. It is almost as if υἱὸς θεοῦ acts as a vocative of κληθήσεται so that Gabriel announces, "The holy One shall be called—Son of God!" This exact anarthrous phrase is found elsewhere only at Mark 15:39, "When the centurion, who was standing right in front of Him, saw the way He breathed His last, he said, 'Truly this man was the Son of God!'" (ἀληθῶς οὗτος ὁ ἄνθρωπος υἱὸς θεοῦ ἦν). The lack of the definite article is also notable at Heb 1:2, "God ... in these last days has spoken to us in *His* Son" (ἐλάλησεν ἡμῖν ἐν υἱῷ), The lack of the definite article before υἱός ought to be understood the same way as the anarthrous appearance of πνεῦμα ἅγιον and δύναμις ὑψίστου earlier in the verse, as emphasizing quality of being.

41. Bock, *Luke*, 124, ties "Son of God" to the Davidic reference in Luke 1:32, insisting that the title defines role and not necessarily nature. While he admits that Luke's language may imply ontology, he insists it is only "later texts [which] will make it clear that his messiahship and sonship have even greater connections, which transcend Jesus' earthly sonship ties, but Luke does not make such points explicit here" (p. 125). That observation is certainly true enough, even if Luke "merely" quotes what Gabriel said, but if this verse is not the source text for the divine Sonship of Jesus, what else is?

said of those who trust *YHWH* in Ps 5:11, thus giving equal prerogatives of deity to this Son. Gabriel's announcement of a Son of God, then, should not have been altogether foreign to first-century Jewish readers.[42]

> In terms of its theological significance, the virginal conception explains how the incarnation transpired, though Matthew and Luke do not speak of the event in terms of the incarnation of a pre-existing being. Later theological reflection was also to see in the virginal conception the explanation of how Jesus could be born with a human nature not tainted by original sin.[43]

If a new person is not created, what then is created by the conception of the Son of God?

To use the words of Jesus, He had existed with the glory He had with the Father before the world was (τῇ δόξῃ ᾗ εἶχον πρὸ τοῦ τὸν κόσμον εἶναι παρὰ σοί, John 17:5), so it is not life that His conception engendered, but, at the least, it was His body of flesh (John 1:14), or as Heb 10:5 quotes the Messiah, "a body Thou hast prepared for Me."[44] However, the incarnation does not mean that the divine Son assumed a human body, as Nestorianism teaches: His coming to Mary would be no different from the indwelling of the Holy Spirit in the body of the believer (1 Cor 3:16). Instead, the Son of God also assumed what is essential to human nature, which does not include a propensity to sin.[45]

---

42. There is another OT reference to a Son of God coming from the astonished lips of Nebuchadnezzar, when he exclaims, "Look! I see four men loosed *and* walking *about* in the midst of the fire without harm, and the appearance of the fourth is like a son of *the* gods!" Some versions of the LXX translate the Aramaic *Bar-Elahin* as ὁμοία υἱῷ θεοῦ (Dan 3:25), but it may be assumed that the Babylonian king spoke with polytheistic overtones rather than with Trinitarian indications. Even so, Young, (*Prophecy of Daniel*, 94), reviews how many Christian commentators understand this appearance as a Christophany.

43. Witherington, "Birth of Jesus," 72.

44. Erickson observes, "There is no need nor indication that the Word became sinful flesh—Paul states that God sent His own son in likeness of flesh of sin (ἐν ὁμοιώματι σαρκὸς ἁμαρτίας, Rom 8:3). Likeness is certainly not equality, for the angel's announcement confirms the baby's holiness" (*Word Became Flesh*, 546).

45. Ibid., 547. Erickson suggests that the VB deals with one of problems of the incarnation, how a perfectly holy God could become united with sinful human nature. He notes that in the VB, God is united with sinless humanity in agreement with 1 John 3:5, "Ye know that he was manifested to take away our sins; and in him is no sin."

CONCLUSION: WHAT DOES LUKE 1:35 TEACH?

Despite those who speak of "unhistorical fantasy of a virginal conception,"[46] the fact is that the united witness of the NT presents the Virgin Birth as the human origin of Jesus, leading the reader to ask, what is the point of it? If it is historically true (as this article argues), why did God deem it necessary for His Son to be born of a virgin?

In particular, the VB is essential in confirming the careful investigative research of Luke, as he claimed in his prologue (Luke 1:1–4). If the evangelist is wrong in his opening narrative, how can he be trusted with anything else he records about Jesus?[47]

In addition, this article has shown that Luke 1:35 is the seedbed for the doctrine of the Trinity. Gabriel announces three divine Persons involved in this conception: the Holy Spirit, the Highest, and the Son of God, and a perceptive reader should ask, what is the relationship within this triunity?[48] Despite the contention that "there is no evidence here in the Lucan infancy narrative of Jesus' pre-existence or incarnation,"[49] Gabriel's announcement implies those precise concepts, because "Son of God" describes a divine Person who of necessity has existed eternally.

Furthermore, the language of conception confirms the true humanity of Jesus, that He had a normal human gestation and birth of a human mother. As a human, Jesus developed physically (Luke 2:40) and matured normally (Luke 2:52), so that others assumed He was human (John 7:27) while He even described himself as a Man (John 8:40).

However, Luke 1:35 emphasizes a profound difference of Mary's baby, that He is conceived as the "holy One," so that by the overshadowing of the Spirit and power of the Highest, Jesus assumes a sinless human nature, as confirmed in 1 John 3:15 ("Sin in him not is"). The virginal conception,

---

46. Bostock, "Divine Birth," 332. It is astounding how he can turn the plain meaning of the text on its head. He even insists that the uniqueness of the VB would impugn the humanity of Jesus when the NT texts clearly links the VB to Jesus' humanity.

47. This deduction comes despite the contention of Brown, *Virginal Conception*, 42: "It is doubtful that if there had been no infancy narratives, the Christian faith in Jesus as God's Son would have been really different." The evidence from Scripture and history proves otherwise, for would Brown have written his monumental book, *The Birth of the Messiah*, had there been no infancy narratives?

48. Fitzmyer rightly notes, "The collocation in this verse of 'the Most High,' 'the Son of God,' and 'the holy Spirit' prepared in its own way for the Trinitarian doctrine of a later date," but then he detracts from his observation by commenting, "Only the elements of that doctrine are found here, not the doctrine itself" (*Luke*, 350). If the elements are present, then in elementary form, the doctrine necessarily must also be present.

49. Ibid., 351.

then, was necessary to protect Jesus from the original sin infecting every other progeny of Adam ("that which is born of flesh is flesh," John 3:6) and grant to him the proto-type of every other regenerated nature, "created in holiness of the truth" (Eph 4:24).

Rather than remove Jesus from real humanity, his sinlessness enabled him to give an example of perfect humanity (1 Pet 1:22), to resist all temptation to sin (Heb 2:18), to sympathize with human weakness (Heb 4:15), to offer himself "without blemish to God" (Heb 9:14), and to rise to dwell in bodily form forever (Col 2:19). He performed all these works flawlessly so that he may present his bride "holy and blameless" (Eph 5:27) as believers who share in his holiness by virtue of their union with him.

This doctrine is so imperative that 2 John 1:7 warns that the "deceiver and antichrist" are "those who do not acknowledge Jesus Christ *as* coming in the flesh," but conversely, 1 John 4:2 proclaims, "By this you know the Spirit of God: every spirit that confesses that Jesus Christ has come in the flesh is from God." Thus, the Virginal Conception lies at the heart of a saving confession, as the Nicene Creed recognizes it as the unique entry for the unique Person, God the Son incarnated as the Sinless Man, born of the Virgin Mary, "for us and for our salvation."

BIBLIOGRAPHY

Anselm of Canterbury. *The Major Works*. Edited by Brian Davies and G. R. Evans. Oxford: Oxford University Press, 1998.
Bock, Darrell. *Luke*. Vol. 1, *1:1—9:50*. Edited by Moisés Silva. Baker Exegetical Commentary on the New Testament. Grand Rapids, MI: Baker, 1994.
Bostock, G. "Divine Birth, Human Conception?" *Expository Times* 97 (1986) 260–263.
Brown, Raymond E. *The Birth of the Messiah: A Commentary on the Infancy Narratives in the Gospels of Matthew and Luke*. New Updated edition. New York: Doubleday, 1993.
———. *The Virginal Conception and Bodily Resurrection of Jesus*. Philadelphia: Paulist Press, 1973.
Bultmann, Rudolph. *The History of the Synoptic Tradition*. Peabody, MA: Hendrickson, n.d.
Clark, Alan C. "The Virgin Birth: A Theological Reappraisal." *Theological Studies* 34 (1974) 576–93.
Erickson, Millard J. *The Word Became Flesh*. Grand Rapids, MI: Baker, 1991.
Fitzmyer, Joseph A. *The Gospel According to Luke (I–IX)*. Anchor Bible Series 28. Garden City, NY: Doubleday, 1981.
———. "The Virginal Conception of Jesus in the New Testament." *Theological Studies* 34 (1973) 541–75.
Funk, Robert Walter. *The Acts of Jesus: What Did Jesus Really Do?* San Francisco: Harper, 1998.

Geldenhuys, Norval. *Commentary on the Gospel of Luke*. Edited by F. F. Bruce. The New International Commentary on the New Testament. Grand Rapids, MI: Eerdmans, 1983.

Godet, Frederich. *A Commentary on the Gospel of St. Luke*. Translated by E. W. Shields and M. D. Cusin. New York: Funk and Wagnalls, 1890.

Gromacki, Robert. *The Virgin Birth of Christ*. Grand Rapids, MI: Baker, 1981.

Gundry, Robert. *Matthew*. Grand Rapids, MI: Eerdmans, 1982.

Lange, John Peter. *Commentary on the Holy Scriptures: Critical, Doctrinal, and Homiletical: Mark and Luke*. Translated and edited by Philip Schaff. Grand Rapids, MI: Zondervan, n.d.

Machen, J. Gresham. *The Virgin Birth of Christ*. Grand Rapids, MI: Baker, 1971.

McCready, Douglas. *He Came Down from Heaven*. Downers Grove, IL: InterVarsity, 2005.

Metzger, Bruce M. *A Textual Commentary on the Greek New Testament*. 4th rev. ed. Deutsche Bibelgesellschaft: United Bible Societies, 1994.

Moule, C. F. D. *An Idiom Book of New Testament Greek*. Cambridge: Cambridge University Press, 1953.

Nolland, John. *Luke 1—9:20*. Word Bible Commentary 35a. Dallas: Word, 1989.

Plummer, Alfred. *A Critical and Exegetical Commentary on the Gospel According to St. Luke*. International Critical Commentary. Edinburgh: T&T Clark, 1953.

Robertson, A. T. *A Grammar of the Greek New Testament in the Light of Historical Research*. Nashville: Broadman, 1934.

Sanders, E. P. *The Historical Figure of Jesus*. New York: Penguin, 1993.

Schaberg, Jane. *The Illegitimacy of Jesus: A Feminist Theological Interpretation of the Infancy Narratives*. San Francisco: Harper, 1987.

Schaff, Philip. *The History of Creed*. Vol. 1, *Creeds of Christendom, with a History and Critical Notes*. 6th ed. Grand Rapids, MI: Baker, 1977.

Stein, Robert. *Luke*. New American Commentary 24. Nashville: Broadman, 1992.

von Campenhausen, Hans. *The Virgin Birth in the Theology of the Ancient Church*. Translated by Frank Clarke. Studies in Historical Theology 2. Napierville, IL: Alec R. Allenson, 1964.

Wilson, Robert Dick. "The Meaning of 'Alma' (A.V. 'Virgin') in Isaiah vii.14." *Princeton Theological Review* 26 (1926) 308–16.

Witherington, Ben, III. "Birth of Jesus." In *Dictionary of Jesus and the Gospels*, edited by Joel B. Green and Scot McKnight, 70–72. Downers Grove, IL: InterVarsity, 1992.

Young, Edward J. *The Prophecy of Daniel: A Commentary*. Grand Rapids, MI: Eerdmans, 1949.

Chapter 8

Is Relevance Theory Relevant for Biblical Studies?

—MARGARET SIM
Translation Consultant for SIL

THIS PAPER TACKLES THE usefulness or otherwise of a theory of communication, namely Relevance Theory[1] in relation to biblical studies. It deals with the areas in which a fresh approach to issues such as allusion, quotation, metaphor and irony may enliven debate about the communicatory effect of a text. The intention to communicate is an intrinsic part of human interaction. The question is whether or not it may be applied to the understanding of ancient texts. This theory also examines strategies which humans commonly employ as they interpret utterances ranging from naive optimism to sophisticated understanding. Are there examples of this in the biblical texts itself as well as on the part of its interpreters?[2]

Biblical Studies scholars have been very leery of linguistic approaches to the text and frequently adopt an eclectic approach: an author will select

---

1. The classic text is Sperber and Wilson, *Relevance*. This edition is a review of the original text of 1986 with certain theoretical debates being refined.

2. Recently, SBL reviewed a study purporting to use RT (Relevance Theory will be referred to as RT in this chapter) in interpreting Song of Songs. In fact, the author was using a traditional rabbinical approach and was imposing certain principles of RT on top of this approach. It was not convincing. Also, a new study of Luke-Acts by Steve Smith has been published in which a chapter is devoted to RT as a methodological approach. Of course, others have used RT in the past to good effect — Stephen Pattimore on Revelation — and currently a serious study of the use of the particle γάρ in Romans from the perspective of Relevance Theory is almost complete (Sarah Cassons at King's College, London).

one part of a linguistic theory which they want to use but will ignore the overall view which the theory imposes. The confusion which arises when interpretations are linked to grammatical structures rather than to the pragmatics of the context is another reason for a new approach to the text from the perspective of a cognitive theory of communication. Of course, grammatical structures do impose constraints on interpretation but there has to be a pragmatic interface which interprets such structures. For example, an imperatival form may indicate a wish rather than an actual "command" as in the casual farewell greeting: "have a nice day"!

The areas which I will seek to explore in investigating the usefulness or otherwise of RT are these: 1) intention to communicate: signals of intention; 2) underdeterminacy and inference; 3) strategies for communication; 4) representation of previous utterances as ubiquitous in human communication; 5) literal versus non-literal language: metaphor, irony and 'loose talk'; 6) particles as giving procedural instructions to a reader; 7) syntactic structures as constraints which guide interpretation: what signals do we recognize in the use of subjunctive vs indicative?

INTENTION TO COMMUNICATE

It is a basic assertion of Relevance Theory that an utterance or a text presupposes a desire or intention to communicate:

> Every utterance starts out as a request for the hearer's attention. As a result, it creates an expectation of relevance. It is around this expectation of relevance that our criterion for evaluating possible interpretations is built.[3]

The hearer may decide that the communication is not relevant but the entire enterprise of human interaction is predicated on the belief that we do not throw words in the air but anticipate giving or receiving relevant information. In order to promote the reception of this communication, a speaker or writer may use clues, sometimes small words, which direct the hearer to process the utterance in a particular way, either by blocking a potential interpretation or by increasing the salience of information. This will be dealt with below but is raised here as an integral part of the desire to communicate on the part of humans.

This assumption of a desire to communicate makes the whole enterprise of interpretation of a text possible. Deconstruction may leave us

---

3. Sperber and Wilson, *Relevance*, 8; see also Wilson and Sperber, "Pragmatics and Time."

uncertain if there is any possibility of meaning in a text but RT is based on this belief in a human ability and desire to engage with others in a communicative enterprise.

STRONG ROLE OF INFERENCE IN COMMUNICATION

In spite of a general conviction that we "mean what we say," in fact, meaning is derived from inferences which the speaker or writer intended — or sometimes did not intend — the hearer to draw from the actual words spoken. We do not communicate merely by words which involve a code to be unlocked but by bringing inferences drawn from our own encyclopedic and contextual information. From the trivial but enigmatic example of "Coffee?" to the more complex biblical example of "They did not enter the praetorium so that they would not become polluted,"[4] a hearer or reader brings her[5] own contextual information to the utterance. If a speaker includes *all* the encyclopedic or contextual information in his utterance the hearer will switch off, weighed down under the burden of information which she could access by inference. Of course, a hearer does not always have the necessary contextual or encyclopedic information, at which point communication may fail or be less than completely successful.

Now in stating that we do not communicate by code but by inference, we are recognizing that human communication, from word level to sentence level, is *underdetermined*. In the example above of "Coffee?" a hearer will usually infer that the speaker is offering her a cup of coffee. Of course, in another, less common context, the speaker could be inquiring about the contents of a jar or even the flavor of an ice cream. Context is crucial for a hearer in determining how she will understand the speaker's utterance. The concept of χαρίς in Koine Greek is a wonderful example of underdeterminacy operating at word level.[6]

Recognition of such underdeterminacy is also valuable in our interpretation of participles in Koine Greek. Our predilection for specifying the "type" of each conditional participle masks the fact that the writer or speaker left the relationship between the participle and the main clause of the sentence open.[7] In many examples the relationship might be one of time or

---

4. John 18:28.

5. In this paper the speaker or hearer will be referred to as "he" and the hearer or reader as "she."

6. John Barclay's magisterial study of this topic in *Paul and the Gift* gives an excellent example of the way in which context and presupposition guide interpretation.

7. Wright ("ἁρπαγμός," 321–52), gives a good example of this in his discussion

cause, and often both would be relevant. Constraints on such relationship may be imposed of course, and this will be dealt with below as we consider καίπερ as a constraint on relevance.

A hearer may even infer from actions with no verbal communication. A clear example of this is seen in the presentation in John's Gospel of the Jews/Judeans who had come to mourn with Mary and Martha. Since they assumed that Mary the brother of Lazarus was hurrying out to weep at her brother's tomb, they followed her, but in reality she was making her way to the place where Jesus was waiting.[8] A more serious misunderstanding arose when some Jews from Asia watched Paul enter the temple and assumed that he had taken a Gentile in with him,[9] this on the grounds that they had seen him in the city earlier in the company of an Ephesian man.[10] Do humans infer? All the time.

REPRESENTATION OF UTTERANCE OF ANOTHER

In addition to the issues of underdeterminacy and inferencing we may find RT a useful model to unpack the topic of representation, which is the use of the words or thoughts of another, either directly, indirectly, with or without acknowledgement or with a distancing attitude on the part of the one who is representing.

Intertextuality has been a hot topic in biblical studies for many years now with the focus being on whether or not the representation of a previous utterance or text was intentional or unconscious on the part of the implied author. Another issue has been the extent to which an implied audience might have recognized such representation. In the case of the inclusion of whole sections from the Hebrew Bible, representation is obvious, whereas "allusions" or similarities with an older text may be more problematic in showing intention.

Relevance Theory considers the transference of thought to utterance as being "representation" and further transference, allusion or quotation as being "metarepresentation." I am using the term "representation" in this paper to describe *all* levels of reporting, whether conscious or unconscious

---

of the logical connection of ὑπάρχων to the rest of the sentence in Phil 2:6. The topic of underdeterminacy in participles is dealt with in considerably more detail in Sim, "Underdeterminacy," 348–59.

8. John 11:28–31.

9 Acts 21:27–29.

10. It is interesting to note that the author gives this background information with the addition of γάρ, thus indicating support for the inference that had been drawn, albeit wrongly.

since terms such as "metarepresentation" raise unnecessary emotional barriers for biblical scholars although linguists regard them as essential!

By dealing with this issue as the representation of material or utterances RT is able to highlight a regular human action of representing earlier material with no attribution and no knowledge of the original context. So much of our communication involves representation and advertisements and humor rely on this activity. We may also in addition to representing distance ourselves from the utterance by evidentials[11] such as "apparently," "they say," and "it seems." In this case a speaker or writer is not accepting responsibility for the statements uttered but is attributing them to another source, although that source need not be specified.

Of course, RT literature frequently uses examples from modern oral communication, but it will have already been apparent to you, the reader, that the biblical text is full of such examples. The use of evidentials such as "they say" or "it is said" is ubiquitous in such texts. One clear example from Gal 2:2, 6, 9 of the use of "it seems" or "they seemed" indicates Paul's distancing himself from the opinions of others, the usage in verse six being particularly pointed:

ἀπο δὲ τῶν δοκούντων εἶναί τι, ὁποῖοί ποτε ἦσαν οὐδέν μοι διαφέρει· πρόσωπον ὁ θεὸς ἀνθρώπου οὐ λαμβάνει ἐμοὶ γὰρ οἱ δοκοῦντες οὐδὲν προσανέθεντο, ἀλλὰ τοὐναντίον.

"But from those who seemed to be something—whatever they once were is of no account to me; God does not look on outward appearances/ does not look on the face of man—for those seeming to be something[12] did not place any further requirement on me, but rather. . . ."

The use of "so-called," or even merely "called" in relation to the concept of "gods" in 1 Cor 8:5 also indicates a distancing on the part of the writer. There is also an interesting example in Eph 2:11 of a distancing which is more gentle: "called 'the uncircumcision' by what is called 'circumcision' made by hands in the flesh."

In literal terms these expressions would be an accurate statement of fact but the writer hints at his moving away from such terminology because of the work of Christ by which the two groups might be made one.

---

11. A useful guide to this topic is Ifantidou, *Evidentials*.
12. "Seemed to be something" is the ESV translation of δοκούντων.

USING REPRESENTATION FOR DIFFERENT COMMUNICATORY EFFECTS

Many representations, particularly utterances from the Hebrew Bible used in the New Testament, are prefaced by phrases such as "as it is written," "Isaiah says," "Moses says," "David says," and of course "you have heard it was said." This we may understand as direct representation. The representations which attract attention, however, are those such as "All things are lawful for me"[13] which are now understood to be not the words of Paul the writer, but of some of those in Corinth with whom he is beginning to dialogue. The recognition of such representation makes the argument clearer. An even more interesting phenomenon is a speaker's use of such earlier material with a distancing attitude which is not overtly expressed but which results in verbal irony.

VERBAL IRONY AS REPRESENTATION

It may be more difficult for scholars to accept, however, that when Paul (in particular) represents the words or thoughts of others he is distancing himself from the belief encapsulated in the utterance. Of course, some examples such as "You have enough already, you are rich already, without us you ruled/were kings!"[14] would be widely acknowledged as verbal irony,[15] but the point I want to make is that RT provides a framework for such an interpretation. RT considers verbal irony to be a representation of an utterance from which the speaker distances himself. In examining the above examples from the Corinthian letter, we can see that although Paul did not think that his readers or hearers were rich in spiritual terms they themselves *did* have such an opinion of themselves.

Now in that particular example the second half of the verse makes his thought clear, but that is not always the case. So that we may not be accused of getting out of difficult verses by analyzing them as verbal irony and not the writer's own thought, we can apply three simple criteria in identifying such irony: 1) Is there evidence that the speaker believes the statement he is uttering?; 2) Are we able to identify whose thought or utterance the speaker

---

13. 1 Cor 6:12 and 10:23. Many modern English translations now mark this phrase with quotation marks.

14. 1 Cor 4:8.

15. It is important to recognize that this is only one form of irony and is distinct from the situational irony that may be seen, for example, in John 18:28 mentioned earlier.

is echoing?; 3) Does the context give clues for such identification OR is there a small syntactic signal in the form of a particle which alerts a discerning hearer?

The use of such criteria limits the possible identification of verbal irony because it gives evidence of both the original presentation and also of the writer's dissociative attitude. We may apply these criteria first to examples which are generally accepted to be ironic:

"For you gladly bear with foolish people since you are so wise! Indeed you put up with it if anyone enslaves you, if anyone devours you, if anyone takes (from you), if anyone puts on airs, if anyone hits you in the face. I say in shame, we have been weak!"[16]

English translations put an exclamation mark after "wise" and "foolish" to indicate that Paul did not believe this, but what is not always recognized is that the Corinthians *did* think this. One major issue that stands out in the Corinthian correspondence is the focus on wisdom and their admiration of it. In the very next paragraph of this letter Paul shows that although boasting is foolish, he will in fact boast because that seems to be not only admired but accepted by his audience.[17] There are so many hints of contextual information which we are unable to access almost two thousand years after these events took place, but nevertheless the presence of "false apostles"[18] in the churches of Corinth seems to be an accepted fact. Against this background we can see that the context *does* give clues for interpreting this verse as verbal irony.

A further example accepted as ironic by many scholars is found in 2 Cor 12:13 where there is also a hint of Paul's "weakness" alluded to in the earlier example. I give the example in Greek first and then my own translation since I wish to comment on a vocabulary choice there: τί γὰρ ἐστιν ὃ ἡσσώθητε ὑπὲρ τὰς λοιπὰς ἐκκλησίας, εἰ μὴ ὅτι αὐτὸς ἐγὼ οὐ κατενάρκησα ὑμῶν; χαρίσασθέ μοι τὴν ἀδικίαν ταύτην, "So how did you lose out among (beyond) the other churches apart from the fact that I did not burden you? Forgive me this wrong!"

Now a burden is not a gain but a loss. Paul does not believe that he was burdening the Corinthian churches by refusing to accept support from them, but the idea of patronage may lie behind this complaint from the Corinthians. Ben Witherington[19] suggests that by refusing financial help Paul was also refusing to accept their patronage and this rankled with them.

---

16. 2 Cor 11:19.
17. Note also 1 Cor 5:6 in a different context.
18. 2 Cor 11:14 and "super apostles" in 11:5.
19. Witherington, *Conflict and Community*, 412.

Note also the use of the verb χαρίζομαι. This word is used only in the Pauline correspondence and Luke-Acts although the root χάρις is ubiquitous. The two aspects of meaning found there are "give graciously" and "forgive" (also with the idea of extending favor to someone). Here I suggest that Paul is playing on this double meaning and accepting a mutual relationship, but not as one dependent on receiving their financial support.

These criteria for discerning irony make RT a very useful tool, particularly for the Corinthian correspondence, but also for certain utterances in the Gospel narratives. I mention only two here, Mark 7:9 and Matthew 15:26 with the parallel in Mark 7:27. The words of Mark 7:9 are so close to an ironic statement in the *Discourses* of Epictetus that I include both here for comparison: καὶ ἔλεγεν αὐτοῖς· καλῶς ἀθετεῖτε τὴν ἐντολὴν τοῦ θεοῦ, ἵνα τὴν παράδοσιν ὑμῶν στήτε, "He said to them ‹You have set aside the command of God well, that you might keep your tradition!›"; καλὸς συμπότης καὶ σύνδειπνος Σωκρατικός, "A fine dining companion you would be for Socrates!"

In both cases the context shows that the speaker did *not* think that this behavior was good, but we should also recognize that those to whom the statements were addressed *did* think that their behavior was acceptable.

In the wider discourse of Matthew 15 and Mark 7 the topic of clean and unclean practices are in focus. It is into this discussion that the narrative of the Canaanite or Syro-Phoenician woman has been placed and with that context the irony becomes clearer:

οὐκ ἔστιν καλὸν λαβεῖν τὸν ἄρτον τῶν τέκνων καὶ βαλεῖν τοῖς κυναρίοις,[20] "It isn't good to take the children's bread and throw it to the dogs."

Of course, this has always been a very troublesome verse as Jesus seems to be saying something which his behavior denied, particularly in this wider context in which he both healed and produced food for 4,000 in an area widely assumed to be non-Jewish or at least inhabited by those thought to be of 'suspect' birth. We should be able to recognize that Jesus was in fact representing the common Jewish view of that time, in relation to "Gentiles." Although the sending out of the disciples in chapter 10 of Matthew's Gospel limits their mission to "the lost sheep of the house of Israel," the final verses of the book indicate that the mission is now 'to all nations.'[21]

---

20. Matt 15:26 and Mark 7:27 with slight variation in word order.

21. This topic has been dealt with much more fully and with commentary engagement in Sim, *Relevant Way*.

NON-LITERAL LANGUAGE

Anecdotal evidence suggests that humans assume that most language is to be taken literally, "the meaning" being encapsulated in words which we decode. I have already dealt with the very real fact of inference and contextual and encyclopedic knowledge, but in addition, we should recognize that literalness is *not* privileged. In other words, most human communication, apart from technical papers and scientific dialogue, is couched in non-literal terms. We use metaphor, simile and other tropes with no conscious awareness that we are doing so. RT claims that "literalness in verbal communication is not assumed to be a norm occasionally departed from for specific purposes."[22] This approach enables us to approach human communication in a more unified manner. Rather than having metaphor, simile, and irony as a separate way of communicating, we can see it as a "loose representation" of a literal state of affairs.

LOOSE REPRESENTATION AS A NORMAL COMMUNICATORY PRACTICE

In the previous section, we considered the human capacity for representation, looking at the ways in which this may be seen in the biblical text when an author represents the utterances or writings of another. It is also true that we may represent our own thoughts or those of others in a "loose" way. We should appreciate at the outset of this discussion that the academic preoccupation with accurate and acknowledged quotation is a modern phenomenon. The ancients were much more relaxed about the way in which they represented utterances,[23] as indeed are most people today, apart from an academic context. In the biblical text this is also a very real fact to be taken into consideration.

If we take as an example the pericope of the healing of the young girl as presented by Matthew, Mark and Luke we will see that for them the most relevant information is not identical in each case. The identity of the father of the child is slightly different in each writer, with the child's age only being given by Luke. For the actual healing and the representation of Jesus' words there is "loose" resemblance. Matthew's account is the most succinct with

---

22. Clark, *Relevance Theory*, 257.

23. The comments of Thucydides on his reporting of speeches is pertinent here (*History of the Peloponnesian War*).

the direct speech being omitted:[24] εἰσελθὼν ἐκράτησεν τῆς χειρὸς αὐτῆς, καὶ ἠγέρθη τὸ κοράσιον, "Going in he took her hand and raised the little girl."

Mark includes an Aramaic utterance which we may infer to be presented as the original speech of Jesus, together with a translation into Greek:[25] καὶ κρατήσας τῆς χειρὸς τοῦ παιδίου λέγει αὐτῇ· ταλιθα κουμ, ὅ ἐστιν μεθερμηνευόμενον· τὸ κοράσιον, σοὶ λέγω, ἔγειρε, "And taking the child's hand he says to her, '*Talitha Koum*' which is interpreted as 'Little girl, I am telling you, get up.'"

Finally, Luke[26] is somewhere in between the accounts of Matthew and Mark: αὐτὸς δὲ κρατήσας τῆς χειρὸς αὐτῆς ἐφώνησεν λέγων· παῖς, ἔγειρε, "But taking her hand he called her saying, 'Child, get up.'"

This is loose resemblance, or interpretive resemblance, a cognitive capacity which not only the writers of the New Testament possessed but which we all display on a regular basis in our normal communications with one another. This now leads on to the way in which we view other non-literal language.

THEORETICAL APPLICATION IN TERMS OF METAPHOR

Such "loose" resemblance is an ideal base from which to consider the use of non-literal language such as metaphor, simile and irony. This "loose talk" is not the exact representation of a proposition but it has other very useful effects. Billy Clark claims that metaphoric utterance "achieves its effects not by giving rise to evidence that the communicator intended to convey one strong implicature,[27] or a small set of strong implicatures, but rather by marginally increasing the manifestness of a very wide range of weak implicatures."[28] This may seem overly complicated, but if we examine the communicatory effects of a metaphor as against a literal expression we may find it hard to pin down these communicatory effects but their impact is frequently profound. The picture remains in the memory. Parabolic material is good evidence of this, but perhaps the use of pictures used by John the Baptist of an axe laid to the root of trees and unproductive trees being

---

24. Matt 9:25.
25. Mark 5:41.
26. Luke 8:54.

27. Implicatures are communicated propositions that are not stated explicitly (Clark, *Relevance Theory*, 78).

28. Ibid., 238.

burned is particularly apposite.[29] The effects were so diverse: Herod's response was to put John in prison, but John had 'preached good news to the people.' Clearly this strong metaphor worked but the audience reacted in different ways. Luke's narration of Paul's prediction of what might happen to the churches after he had disappeared from the scene was couched in a vivid metaphor: "I know that fierce wolves will come into you after my departure. They will not spare the flock."[30]

We can interpret this as a warning that false leaders will infiltrate the church for personal gain and that the members of the church will suffer, but this has nothing of the dynamism of the original metaphor. The wider metaphor of believers as a flock with the leaders as shepherds is the background for this warning, but it also may bring to the hearers resonances of Jesus as the 'good shepherd.' Weak implicatures bring wider images.

We are so familiar with the Sermon on the Mount that we do not appreciate the extensive use of metaphor in this discourse. Perhaps an exception might be the exhortation 'If your eye causes you to stumble/sin, take it out and throw it away from you!' We may refuse to take that injunction literally but the picture offered is very strong. A wider context for this metaphor is presented later in this Gospel,[31] with warnings of the extensive damage that can be caused by looking, going, or acting in a manner which causes someone else to sin. The strength of the warning is presented as the need for drastic action if such behavior cannot be stopped, but the use of metaphor highlights that danger and makes it one of the most memorable sayings in this Gospel.

STRATEGIES FOR INTERPRETATION

What has been said so far regarding a communicator's intention to communicate has been predicated on that communicator's integrity and ability. It may be the case that a communicator is anxious to communicate with integrity but is not as competent as he might be. It is also possible that this communicator may wish to communicate in a more manipulative way. Dan Sperber[32] has suggested strategies for interpreting such intentions as follows: *naive optimism* is when a hearer assumes that the speaker is honestly communicating. If this does not produce an utterance which is relevant to her then she may move on to another strategy, namely *cautious optimism*, in

---

29. Luke 3:18–20.
30. Acts 20:29.
31. Matt 18:7–9.
32. Sperber, "Understanding Verbal Understanding."

which she suspects that the speaker may be honest but less than competent in his utterance. This is frequently the case where speaker and hearer do not share the same cultural background, since encyclopedic knowledge and contextual information always play a part of communication.

Of course, it may be the case that the hearer knows that the speaker wants her to derive a certain understanding from his utterance and is aware that he has guided her in this direction *but* she suspects that she is being manipulated. She will then employ a strategy of *sophisticated understanding* which may be interpreted as "he wants me to think that. . .but. . ." This is not the same as an outright lie but a manipulation of facts. We can see a good example of this narrated in John's Gospel.

After Mary has anointed Jesus' feet with very expensive ointment Judas is presented as complaining "Why wasn't this perfume sold for three hundred denarii and given to the poor?" John then contrasts the ostensive utterance — what Judas wanted hearers to think of as his motivation — with his actual motive: εἶπεν δὲ τοῦτο οὐχ ὅτι περὶ τῶν πτωχῶν ἔμελεν αὐτῷ, ἀλλ' ὅτι κλέπτης ἦν καὶ τὸ γλωσσόκομον ἔχων τὰ βαλλόμενα ἐβάσταζεν, "He didn›t say this because he cared for the poor, but because he was a thief and being the treasurer/holding the bag took away what was in it."

John presents Judas as wishing to communicate his care for the poor, but a sophisticated understanding derives a very different interpretation. The statement was not a lie — no doubt the sale of the ointment would have brought a large sum — but the motivation for the statement was doubted. The two divergent interpretations are clearly marked by οὐχ ὅτι . . .ἀλλ' ὅτι. In addition, there is the implicature that *if* the perfume had been sold and the money "put in the bag," then Judas would have benefitted. This is not stated but it is a good example of what RT calls "implicature." The responsibility for deriving this implicature rests with the interpreter.

Clark[33] summarizes these strategies as "an interpreter who is a naive optimist will expect actual relevance, a cautious optimist will expect attempted relevance and a sophisticated understander will expect purported relevance."

It should be understood, however, that a speaker may be mistaken, but that is a different matter. In these strategies, it is the communicatory intention which is being examined. These are strategies which we can recognize as being a part of normal human communication today particularly the propensity to finish off a sentence for someone who hesitates but also correcting a word which we assume has been wrongly used by the speaker.

---

33. Clark, *Relevance Theory*, 351.

These strategies go a good way towards explaining the misunderstandings which arise regularly in human communication and in addition may be seen to illuminate the misunderstandings which arose between Jesus and his disciples. Some of these would also be attributable to the use of metaphorical language but the strategy employed was one of "naive optimism."[34]

SIGNALS GUIDING INTERPRETATION

The human ability to guide interpretation by using small semantic clues is also widespread although we do not always recognize these small markers for what they are, particularly in a language which is not our own. In English, the use of "but" makes us process what follows as an exception to what has been said previously, or at least makes us more aware of the content to follow.[35] In Koine Greek there are particles such as ὅτι, ἵνα, καίπερ, γάρ, οὖν which give procedural instructions to a hearer or reader. I suggest that dealing with such particles in this way rather than insisting on a fixed lexical meaning for them is a much more helpful way of understanding the communicative intention of the speaker or writer. There is no space in this paper to discuss all of these at length but I have dealt with them in detail elsewhere.[36]

A FRESH ANALYSIS OF INA AND OTI AS GIVING INSTRUCTIONS TO THE READER

The second of these two particles may be described as indicating an actual state of affairs. That means that when a writer intends to show what someone has thought, said, or believed, he will introduce this by the particle ὅτι, but when showing what might be the case — a potential state of affairs — he will introduce this potential state of affairs by using the particle ἵνα. If we see a speaker as giving us procedural instructions then we may avoid the crass translations which result when we insist on a fixed lexical meaning for one of these particles.[37]

---

34. For example, Matt 16:5–12.

35. In RT studies, many articles have been written about this small word but I do not wish to be sidetracked by this when the real focus is on Koine Greek.

36. Sim, *Marking Thought and Talk*, deals with ἵνα in depth, and ὅτι more briefly; Sim, *Relevant Way to Read*; οὖν and γάρ is dealt with in Sim, "Καίπερ," and also in a forthcoming thesis by Sarah Cassons.

37. Theologically driven interpretations have been pressed into service for several texts, but one of the most outstanding is Mark 4:12. This together with the multiple

One very obvious example of this in the case of ἵνα is found in 1 John 1:9:

ἐὰν ὁμολογῶμεν τὰς ἁμαρτίας ἡμῶν, πιστός ἐστιν καὶ δίκαιος, ἵνα ἀφῇ ἡμῖν τὰς ἁμαρτίας καὶ καθαρίσῃ ἡμᾶς ἀπὸ πάσας ἀδικίας, "If we confess our sins he is faithful and just *in that* he may/should forgive our sins and cleanse us from all wrong."

It is because God is just and faithful that he forgives our sins, not "in order that" which is usually taken as the "root" meaning of this particle. The solution to this is not by deciding that this particle may mean "so that" but to look for a wider explanation for its work. Such an approach gives greater clarity to a verse such as John 9:3: ἀπεκρίθη Ἰησοῦς· οὔτε οὗτος ἥμαρτεν οὔτε οἱ γονεῖς αὐτοῦ, ἀλλ' ἵνα φανερωθῇ τὰ ἔργα τοῦ θεοῦ ἐν αὐτῷ. ἡμᾶς δεῖ ἐργάζεσθαι τὰ ἔργα τοῦ πέμψαντός με ἕως ἡμέρα ἐστίν, "Jesus replied, 'Neither this man sinned nor his parents, but the works of God must be made/become clear in him. We must do the works of the one who sent me while it is day.'"

As seen in this example, frequently there is a deontic aspect to the utterance which this particle introduces. The various examples in the Gospel of John following the verb "to be" show this clearly. To find a purposive function for the particle when it follows a stative verb is obtuse, but taking it as giving instructions to process the utterance as deontic (what should be done) is both logical and linguistically justifiable. I give only two examples below and a few others in the footnote: αὕτη ἐστὶν ἡ ἐντολὴ ἡ ἐμή, ἵνα ἀγαπᾶτε ἀλλήλους καθὼς ἠγάπησα ὑμᾶς,[38] "This is my command, that you should love one another as I loved you."

The clause introduced by ἵνα explicates the content of the command, namely what a disciple 'should' do. Another example of a similar explication occurs after the verb συμφέρει:

συμφέρει ὑμῖν ἵνα ἐγὼ ἀπέλθω,[39] "It is necessary for you that I go away."

Further examples may be seen throughout the New Testament[40] but the heavy occurrence of this particle in the Johannine material makes the need for a fresh analysis much clearer.

---

interpretations offered by commentators is dealt with at length in Sim, "Καίπερ."

38. John 15:12, with other examples in the same chapter in verses 8, 17, and 34.

39. John 16:7, but other examples may be found, such as in 11:50 and with συνήθεια in 18:39.

40. Matt 5:29, 30; 18:6.

ΚΑΙΠΕΡ AS A GUIDE TO INTERPRETATION

This small particle occurs only five times in the New Testament and three of these occurrences are found in Hebrews. It occurs with participles which in Koine Greek are underdetermined, in other words the logical relationship of the participle to the main clause, or the rest of the sentence is left to the reader to identify. This relationship may be causal, temporal, conditional, concessive, or may even indicate purpose, especially if the participle is in the future tense. Καίπερ guides the reader to a concessive interpretation. This has been dealt with in detail in Sim, "Καίπερ As a Constraint on Relevance," but I offer one example here to make my meaning clear: καίπερ ὢν υἱός, ἔμαθεν ἀφ' ὧν ἔπαθεν τὴν ὑπακοήν, "Although he was a son he learned obedience through the things he suffered."

Now, for modern Westerners this particle might be seen as superfluous but in a culture where fathers were expected to discipline their sons this particle is necessary. A reader from another culture could easily read the relationship as causal: "because he was a son he learned obedience. . ." The author even discusses this in 12:5–11. The point at issue is the special nature of the Son who through suffering was "made perfect." The particle guides the reader to this interpretation.

SYNTACTIC GUIDES TO RELEVANCE

Speakers often make use of syntactic forms to guide a hearer to a relevant meaning of their utterance. The subjunctive form does seem to have disappeared from the normal speech of younger speakers of English but the use of an introductory "like" often signals potentiality or lack of specificity. Somehow it functions as a step back from a definite statement.

In Koine Greek or older or formal English, however, the subjunctive has been used to good effect in indicating some indefiniteness about a proposition. The mood has been described like this in traditional grammars and I would suggest that it is used to describe a potential state of affairs. An actual state of affairs would be couched in the indicative mood. This could be seen in the previous section when we considered the different functions of the particles ἵνα and ὅτι as giving procedural instructions to a hearer to process the utterance introduced as a potential or actual state of affairs.

The relevance of this may be seen in the way in which different cultures deal with the concept of "hope," because the strength of ἐλπίς, ἐλπίζω is so much weaker at least in a modern British context. In that setting "hope" is a general understanding that something might happen, but there is no sense of probability that it will happen. In Koine Greek, however, as well as other non-British contexts hope is a much more positive concept. The verb ἐλπίζω is followed by ὅτι in Luke 24:21 to introduce not only what they "hoped" for in a weak "British" sense, but what they expected. If the verb had indicated a less certain outcome, then another particle would have introduced the statement and a subjunctive verb would have followed.[41] Indeed Paul's explanation of what "hoping" involves is laid out in Rom 8:25 ("we wait for it with patience.")

SIGNALS OF TIME AND TENSE

We can say that there is no fixed time in tense forms, but pragmatically, we are compelled to make decisions. Such decisions are influenced by context and our own presuppositions. Temporal intervals are "left open in semantics and narrowed down in pragmatics."[42] This is hugely relevant for the tense/aspect debate because it takes the heat out of the false dichotomy concerned with these terms and picks apart the way in which we actually understand the time frame. I have huge respect for Stanley Porter and the way in which he has brought this debate into mainstream discussion, but I have noticed that he himself makes pragmatic decisions without always acknowledging this. In his *Idioms of the Greek New Testament*[43] he gives translations which are certainly possible but far from the only ones which might be entertained. The translator's or exegete's own presuppositions also play a major part.[44]

Of course, adverbs and accompanying phrases may make a time reference clear, but in Koine Greek there are many verbs which only display certain tense-forms, making the issue of choice on the part of the writer much less relevant. Further, as Basil Mandilaras points out, the semantic field of a particular verb may limit the possible options open to a speaker: "Aspect depends not only on the use of the particular tense, but also on the meaning of the particular verb involved. Sometimes, too, adverbial expressions in the sentence point to a differentiation of aspect, which tense alone could not determine definitely."[45] It is always important to take into account the view of a speaker of Greek, even if he is temporarily distanced from the

---

41. Other examples of this construction may be seen in Acts 24:26; 1 Cor 1:10, 13; Phlm 22.

42. Clark, *Relevance Theory*, 150.

43. Porter, *Idioms*.

44. Porter does recognize this in some of his examples, but the role of pragmatics is frequently ignored. Among several pertinent examples are Rom 5:11 and Eph 5:29.

45. Mandilaras, *Verb in the Greek*.

period of Koine. What is interesting about the work of Mandilaras is that it is based not on the literary Koine but on everyday communications such as letters, instructions, contracts, etc.

CONCLUSION

This piece is not presented as suggesting that Relevance Theory has the answer to every exegetical problem, but RT is offered as an introduction to a different approach to the way in which humans communicate. This has also been a very cursory introduction to the potential of the theory, with more detailed analysis and heavy linguistic vocabulary being avoided. From my own perspective, I find that RT gives particularly useful insights into the text of the Hebrew Bible and the Greek New Testament. The most useful of these insights are as follows: 1) the intention to communicate the bringing together of text, author, and reader; 2) the crucial role of underdeterminacy and inference; 3) representation as ubiquitous and giving a good account of verbal irony; 4) limited use of literal language versus 'loose' representation; and 5) explanation for failure of communication. More than this, however, it actually works in everyday situations of life. It describes rather than prescribes the way in which we actually communicate with one another, even when we have never heard of Relevance Theory.

BIBLIOGRAPHY

Arrian, Flavius. *Epictetus, The Discourses.* Translated by W. A. Oldfather. Loeb Classical Library 131. Cambridge: Harvard University Press, 1998.
Barclay, J. M. G. *Paul and the Gift.* Grand Rapids, MI: Eerdmans, 2015.
Clark, Billy. *Relevance Theory.* Cambridge: Cambridge University Press, 2013.
Ifantidou, Elly. *Evidentials and Relevance.* Amsterdam: John Benjamins, 2001.
Mandilaras, Basil. *The Verb in the Greek Non-literary Papyri.* Athens: Hellenic Ministry of Culture and Sciences, 1973.
Pattemore, Stephen "The People of God in the Apocalypse: A Relevance Theoretic Study." PhD diss., University of Otago, Dunedin, 2001.
Porter, Stanley E. *Idioms of the Greek New Testament.* Sheffield: JSOT, 1992.
Sim, Margaret G. "Καίπερ as a Constraint on Relevance." In *Festschrift for Stephen Levinsohn.* Logos Biblical Software, 2011.
———. *Marking Thought and Talk in New Testament Greek.* Eugene, OR: Wipf and Stock, 2010.
———. *A Relevant Way to Read.* Cambridge: James Clarke, 2016.
———. "Underdeterminacy in Greek Participles." *Bible Translator* 55 (2004) 348–59.
Sperber, D. "Understanding Verbal Understanding." In *What is Intelligence?*, edited by J. Khalfa, 179–98. Cambridge: Cambridge University Press, 1994.

Sperber, D., and D. Wilson. *Relevance: Communication and Cognition.* Oxford: Blackwell, 1995.

Thucydides. *History of the Peloponnesian War.* Loeb Classical Library 108. Cambridge: Harvard University Press, 1919.

Wilson, D., and D. Sperber. "Pragmatics and Time." In *Relevance Theory: Applications and Implications,* edited by R. Carston and S. Uchida, 8. Amsterdam: John Benjamins, 1998.

Witherington, Ben, III. *Conflict and Community in Corinth.* Grand Rapids, MI: Eerdmans, 1995.

Wright, N.T. "ἁρπαγμός and the Meaning of Philippians 2:5–11." *Journal of Theological Studies* 37 (1986) 321–52.

Chapter 9

Disarming Significant Textual Issues in Jude

*A Text Critical Study and Interpretation of Jude 5 and 12**

—HERBERT W. BATEMAN IV
Cyber-Center for Biblical Studies, Kregel Publishers

INTRODUCTION

WHILE JUDE IS A short letter with 452 to 464 Greek words,[1] Bauckham considers, "the textual critical problems are remarkably numerous and difficult."[2] Nevertheless, several significant text critical studies have been published that have advanced the reliability of the text of Jude.[3] Yet two text critical issues continue to plague commentators. Determining the variant of

---

* This chapter incorporates edited portions from Bateman, *Interpreting the General Letters*, 148–69, 250–69; and Bateman, *Jude*, 3–10, 160–65, 237–38, 274–91. Both are used by permission.

1. Jude's actual size depends on the Greek text. In NA28, Jude has 464 Greek words. In the Majority Text, Jude has 452 Greek words. In Robinson and Pierpont's Greek text, Jude has 452 Greek words. In SBL's Greek text, Jude has 459 Greek words (*Nestle-Aland's Novum Testamentum Graece*, 28th ed; Hodges and Farstad, *Greek New Testament*, 720–21; Robinson and Pierpont, *New Testament*, 351–52; Holmes, *Greek New Testament*). For a chart with a total breakdown of the number of words per verse, see Bateman, *Jude*, 3–4.

2. Bauckham, *Jude and the Relatives*, 135.

3. Wasserman, *Epistle of Jude*; Albin, *Judasbrevet*; and Landon, *Text-Critical Study*.

"Lord" (κύριος) or "Jesus" (Ιησοῦς) in verse 5 and "your love-*feasts*" (ἀγάπαις ὑμῶν) or "your deceptions" (perhaps translated "your pleasures"; ἀγάταις ὑμῶν) in verse 12 remains a challenge and is the focus of this chapter. But first a brief discussion about how to approach these text critical issues is warranted.

As presented in his *New Testament Textual Criticism: A Concise Guide* as well as his edited volume: *Rethinking New Testament Textual Criticism*,[4] David Alan Black's reasoned eclectic approach is followed — an approach practiced by several well-known exegetes and text critical scholars — the results of which are often reflected in NA[28], UBS[4], and SBL Greek texts.[5] Consequently, the variant readings in Jude 5 and 12 are evaluated first based upon *manuscript evidence* provided in the chart entitled "Jude's Manuscript Evidence." Consideration is given to the manuscript's date and character, the geographical distribution of the manuscript evidence, and genealogical solidarity of a variant reading. Second, *internal transcriptional* and *intrinsic* probabilities are evaluated because accidental scribal errors abound in Jude.[6] As a result, we look at the variants in Jude 5, 12, and 22-23 from every possible angle in order to determine what may be the *best* textual reading before addressing their significance for interpretation.

JUDE 5: JESUS (ΙΗΣΟΥΣ) OR LORD (ΚΥΡΙΟΣ)

While there are two rather significant text critical issues in Jude 5, we will focus attention on one.[7] Does Jude 5 read "Jesus" (Ιησοῦς) or does it read

---

4. Black, *New Testament Textual Criticism*; Black, *Rethinking New Testament Textual Criticism*.

5. Metzger, *Text of the New Testament*; Fee, "Rigorous or Reasoned Eclecticism," 174-97; Holmes, "Case for Reasoned Eclecticism," 77-100; Wallace, "Majority Text," 150-69; Wallace, "Laying a Foundation," 33-56; and Ehrman, "Methodological Development," 22-45.

6. There are *transcriptional* errors: homoeoteleuton (= similar ending; e.g., vv. 1, 15), metathesis (= changing the order of a letter or a word; e.g., v. 1, 17, 23), and parablepsis (= a looking to one side; e.g., vv. 1, 18, 21). *Intentional* scribal errors also exist: grammatical improvements (e.g., vv. 3, 19), harmonization of parallel passages (e.g., vv. 3, 9, 14, 17, 25), elimination of apparent discrepancies (e.g., vv. 1, 8, 18, 25), and a scribe's gloss or perhaps clarification for *possible* doctrinal reasons (e.g., vv. 3, 4, 14, 15). Furthermore, the more difficult readings or the awkward readings, whereby an explanation for the variant cannot be offered, are evident (e.g., vv. 8, 18) as well as some more compelling shorter readings (e.g., vv. 14, 19).

7. The other significant text critical problem is a grammatical and theological issue. Does the text read "that the Lord delivered once" (ὅτι ὁ κύριος ἅπαξ ... σώσας) or does it read "although you know all things once for all" (εἰδότας ὑμᾶς ἅπαξ πάντα)? Grammatically, the question is whether ἅπαξ modifies σώσας: "delivered once" and

"Lord" (κύριος)? This is a theological issue in that the presence of "Jesus" (Ἰησοῦς) would appear to support the deity of Jesus.[8]

ὅτι Ἰησοῦς . . . τὸ δεύτερον τοὺς μὴ πιστεύσαντας ἀπώλεσεν,

that Jesus . . . *later* destroyed those who did not believe the second time

ὅτι κύριος . . . τὸ δεύτερον τοὺς μὴ πιστεύσαντας ἀπώλεσεν,

that the Lord . . . *later* destroyed those who did not believe the second time

Manuscripts supporting the first reading, [ὁ] Ἰησοῦς is impressive. "Jesus" (Ἰησοῦς) or "Lord Jesus" (κύριος Ἰησοῦς) has significant support from the Alexandrian (A B 33 81 1241 1881 2344; cf. cop^bo; Lord Jesus 1735), Byzantine (eth Cyril), Western (it^ar vg Jerome), and Independent (6 88 322 323 915) texts. Of these, four manuscripts are of great value because they are believed to preserve an ancestral textual reading whose dates range from as early as the fourth century (uncial: B) to the fourteenth-fifteenth century (minuscules: 322 915 1881).[9] The "Jesus" (Ἰησοῦς) reading is favored and represented in several Greek texts (NA[28] SBL[ed] cf. Alford[1894]), English translations (RSV ESV NET NLT[SE]), and commentaries.[10]

The manuscripts supporting the second reading, "Lord" (κύριος) without the article, is equally significant. It has support from the Alexandrian (*a* Y), Byzantine (177 337 465), and Independent (618 633 1149 1738) texts. An overwhelming amount of support for "the Lord" (ὁ κύριος) reading with the article appears in the Alexandrian (1409 1292), Byzantine (K L 049 056 0142 18 76 82 90 97 105 110 133 141 201 203 204 223 226 250 302 308 309 314 . . . 1175 . . . 1727 and others), and Independent (61 254 307 326 436 453 620 630 1067 1726 1836 1902 2200 2374) texts. Of these, five manuscripts are of great value because they are believed to preserve an

---

thereby part of the ὅτι clause; or whether ἅπαξ is an adverb of manner to "knowing" (εἰδότας) within the participial clause: "although you know once *for all*." The latter view appears to draw attention to faith and known teaching. Does Jude make a parallel and thereby reinforcing statement about the faith passed down *once for all* mentioned in verse 3 as a way to underscore that Jude's readers already know the teaching of the faith? For a complete discussion of this issue, see Bateman, *Jude*, 162-65.

8. A more detailed discussion of this textual issue appears in Bateman, *Interpreting the General Letters*, 148-69, which was later revised for *Jude*, 160-62.

9. For an exhaustive listing of manuscripts and their dates supporting a "Jesus" (Ἰησοῦς) or "Lord Jesus" (κύριος Ἰησοῦς) reading, see Wasserman, *Epistle of Jude*, 148-49, 106-17.

10. For a defense for "Jesus" as the original reading see Hanson, *Jesus Christ*, 136-38; Fossum, "Kyrios Jesus," 226-43; Osburn, "Text of Jude 5," 107-15; cf. Metzger, *Textual Commentary*, 724; Sellen, "Die Häretiker," 206-25, esp. 212-13; Paulsen, *Der Zweite Petrusbrief*, 60-61; Green, *Jude and 2 Peter*, 63, 65, 77-78.

ancestral textual reading whose dates for reading "Lord" (κύριος) with or without the article range from as early as the fourth century (uncial: a) to the fourteenth-fifteenth century (minuscules: 254 322 1067 2200).[11] Several Greek texts (NA[27] UBS[4] MT[2] RP[2005]; cf. Tisendorf[1872] Nestle[1816] *Hexapla*[1841] WH[1885]) and translations (KJV, ASV, NRSV, NASB[95] NIV, CEB, WEB; cf. Tyndale[1526] Bishops) are decidedly in favor of "Lord" (κύριος) or "the Lord" (ὁ κύριος).[12]

Jude's Manuscript Evidence[A]			
Alexandrian	Western	Byzantine	Independent
Papyri P[72] (3rd 4th c.) P[74] (7th c.) P[78] (3rd 4th	No papyri	No papyri	No papyri
Uncials a 01 (4th c.) A 02 (5th c.) B 03 (4th c.) C 04 (5th c.) Y 044 (8th-9th c.)	No uncials	**Uncials** K 018 (9th c.) L 020 (9th c.) P 025 (9th c.) 049 (9th c.) 056 (10th c.) 0142 (10th c.)	**Uncials** 0251 (6th c.)

---

11. For an exhaustive listing of manuscripts and their dates that support "Lord" (κύριος) or "the Lord" (ὁ κύριος) reading, see Wasserman, *Epistle of Jude*, 148–49, 106–17.

12. For a defense of "Lord" as the original reading, see Metzger, *Textual Commentary*, 657; Landon, *Text-Critical Study*, 75–76.

Minuscules	No minuscules	Minuscules	Minuscules
33 (9th c.)		18 (1364)	5 (13th c.)
81 (1044)		596 (11th c.)	6 (13th c.)
1241 (12th c.)		1175 (11th c.)	61 (16th c.)
1243 (11th c.)		2144 (11th c.)	88 (12th c.)
1292 (13th c.)		*Byz* = a UBS group symbol	254 (14th c.)
1409 (14th c.)			307 (10th c.)
1735 (10th c.)		*M* = a NA group symbol	322 (15th c.)
1739 (10th c.)			323 (12th c.)
1852 (13th c.)			326 (10th c.)
1881 (14th c.)			431 (12th c.)
2344 (11th c.)			436 (11th/12th c.)
			453 (14th c.)
			621 (11th c.)
			623 (1037)
			630 (12th/13th c.)
			915 (13th c.)
			1067 (14th c.)
			1836 (10th c.)
			1845 (10th c.)
			1846 (11th c.)
			2200 (14th c.)
			2298 (11th c.)
			2374 (13th/14th c.)
Versions	**Versions**	**Versions**	
cop^{sa} (3–5th c.)	it^{ar} (9th c.)	syr^{ph} (615/616)	
cop^{bo} (3–5th c.)	it^{t} (11th c.)	syr^{h} (507/508)	
	vg^{cl} (1592)	arm (5th c.)	
	vg^{ms} indep. readings	eth (5th c.)	
		geo (5th c.)	
	vg^{ww} (1889–1954)	slav = Old Church Slavonic (9th c.)	

Church Fathers	Church Fathers	Church Fathers	
Didymus of Alexandria (398)	Augustine (430)	Eusebius (339–40)	
	Jerome (420)	Chrysostom (407)	
Clement of Alexander (215)	Lucifer of Calaris (370/371)	Cyril of Jerusalem (386)	
Clement^{lat} Latin trans. (540)	Priscillian (385)	Fulgentius (532)	
Cyril of Alexander (d. 444)			
Origen^{lat}, Latin translation			

A. The dating of all the manuscripts is based upon Wasserman, *Epistle of Jude*, 106–17 and Aland and Aland, *Text of The New Testament*, 96–159. Generally, Wasserman (W) and Aland/Aland's (AA) manuscript dates are in agreement with eleven (11) exceptions: 5 (W 13th; AA 14th), 18 (W 1364; AA 14th), 323 (W 12th; AA 11th), 326 (W 9th; AA 12th), 431 (W 12th; AA 11th), 436 (W 11th/12th; AA 11th), 621 (W 11th; AA 14th), 630 (W 12th/13th; AA 14th), 1175 (W 10th; AA 10th), 1735 (W 10th; AA 11th/12th), 2374 (W 13th/14th; AA 13th). Since Wasserman's dates are newer and based on new examinations of the MSS, they are considered more reliable than Aland's. This chart first appeared in Bateman, *Interpreting the General Letters*, 148–69 and later revised for *Jude*, 7–9.

Unfortunately, the manuscript evidence is less than conclusive. While several dependable uncial texts favor a "Jesus" (Ἰησοῦς) reading (A B), the "Lord" (κύριος) reading with or without the article has some consistent uncial support (א Y K L 049). Yet the "Lord" (κύριος) reading has greater geographical support in that the reading is represented among the Alexandrian, Western, and Byzantine geographical regions. Furthermore, the split reading between "Jesus" (Ἰησοῦς) (A B) and "Lord" (κύριος) (א Y K L 049) within the Alexandrian family ought not to be overlooked because it weakens support for both readings. Nevertheless, a slight edge appears to exist for the "Lord" (κύριος) reading.

Evaluating internal evidence begins with a contextual observation. Verse 5 is part of a collection of verses that recalls three past rebellions: the rebellion of the Jewish people *against God's* (or is it *Jesus'*) *leading* in the wilderness (v. 5c-d), the rebellion of angelic beings *against God's residential placement* (v. 6), and the rebellion of Gentiles living in urban centers *against God's marital norms* (v. 7).[13] All three rebellions share the same outcome: divine judgment. In evaluating the intrinsic probabilities against the "Jesus" reading is twofold: (1) the mention of "Jesus" without the title "Christ" is

---

13. Bateman, "Rebellion and God's Judgment," 454–78.

unparalleled in Jude and (2) the mention of Jesus as the one who delivers the Exodus generation is unparalleled in the New Testament (yet cf. 1 Cor 10:4). The intrinsic probability in favor of "Lord" is also twofold: (1) the second example of divine judgment on angelic beings kept for judgment is executed by God in that just as believers are kept for Jesus by God (1:1b) fallen angels are kept for judgment by God (v. 6a) and (2) the presence of "Lord" (κύριος) without the article occurs elsewhere in Jude as the one who executes judgment against Satan (v 9) and against all the godless (v. 14). Consequently, it seems that a scribe may have intentionally inserted "Jesus" into the text. Why? Perhaps he wanted to underscore the deity of Jesus. Furthermore, the shorter reading "Lord" (κύριος) seems more than likely because "Lord" (κύριος) appears elsewhere in Jude without the article (vv. 9, 14); yet over time, an article was inserted for grammatical clarification.[14] Thus based upon both the external and internal evidence, the preferred reading is "Lord" (κύριος).

So how does this textual decision affect interpretation? While some commentators may argue that "Lord" is a reference to Jesus,[15] it seems Jude recalls God's indiscriminant judgment of three groups: the Exodus generation (v. 5c),[16] fallen angels (v. 6), and Gentile cities (v. 7). These three historical rebellions and outcomes were part of Judea's Jewish literary tradition that appear in *Sirach* 16:5–8, 3 Maccabees 2:4–7, *Damascus Document* 2:17—3:12, and other Jewish literature. They are foundational to Jude's ultimate argument whereby he denounces rebellion among his contemporary audience. Thus, the textual reading "Lord" (κύριος) underscores God's condemnation of all rebellion.

JUDE 12: LOVE-FEASTS OR DECEPTIONS

Whether the text reads "your love-*feasts*" (ἀγάπαις ὑμῶν) or whether it reads "your deceptions" (perhaps translated "your pleasures"; ἀγάταις ὑμῶν) in verse 12 is a lexical challenge.

---

14. Definite nouns need no article. Wallace, *Greek Grammar*, 243. Omission of the article with "Lord" is common in the New Testament. (Turner, *A Grammar*, 174). Textual evidence supports an anarthrous reading. (Wasserman, *Epistle of Jude*, 266).

15. Bigg, *Epistles of St. Jude*, 328; Bauckham, *Jude*, 42–43, 49; Horrell, *Epistles of Peter*, 120; Davids, *Letters of 2 Peter*, 48; Senior and Harrington, *1 Peter*, 195–96.

16. Exodus Advocates: Chaine, *Les épîtres catholiques*, 300; Green, *2 Peter and Jude*, 163; Kelly, *Commentary*, 255; Cantinat, *Les épîtres de Saint Jacques*, 302; Fuchs and Reymond, *La deuxiéme épître de saint Pierre*, 160–62; Kistemaker, *Peter and Jude*, 376; Hiebert, *Second Peter*, 231; Vögtle, *Der Judasbrief*, 35, 39; Moo, *2 Peter and Jude*, 239–40; Schreiner, *1, 2 Peter*, 445; Donelson, *I & II Peter*, 177–78.

Οὗτο εἰσιν ... ἐν ταῖς ἀγάταις ὑμῶν σπιλάδες,

These *godless people* are ... hidden reefs at your deceptions (or pleasures)

Οὗτο εἰσιν ... ἐν ταῖς ἀγάπαις ὑμῶν σπιλάδες

These *godless people* are ... hidden reefs at your love feasts

Manuscripts supporting the first reading, "your deceptions" or "your pleasures" (ταῖς ἀγάταις ὑμῶν), has minimal support from the Alexandrian (A 1243), Byzantine (337 618 1738), and Independent (88 104 459 460 915 1425 1842 1845 1846 2492) manuscripts. Of these, several manuscripts are of great value because they are believed to preserve an ancestral textual reading whose dates range from the fourth century (uncial A) to the twelfth and thirteenth centuries (minuscules 88 915).[17]

The manuscripts supporting the second reading "your love-*feasts*" (ταῖς ἀγάπαις ὑμῶν; literally, "at your love") has substantial manuscript support from the Alexandrian (P[72] a B 044 33 81 1175 1241 1292 1409 1735 1739 1844 1881 2344), the Byzantine (K L 3 18 57 76 97 105 110 141 ... 2431 2466 2483 etc.), Independent (322 323 436 945 1067 1505 1611 2138 2298) manuscripts, contemporary Greek texts (NA[27] UBS[4] RP[2005] MT[4]; cf. Nestle[1816] Tischendorf[1872] WH[1885] Alford[1894]), and numerous English translations (KJV ASV NASB[95] NRSV ESV NET WEB; cf. Tyndale[1526] Geneva[1559] Bishop). Of these, several manuscripts are of great value because they are believed to preserve an ancestral textual reading and whose dates range from the fourth century (papyri: p[72]; uncials: *aleph* B) to the fifteenth century (minuscule 322).[18] Despite the strong external evidence in favor of "your love-*feasts*" (ταῖς ἀγάπαις ὑμῶν), the geographical support for both readings as well as the genealogical split within the Alexandrian (A versus p[72]; uncials: a B) and Byzantine (K L versus 1738) families are problematic. Nevertheless, the "love-*feasts*" (ἀγάπαις) reading has a slight edge.

Evaluation of the internal evidence often involves 2 Peter 2:13. Based upon the presupposition that Peter used Jude, Kilpatrick argues that a scribe would not intentionally change "love-*feasts*" (ἀγάπαις) to "deceptions / pleasures" (ἀγάταις), but rather a scribe copying Jude accidentally transcribed "deceptions / pleasures" (ἀγάταις) as "love-*feasts*" (ἀγάπαις).[19] However if Peter used Jude, why then the multiple alterations and rearrangements in 2 Peter 2:11? Sidebottom observes, "The language [of Jude 10] is rearranged

---

17. For an exhaustive listing of manuscripts and dating for "your deceptions" or "your pleasures" (ταῖς ἀγάταις ὑμῶν), see Wasserman, *Epistle of Jude*, 169, 106–17.

18. For an exhaustive listing of manuscripts and dates for "your love-*feasts*" (ταῖς ἀγάπαις ὑμῶν) see ibid., 169, 106–17.

19. Kilpatrick, "AGAPH," 79, 178.

until the verse becomes virtually unintelligible."[20] Yet in all probability, Peter did not copy Jude but rather each reflect their shared Jewish oral tradition. Wasserman avers, "ἀγάταις probably entered Jude's manuscript tradition due to a poor transcription of ἀγάπαις and should be rejected" and that "the corrections in Jude 12 and 2 Peter 13, respectively, could stem from different correctors."[21]

Another suggestion offered to support "deceptions / pleasures" (ἀγάταις) over "love-*feasts*" (ἀγάπαις) is derived from a twofold uniqueness of ἀγάπαις in Jude: (1) "love-*feasts*" (ἀγάπαις) is an *hapax legomenon* and (2) the concept of "love-*feasts*" occurs only here in the New Testament. Yet thirteen other *hapax legomena* occur in Jude[22] thereby making the *hapax legomenon* argument tenuous. The second argument is weakened because ἀγάπη / ἀγαπητο are prominent catchwords throughout Jude (vv. 1, 2, 3, 12, 20, 21) and thereby the appearance of ἀγάπαις would be in keeping with Jude's emphasis. Landon adds, "the word ἀγάπαις juxtaposed with ὑμῶν equates to ἀγαπητο in vv. 3, 17 and 20, and ἀγάπαις with ὑμῶν is also part of the antithetical balance in v. 12."[23] Finally, one might argue that Jude confronts sexual or licentious pleasures" (ἀγάταις). Yet it seems highly unlikely that Jude alludes to sexual pleasures. "Clearly, if there is a sinful or immoral aspect to the definition of ἀγάπη as pleasure," according to Landon, "then I cannot defend [it] on contextual grounds at Jude 12 since it suggests that Jude's addressees are engaged in immoral pleasures."[24] In conclusion, it seems both the external and internal evidence supports the variant reading "your love-*feasts*" (ταῖς ἀγάπαις ὑμῶν).

So how does this textual decision supporting "your love-*feasts*" (ταῖς ἀγάπαις ὑμῶν) affect interpretation? Contextually, Jude 12 is a continuation of Jude's condemnation of the godless people he is presently confronting.[25] Jude appears to have coined the term "love-*feast*" as a way of describing Judean meals during the AD 60s. Unfortunately, the term *later* became a

---

20. Sidebottom, *James, Jude*, 115.
21. Wasserman, *Epistle of Jude*, 286–87.
22. See Charles, "Literary," 106–24.
23. Landon, *Text-Critical Study*, 107.
24. Ibid., 105; cf. Wasserman, *Epistle of Jude*, 286–87; Bauckham, *2 Peter, Jude*, 77.
25. Verse 12, a single sentence that stretches into verse 13, exposes the moral flaws of the godless (οὗτοί) by likening them to nature (sea, sky, and land). Jude's use of "these *people*" (οὐαί; cf. vv. 8, 10, 14, 16) without a connective particle suggests a continuation and even expansion of Jude's expressed denunciation of the godless in verse 11. Whereas in verse 11 he condemns them based upon the unbecoming typological patterns of greedy behavior evident in three less than honorable leaders of the past, here Jude 12–13 employs metaphors to underscore several supplemental yet parallel concerns.

distinctive description for celebrating the Eucharist.[26] Yet, "nothing in the present passage," rightly avers Kelly, "indicates whether the meals in question were directly connected with the Eucharist or not."[27] In the *Acts of Paul* (circa 200), a Christian meal consisted of five loaves, vegetables, and water whereby there was much love and joy evident (*Acts of Paul*, 25).

The subsequent phrase "those who eat together with you" (οἱ ... συνευωχούμενοι)[28] would also appear to be a reference to a typical Judean meal. Despite the lack of information about Judean meals in extra-biblical Jewish sources,[29] the Gospels do contain such information.[30] The examples often disclose proper order. For instance Luke recounts how Jesus calls a banquet meal into order (22:7–13), begins it (22:14–15), determines the food and beverage to be consumed (22:17–20), and presides over the conversation (22:21–37).[31] And while the retelling of these mealtime events served

---

26. According to Ignatius (circa 110), an *"agapé feast"* is to be presided over by a Bishop (*Smyrna* 8.2). According to the *Didache* (circa 120–50), no one was to eat of the "thanksgiving meal" (= nonsacramental meal) except those who were baptized (*Didache* 9:5). Tertullian (circa 150–220) declares the meal mirrors its name, *agapé* and a somewhat detailed description is provided (*Apology* 39:16–21). Clement of Alexandria (circa 150–220) *The Instructor* 2.1 discusses Christian love feasts. See Connolly, "Agape and Eucharist," 477–89, esp. 488.

27. Kelly, *Commentary*, 269–70. For other discussions, see Chaine, *Les épîtres catholiques*, 315–16; Green, *2 Peter and Jude*, 175; Fuchs and Reymond, *La deuxiéme épître*, 172–73; Kugelman, *James & Jude*, 98–99; Grundmann, *Der Brief des Judas*, 39; Kistemaker, *Peter and Jude*, 392, among several others.

28. The verb συνευωχέμαι occurs only here and 2 Pet 2:13. Peter uses the participial form of συνευωχέομαι with reference to a regular meal and similar to usage by other Jewish authors (Philo *Laws* 4:119; Josephus *Ant* 1.3.5 §92; 4.8.7 §203).

29. Sirach (circa 180 BC) provides some instructions for table etiquette: be disciplined as well as avoid sitting next to another man's wife, avoid over-eating and monitor wine consumption (e.g., do not be greedy), be sensitive to those around you and speak respectfully, and beware of pride if given a seat of honor and extend acts of kindness to the others (Sirach 9:9; 31:12–32:9). At Qumran, the men ate, blessed, and deliberated in common (cf. 1Q28 6.2–3, circa 125–75 BC; cf. Josephus *War* 2.8.5 §129–31). Participation at a Qumran common meal could also be denied or reduced to rations for speaking angrily or knowingly lying to another (1Q28 7:3–4, circa 125–75 BC).

30. At times meals were *private* as was the case of Jesus dining with Levi the tax collector (Mark 2:14–17, circa AD 58–60), *public* as was the case of Herod Antipas' birthday celebration that included live entertainment (Mark 6:14–29), or *ceremonial* as were Sabbath (Luke 14:1, circa AD mid 60s) and Passover (Luke 22:7–8, 13, 15) meals. Meals were also supervised (Pharisees: Luke 7:36; 11:37; 14:1; Jesus: Luke 22:13–37; 24:27–34).

31. Similarly, in the *Rule of the Community* (= 1Q28a or 1QSa), there is a description of a future messianic banquet (2:11–22). While describing a future banquet, the Messiah of Israel enters the banquet hall after a priest (presumably the Messiah or Aaron; 2:11–13), presides over the community as they sit in some military formation (2:14–17), and signals when to eat (2:17–20). See Schiffman, "Rule of the Congregation," 797–99;

the Gospel writer's literary purposes, they also reveal mealtime etiquette.[32] For instance, refusal to accept an invitation to a banquet celebration *denied solidarity* with another person or group (e.g. the elder son in the parable about the prodigal son: Luke 15:25–32), assuming a place of honor at a banquet meal was ill-advised and perhaps considered a conceited or arrogant presupposition (Mark 12:37b–40),[33] and ignoring the custom of washing the feet of an invited guest was rebuked (Luke 7:44–45).[34] Nevertheless, Jesus also challenged societal norms when he openly ate with sinners (e.g. those who were considered disreputable people of society by religious leaders). What was it about the godless during mealtime that raised Jude's ire? These questions are answered in Jude's next two phrases.

12b οἱ ... συνευωχούμενοι ἀφόβως

12b those who eat together without fear,

12c ἑαυτοὺς ποιμαίνοντες,

12c *and* those who feed themselves.

It seems Jude was concerned about the *unbecoming attitude* and the *unsuitable actions* of the godless during mealtime. First, they lack fear (ἀφόβως) during mealtime. The NIV translates the phrase "they eat without the slightest qualm." While Jude provides no specifics, perhaps there was a disregard for table etiquette. Perhaps it was pride for not being given the seat of honor (Sirach 32:1–2; cf. Mark 12:37b–40). Perhaps the young disrespected the old when speaking during mealtime (Sirach 32:3–4, 7–9). Perhaps arrogant attitudes existed about who was and who was not honored (cf. Josephus *Ant* 18.1.6. 23–24).[35] Whatever they did, "these people do not fear social sanction: they are people without honor."[36] Second, they manifested *unsuitable actions*: "those who feed themselves" (ἑαυτοὺς ποιμαίνοντες). Many commentators create another metaphor here, that of a shepherd (e.g., Ezek 34:2, 8, 10; cf. ASV, ESV, NIV, WEB).[37] Most render it as "feeding only

---

Qimron and Charlesworth, "Rules of the Community," 1–5.

32. One helpful source concerning banquet meals during the first century in Judea is Corley, *Private Women*.

33. Mark 12 appears in the context of retelling Jesus' description of scribes and Pharisees who love places of honor. Parallel texts in other Gospels occur in Matt 23:1–36; Luke 14:7–10.

34. Neyrey, "Ceremonies in Luke-Acts," 374–76.

35. Hengel, *Zealots*, 385.

36. Green, *Jude & 2 Peter*, 95.

37. If the opponents are Gnostics, this interpretation fits especially well because they purported to have "secret knowledge." Some, however, make a connection to 1 Cor 11:12, 33. Chaine, *Les épîtres catholiques*, 315–16; Kugelman, *James & Jude*, 98–99;

themselves" (KJV NRSV NASB⁹⁵ NET NLT^(SE)) as an alternative rendering (cf. Hos 13:5; Micah 5:4; Josephus *Ant* 1.19.9 §309; 2.12.1 §264), Jude's point is simply this: the godless feed themselves. Thus, Jude's concern is about the *attitude* and *actions* of the godless during Judean believers' love-*feasts*. The subsequent metaphors "Sky, land, and sea" according to Moffatt, "are ransacked for illustrations of their character."³⁸ Grundmann argues that they convey the idea of ignoring God's fixed rules and thereby living disorderly lives.³⁹ Through these metaphors, Jude further underscores the character of the godless as harmful people, who appear to promise much but produce little, who act shamefully, and wander aimlessly.⁴⁰

CONCLUSION

As indicated at the beginning of this chapter, there are numerous textual issues in Jude. Consequently, much more could be said about the textual challenges in Jude. There are text critical issues that affect grammatical interpretations. These issues include, but are not limited to: 1.b. Does the text read "to the called, to those who are kept for Jesus, who is the Christ" (Ἰησοῦ Χριστῷ τετηρημένοις κλητοῖς), or "to the called of Jesus, who is the Christ" (Ἰησοῦ Χριστῷ κλητοῖς)? Second, does the text read "Jesus Christ" with Χριστός in the dative Ἰησοῦ Χριστῷ), or in the genitive (Ἰησοῦ Χριστοῦ or Χριστοῦ Ἰησοῦ)? 4.c. Does the text read "our Lord, Jesus" (κύριον ἡμῶν Ἰησοῦν), "your Lord, Jesus" (κύριον ὑμῶν Ἰησοῦν), or simply "Lord Jesus Christ" (κύριον Ἰησοῦν Χριστὸν)?

There are text critical issues that contribute to understanding Jude's style. These issues include, but are not limited to: 3.a. Does the text read "our" (ἡμῶν) or "your" (ὑμῶν), or is the pronoun omitted altogether? 14.a. In Jude 14, does the text read "Behold, [*the*] Lord came" (Ἰδοὺ ἦλθεν κύριος), or "Behold, *the* Lord came" (ἰδοὺ ἦλθεν ὁ κύριος)? 15.c. In Jude 15, does the text read "and to convict *every soul*" (καὶ ἐλέγξαι πᾶσαν ψυχὴν; NA²⁸, UBS⁴) or "and to convict *all the ungodly*" (καὶ ἐλέγξαι πάντας τοὺς ἀσεβεῖς)?

Kelly, *Commentary*, 271; Sidebottom, *James, Jude*, 89; Green, *2 Peter and Jude*, 175; Grundmann, *Der Brief des Judas*, 40; Vögtle, *Der Judasbrief*, 67; Kraftchick, *Jude, 2 Peter*, 49–50. False Teacher View: Bigg, *Peter and Jude*, 335; Bauckham, *Jude, 2 Peter*, 87; Kistemaker, *Peter and Jude*, 392; Moo, *2 Peter and Jude*, 259; Horrell, *Epistles of Peter*, 124; Reese, *2 Peter & Jude*, 58; Schreiner, *1, 2, Peter, Jude*, 466; Davids, *Letters of 2 Peter and Jude*, 70; Green, *Jude & 2 Peter*, 95.

38. Moffatt, *General Epistles*, 239.
39. Grundmann, *Der Brief des Judas*, 40–41.
40. Bateman, *Jude*, 274–91.

There are text critical issues that influence and perhaps even challenge our theological presuppositions. These issues include, but are not limited to: 5.a. Does the text read "Lord" (κύριος) or "Jesus" (Ἰησοῦς)? 1.a. Does the text read "have been sanctified" (ἡγιασμένοις), or "have been loved" (ἡγαπημένοις)? 4.b. Does the text read "Master God" (δεσπότην θεόν) or "Master and Lord" (δεσπότην καὶ κύριον)?

There are text critical issues that contribute to our interpretation of lexical words within Jude's context. 12.a. Does the text read "your lovefeasts" (ἀγάπαις ὑμῶν) or "your deceptions," or perhaps "your pleasures" (ἀγάταις ὑμῶν)? 22.c. In Jude 22a, does the text read, "have mercy" (ἐλεᾶτε or ἐλεεῖτε) or "convince" or "contend" (ἐλέγχετε)?

There are text critical issues that reflect a mixture of challenges that also weigh in our interpretation of Jude. These issues include, but are not limited to: 5.b. Does the text read "that the Lord delivered once..." (ὅτι ὁ κύριος ἅπαξ... σώσας), or does it read "although you know all things once for all" (εἰδότας ὑμᾶς πάντα)? The issue is both a grammatical and theological one. 8.a. Does the text read "authority" in the singular (κυριότητα) or "authorities" in the plural (κυριότητας)? This is a grammatical and commonsource issue. 9.b. Does the text read "to bring" (ἐπενεγκεῖν), or "to bear" or "to submit to" (ὑπενεγκεῖν)? This is a theological and source issue. 22.b. Does the textual evidence support three imperatival clauses or only two? The issue is a grammatical-syntactical structural issue. How is Jude 22–23 to be structurally outlined? And though there are variations within the two-clause and three-clause readings (e.g., case variations, verb variations, and word-order variations, in bold), certain readings are the most textually supported options for a two-clause option versus a three-clause option.

These text-critical variants have been evaluated in my commentary *Jude*, and yet, I owe the methodology employed in my assessment of each and every one of these text-critical challenges to men like David Alan Black who have contributed to and helped move text critical discussions forward. Thank you, Dr. Black.

BIBLIOGRAPHY

Aland, Kurt, and Barbara Aland. *The Text of the New Testament*. Translated by Erroll F. Rhodes. Grand Rapids, MI: Eerdmans, 1987.

Albin, Carl Axel. *Judasbrevet: Traditionen Texten Tolkningen*. Stockholm: Natur och Kultur, 1962.

Bateman, Herbert W., IV. *Interpreting the General Letters*. Edited by John D. Harvey. Handbook for New Testament Exegesis. Grand Rapids, MI: Kregel, 2013.

———. *Jude*. Edited by Hall Harris. Evangelical Exegetical Commentary. Bellingham, WA: Lexham, 2015.

———. "Rebellion and Judgment in Jude." *Bibliotheca Sacra* 170 (2013) 454–78.

———. *Translating Jude Clause by Clause: An Exegetical Guide*. Leesburg, IN: Cyber-Center for Biblical Studies, 2013.

———. "Two First Century Messianic Uses of the Old Testament: Hebrews 1:5–13 and 4QFlorilegium 1:1–19." *Journal of the Evangelical Theological Society* 38 (1995) 11–27.

Bauckham, Richard. *2 Peter, Jude*. Word Biblical Commentary Series 50. Waco, TX: Word, 1983.

———. *Jude and the Relatives of Jesus in the Early Church*. Edinburgh: T&T Clark, 1990.

Bigg, Charles. *Epistles of St. Jude and St. Peter*. The International Critical Commentary. New York: Scribner, 1909.

Black, David Alan. *New Testament Textual Criticism: A Concise Guide*. Grand Rapids, MI: Baker, 1994.

———, ed. *Rethinking New Testament Textual Criticism*. Grand Rapids, MI: Baker, 2002.

Bock, Darrell L. *Luke 1:1—9:20*. Baker Exegetical Commentary of the New Testament. Grand Rapids, MI: Baker, 1994.

Cantinat, Jean. *Les épîtres de Saint Jacques et de Saint Jude*. Sources bibliques. Paris: Gabalda, 1973.

Carson, D. A., and Douglas Moo. *An Introduction to the New Testament*. Grand Rapids, MI: Zondervan, 2005.

Chaine, Joseph. *Les épîtres catholiques: La seconde épître de Saint Pierre, les épîtres de Saint Jean, l'épître de Saint Jude*. Études bibliques 27. 2nd ed. Paris: Gabalda, 1939.

Charles, J. Daryl. "Literary Artifice in the Epistle of Jude." *Zeitschrift für die Neutestamentliche Wissenschaft* 82 (1991) 106–24.

Corley, Kathleen E. *Private Women, Public Meals: Social Conflict and Women in the Synoptic Tradition*. Peabody, MA: Hendrickson, 1993.

Davids, Peter. *The Letter of 2 Peter and Jude*. Pillar New Testament Commentary. Grand Rapids, MI: Eerdmans, 2006.

Donelson, Lewis R. *I & II Peter and Jude: A Commentary*. New Testament Library. Louisville, KY: Westminster John Knox, 2010.

Ehrman, Bart D. "Methodological Development in the Analysis and Classification of New Testament Documentary Evidence." *Novum Testamentum* 29 (1987) 22–45.

———. "New Testament Textual Criticism: Quest for Methodology." MDiv thesis, Princeton Theological Seminary, 1981.

Fee, Gordon D. "Rigorous or Reasoned Eclecticism: Which?" In *Studies in New Testament Language and Text: Essays in Honour of George D. Kilpatrick on the Occasion of His Sixty-Fifth Birthday*, edited by J. Keith Elliot, 174–97. Leiden: Brill, 1976.

Fuchs, Eric, and Pierre Reymond. *La deuxiéme épître de saint Pierre: L'épître de saint Jude*. Commentaire du Nouveau Testament. Paris: Delachauz & Nietlé, 1980.

Green, Gene L. *Jude and 2 Peter*. Baker Exegetical Commentary on the New Testament. Grand Rapids, MI: Baker Academic, 2008.

Green, Michael. *2 Peter and Jude*. Tyndale New Testament Commentaries. Grand Rapids, MI: Eerdmans, 1968.

Grundmann, Walter. *Der Brief des Judas und der zweite Brief des Petrus*. Theologischer Handkommentar zum Neuen Testament. Berlin: Evangelische Verlagsanstalt, 1986.
Hengel, Martin. *The Zealots: Investigations into the Jewish Freedom Movement in the Period from Herod I until 70 AD*. Edinburgh: T&T Clark, 1989.
Hiebert, D. Edmond. *Second Peter and Jude: An Expositional Commentary*. Greenville, SC: Unusual Publications, 1989.
Holloway, Gary. *James and Jude*. The College Press NIV Commentary. Joplin, MO: College Press, 1996.
Holmes, Michael W. "The Case for Reasoned Eclecticism." In *Rethinking New Testament Textual Criticism*, edited by David Alan Black, 77–100. Grand Rapids, MI: Baker, 2002.
Horrell, David G. *The Epistles of Peter and Jude*. Epworth Commentary. London: Epworth, 1998.
Kelly, John Norman Davidson. *A Commentary on the Epistles of Peter and Jude*. Thornapple Commentaries. Reprint, Grand Rapids, MI: Baker, 1981.
Kistemaker, Simon J. *Peter and Jude*. New Testament Commentary. Grand Rapids, MI: Baker, 1987.
Kraftchick, Steven J. *Jude, 2 Peter*. Abingdon New Testament Commentaries. Nashville: Abingdon, 2002.
Kugelman, Richard. *James & Jude*. New Testament Message 19. Wilmington, DE: Glazier, 1980.
Landon, Charles. *A Text-Critical Study of the Epistle of Jude*. Journal for the Study of the New Testament: Supplement Series 135. Sheffield: Sheffield Academic, 1996.
Lenski, R. C. H. *The Interpretation of the Epistles of St. Peter, St. John, and St. Jude*. Commentary on the New Testament 11. Minneapolis, MN: Augsburg, 1945.
Metzger, Bruce M. *The Text of the New Testament: Its Transmission, Corruption, and Restoration*. 3rd ed. New York: Oxford University Press, 1992.
———. *A Textual Commentary on the Greek New Testament*. 2nd ed. New York: United Bible Society, 1994.
Metzger, Bruce M., and Bart D. Ehrman. *The Text of the New Testament: Its Transmission, Corruption, and Restoration*. 4th ed. New York: Oxford University Press, 2005.
Moffatt, James. *The General Epistles: James, Peter and Judas*. Moffatt's New Testament Commentary. London: Hodder & Stoughton, 1928.
Moo, Douglas. *2 Peter and Jude*. The NIV Application Commentary. Grand Rapids, MI: Zondervan, 1996.
Nestle-Aland Novum Testamentum Graece. 28th ed. Stuttgart, Germany: Deutsche Bibelgesellschaft, 2012.
Neyrey, Jerome. *2 Peter, and Jude: A New Translation with Introduction and Commentary*. Anchor Bible Commentary. New Haven: Yale University Press, 1993.
Paulsen, H. *Der Zweite Petrusbrief und der Judasbrief*. Kritisch-exegetischer Kommentar uber das Neue Testament. Göttingen: Vandenhoeck & Ruprecht, 1992.
Richard, Earl J. *Reading 1 Peter, Jude, and 2 Peter: A Literary and Theological Commentary*. Macon, GA: Smyth & Helwys, 2000.
Schreiner, Thomas. *1, 2 Peter, Jude*. New American Commentary Series 37. Nashville: Broadman & Holman, 2003.
Senior, Donald, and Daniel Harrington. *1 Peter, Jude and 2 Peter*. Sacra Pagina 17. Collegeville, MN: Liturgical, 2003.

Sidebottom E. M. *James, Jude, 2 Peter*. New Century Bible Commentary. Grand Rapids, MI: Eerdmans, 1967.

Vögtle, Anton, *Der Judasbrief, der 2 Petrusbrief*. Evangelisch-katholischer Kommentar zum Neuen Testament. Neukirchen-Vluyn: Neukirchener Verlag, 1994.

Wachtel, Klaus. *Der byzantinische Text der Katholischen Briefe: eine Untersuchung zur Entstehung der Koine des Neuen Testaments*. Arbeiten zur neutestamentlichen Textforschung 24. Berlin: de Gruyter, 1995.

Wallace, Daniel B. *Greek Grammar Beyond the Basics: An Exegetical Syntax of the New Testament*. Grand Rapids, MI: Zondervan, 1996.

———. "Laying a Foundation: New Testament Textual Criticism." In *Interpreting the New Testament Text: Introduction to the Art and Science of Exegesis*, edited by Darrell L. Bock and Buist M. Fanning, 33–56. Wheaton, IL: Crossway, 2006.

———. "The Majority Text and the Original Text: Are They Identical?" *Bibliotheca Sacra* 148 (1991) 150–69.

———. "A Textual Problem in 1 Thessalonians 1:10: Ἐκ τῆς Ὀργῆς vs. Ἀπὸ τῆς Ὀργῆς." *Bibliotheca Sacra* 147 (1990) 470–79.

Wasserman, Tommy. *The Epistle of Jude: Its Text and Transmission*. Coniectanea Biblica New Testament Series 43. Stockholm, Sweden: Almqvist & Wiksell, 2006.

Witherington, Ben, III. *Letters and Homilies for Jewish Christians: A Socio-Rhetorical Commentary on Hebrews, James and Jude*. Downers Grove, IL: InterVarsity, 2007.

Chapter 10

The Linguistic Features of Second Timothy and Its Purpose

—DAVID R. BECK
Southeastern Baptist Theological Seminary

INTRODUCTION

THIS STUDY HAD ITS origins in my interest in how the personal tone and character of Paul's second letter to Timothy made it particularly applicable for training leaders in God's church today. However, along with that interest was the awareness that there is little consensus agreement within Pastoral Epistles scholarship on many issues, including authenticity, addressee, purpose, and its overall character. When invited to contribute to this collection, the present writer naturally turned to an exploration of recent scholarship focused on various linguistic elements within the Pastoral Epistles in general, and 2 Timothy in particular to discover how those elements inform the inquiry into its purpose and character. This then would assist in determining how legitimately and faithfully to apply this letter in leadership training in the church. What follows is a survey of several recent contributions to the application of various areas of linguistic analysis to the Pastoral Epistles in general, and 2 Timothy specifically. An exploration of the insights learned from these studies will then be applied to the understanding of the purpose and character of 2 Timothy, and its application for Christian leadership development.

The discussion of Paul's purpose in writing his second letter to Timothy is inextricably linked to questions of authorship, recipient, date, and historicity. This essay is not intended to provide a detailed history of the authenticity debate, but neither can it be completely ignored, because so much hinges on the answer to the question, "Did the historical Paul write this letter to the historical Timothy we know from Scripture, accurately portraying his circumstances at the time of writing?" If not, then the purpose and character of 2 Timothy is very different, as indicated by Hans-Josef Klauck in his recent monograph *Ancient Letters and the New Testament*. He deems all three of the Pastorals to be "'doubly pseudonymous' in that both the sender and the recipients are fictitious."[1] In this view, both the stated author, Paul, and the stated recipients, Timothy and Titus, are no longer living, but in these letters those names "function as typological constructs of ideal Christian ministers."[2] Rather than evidence of authenticity, the inclusion of personal details are considered to be intended to "present the ethos of Paul and his students in order to elicit the pathos of the audience."[3]

This long-held majority scholarly opinion of non-Pauline authorship has been recently challenged on several levels, but still remains the dominant view. Some scholars suggest that pseudonymity of the Pastorals is certain and an almost unanimous consensus. An example of this kind of confident dismissal of Pauline authorship is Raymond Collins' recently published Pastoral Epistles commentary in the New Testament Library. He states that "by the end of the twentieth century New Testament scholarship was virtually unanimous in affirming that the Pastoral Epistles were written sometime after Paul's death." He condescendingly admits "as always some scholars dissent from the consensus view,"[4] citing only George W. Knight III and Luke Timothy Johnson as examples, without acknowledging that they are but representative of a growing number of New Testament scholars writing major commentaries and monographs on the Pastoral Epistles holding to the authenticity of 1 and 2 Timothy and Titus.

The growing support for Pauline authorship of the Pastoral Epistles no longer allows authenticity to be dismissed as an aberrant view barely worth mentioning. The list of recent scholars publishing volumes in major commentary series that advocate, or at least view positively the possibility of Pauline authorship for 1 and 2 Timothy and Titus, is much longer than just Knight and Johnson. Recent volumes in major series supporting

1. Klauck and Bailey, *Ancient Letters*, 324.
2. Aune, "Pastoral Letters," 339.
3. Klauck and Bailey, *Ancient Letters*, 325.
4. Collins, *1 & 2 Timothy*, 4.

Pauline authorship include those published in the Anchor Yale Bible, Catholic Commentary on Scripture, Harper's New Testament Commentary, Interpretation, New International Biblical Commentary, New International Commentary on the New Testament, New International Greek Testament Commentary, Smith & Helwys Bible Commentary, and Word Biblical Commentary.[5] Ben Witherington asks the pointed question,

> Why is it that the majority of Pauline scholars who have *not* done a detailed study of these documents or written a scholarly commentary on the Pastoral Epistles in the last fifty years think that these letters are post-Pauline, while the majority who *have* written such commentaries are either open to the possibility or are convinced that these letters do indeed go back to Paul in some form or fashion?[6]

A major weakness of the Pseudo-Pauline authorship alternative to the authenticity of the Pastoral Epistles is the misconception of many scholars in their portrayal of ancient pseudonymous writing. The practice is characterized as acceptable to early Christians, as illustrated by the following assertion: "Jews and early Christians were not averse to accepting pseudepigraphic material. In fact, a substantial portion of the Bible's prophetic books and a still larger portion of the wisdom literature was not composed by those to whom it is attributed."[7] What mattered to the early church, according to this view, is not whether the real author is the one to whom the letter is attributed, but whether or not "the conviction that what is attributed to that authority is a faithful updating of the tradition. The content, not the literary attribution, was the decisive factor in evaluating the 'authenticity' of the message."[8] What is being claimed is that pseudonymous writings were known to exist in the ancient world (undeniable), approved and utilized with no deception involved (highly questionable), and an accepted practice in the early church (demonstrably false).

The early church always condemned pseudonymous writings when discovered, and Paul himself took precautions against it.[9] While no defend-

---

5. Johnson, *First and Second Letters*; Montague, *First and Second Timothy*; Kelly, *Commentary*; Oden, *First and Second Timothy*; Fee, *1 and 2 Timothy*; Towner, who believes the authorship question must remain open, while nonetheless taking the view that "Paul is the author of these letters however much or little others contributed to their message and composition" (*Letters*, 88); Knight, *Pastoral Epistles*; Gloer, *1 & 2 Timothy*; Mounce, *Pastoral Epistles*.

6. Witherington, *Letters and Homilies*, 50–51.

7. Collins, *1 & 2 Timothy*, 7–8.

8. Ibid., 8.

9. For an excellent detailed summation of the early church's condemnation of

er of authenticity, Bart Ehrman provides a far more accurate assessment of the ancient views on pseudonymous documents in his characterization of them as forgeries and counterfeits, declaring that ancient forgers, including authors of pseudonymous New Testament letters, "were consciously lying about their identity in an effort to deceive their readers."[10] Ehrman asserts that the claim that ancient forgery was an acceptable practice without intent to deceive has been fully refuted by scholars of non-biblical antiquity and its writings. The reason this view still persists among New Testament practitioners is that they are simply not well-versed with scholarship outside of their own discipline.[11]

LINGUISTIC FEATURES

Because of its continuing influence, it is necessary to give attention to the linguistic analysis used to argue against the authenticity of the Pastoral Epistles in the 1921 work of P. N. Harrison, *The Problem of the Pastoral Epistles*. In it he argues statistically for pseudonymous authorship with some genuine Pauline fragments, especially in 2 Timothy. He based his arguments on an examination of the linguistic distinctiveness of the Pastorals, including unique vocabulary, style, and grammar, both in terms of what is present in the pastorals as well as typical Pauline features which are absent from them. He further compared the language of these letters to second-century writings, maintaining that the only reasonable conclusion consistent with the evidence is "the Pastorals were not written by Paul, but by a devout and earnest Paulinist with our ten Paulines and, as many think, other genuine notes before him, during the half century A. D. 95–145."[12] Harrison believed he could identify genuine Pauline fragments whose authenticity was undeniably embedded within these letters.[13] His work was notable for its profusion of statistics, charts, and graphs and is still highly influential today.

The lasting influence of Harrison's linguistic study does not indicate its accuracy, but is more a reflection of the perceived objectivity of statistical studies. Nonetheless, even proponents of pseudonymous authorship note that it needs correction, but tweaking is insufficient to overcome its deficiencies. Harrison's analysis serves to illustrate that while the truism may be that "numbers don't lie," the means by which statistics are derived, the

---

pseudepigraphy, see Mounce, *Pastoral Epistles*, cxxii–cxxvii.

10. Ehrman, *Forgery and Counterforgery*, 4n6.
11. Ibid., 129.
12. Harrison, *Problem of the Pastoral Epistles*, 84.
13. Ibid., 93.

manner in which they are presented, and the interpretation of their significance can be misleading and inaccurate. Scholars were quick to identify problematic methodologies, misleading presentation, and questionable interpretations of the statistics derived. An excellent critique of Harrison tracing the significant scholarly refutations of it is provided by Jermo van Nes. He notes methodological problems, including comparing the Pastorals as a cluster of letters while comparing other Pauline letters individually and counting words per page instead of by document. He identifies how Harrison misleads by failing to explain how statistics were compiled for his graphs and charts, and not mentioning that many of the missing Pauline linguistic features are also absent from letters of Paul deemed authentic.[14]

A different explanation for the semantic distinctiveness of the Pastoral Epistles is provided by Armin Baum's linguistic analysis. He too has an impressive array of charts and graphs which illustrate the semantic richness of these letters beyond that of the other Pauline letters. But he also demonstrates that most of the distinctiveness is in the use of additional synonyms for words already found in the other ten letters of the Pauline Corpus, placing the distinctive vocabulary within the shared semantic domains of the other Pauline letters.[15] As his basis for interpreting this phenomenon, Baum turns to recent studies of oral versus written communication. He concludes that while the other ten Pauline letters are closer to oral communication, the Pastoral Epistles reflect more the linguistic character of written language, as if the author was less spontaneous and had more focused time for the composition of these documents.[16]

The second-century dating of the Pastorals by Harrison through the use of linguistic parallels has also been challenged on the grounds of its exclusion of first-century and LXX parallels for the words Harrison claimed were characteristic of second-century writings.[17] Statistical studies attempting to determine authenticity or pseudonymity of the Pauline Epistles continue, and the varying conclusions they reach indicate the elusiveness of the claim of statistical objectivity in this instance. The results of these studies vary from those "proving" the non-Pauline character of 2 Timothy[18] to the assertion that while the style may be different, the variations are better accounted for by the versatility of a single author, not by pseudonymity.[19]

14. Nes, "Problem of the Pastoral Epistles," 158–61.
15. Baum, "Semantic Variation," 278–87.
16. Ibid., 291–92.
17. Nes, "Problem of the Pastoral Epistles," 161–63.
18. Mealand, "Extent of the Pauline Corpus," 86.
19. Kenny, *Stylometric Study*, 100; Neumann, *Authenticity*, 213.

The fragmentary hypothesis put forth by Harrison is disputed on grounds of a misinterpretation of vocabulary usage and recent examinations of the cohesiveness of the letters to Timothy and Titus, such as represented by Ray Van Neste's 2004 monograph on the Pastorals' cohesion and structure.[20] In his study, Van Neste focuses on how the language used connects the various sections of these letters, demonstrating their essential unity. As with each of the letters, Van Neste works through the text of 2 Timothy unit by unit, identifying their boundaries, as well as showing the connections that bind them together and give them internal coherence.[21] Next, he turns to the larger structure of the book and demonstrates the logical flow from each unit to the next through the use of conjunctions and other transitional devices such as verb person and number, as well as thematic concepts. He highlights the repetition of key words through the use of various cognates for "remembrance," "word/message/gospel," and "God;" and also the significant shift in verb number and tense between 1st person (Paul), 2nd person (Timothy), and 3rd person (opponents/false teachers). This is combined with an emphasis on the relationship between Paul and Timothy.[22] There are also consistent thematic threads which are traceable through the letter, indicated by semantic chains, words carrying the theme. These semantic chains include eschatologically charged words, salvation terminology, the word grouping of message/gospel/word (often qualified by expressions such as "word of truth"), terms reminiscent of suffering, words denoting opposition, and words identifying Paul as Timothy's exemplar.[23]

In the conclusion of his study of the coherence of 2 Timothy, Van Neste emphasizes the consistent connectedness indicating the high degree of cohesion in this letter. He suggests the following basic structure, which highlights a shift between a focus on Paul and Timothy and Timothy and the opponents:

1.3—2.13, Paul and Timothy—'Hold Fast'

2.14—3.9, Timothy and Opponents—'Avoid Them'

[HINGE] 3.10–17

4.1–8, Paul and Timothy—'Do the Ministry'[24]

Van Neste effectively refutes those who deny the structural and linguistic unity of the Pastoral Epistles generally, and those who argue for a

20. Ibid., 163–68; Van Neste, *Cohesion and Structure*.
21. Van Neste, *Cohesion and Structure*, 146–93.
22. Ibid., 194–211.
23. Ibid., 211–32.
24. Ibid., 232.

fragmentary theory of composition for 2 Timothy in particular. His refutation also speaks directly to the character and purpose of 2 Timothy, and its application for contemporary Christians. The cohesion of content, the highlighted relational aspect of the letter, and the personal tone all support the identification of this letter as the final letter of Paul, written to a close colleague who was his personal delegate, representing him in his absence. Unlike his first letter to Timothy and the one to Titus, the focus is not on the church and its proper functioning and structure, but on the character and fidelity of the one who would remain to lead it once Paul was no longer present.

Further discussion of the authorship debate is beyond the scope of this essay, but excellent detailed evidence refuting the claim of Pseudo-Pauline authorship of the Pastorals and defending them as genuine letters of Paul is provided in the Anchor Yale Bible and Word Biblical Commentary volumes by Luke Timothy Johnson and William Mounce.[25] For the purpose of the present study, 2 Timothy is understood according to its own self-attestation, as a genuine letter of Paul, written to his associate Timothy, whom he considered a spiritual son.

Based on the acceptance of authenticity and Pauline authorship, attention can now be turned to the question of Paul's purpose and intent in writing a second letter to Timothy. What prompted this correspondence? Was it a change in Paul's circumstances, a new development in the battle against false teaching in Ephesus, or was it something more personal in the relationship of Paul with this trusted ministry partner whom he had led to faith in Christ, discipled towards maturity in Christ, and mentored for leadership in Christ's church? They had shared together in the hardship of itinerant church-planting ministry, and in persecution for the sake of the gospel.

Several other recent studies utilizing various kinds of linguistic analysis of 2 Timothy have been published that are informative for our task of assessing the character and purpose of 2 Timothy. In her presidential address at the seventieth meeting of the Society for New Testament Studies, Judith Lieu addresses generally the role of ancient letters as cultural symbols. She argues for the application of the study of letter writing in antiquity and the study of early Christianity.[26] She notes three key principles of epistolary theory, all of which are spatial, that are helpful in the analysis of early Christian letters. She articulates this as 1. Absent as if Present: Geographical Distance, 2. Half a Conversation: Social Space, and 3. A Mirror of the Soul:

---

25. Johnson, *First and Second Letters*, 55–90; Mounce, *Pastoral Epistles*, xlvi–cxxix.
26. Lieu, "Letters and the Topography," 169.

Interior Space.²⁷ Lieu observes of ancient letters that they are "built around a relationship, replying to something already initiated, or anticipating some response."²⁸ But they also are revealing in their insight into the sender since "all verbal self-expression reveals the character of the individual."²⁹ This analysis of the relational and self-revelatory understanding of ancient letters fits the nature and character of Paul's second letter to Timothy.

The relational nature of Paul's letters to Timothy and Titus is the focus of a study by Tom Thatcher, who also applies the results of epistolary theory for his analysis. He narrows his focus to the formulaic opening and closing of each letter, because any alterations from the standard form made to them can be understood as intentional and provide insight into the relationship between the author and recipient.³⁰ After examining all the Pastoral letters, he observes that what is revealed is "humble authority on the part of the writer...intense loyalty toward Paul on the part of the reader...a genuine mutual concern...a common faith."³¹ Specifically of 2 Timothy he writes that the opening and closing serves to "communicate the writer's love and concern for the recipient and for the recipient's spiritual health."³²

Another example of the application of epistolary theory to understand 2 Timothy better is provided by Cynthia Westfall. Observing that the body of ancient letters had received the least scholarly attention, she chose 2 Timothy for her analysis. She notes that surviving ancient guides suggest that the conventions of letter writing vary according to the changing circumstances of the individual letter, what modern linguists call "register theory."³³ She concludes that 2 Timothy has often been misidentified as a literary letter for public reading and distribution. The personal and interpersonal features of this letter are inconsistent with that characterization. As a specific example of these features she cites the transition from the opening section of the body of the letter to its middle using the phrase "You therefore my child" (Σὺ οὖν, τέκνον μου) which she identifies as unnecessary "extra words," which "serve as discourse markers, and are particularly interpersonal, communicating a high level of intimacy between Paul and Timothy consistent with personal letters between a father and son, or a mentor and mentoree."³⁴ However, one must be clear that in understanding what constitutes a personal letter in the

27. Ibid., 170–78.
28. Ibid., 174.
29. Ibid., 178.
30. Thatcher, "Relational Matrix," 42.
31. Ibid., 44–45.
32. Ibid., 44.
33. Westfall, "Moral Dilemma," 218.
34. Ibid., 235–36n73.

ancient world, one would be mistaken to confuse a personal letter with one that is private and confidential. That is more a modern construct than an ancient one.[35]

The tone of a letter has also been used to argue against Pauline authorship of the Pastorals. The complaint is that the Pastorals are too "prosaic," unimaginative when compared to Paul's "authentic" letters. For example, Linda Maloney maintains that in his genuine letters Paul attempts to reason with and persuade those with whom he differs, while the author of the Pastoral Epistles refuses to do this; instead, "His weapon is a bludgeon, and he makes no attempt to win over those who disagree."[36] In challenging the validity of this argument, Raymond Massey looks to ancient letter writers and focuses on a comparison of two letters of Cicero, letter 75 to Atticus describing the political turmoil in Rome, and letter 24 to Marius describing the games held by Pompey on the occasion of the dedication of Pompey's temple. After noting that both are deemed authentic by scholars and that they are agreed to be private letters without intent to publish, he begins his comparison of them. His comparison demonstrates that Letter 75 to Atticus is vivid and detailed, utilizing figures of speech, full of descriptive words and phrases, and includes names, dates, and other details. On the other hand, Letter 24 to Marius lacks all of the above, and is best described as dull and "prosaic."[37] Since both are agreed by scholars to be authentic letters of Cicero, serious doubt is cast on the legitimacy of arguing for the authenticity of ancient letters based on difference in tone.

A comparison of the Pastoral Epistles to the anti-Sophist polemic of ancient philosophical writings has led Robert J. Karris to conclude that the polemic aimed at the false teachers in these letters parallels the schema of the philosophers. He lists the elements of the schema, providing an example of each occurring within the Pastorals. The elements include: the greediness of the opponents, their practice of deceit, their hypocrisy in not practicing what they preach, their propensity for verbal disputes, the catalogues of vices cited against them, and the inroad of their teachings among women.[38] According to Karris, the function of this schema for the philosophers was to cause their readers to reject the sophists and sympathize with the writer's position, to disassociate the sophists' teachings from those of the writer, and

---

35. Ibid., 228.
36. Maloney, "Pastoral Epistles," 364.
37. Massey, "Cicero," 73–82.
38. Karris, "Backgrounds and Significance," 552–54.

to demonstrate who had the authority and the truth to be the legitimate teachers of true wisdom.[39]

To illustrate this schema in the Pastorals, one of the passages Karris examines is 2 Timothy 2:14—4:5. In this section Timothy is instructed through a string of imperatives in an almost antithetical style, what he should do, and urged to avoid doing what the false teachers do. Karris observes that in the specific mention of Hymenaeus and Philetus in 2:17-18, there is no direct refutation or correction of their false teaching, but the simple condemnation they have "gone astray from the truth."[40] In his use of this philosophical polemical schema, the author declares the teachings of the opponents to be false, disassociates their teachings from his, and demonstrates that only his gospel is the truth, helping create an aversion to the false teachings of the opponents, and to the opponents themselves.[41]

Benjamin Fiore's is another example of a comparison of the Pastoral Epistles to ancient philosophical writings, specifically the letters of Socrates. He finds parallels with the Socratic Discourses to Young Officials and his Kingship Treatises. He explores how personal example is a major motif in these letters, functioning as a positive role model for the exhortation and instruction.[42] He proposes that Paul presents himself as the model for Timothy's fidelity to the gospel in maintaining the purity of its content and faithfully practicing exemplary behavior befitting one who embraces and proclaims the gospel. He demonstrates how the example of Paul's life bookends the teaching and instruction on the nature, function and ministering of God's Word, explicitly the use of the aorist verb παρηκολούθησας "you closely followed/observed" Paul's proclamation, conduct, and circumstances.[43] The use of this verb indicates not only Timothy's presence as an eyewitness to Paul's life and ministry, but also, more importantly, his understanding of the significance of what he observed.[44]

In this letter, the presentation of Paul himself as the model and example for Timothy is prevalent throughout 2 Timothy. He builds on the familial language to plead as a Father to his son, exhorting him to the proper response to the circumstances, as his own presence is no longer available to address the crisis.[45] He is the example for Timothy of faithfulness to the

39. Ibid., 556.
40. Ibid., 559-60.
41. Ibid., 563.
42. Fiore, *Function of Personal Example*, 192-93.
43. Ibid., 205.
44. Knight, *Pastoral Epistles*, 438.
45. Westfall, "Moral Dilemma," 232-33.

content of the gospel and its proclamation, "Retain the standard of sound words which you heard from me," (1:13), "The things which you heard from me in the presence of many witnesses, entrust these to faithful men," (2:2) and also the standard of godly faithfulness in behavior, "Continue in all the things you have learned, knowing from whom you learned them" (3:14).[46]

Closely linked to Paul's presentation of himself as Timothy's exemplar is the linguistic feature of the repetition of the theme of remembrance. Verbs of remembrance occur prominently in the opening verses of this letter, occurring once in each of verses 1:3–5. Intertwined with this theme are words that are deeply emotive, creating a highly personal tone for this letter, as well as establishing Timothy's recall of his previous experience of ministry with Paul, witnessing Paul's faithfulness in proclaiming the gospel, and in living out the claims of the gospel as the model for the faithful ministry Paul was exhorting him to fulfill.[47] This initial cluster of words that share the semantic domain of remembering in 2:8 where Timothy is exhorted to "remember Jesus Christ" serves to introduce the only occurrence of the "trustworthy saying" formula in 2 Timothy, which functions to introduce and affirm the truth of the statement being made.[48] Here Timothy is to remember the work of Christ, and the "trustworthy statement" undergirds the call to endurance through its declaration of the benefits of salvation and its working out in the believer's life. This hymnic text provides assurance of salvation, exhorts perseverance, warns of the severity of the penalty for apostasy, and declares the absolute faithfulness of God, independent of our faithfulness to Him.[49] It is immediately followed by instruction to Timothy, that even as he is being exhorted by Paul to remember, he must remind the believers at Ephesus in order to fulfill his own calling of which Paul reminded him in 1:6–7.[50] Timothy's reminder to them is a "solemn charge" to hold to the eternal truths of salvation that are the essence of the gospel, and avoid useless word-wrangling.[51]

The failure to recognize the personal character of Paul's second letter to Timothy significantly alters the understanding of its character and purpose. Raymond Collins rejects a personal understanding of the letter, influenced by his rejection of Pauline authorship. Convinced of its pseudonymity, he declares, "In no case can any one of the Pastoral Epistles be considered a

46. Murphy-O'Connor, "2 Timothy Contrasted," 411.
47. Van Neste, *Cohesion and Structure*, 147–48; Swinson, "What Is Scripture?," 150.
48. Marshall, *Pastoral Epistles*, 328.
49. Mounce, *Pastoral Epistles*, 515.
50. Ibid., 523.
51. Montague, *First and Second Timothy*, 169.

truly personal letter" although admitting they have that appearance, but he dismisses these as "clearly rhetorical ploys."[52] He accepts the frequent scholarly identification of 2 Timothy as a representative of the ancient testamentary genre, such as the *Testament of the Twelve Patriarchs*. Collins acknowledges that the characteristics of this genre are not well defined, but nonetheless believes that 2 Timothy belongs to this genre.[53] Others have provided detailed reasons that this identification is not suitable to the character of 2 Timothy. Witherington lists several factors that make it difficult to understand this letter as testamentary. These include the absence of any mention of Paul's death or the end of his ministry, Paul and Timothy being of the same and not successive generations, Paul is not dying, details about the activities of the opponents are vivid, specific, not generic, the presence of direct connections between past and future woes, and the lack of general agreement concerning the structure of 2 Timothy.[54]

Among scholars accepting the authenticity of 2 Timothy as an authentic letter of Paul to the historical Timothy, and recognizing its personal tone and character, an oft-repeated assertion can be found that has limited textual basis. This is the assertion that Paul was prompted to write this letter, at least in part, to address his concern over Timothy's "timidity" and his failure to stand up to the opponents because of his own lack of confidence. Ben Witherington is one who finds in this letter evidence of Timothy's ministry failings and character flaws. He calls the situation at Ephesus at the time of writing "grim" and claims that "Timothy himself has become a problem." Witherington says this letter gives "the clear sense that Timothy is in over his head" and that Timothy "needs jump-starting."[55] Is such a negative assessment of Paul's opinion of Timothy at the time of the writing of this letter warranted? Christopher Hutson rightly cautions "Be wary of a tendency among some interpreters to infer a complete personality profile for Timothy from the merest scrap and then to read this profile into everything that is said about him."[56]

An alternative understanding of Paul's use of this single New Testament occurrence of the Greek word frequently translated "timidity," δειλίας, is offered by William Mounce. He argues that the characterization of Timothy as weak and fearful is not supported by the evidence. Timothy was

---

52. Collins, *1 & 2 Timothy*, 7.

53. Ibid., 182–83.

54. Witherington, *Letters and Homilies*, 303–4.

55. Ibid., 302. See also Knight, *Pastoral Epistles*, 8; Kelly, *Commentary on the Pastoral Epistles*, 160; and Johnson, *First and Second Letters*, 320.

56. Hutson, "Was Timothy Timid?," 58.

"Paul's 'first lieutenant,' someone Paul felt comfortable sending into difficult situations."[57] Furthermore, "timidity" is an unfortunate and questionable translation of the single New Testament occurrence of δειλίας. An examination of its nine LXX occurrences reveal that the force is much stronger, and is more accurately translated "cowardice."[58] This characterization does not fit the biblical portrayal of Timothy as Paul's trusted "troubleshooter" who was sent by Paul into crisis situations to refute error and return the church's focus to Paul's proclamation of God's truth. In 2 Timothy 1:6–7 the mention of cowardice should be understood as a rhetorical device, similar to that of Plutarch and Epictetus as they encourage and exhort their students.[59] Paul is encouraging Timothy to continue acting as he has been, with power, love, and self-control. In that context, "Cowardice is merely a foil that serves to emphasize and define what Paul means by power,"[60] not Paul's assessment of Timothy's character.

Another recent monograph that focuses on changing the common understanding of a specific text in 2 Timothy is Michael Prior's examination of Paul's closing assessment of his circumstances in 4:6–8. After surveying and assessing the authorship debate, Prior concludes that 2 Timothy is an authentic letter of Paul. He accounts for the stylistic variance from other Pauline letters by the fact that, in contrast to many of Paul's other letters, 2 Timothy was written without the assistance of a secretary or contributing co-author (frequently Timothy himself) as a private correspondence to Timothy.[61] In attempting to establish the occasion for Paul's writing this letter, Prior argues that not only is 2 Timothy not testamentary literature, but that "being poured out as a drink offering" does not refer to Paul's impending death.[62]

Through a detailed lexical analysis of the key terms σπένδομαι "being poured out" and ἀναλύσεως "departure" in verse 6, Prior seeks to demonstrate that a reference to Paul's death is not intended. He surveys extrabiblical usage, and the only other New Testament occurrence (Phil 2:17) of ἀναλύσεως and shows that a far more common understanding, and the one best fitting the context of Philippians, is not pouring out one's blood in martyrdom, but

---

57. Mounce, *Pastoral Epistles*, lviii.

58. Ibid., 478.

59. Plutarch, *Rect. rat. aud.*, 47.17 (Babbitt, LCL); Epictetus *Diatr.* 1.24.1–10 (Oldfeather, LCL), cited in Hutson, "Was Timothy Timid?," 70–72.

60. Mounce, *Pastoral Epistles*, 478.

61. Prior, *Paul the Letter-Writer*, 58–59.

62. Ibid., 111–12.

expending one's life in ministry and service.[63] Since the interpretation of its use in 2 Timothy is largely dependent on the understanding of its use by Paul in Philippians, its meaning here in 2 Timothy is likely parallel.

Also, occurring only here in the New Testament is the rare Greek word ἀναλύσεως. Based on Paul's omission of any explicit reference to his death, together with the context of 2 Timothy, particularly Paul's request for Timothy to come to him, Prior concludes this is better understood here as Paul's confidence that his release from prison is coming soon, and he will soon embark on a new ministry endeavor.[64] Whether or not one is convinced that his reconstruction of Paul's circumstances in writing 2 Timothy is convincing, Prior's analysis frees the interpretation of this text from the looming shadow of Paul's imminent death. Even if that is on the horizon for Paul, his choice of language makes the focus of his exhortation not the fact of his death but the pouring out of himself in the ministry of the gospel God had entrusted to him.

CONCLUSION

What are the results of this survey of recent linguistic analyses of 2 Timothy in terms of our interests in its character and purpose? First, it has been established that the linguistic arguments for pseudonymity are not nearly as certain as many of its proponents claim. An acceptance of the authenticity of this letter as a genuine letter of Paul is not an aberrant scholarly position, and cannot be relegated by its opponents to the realm of being uninformed or only necessitated by a particular theological position that flies in the face of the actual evidence. The only alternative to authenticity is that this letter was a successfully perpetrated fraud only exposed some 1,800 years after the fact.

Second, the authenticity of 2 Timothy should be accepted. 2 Timothy should be regarded as a genuine letter of the apostle Paul to his coworker Timothy as this is a very personal correspondence to the one whom Paul led to faith in Christ, discipled to maturity as a believer, ministered alongside of through many difficult and dangerous circumstances, and developed as a leader in God's church—one who helped fill the void created by the end of Paul's life and ministry. It is the most personal of Paul's letters, more so than Philemon which seems intended for public reading, or 1 Timothy and Titus which are written more to address situations in their respective congregations, instructing them through the leaders of those churches. But 2

---

63. Ibid., 92–98.
64. Ibid., 98–106.

Timothy is a personal correspondence whose focus is on Timothy and his circumstances, as well as those of Paul.

The purpose of 2 Timothy is best understood as a letter of encouragement and exhortation to Timothy, knowing the difficulty of the opposition he faced, from Paul who himself knew firsthand about difficult circumstances and suffering. It is an exhortation to faithfulness to the gospel, the word God has revealed. This faithfulness is expressed in the fidelity of the proclamation of the word and in faithfully living out that word in godly behavior, while accepting the suffering that will result. It is a call to remembrance for Timothy, remembering his own salvation and calling, remembering Paul's affection for him, the example of Paul's life and ministry, and acceptance of the suffering that inevitably accompanies faithfulness to God and His word. Finally, it was a request for Timothy to come to him to give Paul comfort by his presence.

What are the implications of the insights of these recent scholarly explorations of various aspects of 2 Timothy? The use of 2 Timothy in leadership development and training in the church today is legitimized by the recognition that there is nothing fictitious about this letter. Its author and recipient were two very real people; one called by God as apostle to the Gentiles, and greatly used of God as missionary, church planter, and theologian. The other was his protégé, ministry partner, and close friend. Its character and tone is personal, and its content provides a legitimate blueprint for those called to ministry today.

In his Anchor Yale Bible, Luke Timothy Johnson does a great service in going beyond the norm of most volumes in critical commentary series when he discusses the application of 2 Timothy to those called to ministry. This is a summary of some of his astute observations. In 2 Timothy Paul reminds us that ministry is not a career we choose, but "a call from God to be holy."[65] It is not a particular skillset, or body of knowledge to acquire, it is learning to live in such a way that our behavior reflects the deep convictions of God's truth in our lives. Ministry is carried out even as those called to it continue to themselves be in the process of being conformed and transformed by the power of the gospel. "Ministry . . . is not measured by success, but by its fidelity."[66] Faithful ministry of the gospel will invariably lead to suffering. It is not done with hope of earthly recognition, but in the sure and certain hope of resurrection life. The message of 2 Timothy "speaks with the urgency of prophecy, calling for witnesses to truth in an age that prefers

---

65. Johnson, *First and Second Letters*, 330.
66. Ibid.

teachers who cater to its desires."⁶⁷ This is a message needed for church leaders today, not just the next generation being raised up and equipped, but all who are called to leadership in God's church and desire to live out that calling in faithfulness.

BIBLIOGRAPHY

Aune, David E. "Pastoral Letters." In *Westminster Dictionary of New Testament and Early Christian Literature and Rhetoric*, 338–39. Louisville, KY: Westminster John Knox, 2003.

Baum, Armin D. "Semantic Variation Within the *Corpus Paulinium*: Linguistic Considerations Concerning the Richer Vocabulary of the Pastoral Epistles." *Tyndale Bulletin* 59 (2008) 271–92.

Collins, Raymond F. *1 & 2 Timothy and Titus: A Commentary*. New Testament Library. Louisville, KY: Westminster John Knox, 2002.

Ehrman, Bart D. *Forgery and Counterforgery: The Use of Literary Deceit in Early Christian Polemics*. Oxford: Oxford University Press, 2013.

Fee, Gordon. *1 and 2 Timothy and Titus*. New International Biblical Commentary. Peabody, MA: Hendrickson, 1988.

Fiore, Benjamin. *The Function of Personal Example in the Socratic and Pastoral Epistles*. Analecta Biblica 105. Rome: Biblical Institute Press, 1986.

Gloer, W. Hulitt. *1 & 2 Timothy, Titus*. Smith & Helwys Bible Commentary. Macon, GA: Smith & Helwys, 2010.

Harrison, P. N. *The Problem of the Pastoral Epistles*. London: Oxford University Press, 1921.

Hutson, Christopher R. "Was Timothy Timid? On the Rhetoric of Fearlessness (1 Corinthians 16:10–11) and Cowardice (2 Timothy 1:7)." *Biblical Research* 42 (1997) 58–73.

Johnson, Luke Timothy. *The First and Second Letters to Timothy*. Anchor Yale Bible 35A. New Haven: Yale University Press, 2001.

Karris, Robert J. "The Background and Significance of the Polemic of the Pastoral Epistles." *Journal of Biblical Literature* 92 (1973) 549–64.

Kelly, J. N. D. *A Commentary on the Pastoral Epistles*. Harper's New Testament Commentaries. New York: Harper & Row, 1963.

Kenny, Anthony. *A Stylometric Study of the New Testament*. Oxford: Clarendon, 1986.

Klauck, Hans Josef, and Daniel P. Bailey. *Ancient Letters and the New Testament: A Guide to Content and Exegesis*. Waco, TX: Baylor University Press, 2006.

Knight, George W., III. *The Pastoral Epistles: A Commentary on the Greek Text*. New International Greek Testament Commentary. Grand Rapids, MI: Eerdmans, 1992.

Lieu, Judith M. "Letters and the Topography of Early Christianity." *New Testament Studies* 62 (2016) 167–82.

Maloney, Linda M. "The Pastoral Epistles." In *Searching the Scriptures: A Feminist Commentary*, edited by Elisabeth Schüssler Fiorenza, 361–80. Vol. 2 New York: Crossroad, 1994.

---

67. Ibid.

Marshall, I. Howard. *The Pastoral Epistles.* International Critical Commentary. London: T&T Clark, 1999.

Massey, Preston T. "Cicero, the Pastoral Epistles, and the Issue of Pseudonymity." *Restoration Quarterly* 56 (2014) 65–84.

Mealand, David L. "The Extent of the Pauline Corpus: A Multivariate Approach." *Journal for the Study of the New Testament* 59 (1995) 61–92.

Montague, George T. *First and Second Timothy, Titus.* Catholic Commentary on Scripture. Grand Rapids, MI: Baker Academic, 2008.

Mounce, William D. *Pastoral Epistles.* Word Biblical Commentary 46. Nashville: Thomas Nelson, 2000.

Murphy-O'Connor, Jerome. "2 Timothy Contrasted with 1 Timothy and Titus." *Revue Biblique* 98 (1991) 403–18.

Nes, Jermo van. "The Problem of the Pastoral Epistles: An Important Hypothesis Reconsidered." In *Paul and Pseudepigraphy*, edited by Stanley E. Porter and Gregory P. Fewster, 153–69. Pauline Studies 8. Leiden: Brill, 2013.

Neumann, Kenneth J. *The Authenticity of the Pastoral Epistles in Light of Recent Stylometric Analysis.* SBL Dissertation Series 120. Atlanta: Scholars, 1990.

Oden, Thomas C. *First and Second Timothy and Titus.* Louisville, KY: Westminster John Knox, 1989.

Prior, Michael. *Paul the Letter-Writer and the Second Letter to Timothy.* Journal for the Study of the New Testament, Supplement Series 23. Sheffield: Sheffield Academic, 1989.

Swinson, L. Timothy. *What Is Scripture? Paul's Use of Graphe in the Letters to Timothy.* Eugene, OR: Wipf & Stock, 2014.

Thatcher, Tom. "The Relational Matrix of the Pastoral Epistles." *Journal of the Evangelical Theological Society* 38 (1995) 41–45.

Towner, Philip. *The Letters to Timothy and Titus.* New International Commentary on the New Testament. Grand Rapids, MI: Eerdmans, 2006.

Van Neste, Ray. *Cohesion and Structure in the Pastoral Epistles.* Journal for the Study of the New Testament, Supplement Series 280. London: T&T Clark, 2004.

Westfall, Cynthia Long. "A Moral Dilemma? The Epistolary Body of 2 Timothy." In *Paul and the Ancient Letter Form*, edited by Stanley E. Porter and Sean A. Adams, 213–52. Pauline Studies 6. Leiden: Brill, 2010.

Witherington, Ben, III. *Letters and Homilies for Hellenized Christians.* Vol. 1, *A Socio-Rhetorical Commentary on Titus, 1–2 Timothy and 1–3 John.* Downers Grove, IL: IVP Academic, 2006.

Chapter 11

Scripture Memorization and Theological Education

καθ' ὑπερβολὴν ὁδός *("A Most Excellent Way")*

—RADU GHEORGHITA
Midwestern Baptist Theological Seminary

INTRODUCTION

UNLIKE YESTERYEAR, THESE DAYS Scripture memorization is a discipline associated almost exclusively with Sunday School activities. Gone are the days when Scripture memorization was considered part of the tool chest of the Christian academia, especially evangelical theological education.[1] The following considerations are intended as an *apologia* for reconsidering Scripture memorization as an indispensable part of the *instrumentarium* of the theologian, the biblicist and the systematician alike, especially during the years of their theological formation. The type of discipline advocated

1. There is anecdotal information about several prominent exegetes who espoused this position. It is said that Professors C. F. D. Moule and G. B. Caird knew the entire Greek New Testament by heart, as did F. F. Bruce, who allegedly knew by heart both Testaments in their respective languages. So contends Hurst with regard to G. B. Caird, in Hurst and Wright, *Glory of Christ*, and Gasque about F. F. Bruce, in "F. F. Bruce, 1910–1990," 3–5. The Southern Baptists too have a representative in this elite group. Professor Dale Moody of Southern Baptist Theological Seminary, according to the recently published history of the seminary, "had a prodigious memory and seemed to be able to quote any verse in the Greek New Testament by heart." Cf. Wills, *Southern Baptist*, 439.

here is not merely memorization of separate verses or even passages, but of entire books of the Bible. Moreover, for those dedicated to the study of the Scriptures in its original languages, the article proposes to use the same approach in memorizing the Scriptures in the original languages.

It seems entirely appropriate to dedicate the following considerations to honor Dave, with whom I share not only Romanian blood, but also a passion for the Scriptures and for Scripture memorization. During his mission trip to Romania a decade ago, he told a group of pastors that his favorite way to test the graduating PhD students was to grill them on ten NT verses that they must know and analyze from memory.

Why is it necessary to advocate bringing back Scripture memorization onto the radar of evangelical theologians? Is this not a universally assumed practice? What are the benefits of recommending a discipline that most consider obsolete today? After all, we live in an age in which the digital revolution has made it all but redundant. What common ground is there between Scripture memorization and theological Academia?

The following reflections have their origin in the perceived danger of a diminishing contact between the divinity student and the Scriptures themselves. Surrounded by a suffocating volume of secondary literature that most theologians, students and teachers alike, must master, there is the real risk that the very source and heart of our theology, the Scriptures themselves, will become a secondary priority or, even worse, a neglected presence.

This article addresses two aspects pertaining to the Scripture memorization. The first part offers a brief introduction to the practice of Scripture memorization book-by-book. In the second part, the focus will be on the outcome of using such an approach to one New Testament book, appropriately for Dave, the Epistle to the Hebrews. The experience of incorporating this discipline in a variety of ways and venues, be they the classroom, the local church, or personal devotion, alongside its benefits over the years prompted the subtitle καθ' ὑπερβολὴν ὁδός, a most excellent way. While this might be viewed as a rather pretentious claim, it has been used because it conveys truthfully the impact Scripture memorization has made on my life and theological journey.

THE PRACTICE OF MEMORIZATION

Since the methodology and the rationale for memorizing books of the Bible have been addressed in several previous articles, the space devoted to such matters here is only minimal.[2] The praxis of memorizing the Scripture

2. Gheorghita, "Ad Fontes Purissimi," 42–69; and Gheorghita, "Scripture

book-by-book is based on my own program of memorization, which I have been using for almost three decades. It claims no universal validity since an approach that works for someone might be unproductive for another.[3] Nonetheless, this is the approach that I have used personally and have encouraged my students to use. So far, it has proven to be very efficient both for me and for them. I always start by choosing one book that will become the focus of my memorization efforts and study for the following several months. The process of memorization then is comprised of four distinct phases.

The first phase, *the acquisition*, has as its goal the ability to recall and recite the entire book with the aid of a prompter. The daily working target is to commit to memory 10–12 new verses, and to review what had been memorized to that point. If done consistently, reaching the goal for this phase is achievable in about three weeks, for a medium size book of 5, 6 chapters, with a daily average time investment of about 30–40 minutes. By the end of the acquisition phase, the entire book can be recalled from memory, using the promptings of an open text whenever needed. It is important to underscore the obvious: the book is not yet known by heart at this stage. In fact, it is not known very well at all, but at least each paragraph was retained separately and reviewed daily.

The second phase, *the consolidation*, extends anywhere between four to six weeks. The goal for this phase is the ability to recite fluently the entire book from memory, without the help of the prompter. During this phase, the daily objective is to recite the book at least once, preferably in one, but no more than two sittings. Both the speed and the accuracy of recalling the content increase day by day. By the end of this phase, after the book had been recited daily for this interval of time, the book is safely stored in memory.

Once the book is known this well, the third phase, *the elation*, commences. I consider this phase to be the most scintillating stage in book

---

memorization," 15. Lifeway Resources did show interest in this approach and incorporated a series on Scripture memorization in their Ministry Grid platform. The material can be accessed at http://www.ministrygrid.com/web/guest/training-viewer/-/training/how-to-memorize-scripture-book-by-book-1.

3. There are very few books in print on Scripture memorization. For a variety of reasons, not least its unimpressive marketability, the topic is avoided by most evangelical publishing houses. Several years ago, I searched the databases of Zondervan, Baker, IVP, B&H, and Eerdmans, for titles on Scripture memorization and the results confirmed the above assertion. While there were plenty of titles on other spiritual disciplines, mainly prayer, I found across the board only a couple of titles dealing with memorization. Amazon inventory fairs a bit better. Among their titles, Davis, *Approach to Extended Memorization*, offers a similar perspective.

memorization. During this phase, I spend the next three or four months on the book, doing not much more than reviewing it daily. The primary goal is to enjoy fully the benefits that come from a text perfectly known by heart. By this stage, the fluency of recitation has reached its peak, and total attention can be devoted exclusively to the text itself. The joy of discovering God's truths in the memorized text reaches its highest intensity, unsurpassed in my experience by any other spiritual disciplines. The last phase, *the hibernation*, starts when the book is no longer reviewed daily, allowing the transition to the next book.

Turning briefly to the rationale for memorizing books of the Bible, there are indeed many solid reasons to engage in this discipline, which is just as much spiritual as it is cognitive. First and foremost, the practice of memorizing God's Word is equally commended and commanded throughout the Bible, either explicitly, as in some well-known passages such as Pss 1:2; 119:11; and Josh 1:8, or implicitly, as in the paramount example of our Lord, who quoted the Scriptures repeatedly in his sermons, teachings, and debates.

Besides the obedience factor implicit in these references, the spiritual/devotional as well as intellectual/academic benefits are also evident. With regard to the former, anyone who has been involved in Scripture memorization can attest to its diverse spiritual benefits. This spiritual discipline has proven its usefulness for countless generations of Christians, and will find in every generation advocates not merely for its usefulness but for its indispensability for a normal Christian life. As to the latter, memorizing an entire book gives a solid, thorough knowledge of the biblical text, something that cannot be achieved at this level by any other exegetical means.

The primary cognitive benefit of memorization is a mastery and a profound grasp of the biblical text in its canonical form. Issues such as vocabulary and style of the author, themes dominating the overall message of the book, the atmosphere of the writing, theological nuances, the structure of the book and the intricacies of the argument, and many other aspects are depicted by book memorization with more ease and precision than by any other exploratory tools. Among the benefits worthy of mention, one must also include a growing ability to assess critically the work of others. To memorize a book does not mean to withdraw from the theological dialogue. On the contrary, memorization is a means of entering that dialogue with vigorous personal convictions. Last, but not least, one surprising and unexpected spiritual benefit of memorization turns out to be the sheer joy accompanying the memorization process. This seemingly insignificant spiritual discipline promises a level of spiritual satisfaction and inner joy that, on a personal level, has been unrivaled by any other spiritual discipline.

When it is done properly, the intense Scripture memorization will lead to a level of spiritual elation and enjoyment that is unsurpassed.[4]

In conclusion to this brief list of benefits from memorization, it should be mentioned in passing that book memorization lends an almost inexhaustible resource for lecturing, preaching and teaching on that particular book, to the delight of both the speaker and the audience. Memorization is indeed one simple tool that can explore the depths of the Word of God in ways in which few other approaches can. The proposal advanced here is a commitment to memorize entire books of the Bible, with nothing less than the entire canon as a lifetime goal.[5] Such a goal might seem unachievable to most, but when one is committed to Scripture memorization, several decades of disciplined memorization can achieve surprising results, as well as be very rewarding. The memorization of Scripture must regain its rightful place among the exploratory methods of Scripture investigation. Where it is present, it should be intensified; where dormant, revived; and where challenged, defended.

THE OUTCOME OF MEMORIZATION: ΠΡΟΣ ΕΒΡΑΙΟΥΣ AS A TEST CASE

The main part of the paper consists of a sampling from a list of exegetical and theological observations gleaned from ΠΡΟΣ ΕΒΡΑΙΟΥΣ, memorized through the stages outlined above.[6] Hebrews scholars will find little new material here; perhaps nothing spectacular to justify the effort required to memorize the entire Greek text of the epistle. Some might even object that any computer program specialized in the analysis of the biblical text could do comparable exploratory work and much more. No counter-argument is

---

4. For a sample of testimonies collected from students in support of this claim, see Gheorghita, "Scripture Memorization," 49.

5. I usually challenge my students to follow either a three/five-year program of memorization, or a seven/ten-year one. The first program includes a sampling from the gospels (the Sermon on the Mount, Matt 5–7, and the Farewell Discourse, John 13–17), alongside a representative segment of Paul's writings (Galatians and Ephesians), the quorum of the apostolic voices found in the general epistles (James; 1 & 2 Peter; 1, 2, & 3 John; and Jude), and a significant portion of apocalyptic literature, Rev 1–5, 21–22. The second program devotes attention to one entire gospel (either the Gospel of Mark or John), alongside the two undisputable NT theological towers (the epistles of Romans and Hebrews), the quorum of the apostolic voices (cf. *supra*), and the book of Revelation.

6. While the following remarks have in view the memorization of the Greek text of Hebrews, they are equally applicable when memorization is done in a translation of one's choice.

offered to this objection: it is a legitimate and substantial one. However, the proof is in the doing: the case for the superiority of memorization will be self-evident to those who will actually do it.

The material that follows traces five domains that emerge as particularly fruitful in the process of memorization: lexical considerations, intratextuality, stylistic features, structure of the book, and theological insights. The classification here is rather loose and somewhat artificial since several of the examples discussed could feature under more than one rubric.[7] Alongside the results of memorization on Hebrews, the second part will also argue that several characteristics of the author's use of Scriptures are congruent with the hypothesis that he worked, at least in part, by making appeal to Scriptures that he committed to memory.

Lexical Stock

One of the first benefits of book memorization is an immediate grasp of the author's lexical stock. Unlike the artificial acquisition of Hebrews' vocabulary by using a lexicon, memorization of Hebrews facilitates acquiring a working knowledge of the author's vocabulary by observing them in an actual literary context. Moreover, as the work of memorization progresses, the important lexical units become apparent, by the sheer frequency of their usage. Naturally, it is safe to assume that there is a direct correlation between the frequency of a word and its contribution to the overall message. Leaving aside articles, conjunctions, prepositions and particles—words of high frequency usage in any writing—memorization will inevitably detect the words with significant contribution to the message.

Given the wide spectrum of Hebrews' lexical stock, numerous examples in this regard could be provided. First, there is the group of core lexical units responsible for the message of the book. Included here are lexical units of high frequency usage, such as the nouns πίστις, αἷμα, ἁμαρτία, or υἱός, as well as those without statistical dominance, such as the adjective κρείττων or the adverb ἅπαξ, which attest to the weightiness of their contribution.

Appreciation will soon emerge for another lexical subgroup, the family of cognates, either in the simple verb/noun pair, μετέχω/μέτοχος or in a larger set of cognates, like those formed around the root τελ: the verbs τελειόω and its compounds ἐπιτελέω, συντελέω, the nouns τελείωσις, τελειωτής, and συντέλεια, and the adjective τέλειος. The focus on the lexical stock will soon turn to other lexical subgroups of interest, notably the pairs of antithetical

---

7. For a similar analysis conducted on Paul's letter to the Galatians, see Gheorghita, "Ad Fontes."

concepts, often explored by the author with great rhetorical impact: υἱός/ θεράπων, ἀπείθεια/ὑπακοή, νήπιος/τέλειος, ἀρχηγός/τελειωτής, as well as those lexical units unrelated lexically, which nevertheless are bound together in the development of the theological argument: ἐπαγγέλλομαι/ἐπαγγελία— to promise/promise, i.e., the act of making a promise and the words of the promise—and κληρονομέω/κληρονομία/κληρονόμος—to inherit/inheritance, i.e., the promise reaching its fulfilment, the promise that has become reality.

As important as the statistically dominant words are in the lexical repertoire of the author, they are not the only lexemes indispensable for the message of the epistle. There are other words that prove to be just as important even though they are not numerically dominant. Words must be weighted, not simply counted, to adapt a dictum from textual criticism. Memorizing a book helps locating these infrequent, yet theologically loaded words, and it does it with more ease than other exegetical probings. One would include here the cognate pair of αἰσχύνη/ἐπαισχύνομαι, distinctly important in factoring the shame/honor balance within the socio-historical milieu. Likewise, the verb καταρτίζω, employed always with God as the subject, shows unequivocally the shared essence of three of God's works: the creation of the universe, κατηρτίσθαι τοὺς αἰῶνας ῥήματι θεοῦ, the creation of the universe (Heb 11:3), the preparation of Christ's body for the incarnation, σῶμα δὲ κατηρτίσω μοι (Heb 10:5), and the equipping of the believers to do God's will, καταρτίσαι ὑμᾶς ἐν παντὶ ἀγαθῷ εἰς τὸ ποιῆσαι τὸ θέλημα αὐτοῦ (Heb 13:21).

Becoming conversant with the author's lexical preferences will occasionally help in making informed decisions on lexical cruces. The usage of the verb γεύομαι in Heb 2:9 with regard to the death of Christ, ὅπως χάριτι θεοῦ ὑπὲρ παντὸς γεύσηται θανάτου, helps clarify its meaning in Heb 6:4–6. The latter passage uses the same verb twice, γευσαμένους τε τῆς δωρεᾶς τῆς ἐπουρανίου (Heb 6:4) and καλὸν γευσαμένους θεοῦ ῥῆμα δυνάμεις τε μέλλοντος αἰῶνος (Heb 6:5). To suggest that in Heb 6:4–6, the author has in mind an incomplete, superficial Christian experience does not square with the author's use of the same lexeme when he describes the death of Christ as a genuine, complete experience. Similarly, the meaning of ὑπόστασις as "substantial reality, essence" in Heb 1:3, ὃς ὢν ἀπαύγασμα τῆς δόξης καὶ χαρακτὴρ τῆς ὑποστάσεως αὐτοῦ, sufficiently clarifies the meaning of the same word both in Heb 3:14, μέτοχοι γὰρ τοῦ Χριστοῦ γεγόναμεν, ἐάνπερ τὴν ἀρχὴν τῆς ὑποστάσεως μέχρι τέλους βεβαίαν κατάσχωμεν, and in Heb 11:1, Ἔστιν δὲ πίστις ἐλπιζομένων ὑπόστασις, πραγμάτων ἔλεγχος οὐ βλεπομένων, without the need to appeal to the unattested lexical meanings of "condition" or "confidence."[8] Faith brings the unseen realities, those things hoped for, which are not yet part of the believer's real experience, into the visible realm. This is not significantly different than the Son, who, by his incarnation, became the visible manifestation of the invisible God. While, indeed, the danger of lexicographic totality transfer is always present, once the safeguards are set in place, lexical ties between passages could help clarify and explore potential theological affinities between them.

Intratextuality

The following discussion focuses on several instances of intratextuality in ΠΡΟΣ ΕΒΡΑΙΟΥΣ, in which phrases that display similarities, when read intratextually, lead to a deeper message than the sum total of each individual usage.[9] Tracing elements of intratextuality ranks among the most profitable aspects in acquiring a fuller understanding of the book's message, as well as one of the most enjoyable results of memorization. I have found memorization to be unparalleled in enabling one to investigate and to appreciate the inner texture of ideas and themes in the book, providing not only the opportunity for a holistic picture of the writing, but also the ability to identify individual nuances of each passage.

At times, the intratextual links are detected with ease, especially when they are located in close proximity. The opening stages of the epistle's argument offer two such examples of intratextuality. In both instances, the similar phrases mark out the well-known procedure of *inclusio*. In chapter 1, the pair is:

Heb 1:5, τίνι γὰρ εἶπέν ποτε τῶν ἀγγέλων,

Heb 1:13, πρὸς τίνα δὲ τῶν ἀγγέλων εἴρηκέν ποτε,

And in chapter 2:

Heb 2:5, οὐ γὰρ ἀγγέλοις ὑπέταξεν τὴν οἰκουμένην τὴν μέλλουσαν,

Heb 2:16, οὐ γὰρ δήπου ἀγγέλων ἐπιλαμβάνεται.

Similarly, intratextuality is easily observable in passages using the well-known rabbinical exegetical procedure *gezerah shavah*. The author draws attention to the verb καταπαύω in Gen 2:3, ὅτι ἐν αὐτῇ κατέπαυσεν ἀπὸ

---

8. BDAG, *ad loc.*, "The interp. *situation, condition* . . . has been suggested for some of the passages . . . Hb 3:14 . . . The sense 'confidence,' 'assurance' . . . must be eliminated, since examples of it cannot be found."

9. In its literary aspect, intratextuality is a more complex phenomenon than it might appear from the above description; cf. Brett, "Intratextuality," 320–21.

πάντων τῶν ἔργων αὐτοῦ, and its link with the cognate noun κατάπαυσις in Ps 95:11, εἰ εἰσελεύσονται εἰς τὴν κατάπαυσίν μου, quoted repeatedly in Heb 3—4.¹⁰ Similarly, the appellative σὺ [εἶ] "you are" in Heb 5:5, υἱός μου εἶ σύ, and in Heb 5:6, σὺ ἱερεὺς εἰς τὸν αἰῶνα, links the two passages on the bases of the verbal analogy.

Other times, however, the intratextual elements are less obvious, as they are separated by several chapters. Rarely seen or referred to by commentators, the quotation from 2 Sam 7:14 in Heb 1:5, ἐγὼ ἔσομαι αὐτῷ εἰς πατέρα, καὶ αὐτὸς ἔσται μοι εἰς υἱόν, and the one from Jer 31:33 in Heb 8:10, καὶ ἔσομαι αὐτοῖς εἰς θεόν, καὶ αὐτοὶ ἔσοντα μοι εἰς λαόν, not only share a common form, but point to an essential link between the Davidic covenant and the New Covenant, which could hardly be a mere textual coincidence.

Author's Style

Familiarization with the author's literary style ranks among the most important benefits of book memorization, especially when done in the original languages. Charting the literary style of an author as well as tracing its imprint on a given writing is a complex matter. It needs to consider a panoply of aspects, including the intrinsic unity of the writing, the relationship between the author and the amanuensis, as well as all issues concerning the writing itself, date, provenance, occasion, etc. Yet, no writing fails to display stylistic constants that could reasonably be considered the marks of the author's literary style.

Most of the stylistic features of Hebrews are well-known to students of the epistle. Whether one takes as a starting point the five-fold literary devices proposed by Vanhoye (announcement of subject, transitional hookwords, characteristic terms, alternation between exposition and exhortation, and inclusio),¹¹ or the long list compiled in Bateman's tally;¹² whether one looks at the distinct rhetorical features of the discourse or considers the place and function of the use of Scriptures in the author's hermeneutics, the epistle is a rich display of stylistic distinctiveness. No commentator captures better the epistle's unique concern for style than Simcox, who contends that the author "deals with the biblical language . . . as a preacher, whose first

---

10. For the sake of brevity, the OT references will follow the Masoretic textual tradition, even when it differs from the Septuagintal textual tradition. The two numbering systems differ substantially in the Psalter and the book of Jeremiah.

11. Vanhoye, *Structure and Message*.

12. Bateman, *Charts*.

duty is to be faithful, but his second to be eloquent."[13] Given the extent of scholarly scrutiny on the style, none of the aforementioned aspects will be presently rehearsed in further support for memorization as a useful tool in revealing the author's style. One case, however, will be presented as a potential instance in which a stylistic feature might be responsible for a series of well-known exegetical cruces.

The case in point is an unusual, perhaps even surprising, sequence of words or phrases in several passages. The first of these passages, and the least difficult, is Heb 1:6, ὅταν δὲ πάλιν εἰσαγάγῃ τὸν πρωτότοκον εἰς τὴν οἰκουμένην, κτλ, in which the adverb πάλιν could be syntactically construed either as supporting the verb εἰσαγάγῃ or as part of the introductory formula marking out the following quotation in the seven-fold catena. A simple metathesis, πάλιν δὲ ὅταν, or a variation of it, would have dispersed any ambiguity.

A second, more difficult example is Heb 3:9, 10 with the problematic segmentation of the quotation from Ps 95:10, καὶ εἶδον τὰ ἔργα μου τεσσεράκοντα ἔτη· διὸ προσώχθισα τῇ γενεᾷ ταύτῃ καὶ εἶπον in Heb 3:9–10. As it stands, the conjunction διό divides the text in such a way that the forty years are associated with the people's witnessing God's works (the sense of the Greek text in Hebrews) and not with God's displeasure with the desert generation (the sense shared by both textual traditions in the Psalm). The fact that the Author did associate the forty years with God's anger is established without ambiguity by the rhetorical question in Heb 3:17, τίσιν δὲ προσώχθισεν τεσσεράκοντα ἔτη. Again, a simple inversion of words in Heb 3:10, διὸ τεσσεράκοντα ἔτη, would have solved the textual conundrum.

The third example comes from the final benediction in Heb 13:20–21, Ὁ δὲ θεὸς τῆς εἰρήνης, ὁ ἀναγαγὼν ἐκ νεκρῶν τὸν ποιμένα τῶν προβάτων τὸν μέγαν ἐν αἵματι διαθήκης αἰωνίου, τὸν κύριον ἡμῶν Ἰησοῦν, καταρτίσαι ὑμᾶς ἐν παντὶ ἀγαθῷ, κτλ. As the text stands, the prepositional phrase ἐν αἵματι διαθήκης αἰων ου must be construed with the participial verbal phrase ὁ ἀναγαγὼν ἐκ νεκρῶν τὸν ποιμένα, κτλ. In this form, the text, while not unintelligible, conveys an unusual and perhaps unlikely meaning than if the prepositional phrase would support the main verb, the subjunctive aorist καταρτίσαι. Contextually, this would be a more fitting reading of the passage, in fact, in congruence with other usages of the phrase "blood of the covenant," (cf. Heb 10:29). In all these cases, if the interpreter would allow the author a greater measure of stylistic flexibility, and not demand adherence to a strict syntactical norm, the above passages would no longer be considered exegetical cruces. In the same way, the interpreter might also

---

13. Quoted by Moffatt, *Critical and Exegetical Commentary*, lxiv.

tease Heb 9:4 and its unusual placement of the θυμιατήριον in the Holy of Holies.[14] The phraseology adjustments in this case would be significantly greater and consequently they would be less likely the solution to the well-known conundrum.

Structure

The memorization of Hebrews, indeed of any biblical book, yields considerable results in sorting out the structure of the epistle. Reviewing the text over and over again gives a better understanding not only of the natural divisions in the text but also of the logic behind their sequence as well as of the flow of the argument as a whole. Given the space confines, no new structure proposal is offered here. Suffice it to say that memorization has consolidated the appreciation for two aspects of structural consequence. First, it confirmed the architectonic role of Ps 110, a psalm unsurpassed by any other Scriptures quoted or alluded in its reverberations throughout the epistle. Second, there is the unequivocal structural importance of Heb 4:14–16; 8:1–2; and 10:19–21. These passages are replete with textual and thematic parallels, all involving theological re-workings of Ps 110.

When considering the structure of Hebrews' argument, memorization could be very helpful also in assessing the strengths and weaknesses of the structures proposed in various commentaries. Craig Koester's magisterial commentary came about the time I finished memorizing ΠΡΟΣ ΕΒΡΑΙΟΥΣ.[15] While the commentary is brimming with fresh insights and analyses, the structure proposed, following the lead of the socio-rhetorical criticism, was unconvincing. Without entering the details for Koester's proposal, the commentary locates the *propositio* in Heb 2:5–9, with the first set of arguments in Heb 2:10—6:20, followed by two more series of arguments. The proposal amounts to breaking Heb 2:5–18 into two parts, an unattractive solution for a passage characterized by a beautifully balanced structure. There is no doubt that the renewed attention to rhetorical criticism has greatly improved our understanding of the argument structure of various NT epistles. Yet, at times the application of the canons of rhetorical criticism appears not to enhance our understanding, but rather to blur it. Koester's proposal comes close to qualifying as one such instance. While locating the *propositio* in Heb 2:5–9 is possible, it is rather improbable, since it raises Ps 8 to a theological predominance which it simply does not have, especially when compared with Ps 110. Furthermore, competing

---

14. See Gheorghita, *Role of the Septuagint*, 87.
15. Koester, *To the Hebrews*.

against Koester's choice stands the intricate microstructure of the epistle in the opening section 1:5—2:18, consisting of two *inclusio*-type expositions, 1:5–13 (marked by similar rhetorical questions in 1:5 and 1:13) and 2:5-16 (marked by similar statements in 2:5 and 2:16), perfectly balancing each other on either side of the first warning passage in 2:1–4. To isolate 2:5–9 from this beautifully constructed passage, and elevate it to the status of the *propositio* for the entire discourse runs against the stylistic pageantry of the author of Hebrews.

Theological Issues—Scriptural Quotations in Hebrews

The fifth aspect of memorization worthy of consideration comes under the broad heading of theological issues. If there is one aspect in which memorization makes the single biggest impact, this would undoubtedly be in the area of biblical theology. Memorization of an entire book is the paramount exercise that helps the exegete to go beyond an atomistic understanding of the writing. It provides a panoramic, holistic understanding of the text and the implicit theology expressed in it, which is arguably unsurpassed by other exegetical soundings. The last part of the paper will give attention to only one such consideration, namely the likelihood that the memorization of the Psalter—if not in its entirety, at least large portions of it—was indeed a factor, if not *the* factor, responsible for the author's selection of the Scriptures used in quotations.

Unfortunately, because of the inherent methodological indeterminacy, a case for quoting from memory can be neither demonstrated nor refuted.[16] Consequently, scholarship has given at best secondary attention to this possibility. To those engaged in large-scale Scripture memorization, however, an explanation of the author's use of Scripture that presupposes dependence on Scripture memorization is among the best hypotheses that fit the data. As Gerhardsson has documented, the memorization of large portions of the Scriptures, customary in early Judaism, significantly increased an author's ability to draw multiple connections between various scriptural passages, leading to an interplay of Scriptures in support of the message to be delivered.[17]

Hebrews scholarship has long recognized the existence of two separate categories of Scriptural texts from which quotations derive.[18] First, there are the texts of primary importance for the development of the epistle's overall

---

16. Ellingworth, "Old Testament in Hebrews," 309.
17. Gerhardsson, *Memory and Manuscript*.
18. The best case was put forward by Caird, "Exegetical Method," 44–51.

argument. While there is agreement on the nature of these primary texts, the number of eligible passages vary considerably, with advocates for one, four, five, or seven main texts.[19] Texts in the second category have a more limited scope, their contribution rarely extending beyond the paragraph in which they are used. Caird's assertion, "all other scriptural references are ancillary to these [four scriptural passages] which control the drift of the argument," continues to guide scholarship on Hebrews in this respect.[20]

As important as this division in primary and secondary texts is, it has often obstructed an awareness of the extensive web of verbal and thematic parallels between the passages quoted in the epistle, not all readily observable. Indeed, a part of these parallels are evident among the texts of the primary Scriptural passages, but they are certainly not restricted to them. Verbal and thematic links surface also in the contexts of the primary and secondary texts, and even among the contexts of the secondary texts.[21] The following considerations maintain that the verbal and thematic overlap, far from being merely coincidental, were an important consideration in the Author's processing Scripture. Even more, the argument advanced here is that the result is both compatible with and explicable on the presupposition that the Author was operating with memorized Scripture.

There were many factors that contributed to the selection of these Scriptural passages, and the number of proposals is increasing with every study on the topic. The early Christian tradition played a significant role, just as the needs of the community addressed did also. The synagogue liturgical readings or the intricacies of the rabbinic hermeneutics also have plausibility on their side.[22] Various theological agendas, whether the "self confessed inadequacy of the old order,"[23] or the "plurality of divine persons,"[24] could also explain facets of the phenomenon. Doubtless, the process responsible for the selection of the Scriptural texts was as complex and diverse as it was their usage. The proposal advanced here is that memorized Scripture also

---

19. Buchanan advocates for one text, Ps 110, in Buchanan, *To the Hebrews*, xxvii; Caird proposes Pss 8, 95, 110; and Jer 31, in Caird, "Exegetical Method," 47; Longenecker revises the list by adding the catena in Heb 1:5–13 (Ps 2 and Deut 32), in Longenecker, *Biblical Exegesis*, 175ff; France upgrades the list to seven passages, Pss 8, 95, 110; Jer 31; Hab 2; Prov 3; and Exod 19–20, in France, "Writer of Hebrews," 245–76.

20. Caird, "Exegetical Method," 47.

21. Gheorghita, *Role of the Septuagint*, 65ff.

22. Docherty, *Use of the Old Testament*. See also Gelardini, "Hebrews," 107–27; and Walser, *Old Testament Quotations*.

23. Astutely proposed by Caird, "Exegetical Method," 47, and developed further by Motyer, "Psalm Quotations," 3–22.

24. Glasson, "Plurality," 270–72. See also Ellingworth, "Old Testament," 41.

played a role. The type and number of parallels between the quoted passages in the epistle point to the writing of an author who was working with a trove of memorized passages in the Greek Psalter and Scriptures.

Space considerations allow for only two arguments in support of the aforementioned proposal. First, there is the evidence inferred from the web of thematic and verbal parallels between quotations. The quotation texts themselves as well as their larger contexts display the type of overlap and similarities congruent with the hypothesis that the author knew by heart the vast majority of them. The process responsible for the texts' selection and grouping, whatever other facets it might have included, should also allow for the contribution of alleged memorized Scripture. Second, evidence in support of the idea that the author depended on memorized Scripture comes from the Scriptural passages quoted more than once. It has long been observed that several passages quoted multiple times display textual variations among themselves. These variations are resonant with the phenomenon of quoting from memory.

We start with the evidence from the parallels among the passages quoted, one of the most noticeable aspects of Hebrews' quotations. The verbal parallels between quotations are often part of the quoted texts and, as such, they most likely triggered the association of the passages. Other times, the similarities are not part of the quoted text per se, but they become evident when the quotations' larger contexts are set side by side.

Examples of the first kind abound. Some of them have already been discussed in the intertextuality section. Textual parallels, similar to the ones displayed by Pss 2 and 110, mentioned earlier, are evident also between Pss 2 and 8, between Pss 110 and 95, or between Pss 110 and 8.[25] Other times, a particular syntactical pattern could trigger the association. This is the case when the demonstrative particle ἰδού is followed by a first person singular unit as in Ps. 40 and in Isaiah 8:18, quoted in Heb 10:7, 9, ἰδοὺ ἥκω, ..., τοῦ ποιῆσαι ὁ θεὸς τὸ θέλημά σου, and, respectively, in Heb 2:13, ἰδοὺ ἐγὼ καὶ τὰ παιδία ἅ μοι ἔδωκεν ὁ θεός. Very likely, the same phenomenon takes place in the quotation from Ps 110:4 in Heb 7:21, ὤμοσεν κύριος καὶ οὐ μεταμεληθήσεται, when grouped with Ps 95:11 in Heb 3:11, ὡς ὤμοσα ἐν τῇ ὀργῇ μου.

The verbal parallels between the quoted texts thus offer a reasonable explanation to account for the author's selection and combination of texts, a fact indirectly acknowledged throughout the epistle.[26] The textual parallels in the quotations, however, are only the tip of the iceberg. Less visible to

---

25. Gheorghita, *Role of the Septuagint*, 66ff.
26. cf. Heb 5:6, *inter alia*.

the reader, there stand extensive thematic and verbal parallels, drawn from the immediate contexts of the quotation passages. When read side by side, there are at least a dozen verbal parallels between Pss 2 and 110, and half a dozen or more between many of the psalms quoted: Pss 110 and 8; Pss 110 and 95; Pss 8 and 95; and Pss 2 and 95.[27] This is not limited to the quotations from the Psalter. The original context of the crucial quotation from Hab 2:3-4 in Heb 10:37-38 has multiple verbal and thematic parallels with the contexts of most of the other key quotations: Deut 33, Isa 26, Prov 3, Hag 2, Ps 2, Ps 22, Ps 95, and Ps 110.[28] These textual observations support the hypothesis that the author was working with a virtual network of Scriptural texts, which he selected not merely because they offered theological support for his argument, but also because they resonate with each other and are satiated with verbal and thematic affinities. It is beyond doubt that the author was extremely familiar with these Scriptures. Admittedly, this falls short of a positive proof for the contention that the Author had these passages memorized or that he was quoting from memory. Yet, it suggests a *modus operandi* in the practice of quoting from the Scriptures, which is both realistic and decidedly probable.[29]

The second potential evidence in support for the contention that memorization played a role in Hebrews' quotations is hinted by those passages quoted more than once. While this phenomenon could be traced at various junctures, the best candidates are Ps 40 and Jer 31. Both these passages are first quoted in full, only to be rehearsed again in a summary fashion by the closing stages of the argument. In both cases, the summary quotation displays several deviations from the lengthier quotation, which is precisely the kind of incident resonant with quoting from memory. In the first instance, the text under scrutiny is found in Heb 8:10 quoting from Jer 31:32, as part of the longest quotation in Hebrews.[30] The Hebrews passage, διδοὺς νόμους μου εἰς τὴν διάνοιαν αὐτῶν καὶ ἐπὶ καρδίας αὐτῶν ἐπιγράψω αὐτούς, follows very closely the wording of the Jer 31:33, διδοὺς δώσω νόμους μου εἰς τὴν διάνοιαν αὐτῶν καὶ ἐπὶ καρδίας αὐτῶν γράψω αὐτούς. However,

27. Gheorghita, *Role of the Septuagint*, 66ff.

28. Ibid., 181ff.

29. Throughout the doctoral program, the present author memorized the psalms quoted by the author, to add to the ones previously committed to memory. The mere recitation of any of these psalms triggered spontaneously numerous echoes between various psalms, primarily at the level of individual words or particular phraseology. This can be tested by anyone who memorizes large portions of the psalter.

30. It should be mentioned that the text critical issues that are raised in such cases are enormous. This is not the place to delve into the complexity of the problem discussed, as important as it is. For a thorough investigation of the data, see Steyn, *Quest*, 235.

when the passage is summarily quoted in Heb 10:16, there is an inversion of the two prepositional phrases, διδοὺς νόμους μου ἐπὶ καρδίας αὐτῶν καὶ ἐπὶ τὴν διάνοιαν αὐτῶν ἐπιγράψω αὐτούς. The original pairing διδοὺς/διάνοιαν and ἐπιγράψω/καρδίας, becomes διδοὺς/καρδίας and ἐπιγράψω/διάνοιαν.

In the second case, the quotation from Ps 40 in Heb 10, a similar phenomenon is present. In the first installment of the quotation, in Heb 10:5, the phrase θυσίαν καὶ προσφορὰν οὐκ ἠθέλησας follows closely the source text of Ps 40:7, θυσίαν καὶ προσφορὰν οὐκ ἠθέλησας. However, the ensuing summary in Heb 10:8 includes several changes. The third type of sacrifice, ὁλοκαυτώματα, using a plural, not singular form this time, replaces the first two types of sacrifices, θυσίας καὶ προσφοράς. Moreover, these two types of sacrifices are now referred to in their plural form and not singular, as in the text originally quoted. As in the first evidence, the textual variations between quotations do not amount to an indisputable proof of quotation from memory. Yet, they also resonate very well with such a hypothesis.

CONCLUSION

Memorization of entire book(s) of Scripture, the approach to biblical exegesis proposed in this paper, is potentially one of the most beneficial activities in the exploration of the biblical text, whether by the seasoned scholar or the aspiring apprentice. Memorizing books of the Bible either in the original languages or, more accessibly, in a translation will prove to be an invaluable exercise with guaranteed dividends for the mind and the soul. It offers one of the greatest avenues for mining the biblical text, an endeavor that must remain at the foundation of all theological enterprises. Memorization is indeed one way of ensuring that the well-known dictum *ad fontes* will not go unheeded.

Scripture memorization will not render unnecessary the theological research conducted with the established tools of investigation, and it will never make the theological dialogue superfluous. As it was the case in ancient Judaism, committing the Scriptures to memory should be considered as a most optimum starting point for theological reflection and not an end in itself. Even after the Biblical text has been mastered, the considerable task of theological exploration still awaits to be accomplished. What memorization does, however, is to guarantee that the ensuing stages of theological exercise are not built merely upon familiarity with the biblical text, but rather upon a deep and thorough knowledge of it. The results of a theological education based on the mastery of the biblical text, which comes as the result of intense Scripture memorization, will not fail to produce substantial results. I can only hope that the number of those who will try this approach will increase.

BIBLIOGRAPHY

Bateman, Herbert W., IV. *Charts on the Book of Hebrews*. Kregel Charts of the Bible and Theology. Grand Rapids, MI: Kregel, 2012.

Brett, Mark G. "Intratextuality." In *A Dictionary of Biblical Interpretation*, edited by R. J. Coggins and J. L. Houlden, 320–21. London: SCM, 1990.

Buchanan, George Wesley. *To the Hebrews*. Anchor Bible Commentary. Garden City, NY: Doubleday, 1972.

Caird, George B. "The Exegetical Method of the Epistle to the Hebrews." *Canadian Journal of Theology* 5 (1959) 44–51.

Coggins, R. J., and J. L. Houlden, eds. *A Dictionary of Biblical Interpretation*. London: SCM, 1990.

Davis, Andrew M. *An Approach to Extended Memorization of Scripture*. Kindle Edition, 2014.

Docherty, Susan E. *The Use of the Old Testament in Hebrews: A Case Study in Early Jewish Bible Interpretation*. Wissenschaftliche Untersuchungen zum Neuen Testament 2; Reihe 260. Tübingen: Mohr Siebeck, 2009.

Ellingworth, Paul. "The Old Testament in Hebrews: Exegesis, Method and Hermeneutics." Unpublished PhD diss., University of Aberdeen, 1978.

France, Richard T. "The Writer of Hebrews as a Biblical Expositor." *Tyndale Bulletin* 47 (1996) 245–76.

Gasque, W. Ward, and L. Gasque. "F. F. Bruce, 1910–1990." *The Reformed Journal* 40 (1990) 3–5.

Gelardini, Gabriella. "Hebrews—An Ancient Synagogue Homily for *Tisha Be-Av*: Its Function, Its Basis, Its Theological Interpretation." In *Hebrews: Contemporary Methods, New Insights*, edited by Gabriella Gelardini, 107–27. Biblical Interpretation Series 75. Leiden: Brill, 2005.

Gerhardsson, Birger. *Memory and Manuscript: Oral Tradition and Written Transmission in Rabbinic Judaism and Early Christianity*. Acta Seminarii Neotestamentici Upsaliensis 22. Uppsala: Almqvist and Wiksells, 1961.

Gheorghita, Radu. "Ad Fontes Purissimi: Is There a Place for Scripture Memorization in Biblical Studies?" *Midwestern Journal of Theology* 3 (2004) 69–95.

———. *The Role of the Septuagint in Hebrews: An Investigation of Its Influence with Special Consideration to the Use of Hab 2:3–4 in Heb 10:37–38*. Wissenschaftliche Untersuchungen zum Neuen Testament 2; Reihe 160. Tübingen: Mohr Siebeck, 2003.

———. "Scripture Memorization, Once More." *Midwestern Journal of Theology* 13 (2014) 42–69.

Glasson, T. F. "'Plurality of Divine Persons' and the Quotations in Hebrews 1:6ff." *New Testament Studies* 12 (1966) 270–72.

Hurst, L. D., and N. T. Wright, eds. *The Glory of Christ in the New Testament: Studies in Christology in Memory of George Bradford Caird*. Oxford: Oxford University Press, 1999.

Koester, Craig R. *To the Hebrews*. Anchor Yale Bible Commentary 36. Garden City, NY: Doubleday, 2001.

Longenecker, Richard N. *Biblical Exegesis in the Apostolic Period*. Grand Rapids, MI: Eerdmans, 1975.

Moffatt, James. *A Critical and Exegetical Commentary on Hebrews*. International Critical Commentary. Edinburgh: T&T Clark, 1924.

Motyer, Stephen. "The Psalm Quotations of Hebrews 1: A Hermeneutic-Free Zone?" *Tyndale Bulletin* 50 (1999) 3–22.

Steyn, Gert J. *A Quest for the Assumed LXX Vorlage of the Explicit Quotations in Hebrews*. Forschungen zur Religion und Literatur des Alten und Neuen Testaments 235. Göttingen: Vandenhoeck & Ruprecht, 2011.

Vanhoye, Albert. *Structure and Message of the Epistle to the Hebrews*. Subsidia Biblica 12. Rome: Pontificio Istituto Biblico, 1989.

Walser, Georg A. *Old Testament Quotations in Hebrews: Studies in Their Textual and Contextual Background*. Wissenschaftliche Untersuchungen zum Neuen Testament 2; Reihe 356. Tübingen: Mohr Siebeck, 2013.

Wills, Gregory. *Southern Baptist Theological Seminary, 1859–2009*. Oxford: Oxford University Press, 2009.

Chapter 12

Defining Discourse Analysis as an Important New Testament Interpretive Framework

—STANLEY E. PORTER
McMaster Divinity College, Hamilton, Ontario, Canada

INTRODUCTION

IN HIS 1988 INTRODUCTION to linguistics for students of New Testament Greek, David Alan Black devotes less than two pages to what he calls "Analyzing Discourse."[1] This was not the first time that discourse analysis had been introduced to students of the New Testament,[2] but so far as I know it was the first time that it had been identified and described in a work designed for students and others being introduced to the subject of linguistics for New Testament studies.[3] This is not surprising, as David's book was the first of its kind to provide such an introduction to students of the New Testament. If David were writing this book today, I am sure that there are many things that he would want to do differently. One of the areas I am sure

---

1. Black, *Linguistics*, 138–39.

2. I may be wrong, but the earliest sustained treatment that I can find for New Testament studies is Louw, "Discourse Analysis."

3. He was followed the next year by Cotterell and Turner, *Linguistics*, 230–92, who devote two chapters to discourse analysis and related topics. On the early work of the Scandinavian contingent of continental discourse analysis (see below for discussion), see Olsson, "Decade of Text-Linguistic Analysis."

that he would wish to rethink is the discussion of discourse analysis—not least because he has made several contributions to discourse analysis of the Greek New Testament and has, thereby, been able to appreciate the nature of its possible contribution to New Testament studies.[4]

In fact, one of the areas in which New Testament studies has developed the most in its appropriation of the insights of modern linguistics is the area of discourse analysis. If one were to be writing such a book today, I can imagine that an entire chapter of some substance and length would be devoted to discourse analysis. There has been some heated discussion over phonology in some circles, minimal discussion of morphology in a way that has enlightened the field, more productive work on syntax, and a relatively large amount on semantics, especially in the area of verbal aspect. However, various examples of discourse analysis have probably been the most productive area of New Testament studies, and continue to be such. As a result, in this essay I wish to define discourse analysis by identifying features that make it a robust interpretive method, and then identify why I believe that it is vital for New Testament interpretation. I offer this essay in tribute to my long-time friend David Alan Black. He is one of the few scholars that I have known for the entirety of my professional academic career, and I am pleased to be able to recognize the contribution that he has made to scholarship and the life of the evangelical church through his teaching and scholarship.

DEFINING DISCOURSE ANALYSIS

A Brief History of Discourse Analysis

In the less than two pages that Black devotes to the topic of analyzing discourse, he makes several important observations, especially in the environment in which the book was first written. He first notes that there is much meaning that is conveyed beyond the level of syntax especially as it is represented in the sentence. This points to the importance of discourse analysis, which is concerned with examining instances of language beyond the sentence (or clause). The discourse provides the larger context for understanding the smaller units that are found within it. In his exposition of discourse analysis, Black draws upon one particular model of discourse

---

4. See Black, "Hebrews 1:1–4"; and his contributions, as well as his editing, of Black, Barnwell, and Levinsohn, *Linguistics and New Testament Interpretation*; and Black, *Scribes and Scripture*. Black, in fact, includes a new final chapter in the second edition of his *Linguistics* (170–98) that provides some further comments on discourse analysis and an extended treatment of Philippians.

analysis propounded by the South African scholar Johannes P. Louw.[5] Louw took seriously the findings of James Barr that meaning was not to be found simply in the individual word, but in units of words (syntax) extending up to the paragraph as the largest single unit of meaning in a discourse.[6] Louw's form of discourse analysis concentrates upon what he identifies as the "colon" as the unit that bridges syntax and meaning. The colon consists of a nominal element and a verbal element, and the two of them together constitute the minimal meaningful syntactic unit of a discourse. Within a colon, the various words achieve their significance. The organization and meaningful relationship of these cola constitute both the structure and the meaning of a discourse. This approach to discourse, which came to be identified with a distinctly South African approach (Louw was Professor of Greek at the University of Pretoria), is now not nearly so widely used as it once was.

Even at the time that Black wrote this small section on discourse analysis, other approaches to discourse had already been developed in a variety of circles, even if they were not widely known to biblical scholars. Discourse analysis as a discipline had developed along a variety of different lines in linguistic theory. Much of it originated with conversation analysis, although there were other influences also, such as pragmatics (Gricean conversational implicature and speech-act theory), sociolinguistics (e.g. interactional sociolinguistics, ethnography of communication), written text analysis, and the like.[7] There were also important developments that occurred within the field of Bible translation. The subject has continued to develop over the years, as some areas of linguistics have in many ways become discourse analytic approaches.

The field of New Testament studies has progressed similarly. At the time that Black wrote the first edition of his work, there were already other approaches to discourse analysis that had been employed in study of the New Testament, even if they were not widely known or widely used.[8] The Summer Institute of Linguistics (SIL), under the influence of especially Kenneth Pike and his Tagmemics, had already developed a significant body of literature that could be called discourse analytical mostly related to Bible translation.[9] Tagmemics was characterized by a functional non-cognitive

---

5. See in particular, Louw, *Semantics*. For a treatment of Louw, see Porter and Ong, "Eugene A. Nida and Johannes P. Louw," 303–12.

6. Barr, *Semantics*.

7. See Porter, "Discourse Analysis."

8. For what follows, see Porter, "Discourse Analysis"; and Porter and Pitts, "New Testament Greek Language," esp. 235–41.

9. Pike, *Language*, originally published in parts from 1954–60.

approach to language, in which larger units consisted of smaller units. The major proponent of this work in biblical studies probably was the linguist and biblical scholar Robert Longacre, whose *Grammar of Discourse* continues to have influence in biblical studies,[10] even though it is more and more difficult to identify a single approach to discourse within SIL, as its linguists have either gone in various linguistic directions almost from the start or become more eclectic over time.[11] By the time that Black wrote, a Continental form of discourse analysis was already being developed, pioneered by a number of different scholars in various European countries, especially Scandinavia but also elsewhere (see above). The varieties of Continental discourse analyses included a mixture of elements drawing upon a number of different forms of European discourse analysis (or textlinguistics as it was often called). One of the principal features was attention to the differentiation of syntax, semantics, and pragmatics; another was the use of rhetorical criticism, whether ancient or modern; and a third was invocation of communication theory. Such an approach to discourse analysis continues to be utilized especially by European scholars.[12] By the time Black wrote, there were also a few scholars who were incorporating elements of some other schools of linguistic thought. What came to be called Systemic Functional Linguistics (SFL), even if in some of its earlier forms, had made inroads by the 1970s into some areas of biblical scholarship, including translation studies.[13] One of the early developments of SFL was the notion of cohesion, dealing with non-structural elements that go beyond the sentence.[14] Since Black wrote, SFL-influenced discourse analysis has been one of the most productive areas of New Testament studies, as numerous articles and monographs have been written utilizing such an approach, beginning in the 1990s.[15]

The final type of discourse analysis that has developed since Black wrote has been what might be called an eclectic approach. The eclectic

---

10. Longacre, *Grammar of Discourse*; followed by Booth, *Selected Peak*.

11. E.g., Levinsohn, *Discourse Features*; cf. his *Textual Connections*.

12. See Olsson, *Structure and Meaning*; and Breytenbach, *Nachfolge und Zukunftserwartung*. One of the most interesting studies, though not in New Testament studies but related, is Hellholm, *Visionenbuch*.

13. See, for example, Callow, *Discourse Considerations*. The most important recent book in this regard is Halliday and Webster, *Text Linguistics*.

14. See Halliday and Hasan, *Cohesion*. This book continues to excite much interest, although it has been surpassed in SFL with cohesive harmony analysis.

15. Still one of the best is Reed, *Discourse Analysis*. The first may have been Porter and Reed, "Greek Grammar," 156–62; followed by Porter, *Idioms*, 298–307. There have been many works since.

approach selectively draws upon a variety of features of various types of discourse analysis, along with principles from literary criticism and cognate disciplines. Because such approaches are often not very rigorously linguistic, they are sometimes not viewed as legitimate approaches to discourse analysis but are treated as more traditional exegetical enterprises. Nevertheless, there have been a significant number of instances of such eclectic interpretations that have been offered over the last several years, also beginning in the 1990s.[16]

The Major Features of Discourse Analysis

How to characterize New Testament discourse analysis as an approach to texts? What are the various features of it that have led to its rise in significance within New Testament interpretation? What are the features that it has developed that merit further incorporation within the field of New Testament studies? I believe that there are five features that merit some attention. Along the way, I will make incidental comments about other forms of New Testament interpretation. I do not have space here to discuss these in detail, so I must rely upon some generalizations about them.

1. *Multi-Dimensional/Inclusive Model*

The state of New Testament interpretation may be characterized as fragmented. Whereas with the Enlightenment and the rise of scientific knowledge the historical-critical method was developed and came to dominate mainstream biblical scholarship for over two-hundred years, the situation is radically different today. The current smorgasbord of interpretive approaches offers a bewildering array of options. These include both traditional and non-traditional approaches, with the non-traditional approaches including neo-historical, social-scientific, literary, cultural, and ideological frameworks, among others. The result has been a fragmentation in much of New Testament scholarship, in which either proponents of various approaches do not consider the work of others because they do not agree on their presuppositions, methods, or priorities, or proponents attempt to hierarchicalize the various approaches so that some are subordinate to others—in neither case is there interpretive integration or unity or even understanding.[17]

---

16. See, for example, Guthrie, *Structure of Hebrews*.

17. For my perspective on the history of biblical scholarship, see Porter, "History of Biblical Interpretation," along with the essays in both Porter and Adams, *Pillars*, vols. 1 and 2.

One of the features of discourse analysis—not just the eclectic approach mentioned above—is its multi-dimensionality or inclusive modeling that encompasses many of the features of other exegetical methods. This is a fair characterization of any of the major methods of New Testament discourse analysis mentioned above, even if this characteristic is more clearly realized and expressed by some forms over others. By this, I mean that within virtually all of the major types of discourse analysis used in New Testament studies noted above, there is potential room for encompassing the major exegetical approaches that have come to characterize New Testament studies. I am not saying that this is always done or that it is necessarily a given or easy task (or even always desirable). What I am saying is that because of the nature of discourse analysis, there is a tendency to subsume within its overall conceptual framework many of the major features of these other exegetical approaches. Some examples will make this clear. Virtually all of the discourse analytic frameworks have a place for examination of the typical structures of language examined in exegesis. This usually entails discussion of the sentence or smaller units, something that most of these discourse models handle well within their frameworks. However, they also offer much more. Because much traditional discussion of syntax is confined to the sentence as the maximal unit of investigation (as well as of structure), the result has been the elevation of the sentence and smaller units as of primary linguistic importance. One of the basic orientations of discourse analytic frameworks is that the sentence and related units are to be examined within the larger context of the text in which they are found. Even the eclectic methods, with their literary influences, tend to place instances of language within the context of the larger literary whole.

Discourse analysis goes beyond the sentence, however, as noted above. As a result, while there is not systematic attention devoted to some of the other approaches to New Testament exegesis, nevertheless, a number of them are addressed. For example, a form of ideological criticism is found in SFL, especially in what is called Critical Discourse Analysis (CDA). CDA is influenced by neo-Marxist and Frankfurt School thought, claiming that the use of language is an exercise in power.[18] Other forms of discourse analysis are probably not so explicitly ideological as is CDA, but they are nonetheless reflective of and able to include within their conceptual framework various ideological approaches, including various social theories. Many linguistic approaches reflect types of social constructivism, in which there is an

---

18. There have been few instances of CDA in New Testament studies. For an early example, see Porter, "Is Critical Discourse Analysis Critical?"

interplay of facts and interpretation that constitute reality.[19] Even those discourse analytic approaches that champion the distinction between syntax, semantics, and pragmatics must reflect an ideological orientation to reality and the use of language within it, such as action models of language. Many of the approaches noted here have close associations with various types of social-scientific criticism. Almost by definition, discourse analysis is a type of social-scientific criticism, in the sense that as an interpretive framework it emphasizes the social and societal role of language, with a text being the product of that role.

I think that it is accurate to say that the potential of discourse analysis—admittedly some forms of it more so than others—to perform similar interpretive tasks to other exegetical frameworks, while still encompassing other critical elements as well, is a feature that is not reciprocally found within these other interpretive frameworks. If those interpretive frameworks are to include the diversity of interpretive analytics of discourse analysis, they would need to adjust their theoretical framework to include various linguistic elements not currently incorporated.

2. Context

The notion of context is vitally important to a variety of traditional and contemporary approaches to New Testament interpretation. However, that does not mean that these approaches have always been clear on what they mean by context. One of the major trends in New Testament exegesis over the last one-hundred years, as an example, is the shifting exploration of Semitic and Hellenistic backgrounds to the New Testament. This discussion includes a very large and expansive definition of context, that is, context as historical, social, and religious background. Another attempt to define context is what might be called immediate literary or linguistic context. By this, interpreters usually mean the immediate textual environment of the passage, episode, or event under consideration.

These shifting and variable notions of context have been highly problematic in New Testament exegesis, to the point where the use of the term "context" can be so imprecise as to be nearly useless. One of the features of discourse analysis is to provide a more constrained set of parameters for the definition of context. Some of the discourse analytic frameworks do a better job of identifying and even formalizing context than do others, but

---

19. See Berger and Luckman, *Social Construction*. There has been some significant discussions in recent linguistics regarding the ideological commitments of various linguistic models.

they have in common that they are concerned with more precise definitions of it, and using the concept as a positive factor in interpretation. SFL is particularly robust in its definitions of "context," identifying three in particular. These include the context of culture, the context of situation, and the cotext.[20] The cotext, which is the verbal environment, is used to distinguish the parameters of usage that are often identified with the immediate context in traditional biblical studies, but with an emphasis upon that context being one that is entirely linguistic in nature. Instances of language are thereby to be identified and examined according to how they are used in relation to other similar or different instances of language. The context of situation is non-verbal, in the sense that it is not defined in linguistic terms as is cotext, but is a situation in which language is used. For SFL, the context of situation is not to be equated with an actual material situation, although this is an area where probably more theorizing can find points of connection between context of situation and material situation through principled examination of both. This notion of context is very useful not only in linguistics but in biblical studies, where interpreters are often attempting to identify a passage within a context that offers guidelines for interpretation. The notion of context of situation—as distinct from cotext and other types of context—even if it does not answer all of the questions regarding context, provides a more circumscribed and constrained notion of context to guide in the interpretive process. The notion of context of culture is the broadest and most difficult construal of context to define, but its very identification adds robustness to the notion. Context of culture entails the elements of a culture in which the potential activities related to language may occur, including the language system itself. Rather than seeing culture as something distinct from language, the context of culture places language squarely within a robust theory of culture.

Not all of the discourse analytic approaches mentioned here have as well-developed a notion of context as does SFL, and SFL itself could well benefit from further theorizing upon the notion of context (in fact, there are a number of different construals of the notion that have been developed). Nevertheless, many of the discourse analytic frameworks work with a notion of context, even if they do not posit such an explicit articulation of it. However, one must also admit that for most of these discourse models the notion of context is a more localized one that is equivalent to cotext as defined above. This is, on the one hand, a clear limitation of these models, although no more of a limitation than is often found in traditional exegetical models. On the other hand, even if context is limited to cotext, the fact

---

20. The most concise explanation is found in Halliday and Hasan, *Language*.

that the concept is defined and its parameters set by the boundaries of the text adds to the usefulness of the concept.

3. Top-Down and/or Bottom-Up

Traditional exegesis may approach a biblical text from one of two major perspectives, either from that of close attention to the wording of the text or of the surrounding context (see above). However, rarely is such a distinction firmly articulated or grounded in theoretical explanation or justification. In fact, sometimes a variety of perspectivally opposed factors are played off against each other as interpreters move from language to context without apparent controls on the interpretive process. For most exegetes, the notion of whether one takes a local or global approach is not a major interpretive question.

Discourse analytic frameworks, however, are often defined by whether they are what has been called top-down or bottom-up in their orientation. Top-down discourse analysis begins with a large-scale or expansive perspective upon the text as discourse. This may include as broad a perspective as recognizing the context of culture, although it more often means large scale literary patterns, such as the genre and structure of a given text. The approach of Longacre is a top-down approach. Longacre begins with large-scale structural patterns of a discourse, such as the five-part structure of a discourse, and then moves from this large-scale analysis to smaller units by means of progressively smaller intermediate units.[21] SFL is also a top-down approach, beginning with the functions of language and then identifying how these functions are encoded in language. The Continental approach also tends to take a top-down approach, with its concern for macro-structures or superstructures. Communication theory's concern with the communicative framework supports this approach, as does rhetorical analysis with its emphasis upon the persuasive intent of a discourse.

Bottom-up discourse analysis begins at the opposite end of the cline, with a small-scale or constrained perspective upon the text as discourse. This probably includes attention to the smallest usefully examined linguistic units. These can vary in nature, but often include clauses and their components as the foundation for further examination. For colon analysis, a distinctly bottom-up approach, the smallest meaningful unit is the colon, and examination of these cola forms the basis for identifying and analyzing larger meaningful connections up to and including the entire text.

---

21. Longacre, *Grammar of Discourse*, 33–50.

A concomitant part of the opposition of top-down and bottom-up analysis is that most forms of discourse analysis, at least those that are explicit in their methods, take a stratal or stratified approach to language. In other words, most of them recognize that the points of connection between the highest and lowest levels of language are intermediate levels that have relations that connect them together—this is the definition of a stratal approach to language. Some forms of exegesis attempt to define such levels (or are at least organized in what appears to be strata), but it is often difficult to see how the levels are connected or how they are related such that one is seen as either the constituent of a higher level or is constituted by a lower level, and what that line of connection is.

In reality, most approaches to discourse analysis exemplify in practice a combination of both top-down and bottom-up perspectives, in which there is movement both up and down the scale of analysis as a means of control on interpretation. This means that, in effect, smaller units are interpreted within their larger textual cotext, and larger units are analyzed in relation to their individual parts or constituents in increasingly smaller identifiable (usually structural) units. The result may be similar to what is found in more traditional exegetical approaches but has the clear advantage of being explicit and expected within the discourse analytic itself.

This approach distinguishes it from traditional exegesis, which all too often begins with smaller units but experiences a significant break at the point of transition from the substance of language (e.g., syntax) to the meaning of the text. This is why so much exegesis often looks more like the imposition of biblical or even systematic theology upon the fine points of the text—these broad conceptual areas form the interpretive control and are read into the smaller units of structure, even if the connection between the two is not clearly shown. This is not to say that all forms of discourse analysis are able seamlessly to navigate the movement from larger to smaller to larger units. However, they at least are able to see such a movement as part of a larger conceptual interpretive whole. As a result, discourse analysis is more sensitive to identifying and formulating the relations among the linguistic strata. Longacre's Tagmemics, SFL, and even colon analysis are all recognizably stratal in nature, but even Continental and eclectic approaches often posit types of inter-level relations (e.g., syntax, semantics, pragmatics).

4. Beyond the Sentence, or Rather the Sentence and Beyond

As I have noted above, Barr's critique of the linguistics of much biblical studies was directed at the focus upon the word as the optimal unit of meaning, rather than seeing the sentence or clause as that minimal unit. Despite the many important examples of word-study fallacies found within Barr's work, as well as in the work of others who have followed him, the field of biblical studies does not yet appear to have grasped the significance of his admonishments regarding the abuse of words. The result is that commentaries still focus upon the word, and there is a clear lack of sound methodology regarding the study of words and/or concepts, the two of which are often confused even in scholarly writings.

One of the features that all of the models of discourse analysis discussed in this essay have in common is their focus upon moving beyond the sentence in their analysis. For many if not most of these models, the sentence remains the foundational unit for analysis, but they also provide for moving beyond the sentence to larger units. One of the major reasons for a fundamental focus upon the sentence is that the sentence (or perhaps better the clause, even though clauses may appear in analyzable clause complexes) is the largest unit of commonly-agreed syntactical structure.

There are some discourse analytic frameworks—Longacre's being the primary one—that believe that discourse analysis is essentially a type of super-sentential analysis, with structure equivalent to that of the sentence to be found at higher levels, but most discourse analytic models do not hold to this perspective. Most discourse models instead believe that whereas there is structure beyond the sentence, the structure is not of the same type or is not syntactic in the same way. As a result, whereas colon analysis uses the colon as the significant meaning and structure unit, the semantic connections beyond the colon are not based upon the colon, but reflect networks of semantic groupings and relations.

A similar situation is found in SFL, where Halliday's major work on functional grammar uses the clause as the major unit around which he structures his analysis, with one of the major sections being devoted to what is above, below, and beyond the clause.[22] Eclectic models are not uniform in this regard due to their eclecticness, but most of them have a similar relation to the sentence because they incorporate other linguistic models, as well as literary dimensions that push beyond the sentence or proposition.

The significance of using the sentence (or clause) as the fundamental unit of meaningful analysis has not been fully realized by those who draw upon traditional exegetical models. For those who maintain traditional syntactical perspectives, this discourse analytical emphasis upon the sentence and beyond provides a means of incorporating the best features of

---

22. See Halliday, *Introduction to Functional Grammar*. Part 1 is concerned with the clause and Part 2 with "Above, Below and Beyond the Clause."

traditional exegesis into a larger interpretive framework. Most discourse analytic approaches include analysis of structure below the clause as well, even if they see the clause as the focal unit. The Continental, SFL, and SIL models (at least in its Tagmemic approach) all provide for structure up to and including the sentence, as well as moving beyond the sentence. It is the movement beyond the sentence that provides the added benefit of discourse analysis. A recognizable shortcoming of traditional exegesis is that it has very little facility to move beyond the clause in a principled or formalizable way. Some interpretive approaches, such as social-scientific criticism or forms of ideological criticism or literary criticism, are concerned with meaningful concepts that are at or beyond the sentence, but for many if not most of these the line of connection between these concepts and the use of language is tenuous. Discourse analysis, however, is often concerned with not just the content of a passage, but with how the conveyance of this content is arranged and organized. As a result, moving beyond the sentence allows discourse analysis to examine how the message is structured, how and why particular parts of the discourse are emphasized over others, and how the cohesion of the text is established and what its implications for interpretation are. Such notions as the structuring of information, emphasis, and cohesion are all potentially productive concepts in discourse analysis and in New Testament studies.

5. Expanded Definition of Meaning

The concept of meaning is a difficult one in linguistics, to say nothing about its complexity in other disciplines. There are various ways in which meaning is identified, analyzed, and then described. One of the major issues in contemporary biblical interpretation regards the meaning of texts, and whether such meanings are to be found in relation to the author, the reader, or the text, as the three major hermeneutical foci.[23] To summarize briefly, exegesis focused upon the author up until the twentieth century, when interpretation was re-oriented with the text becoming the center, and then, for a relatively brief period, the reader. This shift in focus is reflected in the expansion of critical methods and their own orientations to meaning and significance. In the current interpretive scene, there is a wide variety of opinion on the locus of meaning, with some interpretation still being focused upon the reader.

Linguistic meaning itself is a flexible and varied concept. For some, meaning is minimally identified with small linguistic structures, while for others meaning is maximally identified with broad and expansive units and

23. See Porter, "History of Biblical Interpretation," 24–25.

even concepts. One of the features that all of the forms of discourse analysis discussed here have in common is that they maintain an expanded definition of meaning, one that moves beyond the kinds of limited definitions of meaning often associated with traditional exegesis. This expansion of meaning is perhaps most readily seen in the use of the syntax, semantics, and pragmatics framework of Continental discourse analysis. The way that these categories are defined and handled, there are layers of meaningful interpretation, the first related to the structures of language (syntax) and then to the meanings of these structures (semantics) and finally to meanings as they are found in their use in context (pragmatics). The notion of pragmatics is a fluid and somewhat embattled one in contemporary linguistics, but it is generally seen as encompassing the meanings that go beyond what is simply conveyed by the form and including those meanings that are gained from the situation and context in which the language itself is used (utterance meaning, as opposed to sentence meaning). Pragmatics often includes such things as principles by which conversations occur, action models of language (speech act theory), and the non-essential or implicated meanings of the use of a particular form or structure.

SFL does not use the notion of pragmatics in the same way as other linguistic models. Instead, because of its top down approach that begins with meanings, SFL subsumes what is usually placed in the area of pragmatics in the area of semantics. The semantics or meaning of a text include by definition consideration of the contextual factors (see above on contexts of situation and culture). The semantics are realized in the lexicogrammar of the language, which consists of the various systems of potential meaning that can be expressed by the structures of the language. Even colon analysis, which may be among the most abstract regarding meaning, organizes the meaningful relations among cola according to a hierarchy of integrated meaning relations that finally converge in the overall meaning of the text.

Even if such varied types of meanings are examined in traditional exegesis, within a discourse analytic framework they are seen as parts of a system of meanings susceptible to interpretation. However, it must be admitted that some forms of exegesis are vague about the relationship between language and meaning. This occurs to the point where it is difficult to see the relationship between form and meaning or the substance of the language that is used and the meaning structures that are used to describe and interpret it. Even in its most abstract frameworks, discourse analysis establishes meaning as a fundamental component. One is either concerned to establish the meanings of the text on the basis of the linguistic substance that is employed or one is intent upon describing how the meaning of the text is expressed in the various linguistic elements available to the language user. In either case, meaning is a pervasive concept that is at play from the top to the bottom and vice versa of the text.

IS DISCOURSE ANALYSIS IMPORTANT FOR NEW TESTAMENT INTERPRETATION?

Discourse analysis within linguistics has been a recognized area within the field since at least soon after World War 2, and arguably much earlier than that.[24] The use of discourse analysis in New Testament studies has taken much longer to become established than it has been in a variety of other fields. There are many possible reasons that one might posit for this reluctance and even outright opposition to it. Many of them seem to revolve around the word-oriented exegetical practices of biblical studies, as well as a hesitancy to adopt and develop new methods of interpretation. In light of the situation, I suppose that the larger question for New Testament interpretation is whether any particular form of interpretation is essential for the discipline. In that regard, the answer is probably no. There was a time before the historical critical method, and there will eventually be a time after it. In the meantime, there has been a variety of other methods that have been developed and implemented, many of them derived from other academic areas (e.g. literary criticism, social-scientific criticism, etc.). The discipline of New Testament studies does not seem therefore necessarily to require any particular interpretive method as essential for its continuing function. This does not mean that there are not reasons why discourse analysis should be viewed as interpretively important for the present and future of the discipline of New Testament studies as we currently know it.

On the basis of what I have said above, I believe that there are significant reasons why discourse analysis might be viewed as important, even if not ultimately essential, for the continuing work of contemporary New Testament interpretation—and here I continue to draw on an idealized conception of discourse analysis, based upon the common features that I have outlined above. The first is that discourse analysis is focused upon the text. New Testament studies, no matter what else it may be, is fundamentally a textual discipline, and so requires text-oriented approaches. There has been an unfortunate history of biblical interpretation that has relied upon theological categories (even if they are sometimes called something else, such as ideology) to determine the parameters of legitimate interpretation of the Bible. This is a top-down form of interpretation taken to extreme lengths—and it is widely found in contemporary commentaries (even if

24. See Porter, "Discourse Analysis and New Testament Studies," 19–21.

they unload those theological meanings on individual words). A re-focus and re-emphasis upon text and upon understanding the New Testament as a text within a context could help to re-invigorate avenues of New Testament interpretation. The second reason for discourse analysis, even with its wide divergences in schools of thought, is that the field has developed not just an approach but a principled framework or set of frameworks that attempt to encompass the wide variety of data found within a text. As a result, discourse analysis pays attention to the smallest units of language all the way up to the largest units of language—and beyond. Discourse analysis goes beyond syntax and structure to encompass the ideas, world, and environment in which such a text might have been conceived and executed. This is an important realization especially when dealing with ancient texts, where they are often treated as if they have lives of their own—and many of them do have interpretive lives of their own based upon tradition—but where they need to be grounded in linguistic and related environments appropriate for their examination. A third reason for the use of discourse analysis is that the conceptual framework encompasses many if not all of the enduring values from traditional exegesis, but does so within a more robust and theoretically well-grounded framework of understanding based upon the latest linguistic thought. Much research in biblical studies continues to examine questions of language from the viewpoint of previous generations of language scholarship, ones dominated by diachronic perspectives and comparative mindsets. Contemporary linguistics has re-oriented this perspective to emphasize the importance of synchronic and systematic investigation as more suitable to understanding the functions of language, and discourse analysis is perhaps the most inclusive exemplification of this interpretive framework. There are no doubt other reasons as well, but these suffice to make the point that discourse analysis, while perhaps not essential, is important to the future of New Testament interpretation.

CONCLUSION

In this essay, I have attempted to define discourse analysis by drawing upon some of the common features of the variety of discourse analytical frameworks that have been current in New Testament studies. While these four or five different models each have some identifiable differences from each other, they also have a number of common features that, examined as a whole, point in potentially new directions for New Testament interpretation. In some cases, New Testament studies is already making some of the interpretive moves that are central to discourse analysis. In other cases, New

Testament studies would probably benefit from adopting forms of discourse analysis in order to enhance its interpretive possibilities. One of the most important observations is that discourse analysis is far more systematic and principled in its approach to the text. As a result, discourse analysis in its focus upon the sentence or clause and beyond has the potential to take New Testament exegesis into new areas of understanding, without losing the co-textual or contextual grounding (a distinction that is made in some forms of discourse analysis) that is so important for textual interpretation, including and perhaps especially interpretation of an ancient text.

I would hesitate, but perhaps only slightly, to say that discourse analysis is essential for New Testament interpretation; however, I believe that there are many features of discourse analysis that make it an incredibly productive interpretive framework from which New Testament studies could continue to benefit. Some of these issues and even advantages were first raised in my friend David Alan Black's *Linguistics for Students of New Testament Greek*. Even though the field of discourse analysis has continued to develop in ways that David probably did not imagine at the time, we can all be thankful that he was one of the first to indicate its importance. I want to congratulate David for the blessing that he has been to the field of New Testament studies, and especially to his students and friends, during the course of a very important and productive career.

BIBLIOGRAPHY

Barr, James. *The Semantics of Biblical Language*. London: Oxford University Press, 1961.

Berger, Peter L., and Thomas Luckmann. *The Social Construction of Reality: A Treatise in the Sociology of Knowledge*. New York: Doubleday, 1966.

Black, David Alan. "Hebrews 1:1-4: A Study in Discourse Analysis." *Westminster Theological Journal* 49 (1987) 175-94.

———. *Linguistics for Students of New Testament Greek: A Survey of Basic Concepts and Applications*. Grand Rapids, MI: Baker, 1988.

———, ed. *Scribes and Scriptures: New Testament Essays in Honor of J. Harold Greenlee*. Winona Lake, IN: Eisenbrauns, 1992.

Black, David Alan, Katherine Barnwell, and Stephen Levinsohn, eds. *Linguistics and New Testament Interpretation: Essays on Discourse Analysis*. Nashville: Broadman, 1992.

Booth, Steve. *Selected Peak Marking Features in the Gospel of John*. New York: Peter Lang, 1996.

Breytenbach, Cilliers. *Nachfolge und Zukunftserwartung nach Markus: Eine methodenkritische Studie*. Zürich: Evangelischer, 1984.

Callow, Kathleen. *Discourse Considerations in Translating the Word of God*. Grand Rapids, MI: Zondervan, 1974.

Cotterell, Peter, and Max Turner. *Linguistics and Biblical Interpretation.* Downers Grove, IL: InterVarsity, 1989.
Guthrie, George H. *The Structure of Hebrews: A Text-Linguistic Analysis.* Novum Testamentum, Supplements 73. Leiden: Brill, 1994.
Halliday, M. A. K. *Halliday's Introduction to Functional Grammar.* Revised by Christian Matthiessen. London: Routledge, 2014.
Halliday, M. A. K., and Ruqaiya Hasan. *Cohesion in English.* London: Longman, 1976.
———. *Language, Context, and Text: Aspects of Language in a Social-Semiotic Perspective.* Geelong: Deakin University Press, 1985.
Halliday, M. A. K., and John J. Webster. *Text Linguistics: The How and Why of Meaning.* Sheffield: Equinox, 2014.
Hellholm, David. *Das Visionenbuch des Hermas als Apokalypse: Forgeschichtliche und text-theoretische Studien zu einer literarischen Gattung. I. Methodologische Vorüberlegungen und makrostrukturelle Textanalyse.* Coniectanea biblica, New Testament Series 13. Lund: C. W. K. Gleerup, 1980.
Johanson, Bruce C. *To All the Brethren: A Text-Linguistic and Rhetorical Approach to 1 Thessalonians.* Coniectanea biblica, New Testament Series 16. Stockholm: Almqvist & Wiksell, 1987.
Levinsohn, Stephen H. *Discourse Features of New Testament Greek.* Dallas: Summer Institute of Linguistics, 1992.
———. *Textual Connections in Acts.* Atlanta: Scholars, 1987.
Longacre, Robert E. *The Grammar of Discourse.* New York: Plenum, 1983.
Louw, J. P. "Discourse Analysis and the Greek New Testament." *The Bible Translator* 24 (1973) 101–18.
———. *Semantics of New Testament Greek.* Philadelphia: Fortress, 1982.
Olsson, Birger. "A Decade of Text-Linguistic Analyses of Biblical Texts at Uppsala." *Studia Theologica* 39 (1985) 107–26.
———. *Structure and Meaning in the Fourth Gospel: A Textlinguistic Analysis of John 2:1–11 and 4:1–42.* Coniectanea biblica, New Testament Series 6. Lund: C. W. K. Gleerup, 1974.
Pike, Kenneth L. *Language in Relation to a Unified Theory of the Structure of Human Behavior.* The Hague: Mouton, 1967.
Porter, Stanley E. "Discourse Analysis." In *Dictionary of the Bible and Ancient Media*, edited by Tom Thatcher, Ray Person, Chris Keith, and Elsie Stern, 83–87. London: Bloomsbury, 2017.
———. "Discourse Analysis and New Testament Studies: An Introductory Survey." In *Discourse Analysis and Other Topics in Biblical Greek*, edited by Stanley E. Porter and D. A. Carson, 14–35. Journal for the Study of the New Testament, Supplement Series 113. Sheffield: Sheffield Academic, 1995.
———. "The History of Biblical Interpretation: An Integrated Conspectus." In *Pillars in the History of Biblical Interpretation.* Vol. 1, *Prevailing Methods before 1980*, edited by Stanley E. Porter and Sean A. Adams, 1–70. McMaster Biblical Studies Series 2. Eugene, OR: Pickwick, 2016.
———. *Idioms of the Greek New Testament.* Sheffield: Sheffield Academic, 1992.
———. "Is Critical Discourse Analysis Critical? An Evaluation Using Philemon as a Test Case." In *Discourse Analysis and the New Testament: Approaches and Results*, edited by Stanley E. Porter and Jeffrey T. Reed, 47–70. Journal for the Study of the New Testament, Supplement Series 170. Sheffield: Sheffield Academic, 1999.

Porter, Stanley E., and Sean A. Adams, eds. *Pillars in the History of Biblical Interpretation*. 2 vols. McMaster Biblical Studies Series 2. Eugene, OR: Pickwick, 2016.

Porter, Stanley E., and Hughson T. Ong. "Eugene A. Nida and Johannes P. Louw and Their Linguistic Contribution." In *Pillars in the History of Biblical Interpretation*. Vol. 2, *Prevailing Methods after 1980*, edited by Stanley E. Porter and Sean A. Adams, 291–318. McMaster Biblical Studies Series 2. Eugene, OR: Pickwick, 2016.

Porter, Stanley E., and Andrew W. Pitts. "New Testament Greek Language and Linguistics in Recent Research." *Currents in Biblical Research* 6 (2008) 214–55.

Porter, Stanley E., and Jeffrey T. Reed, eds. *Discourse Analysis and the New Testament: Approaches and Results*. Journal for the Study of the New Testament, Supplement Series 170. Sheffield: Sheffield Academic Press, 1999.

———. "Greek Grammar since BDF: A Retrospective and Prospective Analysis." *Filología Neotestamentaria* 4 (1991) 143–64.

Reed, Jeffrey T. *A Discourse Analysis of Philippians: Method and Rhetoric in the Debate Over Literary Integrity*. Journal for the Study of the New Testament, Supplement Series 136 Sheffield: Sheffield Academic, 1997.

Chapter 13

Legal Metaphors in 2 Thessalonians 1 and 2

God's Just Judgment on the Day of the Lord

—TERRY WILDER
Southwestern Baptist Theological Seminary

I HAVE ALWAYS ADMIRED David Alan Black. He is an exemplary New Testament scholar, but he is also missions-minded and burdened for the souls of people. That combination is rare in the academy nowadays, and is what I appreciate most about him. I first met David, as I recall, in the late 1990s at one of the Evangelical Theological Society's annual meetings. He was present in a breakout session to hear a version of this article. He also allowed me near that time, along with David Dockery and the late Thomas Lea, the honor of contributing an essay to a book that he edited on New Testament interpretation—my very first published piece in the field. I consider it now a privilege to contribute this essay to this volume in his honor. Congratulations, David!

INTRODUCTION

Did Paul portray the scene of an eschatological court day in 2 Thessalonians?[1] Though some scholars have alluded to the use of legal language in 2

---

1. This essay attributes 2 Thessalonians to Paul. The letter presents him as the author. I maintain that (1) the apostle wrote the letter, (2) Acts is historically trustworthy, and (3) the events in 2 Thessalonians can be related to those in Acts. For defenses of

Thessalonians,[2] and others, though not specifically touching upon this topic, have done work along these lines with the New Testament,[3] the present writer knows of only one person who specifically treats the latter hypothesis in any great detail.[4] Thus, the subject merits another look. Might the apostle have painted with legal metaphors a picture of believers in the Lord Jesus Christ having their day in court and being vindicated by a just judge?[5] This paper explores the latter theme by examining whether Paul used any legal words or phrases in 2 Thessalonians 1 and 2 that paint such a judicial scene. After providing some answers to the latter inquiry, the present writer will offer an exposition of 2 Thess 1:3—2:3 that is informed by the forensic language discovered in our research.[6] Consequently, a fresh theme for the book of 2 Thessalonians will be suggested.

Though a first-century judicial scene does not necessarily have to include all of the following elements, these typical components do appear to be present in 2 Thessalonians. First, if court is to be held, the presence of a judge is required. Second, one needs to know the appointed day on

---

the authenticity of 2 Thessalonians see Marshall, *1 and 2 Thessalonians*; Wanamaker, *Epistles to the Thessalonians*; and most recently, MacDougall, *Authenticity of 2 Thessalonians*. Luke shows remarkable accuracy as a historian, especially in matters of detail. See Sherwin-White, *Roman Society*; Marshall, *Luke*; Gasque, "Book of Acts," 54–72; Hengel, *Earliest Christianity*; Hemer, "Luke the Historian," 28–51; and Hemer, *Book of Acts*.

2. For example, Wanamaker, *Epistles to the Thessalonians*.

3. For example, Turner, "Metaphors"; Lyall, *Slaves*; and Williams, *Paul's Metaphors*.

4. Aernie, *Forensic Language*. However, the first version of the present paper was done independently, written long before Aernie's monograph, and read at the Evangelical Theological Society's annual meeting in Danvers, MA, November 17–19, 1999, and then later at the Society of Biblical Literature's Central States regional meeting in Kansas City, MO, April 7–8, 2002; it appears here now with slight modification. I am indebted to my friend and former colleague, F. Alan Tomlinson, whose ideas on 2 Thessalonians helped provide some impetus for this project. Aernie was a student of both Tomlinson and me.

5. Why would Paul paint such pictures using extended metaphors in his letters? The first century was largely an oral culture with most people being illiterate; thus, it would make sense that in his letters written to churches, Paul may have employed lucid, colorful, and extended metaphors using everyday language to communicate truth so that the recipients would understand and remember content when those letters were read to them. For a detailed study on ancient literacy, see Harris, *Ancient Literacy*, whose findings, though recently challenged, suggest that literacy rates were 10 percent at best in Greco-Roman antiquity.

6. Bible translations are my own. Also, although the present writer's eschatological viewpoint can easily be discerned in this paper, the time of Christ's return is *not* our particular focus.

which court will take place. Third, a crowd or gathering at court is expected.[7] Fourth, persons who have been accused of a particular charge come before the court. Fifth, a judicial session includes people who may or may not be vindicated in court. Sixth, a crucial component of a day in court is the evidence that will be presented. Seventh, after the evidence is considered, a verdict is reached, and the sentence or punishment is administered.[8]

These select elements from a court scene seem to be evident in the texts that follow from 2 Thessalonians. For example, God and the Lord Jesus Christ are present as both judge and jury (1:5–8; 2:1). The day on which court takes place is one of judgment fixed by the judge (1:10; 2:2). On this day, many will be gathered at court (2:1). Evidence is presented (1:5) in court on that day which vindicates persons who have been afflicted (1:5–7). Finally, punishment is meted out (1:6, 8, 9) to those who have been accused and found guilty (1:6, 8; 2:3). In the paragraphs that follow, the present writer will draw attention to some legal words and phrases in 2 Thessalonians 1 and 2, which may support the picture of a judicial setting.

ANALYSIS

Paul seems to have described a day in court with several Greek words and phrases. All of the following can have legal connotations:[9] ἔνδειγμα (1:5), δίκαιος (1:5, 6), παρὰ θεῷ (1:6), ἀποκάλυψις (1:7), ἐκδίκησις (1:8), δίκη (1:9), μαρτύριον (1:10), παρουσία (2:1), ἐπισυναγωγῆς ἐπ' αὐτόν (2:1), ἡμέρα (1:10; 2:2), ἀποκαλύπτω (2:3), and ἀνομία (2:3).[10] When used in and of themselves, the latter words are not so distinctive that they would have automatically made Paul's readers think of a judicial scene; cumulatively, however, this matrix of terms may very well paint that kind of picture.[11] An analogy demonstrating the latter point can be found with the colors red, white, and green. In and of themselves these colors do not make one think of, say, the flag of Mexico, but when used together, and in a particular context, they do have a definite meaning. The point is *context determines meaning*. With this

---

7. For other examples of a gathering at court, i.e., an "acclamatory assembly," cf. Matt 27:15–23; Luke 23:13–25; and Suetonius, *Lives of the Caesars*, Claudius 5.15.2.

8. For further information concerning judicial elements, see Berger, *Encyclopedic Dictionary*, and Jones, *Criminal Courts*.

9. This list is not exhaustive.

10. 2 Thess 2:3 refers to ὁ ἄνθρωπος τῆς ἀνομίας ("the man of lawlessness").

11. Some scholars would perhaps critique this article with the claim that it is nothing but a string of several word studies. Exegesis, however, includes studying, among other things, words.

principle in mind, the present writer will now highlight some of the legal terms that the apostle used in 2 Thessalonians 1 and 2.

Bible scholars are well acquainted with the word παρουσία ("presence; coming"). On the one hand, this term "served as a cult expression for the coming of a hidden divinity," and on the other, "became the official term for a visit of a person of high rank, especially of kings and emperors visiting a province."[12] When the emperor visited a province, he often held court. (He could hold court wherever he pleased, whether on an official visit, or on the side of the road as he journeyed to a province). The word παρουσία has further judicial import, for, in legal texts παρουσία often referred to the "presence" or "coming" of circuit judges on their official judicial tours/assizes.[13] Like the emperor and judges who dispensed justice,[14] so Paul seems to have used παρουσία in 2 Thess 2:1 to refer to Christ's return when he comes in glory at the end of the age to judge the earth in the great assize (cf. Matt 24:3; 1 Cor 1:8; 15:23; 2 Thess 2:8; 2 Pet 3:4; 1 John 2:28; *Diognetus* 7:6, etc.).[15]

Many readers skim over the word "day" (ἡμέρα) in the NT, not thinking much of it. The term, however, has important nuances. For example, ἡμέρα often occurs in early Christian texts to indicate a "civil or legal day" (cf. Matt 6:34; 15:32; Mark 6:21; Luke 13:14; *Barnabas* 15:3–5), and it is especially used to denote a "day of judgment" which has been "fixed by the judge"—whether "a day appointed by a human court" (1 Cor 4:3), or the day of "God's final judgment" (Luke 17:30; 1 Cor 5:5; 1 Thess 5:2; 2 Pet 3:10, 12; Rev 16:14, etc.).[16] The apostle used ἡμέρα in 2 Thess 1:10 and 2:2 in the latter fashion; namely, to denote the "day" of the Lord—seemingly, a "court day" appointed for judgment—on which Christ's judgment of the earth will take place.

Most commentators say that the phrase "assembling before him" (ἐπισυναγωγῆς ἐπ' αὐτόν) in 2 Thess 2:1 alludes to the OT Jewish hope of gathering the scattered exiles back into Israel and particularly refers in the NT to the taking up of the church to meet Christ. The expression, however, may not refer specifically to the transport of the church—though

---

12. Bauer, Danker, Arndt, and Gingrich, *Greek-English Lexicon*, 780–81; hereafter to be cited as BDAG.

13. Cf. Kittle, "Παρουσία denotes active presence, e.g., in legal documents (BGU, IV, 1127, 37; 1129, 27; P. Gen., 68, 11f.; P. Masp., 126, 15; P. Oxy., VI, 903, 15)" *Theological Dictionary* V: 859).

14. See Millar, *Emperor*, 516–27, especially the sections on imperial hearings (228–40), and the emperor as judge of first instance. The emperor could hold court anywhere he decided to do so.

15. BDAG, 781.

16. Ibid., 437–38.

both 1 Thess 4:17 and Matt 24:31 do teach that such a gathering will take place.[17] Rather, when Paul used ἐπισυναγωγῆς ἐπ' αὐτόν in 2 Thess 2:1 he seems to have had something more specific in mind. Elsewhere in the NT ἐπισυναγωγή occurs only in Heb 10:25 where it refers to an "assembly for worship." In and of itself, ἐπισυναγωγή is not that different in meaning from συναγωγή. Both the latter terms can refer to a "meeting, gathering, or assembling" with someone. However, when ἐπισυναγωγή occurs with the prepositional phrase ἐπ' αὐτόν, something quite striking seems to be in view. For, when ἄγω-type verbs are in the passive voice and occur with ἐπί which has as its object the accusative of a person, then the phrase becomes like expressions often found in law-court language (cf. Luke 12:58; 23:1; Acts 9:21; 16:19; 18:12; etc.).[18] For example, in Matt 10:18 Jesus told his disciples they would be "brought before governors and kings" (ἐπὶ ἡγεμόνας δὲ καὶ βασιλεῖς ἀχθήσεσθε) on account of him; in Luke 21:12 Christ also said that they would be "brought before kings and governors" (ἀπαγομένους ἐπὶ βασιλεῖς καὶ ἡγεμόνας) on account of his name. In legal terminology, the phrase ἐπισυναγωγῆς ἐπ' αὐτόν denotes the "gathering at court"[19]—as the expression seems to be used by Paul in 2:1, a "court gathering before the Lord Jesus Christ," who is coming to judge.

Paul used the word ἔνδειγμα ("evidence") in 1:5; this term is a *hapax* in the NT and is not found in the LXX. The word does occur, however, outside of the NT. For example, in an address to the men of Athens, Demosthenes trusted that certain events under scrutiny in the commonwealth provided it with a new "example/evidence" of the divine favor (cf. also Plato, *Critias* 110b; Iamblichus, *de Mysteriis* 1.11).[20] A related noun form, ἔνδειξις ("sign, demonstration, proof") occurs four times in the NT: Rom 3:25-26 (twice); 2 Cor 8:24; and Phil 1:28. In Rom 3:25-26 Paul discussed the demonstration of God's righteousness "both with respect to the forgiveness of past sins and with respect to the present."[21] In 2 Cor 8:24 Paul "asks the Corinthian church to show ἀγάπη to Titus and the two (unnamed) delegates and thus to give evidence (ἔνδειξιν ἐνδείκνυσθαι) for Paul's boasting about

---

17. Matt 24:31 indicates that Christ's angels will "gather" (ἐπισυνάγω) his elect. The difference here, however, is that ἐπισυνάγω does not occur with ἐπ' αὐτόν, and thus, unlike 2 Thess 2:1, does not refer to a "gathering at court."

18. This phenomenon can also be found when ἐπί occurs with the genitive.

19. Though ἐπισυναγωγή is not an αγω-type verb, the same type of phenomenon can also occur with αγω-type action head nouns, which have a passive sense.

20. Demosthenes, *de falsa Legatione*, 256.

21. Balz and Schneider, *Exegetical Dictionary*, I:450. This work will be cited hereafter as EDNT.

the Corinthians' conduct."²² In Phil 1:28 "the unanimity of the Church becomes a clear proof (ἥτις attracted to ἔνδειξις) to the Church's opponents ... of their destruction and of the presence of salvation in the Church."²³ In 2 Thess 1:5 the term ἔνδειγμα seems to be "used in an analogous way."²⁴ The verbal form of ἔνδειγμα, namely, ἐνδείκνυμι, means "to show or demonstrate something" (Rom 2:15; 9:17, 22; 2 Cor 8:24; Eph 2:7; 1 Tim 1:16; 2 Tim 4:14; Titus 2:10; 3:2; and Heb 6:10, 11).²⁵ Interestingly, outside of the NT ἐνδείκνυμι is often specifically used as a law term meaning: "to inform against" (Isocrates 18.20; Plato, *Leges* 856c; Plutarch, *Solon* 24; Antipho 5.9; Lysias 6.15; Demosthenes 21.182; etc.).²⁶ In the context of 2 Thessalonians, ἔνδειγμα may mean "exhibit A" in court—that is, "evidence" of God's just/righteous (δίκαιος)²⁷ judgment on the day of the Lord. This evidence is used to vindicate believers, finding them worthy of God's kingdom.

Paul used the dative phrase παρὰ θεῷ in his letters more than once to denote the expression: "before the bar of/in the judgment of God"—and for good reason. Figuratively, when παρά occurs with a person in the dative the phrase can mean "before someone's judgment seat" (cf. 2 Pet 2:11). A closely related meaning of this expression is "in the sight or judgment of someone" (cf. 1 Cor 3:19; Gal 3:11; Jas 1:27; 1 Pet 2:4; 2 Pet 3:8, etc.).²⁸ Romans 2:13 furnishes an example of this phrase's latter use when it reads, "For the hearers of the law will not be vindicated 'before the bar of God' (παρὰ τῷ θεῷ), but rather, the doers of the law will be declared righteous." Galatians 3:11 provides a similar case: "Now that no one is vindicated/made righteous by the law 'before the bar of God' (παρὰ τῷ θεῷ) is evident; for the righteous will live by faith." In 2 Thess 1:6 Paul explained that it is "fitting/just" (δίκαιος)²⁹ "before God" (παρὰ θεῷ) to repay with affliction those who have afflicted the Thessalonian believers.

22. Ibid.

23. Ibid.

24. Ibid.

25. This writer is simply using the verb form of the noun to stress, as a point of information, that the verb is used in legal scenarios as well.

26. Liddell and Scott, *Greek-English Lexicon*, 558.

27. The word δίκαιος "is used of God with special reference to his activity as judge" (EDNT, I: 324).

28. BDAG, 757.

29. The neuter δίκαιον also has legal ramifications. The term denotes "what is *fitting* or *to be carried out* according to an established legal requirement. It is used esp. for what is required by God— δίκαιον παρὰ θεῷ (2 Thess 1:6) ... further occurrences of neut. [τὸ] δίκαιον are in Matt 20:4; 20:7 v.1.; Luke 12:57; Eph 6:1; Phil 1:7; Col 4:1; 2 Pet 1:13" (EDNT, I: 324). So also BDAG, 247: the neuter δίκαιον "denotes that which is obligatory in view of certain requirements of justice."

The term ἐκδίκησις ("punishment, retribution, vengeance"), which Paul used in 2 Thess 1:8, is found several times in the LXX (Exod 12:12; Num 31:2–3; 33:4; Deut 32:35)[30] and nine times in the NT (Luke 18:7–8; 21:22; Acts 7:24; Rom 12:19; 2 Cor 7:11; 2 Thess 1:8; Heb 10:30; 1 Pet 2:14);[31] the word often occurs in judicial contexts. For example, in the parable of the judge and the widow (Luke 18:1–8), the widow tenaciously asks the judge to give her legal protection (ἐκδίκησόν με, 18:3). Because of her persistence he did so (ἐκδικήσω, 18:5), and states, "Now will not God 'avenge/execute judgment' (ποιέω τὴν ἐκδίκησιν) for his chosen ones who cry aloud to him day and night" (18:7)? Jesus answered the question, "I tell you that 'he will avenge/execute judgment' (ποιήσει τὴν ἐκδίκησιν) for them quickly" (18:8). The text indicates that this judgment takes place when the Son of Man comes (18:8). When ἐκδίκησις is used with the dative it often denotes "the person who is being punished."[32] Such is the case in 2 Thess 1:8—God deals out "retribution to those not knowing God and to those not obeying the gospel of our Lord Jesus (ἐκδίκησιν τοῖς μὴ εἰδόσι θεὸν καὶ τοῖς μὴ ὑπακούουσιν τῷ εὐαγγελίῳ τοῦ κυρίου ἡμῶν Ἰησοῦ)."[33]

Δίκη ("punishment, penalty, vengeance, verdict") is another word used by Paul (1:9) that is often found in legal/judicial texts; the term occurs several times in the NT (2 Thess 1:9; Jude 7; Acts 25:15; cf. also *Hermas, Mandate* 2.5; *Similitude* 9,19,3),[34] and in the LXX (cf. Est 8:12d; Hos 13:14; Wisdom 12:24; Deut 32:41; Lev 26:25; etc.).[35] In Jude 7, a context of judgment, Sodom and Gomorrah and the cities around them are mentioned as negative examples of those who did not believe, undergoing the "punishment/penalty" (δίκη) of eternal fire. In Acts 25:15 Festus presented Paul's case before Agrippa and related to the king that the chief priests and Jewish elders had brought charges against Paul and asked for a sentence of required "punishment against him" (κατ' αὐτοῦ καταδίκην). When the word δίκη occurs with a verb like τίνω, as Paul used them in 2 Thess 1:9, their combination means: "to pay a penalty."[36] To be sure, on that day when Christ returns

---

30. Texts within parentheses found in Lust, Eynikel, and Hauspie, *Greek-English Lexicon*, 135.

31. See EDNT, I: 408.

32. BDAG, 301.

33. The definite articles in these clauses may indicate that the recipients of divine retribution are two distinct groups, namely, Gentiles and Jews, e.g., as Marshall (*1 and 2 Thessalonians*, 177–78) believes. The latter distinction, however, is not necessary. Arguably, the construction is simply a parallelism denoting any unbelievers.

34. EDNT, I: 336.

35. Lust, Eynikel, and Hauspie, *Greek-English Lexicon*, 116.

36. See BDAG, 250.

to judge—those who have been found guilty, who neither know God nor obey his gospel—will be punished; they "will pay the penalty" of eternal destruction.

EXPOSITION

In the paragraphs above the present writer drew attention to some words and phrases that have legal connotations. If used to inform the text, this matrix of forensic terms may paint a much more cogent picture of the day of the Lord in 2 Thessalonians than one usually sees. To consider further the hypothesis that Paul used legal metaphors in 2 Thessalonians to portray an eschatological court scene, the present writer will offer next a brief exposition of 1:3—2:3 that has been informed by some of the words highlighted earlier. By doing so, this author seeks to explain cogently this part of the text of 2 Thessalonians without importing some of the theological ideas that many often bring to this passage.

Acts 17:1–9 reports the founding of the church in Thessalonica by the apostle Paul. However, his ministry in that city is cut short because some Jewish opponents, along with some "agora men,"[37] incited a riot and sought to bring Paul and his associate Silas before the city magistrates (17:5). These opponents attacked the house of Jason, where Paul was staying, and not being able to find him there, dragged Jason and some other Christian believers before the authorities (17:6), charging them with acting contrary to Caesar's decrees (17:7); i.e., they are charged with treason.[38] The politarchs only release Jason and the others after a legal "pledge" or "bond" (ἱκανός)[39] is secured from them to guarantee the peace (17:9), i.e., that "this missionary group will not break the Roman law."[40] So later, Paul and Silas were sent away by night to Berea (17:10).[41] Paul stayed for a while in that place, but the Jews from Thessalonica followed him there and stirred up trouble. The

---

37. The "agora men" (οἱ ἀγοραῖοι ἄνδρες) were a gang of ruthless, rabble-rousing thugs who frequented the marketplace. These ruffians of the Gentile populace were coarse and unruly people, and loafers.

38. Green, *Letters to the Thessalonians*, 50, contends that the charge was "based on public law and not imperial 'decrees.'"

39. This word is another legal term: "pledge, bond, security"; see BDAG, 472. When a "peace bond" was put up for a person(s), the surety would be forfeited if the infringement occurred again.

40. Bock, *Acts*, 553.

41. Bruce notes that the politarch's demand for security from Jason bound him over "to make sure that Paul, the alleged cause of the rioting, left Thessalonica and did not return" (*1 & 2 Thessalonians*, 55).

brethren sent Paul away from Berea as far as the sea. Silas and Timothy remained there. The apostle went on to Athens and waited for them. Eventually, he made his way to Corinth where he met up with his trusted associates (18:5). Paul sent Timothy back to Thessalonica to encourage and strengthen the church in that place (1 Thess 3:2). Upon receiving Timothy's report of good news (1 Thess 3:6), Paul penned 1 Thessalonians and 2 Thessalonians shortly thereafter from Corinth probably about AD 51.[42]

The posting of the "peace bond" in Acts 17:9 evokes some questions: "When will vindication in court ultimately come for these persecuted Thessalonian believers?,"[43] "When will vindication eventually come for Paul who has been compelled to leave?," "When will vindication eventually come for the gospel?" In 2 Thessalonians, the apostle provides for his readers an answer: *Vindication will come on the day of the Lord when God will exercise his just judgment upon all.* That day has not yet come, but it will certainly come. Paul wrote 2 Thessalonians to encourage the persecuted Thessalonian believers who longed for their vindication with God and from their oppressors.[44] He urged them to remain steadfast as they awaited their vindication at the final assize. He did not encourage the church at Thessalonica to be vindictive, but instructed them that the gospel, and thus their lives lived on behalf of it, would one day be vindicated. This vindication for the gospel and for those who trust the gospel would be in the future assize when Christ the great judge arrives.

After his prescript and greeting in 1:1–2, Paul expressed in 1:3 that he felt compelled always to give thanks to God for the Thessalonian believers. He saw such thanksgiving as fitting for two reasons (ὅτι). First, Paul was thankful because his readers' faith was "growing abundantly" (ὑπεραυξάνω). Second, he was thankful because their love for one another was "increasing" (πλεονάζω).

Paul continued giving thanks in 1:4, using a result clause (ὥστε plus the infinitive) to show that the growing faith and increasing love of the Thessalonians was for him a cause for boasting amongst other churches. Though Paul's praise for his readers resulted from their increasing faith and love, he

---

42. This scenario represents the traditional order of the Thessalonian correspondence. However, for a full treatment that argues that 2 Thessalonians was written first, see Wanamaker, *Epistles to the Thessalonians*, 37–45.

43. Since believers in Thessalonica are under a legal restriction with the "peace bond," it makes sense that Paul would write to them using legal terminology. The questions generated here by the events in Acts 17 may be key for understanding the theme of 2 Thessalonians.

44. This is not to say that believers do not currently enjoy vindication with God, but that their ultimate vindication comes on the day of the Lord.

gave a more precise basis for his boasting in 1:4—namely, their perseverance and faith despite the persecutions and afflictions they were suffering.

After Paul mentioned the Thessalonians' persecution and his praise concerning their perseverance, he stated in 1:5 that their affliction was "evidence" (ἔνδειγμα) of the "just" (δίκαιος) judgment of God.[45] That is to say, the persecution and affliction of the Thessalonians for their faith is "evidence" in God's court, in which he will exercise his just judgment on the day of the Lord.[46] This evidence serves as "exhibit A" and has the effect (εἰς τὸ καταξιωθῆναι ὑμᾶς, an infinitival construction expressing result) of making the Thessalonians worthy of God's kingdom. Though not redemptive in and of itself, suffering for the kingdom is indeed "evidence" of the genuineness of one's faith.

These persecuted believers are counted worthy of the kingdom of God since (εἴπερ, "if indeed") it is "fitting/just before the bar of God" (δίκαιον παρὰ θεῷ) to repay with affliction those who have been afflicting them (1:6). Not only does the just judgment of God repay with affliction those who are persecuting the church, but it also grants rest/relief (perhaps relief in court) to those who are afflicted (1:7).

The judgment of the church's oppressors and the relief granted to persecuted believers will take place when Jesus is revealed from heaven (1:7b–9)[47] "with the angels of his power/force."[48] In 1:8 the phrase "with flaming fire" describes how God deals out retribution[49] (cf. Isa 66:15–16). The recipients of his divine vengeance/retributive justice are "those who do not know God and who do not obey the gospel" (1:8). Such people, namely, those who reject God, will "pay the penalty" of eternal destruction (1:9). This terrible punishment is not only everlasting,[50] but is described further

---

45. For a fuller discussion of what comprises the "evidence" of the righteous judgment of God, see Wanamaker, *Epistles to the Thessalonians*, 220–23.

46. This reference is to the future judgment on the day of the Lord. One thing that Aernie, *Forensic Language*, did in his work that I had not the space to do in this previous article was to study in detail the day of the Lord theme found in the OT. He concurs that Paul understood the day of the Lord motif as an appointed day when the Lord would execute his just judgment upon all.

47. That is, "at the revelation of Jesus Christ." Martin appropriately notes that the tone of these verses is "unusually retributive, almost celebrating the judgment upon the wicked. It is a tone that a people suffering unjustly at the hands of wicked persecutors could well appreciate" (*1 and 2 Thessalonians*, 210); (cf. Ps 137).

48. Other possibilities just as easily could be: "with his powerful angels," or "with the angels through whom he exercises his power," or "with his angels of power."

49. Though it may depict Christ and his angels as coming "in flaming fire."

50. As to whether the everlasting punishment is to be taken at face value or is instead referring to annihilation is beyond this article's scope. This author holds to the former

as banishment away from the Lord's presence and the majesty of his power (1:9). Those who are not acquitted by the "evidence" of a genuine faith will stand condemned and suffer dire consequences. This extreme punishment is the flip side of salvation, the recipients of which will be delivered at court and will always enjoy the presence of the Lord.

Paul brought up again the topic of the παρουσία, which he had mentioned earlier in 1:7b. In 1:10 he taught that the punishment of those who persecute the church will occur when (ὅταν introduces here a compound temporal clause) the Lord comes. Two infinitival clauses express some purposes of Christ's coming: (1) "to be glorified among his saints," and (2) "to be marveled at among all those who have believed." Paul then reminded the church that they would participate in the latter actions "because our testimony to you was believed." That is to say, the reason the Thessalonians will take part in glorifying Christ at his coming is because (ὅτι) they believed the apostolic proclamation of the gospel—unlike their oppressors.

In 1:11 Paul informed his readers that to this end[51] he constantly prays for them. The content (ἵνα) of Paul's prayer is twofold. First, the apostle asks that God would make the church worthy of its calling. That is to say, he prays that God would further validate his call in their lives—that the evidence of membership in God's kingdom would continue and be further authenticated/confirmed in them. Second, Paul asks God to fulfill in them every good intention and work which springs forth from faith[52] with power. In other words, he requests that the Lord will work powerfully in the Thessalonians' lives. The apostle prays that God will bring to full maturity what is already operative in the Thessalonian believers. The apostle's second request on behalf of the church clearly shows Paul's concern for ethical conduct, which fact may be pointing ahead to 2:13—3:13.

In 1:12 Paul's prayer has as its intended result/aim (ὅπως) the glorification of both the name of Christ (i.e., the enhancement of his reputation) and the Thessalonian church. That is to say, the glorification of Christ's name and the church results only if what Paul has prayed for in 1:11 comes to fruition. Indeed, "a church that God makes/counts worthy and in which God is working powerfully will as a result bring glory to the name of Christ and be glorified themselves in his name."[53]

---

viewpoint, i.e., the traditional, historic understanding of hell that is eternal punishment and not annihilation. For a fuller defense of the historic doctrine of hell, see Morgan and Peterson, *Hell Under Fire*.

51. This statement likely looks to the preceding passage. Thus, Paul seems to have in mind their salvation and perseverance through persecution.

52. Faith (πίστεως) is taken as a subjective genitive.

53. As Martin, *1 & 2 Thessalonians*, 219, has well said. Glorification reaches its

The oppressors of the Thessalonian church will reap their harsh punishment, and these persecuted believers will be vindicated on the day of the Lord, which Paul went on to discuss further in chapter 2. To be sure, the coming of Christ will be a day of judgment—seemingly, an eschatological day in court.

When Paul introduced chapter 2 with the theme of the "coming" (παρουσία) of our Lord Jesus Christ and our "gathering before him" (ἐπισυναγωγῆς ἐπ' αὐτόν), he likely viewed Christ's "coming" and our "gathering before him" as two aspects of one event.[54] Though the following viewpoint is not without its problems, the picture in this text seems to portray Christ coming to judge the world, with believers also "gathered together at court before Christ" for judgment. At this judicial gathering, the Thessalonian believers will be acquitted before Christ based on the "evidence" of their faith—namely, the persecution they have undergone for their faith, while those who reject God and his gospel will not be acquitted. The latter persons will instead suffer the verdict of eternal punishment. After voicing his concern that the Thessalonians not be quickly shaken, Paul made it clear that he and his associates were not the origin of the false teaching that the day of the Lord had already come (2:2).

SUMMARY

In sum, the interpretation offered above has its advantages; namely, it may solve two problems for interpreters of 2 Thessalonians. First, the proposed theory provides an answer to the difficult question: "What led the Thessalonians to believe that the day of the Lord (2:2) either had already come (extensive perfect) or was indeed present (intensive perfect) in spite of the instruction they had received from Paul (2:5)? With the hypothesis of this paper, perhaps the question that should instead be asked is the one posed earlier: "When will vindication eventually come for these persecuted believers?" The apostle Paul encouraged the persecuted Thessalonian church, which was wondering when and whether they would ever be vindicated. Paul assured them that they would be—on the day of the Lord. That day has not yet come, though some have apparently been telling the church that it has already come (2:2), and thus, they have received all the vindication that they are ever going to get. Paul responded that from whatever means you got that information—whether from a spirit (inspired utterance, prophecy)

---

climax at the παρουσία.

54. In Greek, both nouns are governed by one article and one preposition in addition to being joined by καί.

or a word (oral teaching, message) or an epistle (letter)—you did not receive it from us. He went on to explain in 2:3 that they should not let anyone deceive them in any way along those lines, i.e., to the effect that the day of the Lord—the day of their vindication/acquittal—has already come (2:2). Support that the "court day" has not yet come is found in 2:3–8. Certain events must transpire first; namely, the general apostasy and rebellion, featuring the revelation of "the man of lawlessness" (ὁ ἄνθρωπος τῆς ἀνομίας), the son destined for destruction (2:3).[55] The restrainer is removed (2:7), and then "the lawless one" is revealed; he comes with Satan's power to deceive and to render injustice (2:9–12), but is destroyed at the Lord's coming (2:8). Paul concluded chapter 2 by exhorting the church to stand firm and hold fast (2:13–15).

Second, the interpretation above seems to supply an answer to the difficult question: "What factor(s) motivated believers in Thessalonica to be unruly and idle (3:6–13)?" The most common explanation given in response to this perplexing question is that the belief in an imminent παρουσία led the Thessalonians to abandon their commonplace material pursuits. This latter notion presupposes that 2 Thessalonians connects the expectation of an imminent παρουσία with the actions of the idle—*but the text never seems explicitly to make this link.*[56] Rather than saying that the παρουσία led to idleness by the church, might one argue instead that in chapter 3 Paul warned the Thessalonian church as a whole not to be unruly and idle?[57] That is to say, after the apostle has discussed the day of the Lord in chapters 1 and 2, is it possible that in chapter 3 he admonished the Thessalonian church to protect their corporate witness until their day of vindication comes? If so, the unruly persons mentioned by Paul in chapter 3 seem to be just a few isolated instances in the church, and not the body as a whole.[58] With such unruly people, the church is not to associate (3:6). This latter action will help protect their corporate testimony—and this observation is important—from the charge made by the Jews in Acts 17 that they are treasonous.

---

55. Few, if any, temporal indicators are in the text to indicate when these events will take place. Only the word "first" (πρῶτος) specifies that these proceedings will occur before the day of the Lord. Paul made it clear that the church already knew about these things (2:5).

56. Though psychologically convincing, Paul nowhere in 1 or 2 Thessalonians makes an explicit link between idleness and eschatology.

57. Perhaps he is saying that they should not be like the "agora men," e.g., who have helped Paul's Jewish opponents in Acts 17.

58. Instead of speaking of the church here in the plural, Paul uses the singular "every brother" (3:6), and says that "some among you" are leading an unruly life (3:11). The non-use of the plural is very much in keeping with this paper's theory.

Consequently, they can be presented blamelessly, i.e., irreproachably, without any charge or legal accusation, on that day (cf. 1 Thess 3:13; 5:23).

To recap, the picture in 2 Thessalonians seems to be that on the day of the Lord—an eschatological "court day"—all are gathered at court, believers and unbelievers alike. They are assembled before the coming judge, Jesus Christ. Believers, those who obeyed the gospel, are acquitted on the basis of "exhibit A"—evidence (their persecutions and afflictions for the faith) which shows that their faith is genuine—while unbelievers, namely, those who do not know God nor obey his gospel, suffer punishment. The verdict is eternal destruction.

CONCLUSION

In the light of the conclusions of this paper, one might ask whether this study makes any difference. An answer to this question is that the judicial setting explored in this paper challenges some long-held viewpoints about the interpretation of 2 Thessalonians and may lend a coherence to the text that scholars do not always catch.

Aernie's monograph agrees—at least in concept—with the conclusions of this article. Thus, his work is another strand of research that supports the theory pointed out earlier—that a judicial setting is present in 2 Thessalonians, and that Paul wrote the letter to encourage the persecuted believers at Thessalonica to remain steadfast in their faith as they awaited the return of Christ in the great assize.

The practical applications of this exposition are several, with particular comfort for the persecuted church. First and foremost, believers can rest assured that God is in control. Second, Christians can know that they are well within the will of God, not outside of it, when they suffer for their faith. Third, persecuted believers can know that they will be vindicated for their faith, and that those who persecute the church will reap their just reward. Fourth, unbelievers, particularly those who persecute the church, need to know that God will exercise his retributive justice upon them one day. Fifth, believers should neither be shaken in confidence nor easily led astray concerning Christ's coming, nor should they make hasty eschatological conclusions concerning his return. Rather, they should remain alert and sober, i.e., ready, constantly vigilant, and self-controlled, living responsibly active, faithful, and ethical lives, sharing the gospel, knowing that Christ Jesus is coming to judge (cf. 1 Thess 5:6–8; Matt 24:42). Even so, Lord Jesus, come quickly.

BIBLIOGRAPHY

Aernie, Matthew D. *Forensic Language and the Day of the Lord Motif in Second Thessalonians 1 and the Effects on the Meaning of the Text.* WEST Theological Monograph Series. Eugene, OR: Wipf & Stock, 2015.

Balz, Horst, and Gerhard Schneider. *Exegetical Dictionary of the New Testament.* 3 vols. Grand Rapids, MI: Eerdmans, 1990–1993.

Bauer, Walter, Frederick W. Danker, William F. Arndt, and F. Wilbur Gingrich. *A Greek-English Lexicon of the New Testament and Other Early Christian Literature.* 3rd ed. Chicago: University of Chicago Press, 2001.

Berger, Adolf. *Encyclopedic Dictionary of Roman Law.* Transactions of the American Philosophical Society 43, Part 2. American Philosophical Society: Philadelphia, 1953.

Bock, Darrell L. *Acts.* Baker Exegetical Commentary on the New Testament. Grand Rapids, MI: Baker, 2007.

Bruce, F. F. *1 & 2 Thessalonians.* Word Biblical Commentary 45. Rev. ed. Grand Rapids, MI: Zondervan, 2015.

Gasque, W. Ward. "The Book of Acts and History." In *Unity and Diversity in New Testament Theology*, edited by Robert A. Guelich, 54–72. Grand Rapids: Eerdmans, 1978.

Green, Gene L. *The Letters to the Thessalonians.* Pillar New Testament Commentary. Grand Rapids, MI: Eerdmans, 2002.

Harris, William V. *Ancient Literacy.* Cambridge: Harvard University Press, 1989.

Hemer, Colin J. *The Book of Acts in the Setting of Hellenistic History.* edited by Conrad H. Gempf. Wissenschaftliche Untersuchungen zum Neuen Testament 49. Tübingen: Mohr, 1989.

———. "Luke the Historian." *Bulletin of the John Rylands Library* 60 (Autumn 1977) 28–51.

Hengel, Martin. *Earliest Christianity.* Translated by J. Bowden. London: SCM, 1986.

Jones, A. H. M. *The Criminal Courts of the Roman Republic and Principate.* Edited by J. A. Crook. Blackwell: Oxford, 1972.

Liddell, Henry George, and Robert Scott, eds. *A Greek-English Lexicon.* Oxford: Clarendon, 1996.

Lust, J., E. Eynikel, and K. Hauspie, eds. *Greek-English Lexicon of the Septuagint.* 2 vols. Stuttgart: Deutsche Bibelgesellschaft, 1992.

Lyall, Francis. *Slaves, Citizens, Sons: Legal Metaphors in the Epistles.* Grand Rapids, MI: Zondervan, 1984.

MacDougall, Daniel W. *The Authenticity of 2 Thessalonians.* Paternoster Biblical Monographs. Milton Keynes, UK: Authentic, 2016.

Marshall, I. Howard. *1 and 2 Thessalonians.* New Century Bible Commentary. London: Marshall, Morgan, and Scott, 1983.

———. *Luke, Historian and Theologian.* Grand Rapids: Zondervan, 1970.

Martin, D. Michael. *1 and 2 Thessalonians.* New American Commentary 33. Nashville: Broadman & Holman, 1995.

Millar, Fergus. *The Emperor in the Roman World.* Ithaca, NY: Cornell University Press, 1977.

Morgan, Christopher W., and Robert A. Peterson, eds. *Hell Under Fire: The Modern Scholarship Reinvents Eternal Punishment.* Grand Rapids, MI: Zondervan, 2004.

Sherwin-White, A. N. *Roman Society and Roman Law in the New Testament*. Oxford: University Press, 1965.
Wanamaker, Charles A. *The Epistles to the Thessalonians: A Commentary on the Greek Text*. New International Greek Testament Commentary. Grand Rapids, MI: Eerdmans, 1990.
Williams, David John. *Paul's Metaphors: Their Context and Character*. Peabody, MA: Hendrickson, 1999.

Chapter 14

"Participatory" Language in Ephesians Mediated through Σύν Compounds

—MEL WINSTEAD
Southern Evangelical Seminary

I RELOCATED TO SOUTHEASTERN Baptist Theological Seminary in 2001 for the express purpose of studying under Dr. David Alan Black. My time under his tutelage helped me to expand my understanding of Koine Greek and forced me to remember that good research can be accomplished when one goes where the evidence leads, even if it takes the student where others were too fearful or indolent to go. I am thankful for Dr. Black's passion to teach Greek, and as I have taught New Testament studies for the last ten years, he has greatly inspired me in that direction. In my classes with Dr. Black, I was forced to research and write on philological concerns that really stretched me as a seminary student. I originally wrote this essay on σύν-compounds in Ephesians chapters 2 and 3 for a class with Dr. Black in 2006. Since then, scholars such as Constantine Campbell have added valuable insights to the topic of Greek prepositions so that I have had to update my research.[1]

INTRODUCTION

The apostle Paul used compound words that involved the preposition σύν ("with") to broker the depths of *soteriology* in Ephesians chapter 2 and to display the outworkings of *ecclesiology* in Ephesians chapter 3. What follows is not a marginalizing of the works of scholars and theologians who

---

1. Most notably, Campbell, *Paul and Union*.

have observed the union between Christ and the repentant believer,[2] but to bring attention to the participation among believers that is also being called for by the apostolic writer.

Mine is a very modest proposal.[3] In this and other letters, Paul used stand-alone prepositions and compound words that utilized prepositions in order to communicate the unique message of Christianity. I intend to demonstrate that Paul's use of σύν compounds[4] lends itself to a little more than the popular understanding of "participation with Christ" and that it is demonstrating the union between and among believers, thereby pointing up the notion of community.

Additionally, I want to demonstrate the explanatory and clarifying power of philological research (paying attention to the grammar, structure, and linguistic phenomena of Koine Greek). We will observe how searching out the intricacies of New Testament Greek and utilizing tools of modern linguistics can provide us with a more robust understanding of the composition of the text and consequently, a clearer understanding of the message (with a view to being internally changed by it). This should successfully demonstrate the cash value of philological (and linguistic) studies. I will proceed by mentioning the relationship between prepositions and theology, and by offering a linguistic, exegetical, and grammatical analysis of several SCs in Ephesians.

A NOTE ON HOW PREPOSITIONS INFORM THEOLOGY

The first thing to remember for students (and remind other readers) is that prepositions are small words after all, but they can help to move a lot of theological freight. The preposition κατά is a case in point. In Table 1 below, we should notice the depth of theology being explained by use of this preposition.

---

2. In fact, I am building on what these scholars have built before.

3. In this essay, I am writing from the view that Paul of Tarsus authored the Letter to the Ephesians. Thielman concludes in his discussion of authorship that the text "makes sense as an authentic letter from Paul to Christians in Ephesus" (*Ephesians*, 5).

4. Hereafter referred to as SC or SCs.

Table 1.[5]

Κατα	Comments
κατενώπιον (Eph 1:4)	God chose us for the purpose of us being blameless **in his presence**
κατὰ τὴν εὐδοκίαν τοῦ θελήματος αὐτου (Eph 1:5)	God predestined us for adoption **influenced by** his will
κατὰ τὸ πλοῦτος τῆς χάριτος αὐτοῦ (Eph 1:7)	we have forgiveness **influenced by** the riches of his grace
κατὰ τὴν εὐδοκίαν αὐτοῦ ἣν προέθετο ἐν αὐτω (Eph 1:9)	He made known to us the mystery of his will **influenced by** his kind intention
κατὰ πρόθεσιν τοῦ τὰ πάντα ἐνεργοῦντος (Eph 1:11)	We obtained an inheritance having been predestined, **influenced by** his purpose
κατὰ τὴν βουλὴν τοῦ θελήματος αὐτου (Eph 1:11)	God works all things **according to** his will
κατὰ τὴν ἐνέργειαν τοῦ κράτους τῆς ἰσχύος αὐτου (Eph 1:19)	The **influence of** the working of the strength of his might that he used to raise Jesus from the dead is also shown in some way to us
κατὰ τὸν αἰῶνα τοῦ κόσμου τούτου (Eph 2:2)	We walked in sins because we were **influenced by** the world system
κατὰ τὸν ἄρχοντα τῆς ἐξουσίας τοῦ ἀέρος (Eph 2:2)	… and because we were **influenced by** the Devil
κατὰ ἀποκάλυψιν ἐγνωρίσθη μοι τὸ μυστήριον (Eph 3:3)	The mystery of the gospel was made known, **influenced by** divine revelation
κατὰ τὴν δωρεὰν τῆς χάριτος τοῦ θεοῦ τῆς δοθείσης μοι (Eph 3:7)	Paul was made a minister **according to** the gift of God's grace
κατὰ τὴν ἐνέργειαν τῆς δυνάμεως αὐτοῦ (Eph 3:7)	… and it was given to Paul **according to** the working of God's power
κατὰ πρόθεσιν τῶν αἰώνων (Eph 3:11)	The mystery of the gospel will be made known **in accordance with** God's eternal purpose
ἵνα δῷ ὑμῖν κατὰ τὸ πλοῦτος τῆς δόξης αὐτοῦ (Eph 3:16)	May they be granted strength **influenced by** the riches of God's glory

5. I have used the NASB as a base translation but have translated κατά and other words and phrases on my own. Also, I am aware that my translation using the word "influence" will perhaps sound "soft" to some, but I am at this point simply trying to reach for the best translation of this preposition. Besides, while God's work in salvation is more than "influence," it is not less than "influence." This being said, I am certainly open to a more suitable word with which to translate this preposition in these passages.

κατὰ τὴν δύναμιν τὴν ἐνεργουμένην ἐν ἡμῖν (Eph 3:20)	**influenced by** the power that works within us
κατὰ τὸ μέτρον τῆς δωρεᾶς τοῦ Χριστοῦ (Eph 4:7)	We were given grace **influenced by** Christ's gift
κατὰ τὴν προτέραν ἀναστροφὴν τὸν παλαιὸν ἄνθρωπον (Eph 4:22)	**in reference to** your former conduct, lay aside the old self
κατὰ τὰς ἐπιθυμίας τῆς ἀπάτης (Eph 4:22)	…this old self is being corrupted, **being impacted by** the lusts of deceit
τὸν κατὰ θεὸν κτισθέντα ἐν δικαιοσύνῃ (Eph 4:24)	put on the new self, which being **influenced by** God's image…

As the lexicons indicate, κατά is usually going to be translated "down," "against," or "according to."[6] The point of Table 1 is simply to demonstrate that, at least in the case of Ephesians, a particular preposition might be used to carry particular information in order to most clearly convey the desired message. Can we consider, as with the comments in Table 1, that translating κατά as "influenced by" (or "impacted by") might more clearly decode the message for English readers? Additionally, as evidenced from Table 1, prepositions can say a lot, as already asserted.

PROPER / IMPROPER PREPOSITIONS AS LISTED IN BLACK'S IT'S STILL GREEK TO ME:[7]

The second thing to think about is that some prepositions in the Greek New Testament can be compounded with other words, while others cannot. Those prepositions that can be compounded with other words are called "proper prepositions," while those that cannot be compounded are called "improper prepositions."[8] The improper prepositions used in Ephesians are: κατενώπιον, χωρὶς, χάριν, ἔσω, ὑπεράνω, and μέχρι. The proper prepositions used in Ephesians are: διά, ἐν, ἀπό, εἰς, κατά, ὑπέρ, ἐπί, ἐκ, ὑπό, πρό, πρός, σύν, μετά, ἀντί, παρά, and περί.

---

6. To give credit where credit is due, I first heard a sermon on the preposition κατά as found in Ephesians chapters one and two back in the mid 1990s at the Wild's camp in Brevard, NC. The speaker was the Rev. Frank Hamrick. His sermon encouraged me to dig a little deeper than most other preachers that I was hearing at the time.

7. Black, *It's Still Greek*, 84–85 (for *improper* prepositions, see *It's Still Greek*, 86). See also Porter, Reed, and O'Donnell, *Fundamentals*, 132n1.

8. See footnote above.

ANALYSIS

Prepositions not Compounded

Paul used twelve different SCs in Ephesians to discuss his theology of "association" or "participation."[9] Along with these tools, he employed other grammatical tools which include the preposition ἐν which occurs 122 times, μετά, seven times (his choice over the only twice used σύν alone), some variation of ἐν Χριστῷ, ἐν αὐτῷ, ἐν ᾧ, etc. roughly twenty-eight times.[10]

C. F. D. Moule made the following observations concerning the preposition σύν: The proper prepositions do not "govern" an object, but only strengthens the idea of the verb used;[11] σύν is used sometimes in a sense which defies explanation. The examples are συμβιβάζω and συστρεφόμαι (Matt 17:22).[12] At other times, it is used without further prepositions, sometimes with the same prepositions, (Col 2:13 is the only NT instance of σύν being repeated). Then at other times, it is used with a different preposition.[13] A. T. Robertson comments, "The associative instrumental is the case used with σύν as with ἅμα and it is just that idea that it was used to express originally."[14] He explains further that "As applied to Christ, σύν, like ἐν, may express the intimate mystic communion . . ."[15] So goes the comments by philologists of days gone by.

Recent philologists and linguists have had the following to say concerning the σύν preposition and its compounds: "σύν seems to imply at least in its fundamental sense the idea of like things being 'with' each other . . . . This does not mean that they are exactly the same thing, but that the way they are being characterized by the author implies points of similarity,"[16] and "The function of the preposition is to express accompaniment and association, and the result is that believers share or participate in this Christ-event in a

---

9. This statistic might be similar within the Pauline corpus, but it demonstrates the range of tools within Greek lexicography, and the versatility of prepositions in compounds.

10. Statistics drawn using BW10 (BW10 = Bible Works 10, Norfolk, VA: Bible-Works, LLC, 2014). The total count for prepositions in Ephesians is 278, excluding those used in compounds.

11. Moule, *Idiom Book*, 87.

12. Ibid., 90.

13. Ibid., 90–92.

14. Robertson, *Grammar*, 627.

15. Ibid., 628. Wedderburn says that Paul's association language (specifically σύν) in connection with Christ is "a more profound identification of oneself with the pattern of his life." ("Some Observations," 91).

16. Porter, *Idioms*, 174.

conceptual or spiritual manner."[17] Metzger defines the root meaning of σύν as "together with."[18] After this study, perhaps we can tweak our understanding of the SCs in Ephesians to emphasizing the fellowship or communion of the saints (the fact that Christianity is not a spectator nor a lone wolf sport, but instead a participatory community). Exegesis will supplement the linguistics in this passage.

Compounds with Μετά and Σύν

Murray J. Harris relates that in Attic Greek, "σύν meant "including" and "with the aid of" and μετά, "(in company) with."[19] But, he argues, in Hellenistic Greek, the two prepositions are synonymous.[20] Harris does agree with Moule that μετά is more common than σύν, but μετά is rarely used in compound verbs.[21] Therein lies that major difference between the two.[22] Harris also notes that "Both prepositions are used in connexion with Christian discipleship, fellowship meals, and eschatology."[23] But since σύν is used in compound verbs, this preposition is able to refer to many more nuances of Paul's theology as this study will demonstrate.[24]

---

17. Campbell, *Paul and Union*, 228.

18. Metzger, *Lexical Aids*, 84.

19. Harris, "Prepositions," 1206. Harris' work has been published as a monograph: *Prepositions and Theology in the Greek New Testament* (Grand Rapids, MI: Zondervan, 2012).

20. Ibid.

21. Ibid. Robertson says that σύν in composition is "extremely common," but not so common in σύν alone; *Grammar*, 627. Μετά is used in Eph 4:28 in reference to sharing one's goods, and a few times (and relevant to our discussion) in Hebrews.

22. Within the SCs, I hope to demonstrate the need for more research to see if, as I think might be the case, or is at least the case in Ephesians chapters 2 and 3, σύν compounded with a verb yields the understanding "with . . ." and σύν compounded with the noun yields the understanding "fellow . . .," or "co- . . ."

23. Harris, "Prepositions," 1206.

24. According to Moule, σύν is used less than μετά, and mostly in Luke-Acts, and is absent from the Johannine epistles, Revelation, Hebrews, 1 Peter, 2 Thessalonians, Philemon, 1 & 2 Timothy, and Titus (*Idiom Book*, 81). A search of BW10 affirms the absence of σύν (alone) in these epistles, while μετά, (alone) is used sixty-seven times (BW10). The same search engine shows that in the rest of Paul's epistles, he used σύν (alone) and μετά (alone) about the same (σύν—thirty-nine times, μετά—thirty-seven times) (BW10).

Exegesis of Relevant Ephesians Passages — Soteriology

Table 2 shows the distribution of SCs by chapter throughout the epistle.

Table 2.

1	2	3	4	5	6
N/A	συνεζωοποίησεν συνηγείρεν συνεκάθισεν συμπολῖται συναρμολογουμένη	συγκληρονόμα σύσσωμα συμμέτοχα	N/A	συγκοινωνεῖτε	N/A

According to the Table 2, Paul clusters these SCs in the two chapters in which he most clearly and forcefully paints a picture of soteriology and ecclesiology. Greek is his brush and the prepositions are the colors on his palette. Following on the heels of this pedagogy, the apostle begins to offer his ethical injunctions based on the point made by the SCs. Hence, as chapter four begins, Paul uses the structure marker οὖν, which he uses seven times in this letter, all but one coming at 4:1 and after. This marker denotes inferences that should be drawn based on previous assertions.

2:5: καὶ ὄντας ἡμᾶς νεκροὺς τοῖς παραπτώμασιν συνεζωοποίησεν τῷ Χριστῷ— χάριτί ἐστε σεσῳμένοι.[25]

συζωοποιέω.[26]

This is the first use of the SC that demonstrates my thesis (showing participation) in the book of Ephesians. It is the first of three aorist active indicatives with the SC used in verses 5–6. The lexical form is συζωοποιέω and means "to raise to life with," according to Louw and Nida (hereafter I will

---

25. Holmes, *Greek New Testament*.

26. Porter, Reed, and O'Donnell wisely note that the preposition σύν is often altered when attached to another word. The preposition σύν will become συμ with labials, συλ before λ, συγ before velars, and συ with σ or ζ (*Fundamentals*, 133). He states that "these variations can be learned by observation in the vocabulary lists." (133). Of course, they can also be observed as one completes a wildcard search on software such as Bible Works 10 or Logos or in reading (or stumbling) through the Greek New Testament. It is informative for the student to see some of these variations in the σύν compounds.

refer to this resources as "LN").²⁷ Συνεζωοποίησεν is used with a dative as its object as are the other two words συνήγειρεν and συνεκάθισεν.

Timothy Gombis notes here that we are "co-crucified with Christ, co-resurrected, and now brought into the new age along with Christ to enjoy the life of God."²⁸ I am proposing, however, that the SCs are offering a little more than this—that being the demonstration of believers' participation with one another, in effect, calling for a more robust unity within the Christian family.²⁹

Perhaps the modern scholar of which I am aware who is nearest to this concern is Campbell and his comment that,

> The σύν-related language indicates participation with Christ, which has clear implications for Christian living. They are regarded as suffering with Christ, having died with Christ, being raised with him, living with Christ, ascending with him to the heavens, and being glorified with Christ, among other things. Paul understands these profound realities to have essential significance for the ways in which believers are to live and identify themselves.³⁰

The following exegesis section will show what these realities and the significances are for the modern church.

2:6: καὶ συνήγειρεν καὶ συνεκάθισεν ἐν ἐπουρανίοις ἐν Χριστῷ Ἰησοῦ.³¹

συνεγείρω.

Paul's second use of a SC in Ephesians is συνήγειρεν, which is also an aorist active indicative verb of whom the subject is still God. The verb's lexical form is συνεγείρω which means "to raise to life with." Note that LN give the exact same definition as they do to the previous verb συνεζωοποίησεν.³² But BDAG gives some distinction probably based off of the two roots (to

27. Holmes, *Greek New Testament*.

28. Gombis, "Ephesians 2," 95. Perhaps even more clearly, Gombis states, "Paul is saying that Christians already participate in the reality of the age to come, even though it is not fully here yet" ("Ephesians 2," 96).

29. One could compare Paul's "body language" in 1 Cor 12 for another explanation of our need for each other.

30. Campbell, *Paul and Union*, 372.

31. Holmes, *Greek New Testament*, (Eph 2:6).

32. BW10.

make alive and to raise up). BDAG gives the definition and comments for συνεγείρω as "fig., of participating in the resurrection of Jesus; the believer, in mystic union w. him, could experience this..."[33] Abbott goes so far as to suggest that though there is synonymy, συνεγείρε "suggests more distinctly physical resurrection."[34] He goes on to compare the verb with its parallel in Col 3:1 (there, in the aorist passive)[35] where the being raised is "made the motive for seeking those things which are above."[36] As Hoehner comments, "The new resurrected life demands new values."[37] These values are spelled out for us in Eph 4:2ff., and in the parallel in Col 3:1ff. These selections of Scripture call for specific behavior within the body of Christ.

συγκαθίζω.

This verb is an aorist active indicative as are the previous two SCs. The lexical form of this verb means "to sit down with" or "to cause to sit down with."[38] In Eph 1:20, Paul already alerted us that Jesus had been made to sit at God's right hand. And in the parallel passage to Eph 2:6, found in Col 3, believers are exhorted to "keep seeking the things above, where Christ is, seated at the right hand of God." For some reason, Paul used the different but related verb κάθημαι. Bruce denotes the distinction. He states that in Eph 2:6 "believers are viewed as already being seated there with Christ...."[39] He comments further: "Temporally, indeed, we live on earth so long as we remain in this body; but 'in Christ Jesus' we are seated with Christ where He is. And God, who sees all His creatures as they really are, sees believers 'in Christ Jesus.'"[40]

---

33. BDAG, 786. Abbott-Smith also gives the distinction: συνεζωοποίησεν = "to make alive or quicken together with" (429), συνήγειρεν = "to raise together" (*Manual Greek Lexicon*, 426).

34. Abbott, *Critical and Exegetical Commentary*, 49. Du Toit suggests that the Jews preferred ἐγείρω over ἀνίστημι perhaps because "it was better suited to portray God's initiative," contra the Greek writers who preferred ἀνίστημι ("Primitive Christian Belief," 316–17).

35. I would definitely term this use in Colossians as a "divine passive" for it is God who has raised us and not we ourselves. A dead man cannot raise himself (only Jesus could do that—John 10:18).

36. Abbott, *Critical and Exegetical Commentary*, 49–50.

37. Hoehner, *Ephesians*, 334.

38. BW10.

39. Bruce, *Epistle*, 50.

40. Ibid.

Patzia says that since Christians participate in the enthronement (the seating), they already share in His rule.[41]

THEOLOGY OF THREE SCS IN 2:5–6

The theology brokered in Eph 2:5–6 by use of the three SCs is that of soteriology. Paul is still describing something that he began to do in chapter 1 of Ephesians, something that's indescribable. This salvation was according to God's kind intentions, was for the purpose of bringing glory to God, was a grace gift bestowed upon spiritually dead folks, led to a "building" belonging to God, and is now described as an enlivening, a resurrection, and a seating. The SCs in this selection involve compounded verbs and tend toward the English rendering "with . . ..," as in "made alive together with," "raised up together with," and "seated with." It might be the case, therefore, that along with the soteriology being brokered by use of the SCs, the SCs themselves, when containing a verb, are to be translated with the helping word "with." This suggestion certainly needs more research.

2:19 συμπολῖται.

The next few participatory uses of a SC that we briefly mention are συμπολῖται (Eph 2:19), συναρμολογουμένη (Eph 2:21), and συνοικοδομεῖσθε (Eph 2:22). With συμπολῖται ("fellow citizens"), the preposition is used with a noun. This particular usage more directly addresses the notion of believers being members with one another, members of a community or of some other participation together. The word συναρμολογουμένη is a present passive participle meaning "fitted together." One should note the passive as both denoting and connoting the fact that God has done the work in Christ.[42]

The major verb of this passage, αὔξει, "to grow," is placed alongside the participle συναρμολογουμένη. The verb is in the present tense so the idea could be an emphasis on the continual growth of the building.[43]

---

41. Patzia, *Ephesians*, 180.

42. This use of the passive in the New Testament echoes the OT truth "Salvation is of the Lord" (Jonah 2:9; Ps 3:8). Eduard Schweizer refers to Paul's participatory usage as "mystical" and submits that this mystical language is used in such a way that God is even involved in our sanctification. It is when faith is yielded to God and allows His Spirit to take over that sanctification occurs. ("Dying and Rising," 14).

43. This is an issue explored and answered by verbal aspect: see, among others, Campbell, *Advances*; Campbell, *Verbal Aspect and Non-Indicative Verbs*; Fanning, *Verbal Aspect*; Porter, *Verbal Aspect*; Porter, *Linguistic Analysis*; Picirilli, "Meaning," 533–55; Runge, "Verbal Aspect"; Runge, *Discourse Grammar*; Decker, *Temporal Deixis*;

Regardless, the building that is being built into a holy temple *is growing*. Tet-Lim Yee declares "The sense of a commonality is made abundantly clear by the term συναρμολογουμένη, denoting that the various parts of the building-community are 'fitted' or joined together."[44] He also says that the building is made a unity and that "in Christ" this community is held together.[45]

The connotation of the verb, and the tense-form of both the participle and of the verb αὔξει lends itself quite nicely to the thesis that the focus here should be seen as being not only upon the oneness with Christ but on the co-unity with other believers. The verbal aspect (imperfective) of the present tense of the participle and the indicative verb connotes (and probably denotes) the ongoing nature of the growth.[46] It is this precise nature of growth of this body that demonstrates this it is not emphasizing the union with Christ at this point, but union with other parts of our body (the universal and local church community). Hoehner, as cited above, was accurate in noting the previous enmity believers had toward one another; but after Christ, believers are in harmony and must maintain that attitude and lifestyle.

Finally, συνοικοδομεῖσθε is a present passive indicative verb, the same tense and voice as συναρμολογουμένη. The nuance is that God has done this work and the work is ongoing which demonstrates that this is not emphasizing the nature of union with Christ as much as it is emphasizing the union among believers.

VERBAL ASPECT[47]

Without using excessive space on this topic, I want to introduce or at least make mention of "verbal aspect" and how it applies to the Greek verb in the New Testament. To keep it very simple, verbal aspect is the tense-form of a

---

and Winstead, "Significance," 109–21.

44. Yee, *Jews, Gentiles*, 208–9.

45. Ibid. Hoehner gives the connotation of the σύν as intensification of the verb ἁρμολογέω. The verb "speaks of the inner unity or harmony among believers who, before their conversion, were at enmity with one another" (Hoehner, *Ephesians*, 409). See also Williams, *Paul's Metaphors*, 18, and Best, *Critical and Exegetical Commentary*, 287, for comments on the history of this term. They explain the intricate process of ancient stone-working that was responsible for shaping and fitting stones into place.

46. I have dealt with verbal aspect and its effects on the participle in my yet-to-be-published dissertation. Dissertation can be accessed at http://gradworks.umi.com/34/97/3497133.html.

47. Verbal Aspect here really ought to be made a subpoint under "Exegesis," because this grammatical phenomenon should be seen as a tool (one of several handmaids) for exegetes.

verb that the writer chose to get his viewpoint across.[48] Basically, an aorist tense-form denotes that something happened, with no further comment on the duration of the action. Any departure from the aorist possibly becomes exegetically important.

Having this truncated understanding, when we come to the three SCs in Eph 2:5–6, we should understand that the apostle is saying we have been made alive, raised up, and seated with Christ, and these actions are those whose essence requires that they be performed only once. The apostle is offering no teaching here that the actions of these verbs are imperfective, ongoing. Neither is he adding to the teaching of a "once in point of time" kind of notion (contrast this with the verbal aspect of the verb αὔξει in the "theology" section above).

STRUCTURAL AND TEXTLINGUISTIC ANALYSIS

I will also offer a brief note on discourse analysis. Dr. Varner has applied this area of linguistics quite nicely to *James*.[49] Here, I wish to offer a short definition and what it can look like when applied to Eph 2:5–6 and 3:6.

Discourse Analysis is concerned with the relationship between words. A more detailed explanation is given by Guthrie, "Discourse analysis is an approach to examining a text by which the critic seeks to understand the paragraphs in the discourse."[50] The paragraphs and relationships among the words in the paragraph can be analyzed and understood through cohesion, coherence, prominence, various rhetorical features such as the head/tail links in "being dead" in Eph 2:1 and 5, the conjunction with "but God" in 2:4, the Διὸ in 2:11, the intensive αὐτὸς in 2:14, the use of the prepositional compounds, and much, much more. For more application to the New Testament text, see the several essays on discourse analysis by the honoree of this book, David Alan Black.[51]

---

48. Winstead, "Significance," 2. For more detailed definitions, see Porter, *Dictionary of Biblical Criticism*, 200, and Campbell, *Verbal Aspect, the Indicative Mood*, 1 (reiterated in Campbell's *Verbal Aspect and Non-Indicative Verbs*, 6). As rightly explained by Merkle in this *Festschrift*, the word chosen itself does have a little to do with the choice of tense-form as well; that is, certain types of words almost demand a certain tense-form so that the choice of the writer is limited. This is an area of verbal aspect that will probably see more exploration.

49. See Varner's essay ("Who is Resisting—the Righteous One or Someone Else? James 4:6 and 5:6") in this *Festschrift*, and his *Book of James*.

50. Guthrie, *Structure of Hebrews*.

51. See David Black's CV; see also Winstead, "Integration," 65–85, and the bibliographic references there.

The SCs used in Eph 2 with verbs denote primarily the union a believer has with Christ. At the metaphorical level, we see that the metaphors and the language used in this selection add to the NT description of salvation. The above analysis suggests that at the terminological level, when a verb is used with a SC, the translation of "with . . ." should be considered. And in the following cases, when a SC is used with a noun, the translation of "fellow . . ." or "co- . . ." should be considered.

Exegesis of Relevant Ephesians Passages — Ecclesiology

3:6: εἶναι τὰ ἔθνη συγκληρονόμα καὶ σύσσωμα καὶ συμμέτοχα τῆς ἐπαγγελίας ἐν Χριστῷ Ἰησοῦ/ διὰ τοῦ εὐαγγελίου.

Paul uses three SCs here in succession. These three are all adjectives describing the ἔθνη. He calls the Gentiles "fellow heirs," "fellow members," and "fellow partakers." The three adjectives connected by καί, are plural (and therefore do not fall under the rubric of the Granville Sharp rule),[52] and hence, each adjective will be considered separately.

συγκληρονόμος.

Louw and Nida give their semantic domain analysis for Συγκληρονόμος[53] as belonging to those words which refer to possessing, transferring, or exchanging.[54] We are heirs *together* with those who have received the promise.[55] We are all getting a share, and if this is the case, it behooves us to diminish the enmity among ourselves.

---

52. Wallace, *Greek Grammar*, 270ff.

53. This word, since it is not used elsewhere in the NT or in contemporary Koine of Paul's time, is supposed to have been coined by Paul. But Abbott informs us that Aristotle used the word in another compound form, "it is more probable that the adjective was in use." (*Critical and Exegetical Commentary*, 83.) Patzia also says the word is not used elsewhere in the NT, LXX, or classical writers, so that "the author coined it in order to describe the intimate relation that Jews and Gentiles have to each other in the body of Christ, the church" (*Ephesians*, 212). See also Best, *Critical and Exegetical Commentary*, 311-12.

54. BW10.

55. O'Brien, *Letter*, 236, explains that the promise, being the Holy Spirit (1:13), aligns with the notion of the programmatic nature of the *berakah* of 1:3-14. Since this is probably the case, believers are not only fellow sharers of what is to come, but sharers of the presence of the Spirit.

Westcott offers an insightful comment on this verse. He emphasizes the word "are" denotes the sense of the present tense of the infinitive εἶναι.[56] Gentiles "are fellow heirs," not "will be fellow heirs in the future." Westcott also references Acts 10:45 where the people were awed because the Holy Spirit was poured out on the Gentiles as He had been on the Jews.[57] The union with other believers is thus pointed up for us (without mentioning practical applications, which are legion).

σύσσωμα.

This word comes from σύσσωμος and is an adjective as is the SC just before and after it. Louw and Nida define σύσσωμος as a "co-member."[58] Rogers defines it as "fellow members of a body, belonging to the same body."[59] BDAG gives the same definition "belonging to the same body," and parenthetically says the word is found only in Christian writers.[60] This last notion could possibly be a theological issue. That is, why do only the Christian writers use such a term? Perhaps it is because of the unique doctrine within Christianity of the mystical union of the believer with his Savior, or as emphasized here, the unique communal bond with which followers of Christ were initially charged.

The ἐν Χριστῷ Ἰησοῦ in the phrasing τῆς ἐπαγγελίας ἐν Χριστῷ Ἰησοῦ διὰ τοῦ εὐαγγελίου has a special bearing on Paul's use of participatory language in this epistle. A statistical analysis of Paul's use of the preposition ἐν shows that Paul uses the preposition 122 times in Ephesians. He uses it also in combination with objects, one example being Χριστῷ Ἰησοῦ, etc. Here in Eph 3:6 Paul uses ἐν Χριστῷ Ἰησοῦ. He used this same phrase or the ones like it (ἐν Χριστῷ Ἰησοῦ, and ἐν Ἰησοῦ) roughly fifteen times. Concerning the phrase ἐν Χριστῷ Ἰησοῦ διὰ τοῦ εὐαγγελίου, Hoehner has a concise yet sufficient explanation.

> The second of these two prepositional phrases modifies the first and the two depend on the three adjectives just discussed. Therefore, the first prepositional phrase (ἐν Χριστῷ Ἰησοῦ) shows the locale of the three adjectives, namely, "the Gentiles are fellow heirs in Christ, and fellow members of the body in Christ, and fellow participants of the promise in Christ." The

56. Westcott, *Saint Paul's Epistle*, 46.
57. Ibid.
58. BW10.
59. Rogers, *New Linguistic and Exegetical Key*, 439.
60. BDAG, 794.

second prepositional phrase (διὰ τοῦ εὐαγγελίου) shows the means by which believing Gentiles become one with believing Jews in Christ.[61]

We participate with Christ and we participate with the other members of His body.

συμμέτοχα.

Believers are fellow participants or fellow partakers in the Holy Spirit (1:13), which is one of the blessings of the new covenant, Ezek 36:26–27; 37:14; Joel 2:28–30.[62] Arnold writes, "Although the term Paul uses here (συμμέτοχα) is unique in the Bible (it appears only here and in Eph 5:7), the unprefixed term is common and can refer to a business partner (such as partners in the fishing business; see Luke 5:7)."[63]

Christianity is surely a community organism. It is a participatory religion. We participate in spiritual blessings, but these expand to include a daily life and subsistence of mutual love and consideration. That's why Paul began this section with "Therefore I, the prisoner of the Lord, implore you to walk in a manner worthy of the calling with which you have been called." (4:1).

Believers have a particular identity in belonging to Jesus Christ. This identity changes everything. This change begins with the membership they have with other believers. The church universal is a living organism, one to which individuals belong, and to whom some level of responsibility is expected.[64]

---

61. Hoehner, *Ephesians*, 448. Patzia says, "Once again, the author uses a *syn* noun ... to emphasize that the Gentiles participate equally with the Jews in the promises of God" (*Ephesians*, 212.) Best writes, "In Christ Jesus applies to all three adjectives and serves either to stress the idea of fellowship of Jewish and Gentile believers as taking place in Christ or indicates the sphere of God's activity, Christ's death and resurrection by which they were brought together (2:14–17)" (*Ephesians, A Shorter Commentary*, 143).

62. Arnold, *Zondervan Exegetical Commentary*, 192.

63. Ibid. See also Hos 4:17; Heb 3:1, 14; 6:4; and 12:8.

64. Other SCs include συνδούλων ("fellow slaves," Matt 18:28), συμμαθηταῖς ("fellow disciples," John 11:16), συνεργούς ("fellow workers," Rom 16:3), συναιχμαλώτους ("fellow prisoners," Rom 16:7), συγκοινωνός ("fellow partaker," 1 Cor 9:23), συστρατιώτην ("fellow soldier," Phil 2:25), συμπρεσβύτερος ("fellow elder," 1 Pet 5:1).

USES OR CATEGORIES OF PAUL'S ΣΥΝ COMPOUNDS

This section is simply an attempt to categorize in some fashion each of Paul's theologically weighty SCs.

In 2:5 (συνεζωοποίησεν), Paul is giving an explanation of God being rich in His mercy, etc. This use of the SC can be categorized as *"descriptive."* Several of the other SC's are also descriptive. In fact, the next two, συνηγείρεν and συνεκάθισεν, found in 2.6, are expansions of the same theme of the results of God being rich in His mercy. This use seems also to be descriptive as well. Additionally, as has been demonstrated here, this is also a soteriological context. Finally, noting that the SCs involve verbs, the translational helping word should be "with."

The next three SC words are found in the same context together, almost in a cluster in 2:19–22. They are: συμπολῖται (19), συναρμολογουμένη (21), and συνοικοδομεῖσθε (22). These three are in the context of Paul's explanation of the reconciliation man can find through Christ, but also the reconciliation found man to man. These three uses of the SC are *resultant*, they are the results of reconciliation.

In Eph 3:4–6, Paul refers to the "mystery of Christ" and proceeds to give the content of that concept. The triad of SCs he uses in 3:6 all show the contents of the mystery. These uses are *revelatory*, or *explanatory*. Believers are fellow heirs, fellow members, and fellow partakers.

The last of the SC uses in Ephesians is found in 5:11 with the word συγκοινωνεῖτε, and it is negative. It was a prohibition to participating in the unfruitful deeds of darkness. The category can be termed a *prohibition*.

CONCLUSION

This study has sought to contribute to both the technical undertaking of philology with regards to Greek prepositional compounds used by the apostle Paul and to a partial explanation of the apostle's use of the compound terms and what composing his communication with these terms added to his arguments, explanations, or exhortations. Additionally, the research has offered translational helps in regards to the SCs. And, the SCs in Ephesians chapters 2 and 3 have yielded for us a closer look at soteriology (identity) and ecclesiology (community). Finally, this essay has demonstrated the more robust nature of exegesis when applying linguistic tools vis-à-vis traditional exegesis alone.

Additionally, direction from the letter to the Hebrews (3:13–14 and 10:24–25) and from the SCs in Ephesians (and the Colossians parallels) offers help and hope to believers in current society (the postmodern soul, if you will). The soteriology and ecclesiology brokered in Eph 2:5—3:6 offer, in John Feinberg's words, narrative, relationships, relevance, care, and community.[65] In this way, we see the relevance of the gospel through a study of the Greek prepositions in this small epistle.

Table 3. My conclusions may be viewed in chart form:

Reference	SC	Translation	Explanation
2:5	συνεζωοποίησεν	made alive together with	Descriptive
2:6	συνήγειρεν	raised up with	Descriptive
2:6	συνεκάθισεν	seated with	Descriptive
2:19	συμπολῖται	fellow citizens	Resultant
2:21; 4:16	συναρμολογουμένη, συναρμολογούμενον	being fitted together with	Resultant
3:6	συγκληρονόμα	fellow heirs	Revelatory or explanatory
3:6	σύσσωμα	fellow members of the body	Revelatory or explanatory
3:6	συμμέτοχα	fellow partakers	Revelatory or explanatory

In summing up Table 3, I suggest translating "with" when the preposition accompanies verbs, and translating "fellow" when it accompanies nouns.

The outworking of Paul's theology from his use of SCs is multifaceted. Paul mitigates ethical injunctions from his participatory language. The most forceful of these is the negation in 5:11 with the μή and the imperative. Because believers are fellow heirs and have been raised with Christ, etc., believers have an obligation to walk worthy of their calling.

---

65. Feinberg, "Postmodern Themes," 213–28. Feinberg uniquely described the relevance of the Christian faith from Isa 53 in terms that postmoderns would understand. I think the same soteriological and societal relevance can be seen from the Ephesians passages. Incidentally, I used Feinberg's notion in Winstead, "An Overview of Christology," 5–22. Also note Campbell's comment: "The *syn*-related language indicates participation with Christ, which has clear implications for Christian living. They are regarded as suffering with Christ, having died with Christ, being raised with him, living with Christ, ascending with him to the heavens, and being glorified with Christ, among other things. Paul understands these profound realities to have essential significance for the ways in which believers are to live and identify themselves" (*Paul and Union*, 372).

The association is positional but also practical. That is, some of the statements Paul makes are to alert his audience to the fact and the doctrine of their togetherness with Christ and with one another, while other phrases are used to exhort or prod them to flesh out this communion. Thus, there are pedagogical benefits of attending to the SCs in Ephesians. The SCs are part of Paul's rhetoric to argue and explain the participation believers have both with Christ and with one another, and his literary devices place emphases on this oneness as they maintain and expand his motif of body metaphor within this letter.

BIBLIOGRAPHY

Abbott, T. K. *A Critical and Exegetical Commentary on the Epistles to the Ephesians and to the Colossians*. The International Critical Commentary. Edinburgh: T&T Clark, 1953.

Abbott-Smith, G. *Manual Greek Lexicon of The New Testament*. Edinburgh: T&T Clark, 1999.

Allen, Thomas G. E. "Exaltation and Solidarity with Christ Ephesians 1:20 and 2:6." *Journal for the Study of the New Testament* 28 (1986) 103–20.

Arnold, Clinton E. *Ephesians*. Zondervan Exegetical Commentary on the New Testament 10. Grand Rapids, MI: Zondervan, 2010.

Barth, Markus. *Ephesians*. The Anchor Bible 34. Garden City, NY: Doubleday, 1974.

Bauer, Walter. *A Greek-English Lexicon of The New Testament and Other Early Christian Literature*. Translated by William F. Arndt and F. Wilbur Gingrich. Chicago: University of Chicago Press, 1979.

Best, Ernest. *A Critical and Exegetical Commentary on Ephesians*. International Critical Commentary. Edinburgh: T&T Clark, 1998.

———. *Ephesians, a Shorter Commentary*. New York: T&T Clark, 2003.

———. *Essays on Ephesians*. Edinburgh: T&T Clark, 1997.

———. *One Body in Christ*. London: SPCK, 1955.

———. "Who Used Whom? The Relationship of Ephesians and Colossians." *New Testament Studies* 43 (1997) 72–96.

Black, David Alan. *It's Still Greek to Me: An Easy-to-Understand Guide to Intermediate Greek*. Grand Rapids, MI: Baker, 1998.

———. *Linguistics for Students of New Testament Greek*. Grand Rapids, MI: Baker, 1995.

———. "Paul and Christian Unity: A Formal Analysis of Philippians 2:1–4." *Journal of the Evangelical Theological Society* 28 (1985) 299–308.

———. "The Peculiarities of Ephesians and the Ephesian Address." *Grace Theological Journal* 2 (1981) 59–73.

———. *Using New Testament Greek in Ministry*. Grand Rapids, MI: Baker, 1998.

Bruce, F. F. *The Epistle to the Ephesians*. London: Pickering & Inglis, 1961.

Campbell, Constantine R. *Advances in the Study of Greek*. Grand Rapids, MI: Zondervan, 2015.

———. *Paul and Union with Christ: An Exegetical and Theological Study*. Grand Rapids, MI: Zondervan, 2012.

———. *Verbal Aspect, the Indicative Mood, and Narrative: Soundings in the Greek of the New Testament.* Studies in Biblical Greek 13. New York: Peter Lang, 2007.

———. *Verbal Aspect and Non-Indicative Verbs.* New York: Peter Lang, 2008.

Decker, Rodney J. *Temporal Deixis of the Greek Verb in the Gospel of Mark with Reference to Verbal Aspect.* New York: Peter Lang, 2001.

Deissmann, Adolf. *The Philology of the Greek Bible.* London: Hodder and Stoughton, 1908.

Du Toit, A. B. "'In Christ,' 'In the Spirit,' and Related Prepositional Phrases: Their Relevance for a Discussion on Pauline Mysticism." *Neotestamentica* 34 (2000) 287–98.

———. "Primitive Christian Belief in the Resurrection of Jesus in the Light of Pauline Resurrection and Appearance Terminology." *Neotestamentica* 23 (1989) 309–30.

Estes, Douglas. *Questions and Rhetoric in the Greek New Testament.* Grand Rapids, MI: Zondervan, 2017.

Fanning, Buist M. *Verbal Aspect in New Testament Greek.* Oxford Theological Monographs. Oxford: Clarendon, 1990.

Feinberg, John. "Postmodern Themes from Isaiah 53." In *The Gospel According to Isaiah 53*, edited by Darrell L. Bock and Mitch Glaser, 213–28. Grand Rapids, MI: Kregel, 2012.

Gombis, Timothy G. *The Drama of Ephesians: Participating in the Triumph of God.* Downers Grove, IL: IVP, 2010.

———. "Ephesians 2 as a Narrative of Divine Warfare." *Journal for the Study of the New Testament* 26 (2004) 403–18.

Guthrie, George H. *The Structure of Hebrews: A Text-Linguistic Analysis.* Novum Testamentum, Supplements 73. Leiden: Brill, 1994.

Harris, Murray. "Prepositions and Theology in the Greek New Testament." In Vol. 3 of *New International Dictionary of New Testament Theology*, edited by Colin Brown, 1206. Grand Rapids, MI: Zondervan, 1971.

Hoehner, Harold W. *Ephesians: An Exegetical Commentary.* Grand Rapids, MI: Baker Academic, 2002.

Holmes, M. W., ed. *The Greek New Testament: SBL Edition.* Bellingham, WA: Lexham Press, 2011–2013.

Metzger, Bruce M. *Lexical Aids for Students of New Testament Greek.* Grand Rapids, MI: Baker, 1998.

Moule, C. F. D. *An Idiom Book of New Testament Greek.* Cambridge: Cambridge University Press, 1959.

O'Brien, Peter. *The Letter to the Ephesians.* Grand Rapids, MI: Eerdmans, 1999.

Patzia, Arthur G. *Ephesians, Colossians, Philemon.* New International Biblical Commentary. Peabody, MA: Hendrickson, 1990.

Picirilli, Robert. "The Meaning of the Tenses in New Testament Greek." *Journal of the Evangelical Theological Society* 48 (2005) 533–55.

Porter, Stanley E. *Idioms of the Greek New Testament.* Sheffield: Sheffield Academic, 1999.

———. *Linguistic Analysis of the Greek New Testament.* Grand Rapids, MI: Baker, 2015.

———. *Verbal Aspect in the Greek of the New Testament, with Reference to Tense and Mood.* New York: Peter Lang, 1993.

———. ed. *Dictionary of Biblical Criticism and Interpretation.* New York: Routledge, 2007.

———, ed. *The Pauline Canon*. Leiden: Brill, 2004.
Porter, Stanley E., Jeffrey T. Reed, and Matthew Brook O'Donnell. *Fundamentals of New Testament Greek*. Grand Rapids, MI: Eerdmans, 2010.
Robertson, A. T. *A Grammar of the Greek New Testament in the Light of Historical Research*. Nashville: Broadman, 1934.
Rogers, Cleon L., Jr. *The New Linguistic and Exegetical Key to the Greek New Testament*. Grand Rapids, MI: Zondervan, 1998.
Runge, Steven E. *Discourse Grammar of the Greek New Testament*. Peabody, MA: Hendrickson, 2015.
———. "Verbal Aspect and Discourse Prominence Presentation." Pages 1–7. http://www.ntdiscourse.org/docs/Verbal%20Aspect%20and%20Discourse%20Prominence-presentation.pdf.
Schnackenburg, Rudolf. *Ephesians: A Commentary*. Translated by Helen Heron. Edinburgh: T&T Clark, 1991.
Schreiner, Thomas R. "Interpreting the Pauline Epistles." In *Interpreting the New Testament*, edited by David Alan Black and David S. Dockery, 412–32. Nashville: Broadman and Holman, 2001.
Schweizer, Eduard. "Dying and Rising with Christ." *New Testament Studies* 14 (1967) 1–14.
Thielman, Frank. *Ephesians*. Baker Exegetical Commentary on the New Testament. Grand Rapids, MI: Baker Academic, 2010.
Varner, William. *The Book of James: A New Perspective*. The Woodlands, TX: Kress Biblical Resources, 2010.
Wallace, Daniel B. *Greek Grammar Beyond the Basics*. Grand Rapids, MI: Zondervan, 1996.
Wedderburn, A. J. M. "Some Observations on Paul's Use of the Phrases 'In Christ' and 'With Christ.'" *Journal for the Study of the New Testament* 25 (1985) 83–97.
Westcott, Brooke Foss. *Saint Paul's Epistle to the Ephesians*. London: Macmillan, 1906.
Williams, David John. *Paul's Metaphors: Their Context and Character*. Peabody, MA: Hendrickson, 1999.
Winstead, Melton B. "An Integration of Biblical Theology and Some Tools of Discourse Analysis: Hebrews 8:6–13 as a Case Study." *Christian Apologetics Journal* 12 (2014) 65–85.
———. "An Overview of Christology in the Letter to the Hebrews." *Christian Apologetics Journal* 13 (2015) 5–22.
———. "The Significance of Verbal Aspect on the Participles in Hebrews 6:1–12." *Criswell Theological Review* 12 (2014) 109–21.
———. "The Significance of Verbal Aspect on the Participles in Hebrews with Special Reference to 6:1–12." PhD diss., Southeastern Baptist Theological Seminary, 2011.
Yee, Tet-Lim N. *Jews, Gentiles and Ethnic Reconciliation: Paul's Jewish Identity and Ephesians*. Cambridge: Cambridge University Press, 2005.

www.ingramcontent.com/pod-product-compliance
Lightning Source LLC
Chambersburg PA
CBHW050348230426
43663CB00010B/2038